Evidence

Evidence

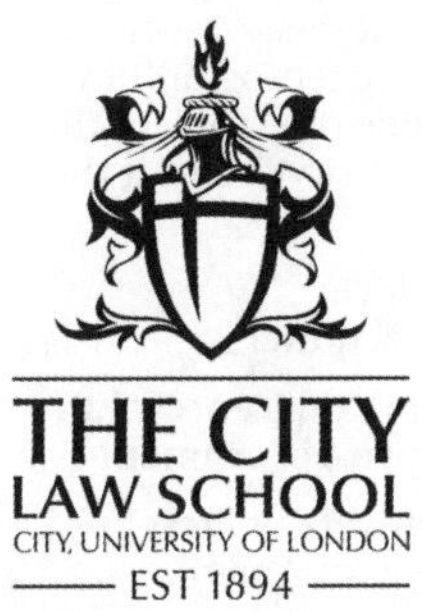

Authors

Romilly Edge, Barrister, Senior Lecturer, The City Law School
James Griffiths, Barrister, formerly Senior Lecturer, The City Law School
Paul McKeown, Barrister, Associate Professor of Law, The City Law School
Robert McPeake, Barrister, Principal Lecturer, The City Law School
Alexander Mills, Barrister, Associate Professor of Law, The City Law School

Editors

Romilly Edge, Barrister, Senior Lecturer, The City Law School
Alexander Mills, Barrister, Associate Professor of Law, The City Law School

Series Editor

Julie Browne, Director of Bar Training, Associate Professor of Law,
The City Law School

Great Clarendon Street, Oxford, OX2 6DP,
United Kingdom

Oxford University Press is a department of the University of Oxford. It furthers the University's objective of excellence in research, scholarship, and education by publishing worldwide. Oxford is a registered trade mark of Oxford University Press in the UK and in certain other countries

Sixteenth edition 2012
Seventeenth edition 2014
Eighteenth edition 2016

Impression: 2

Published in the United States of America by Oxford University Press
198 Madison Avenue, New York, NY 10016, United States of America

British Library Cataloguing in Publication Data
Data available

ISBN 978–0–19–882315–5

Printed in Great Britain by
Bell & Bain Ltd., Glasgow

FOREWORD

These manuals have been written by a combination of practitioners and members of staff of the City Law School (formerly the Inns of Court School of Law), and are designed primarily to support training on the Bar Professional Training Course (BPTC), wherever it is taught. They provide an extremely useful resource to assist in acquiring the skills and knowledge that practising barristers need. They are updated regularly and are supported by an Online Resource Centre, which can be used by readers to keep up to date throughout the academic year.

This series of manuals exemplifies the practical and professional approach that is central to the BPTC. I congratulate the authors on the excellent standard of the manuals and I am grateful to Oxford University Press for their ongoing and enthusiastic support.

Peter Hungerford-Welch
Barrister, Assistant Dean
The City Law School
City University London
2018

PREFACE

The law of evidence regulates the means by which facts may be proved in courts of law. It is for this reason that mastery of its basic principles and rules is essential to the practitioner. All too often, both before a trial and during its conduct in court, the rules of evidence must be applied on the spur of the moment, without the opportunity to consult books or articles. Perhaps instructions have been belatedly received. Perhaps a problem arises at the trial itself: during examination-in-chief, cross-examination, or re-examination; when the admissibility of an item of evidence is suddenly questioned; or when it becomes necessary to deal with a judicial intervention or to make submissions about the contents of a summing-up.

This manual, by its combination of text, materials, and examples, aims to develop not only knowledge of evidence law, but also understanding of the ways in which it is applied in practice.

The law is stated as at 1 March 2018.

GUIDE TO USING THIS BOOK

This manual provides an introduction to the key areas of evidence for the practitioner. The purpose of this guide is to enable you to get the greatest benefit from your reading.

Statutory materials

The law of evidence developed at common law but increasingly the rules are being placed on a statutory footing. Some statutes, such as the Criminal Justice Act 2003, are of particular significance and will be referred to frequently. It will often assist to have a copy of the statute to hand, and you should therefore be familiar with accessing statutory material through hard copy and electronic sources, many of which are available via the Online Resource Centre for this book (**http://global.oup.com/uk/orc/law/bptc//**).

Law reports

You are strongly recommended to read the law reports of the key cases referred to throughout the manual. There is no substitute for reading the full report of a case. Many cases are reported in the ordinary reports with which you are acquainted (eg AC, QB, WLR, All ER). Cases reported in any of the main or specialist series may easily be accessed through the main electronic services: Lawtel, LexisNexis, and Westlaw.

Further reading

You may also find the specialist journals and periodicals useful for keeping up to date with current developments and as a source of insightful commentary. Articles on civil and criminal evidence also appear in all the main general legal periodicals.

(a) Journals

The leading specialist journal is the *International Journal of Evidence and Proof*, containing articles, comment, case notes, reports, and reviews.

Other journals of particular interest include the *Criminal Law Review*, the *Modern Law Review*, and the *Law Quarterly Review*.

(b) Updating services

Updates on key cases in the law of evidence will be provided at the Online Resource Centre at **http://global.oup.com/uk/orc/law/bptc//**.

The monthly and weekly publications, *Legal Action* and *New Law Journal*, are useful for up-to-date information on recent cases, often before they have been reported, and articles surveying a particular topic, often from a highly practical perspective.

Archbold News, published ten times per year, provides access to updated developments including cases, legislation, and commentary in the field of criminal law. Significantly, it includes reports of cases that are not reported elsewhere.

Criminal Law Week, published weekly, is a comprehensive digest of developments in the criminal law. It is available as a printed version and online at www.criminal-law.co.uk.

CrimeLine is the largest circulation criminal law update. Each issue digests the latest cases, legislation, and news. Students can subscribe at the CrimeLine website (www.crimeline.co.uk) where previous editions of the update together with other useful resources are available.

OUTLINE CONTENTS

DETAILED CONTENTS

TABLE OF CASES

TABLE OF STATUTES

International legislation

TABLE OF SECONDARY LEGISLATION

Table of statutory instruments

Practice Directions

Codes of Practice

1

Fundamentals of evidence

1.1 What is 'evidence'?

Before looking at the rules of evidence (ie the law governing what evidence may be adduced), it is useful to be clear about some of the matters of fundamental importance in understanding how evidence works. The subject matter of this chapter is therefore of considerable importance. You will find that the key terms that are being referred to in this chapter are used throughout this book.

1.1.1 Facts and law

The legal sanctions that the court can impose depend upon the proven facts of the case. Therefore, for example, before a judge in the Crown Court can impose a sentence on a defendant, the defendant must be proven to have committed an offence. Further, the type of sentence imposed on the defendant depends on which offence or offences that defendant is proven to have committed: in effect, which factual allegations the court has accepted. Likewise, a civil court could not award damages to a claimant for three breaches of contract if the claimant had only proven a single breach. Furthermore, the amount of any damages awarded would depend on how much loss the claimant could prove flowed from that breach.

It will be seen therefore that the court's power to exercise legal sanctions and to apply legal rules depends on *proof* of particular facts. The function of the law is to establish which facts have to be proven in any given case.

1.1.2 Proof

The word 'proof' is used commonly in discussions about the rules of evidence. Later, in this and the next chapter, you will be introduced to concepts such as 'burden of proof', 'standard of proof', and 'probative value'. Before defining these terms, it is worth attempting a working definition of the key word 'proof'.

The legal meaning of proof is not so different from its ordinary meaning. In ordinary speech 'proof' is most commonly used to mean *either* the process of convincing a person of a particular conclusion by the use of facts and logic, *or* successfully convincing a person of a particular conclusion in that way. Therefore, if A says to B, 'Prove it', A means that B should produce facts and make arguments on the point in question and that the facts and arguments produced should be such as will convince A. It is worth noting the following points.

(a) Proving a fact is achieved by combining supporting material.

(b) There is an implicit standard below which a conclusion would be 'unproven'. Some things are more difficult to prove than others. The more improbable the desired conclusion, the harder it will be to prove it. By 'harder' we mean that better-quality facts and arguments will be required to *convince the person* to reach the conclusion in question.

(c) Facts and arguments are not all equally valuable in proving conclusions. We expect anyone deciding whether something is proven to treat facts and arguments differently for a variety of reasons. Some have less relevance or bearing on the matter in question. Some facts relied upon may be less reliable than others, whether because the source of the fact is suspect or because there is an impression that the fact does not give the whole picture.

(d) In ordinary life, proving something means convincing another human being that a particular matter did or did not happen.

The approach of the courts to proof is essentially the same. However, as one might expect from the formal nature of courts, proof is subject to a system of rules and practices. These rules and practices are at the heart of the rules of evidence and most of this manual will examine how the formal process of proof is based on these rules and practices. It is therefore worth considering some of the ways in which the points noted above are applied in a formal, legal setting.

1.1.2.1 Facts and arguments

The legal process of proof in court requires a combination of evidence and argument to prove cases. The rules of evidence and of court procedure draw a distinction between facts, which are proven by the evidence (usually the calling of witnesses), and arguments, which are advanced later on by the advocates in the case. For example, an advocate in a Crown Court trial should not comment on the evidence given by a witness while conducting cross-examination (see the ***Advocacy*** manual). Rather, he or she will make comments upon that evidence (ie make arguments about it) during a closing speech after all of the facts have been put before the jury, or when addressing the jury immediately after cross-examination, where the cross-examination is of a vulnerable witness or vulnerable defendant (for more on the cross-examination of vulnerable witnesses and defendants, see **7.3.2.1**).

1.1.2.2 Standards of proof

Every allegation in a case must be established to a particular 'standard of proof'. The standard for any particular allegation is set by the law. It is in this context that phrases you may have heard before such as 'beyond reasonable doubt' and 'on the balance of probabilities' are used. The law has also regulated who must prove facts. The requirement 'to prove it' is generally imposed upon the party bringing the case (ie the claimant in civil cases and the prosecution in criminal cases) but, given the complexity of the litigation process, this is not always so. The requirement that a party prove a particular conclusion is called the 'burden of proof'. We shall examine the burden and standard of proof more closely in **Chapter 2**.

1.1.2.3 Facts and arguments are variable

The rules of evidence recognise that facts are not all equally useful in proving conclusions. While the rules of evidence generally seek to allow evidence of all facts that might prove a conclusion ('relevant facts'), there are numerous safeguards that aim to prevent the trial process being undermined by the reception of weak evidence.

The formalised trial process has rules for how facts are proven (see **1.7**) and there are also rules preventing some facts from being proven if the source of the fact in question is in some way potentially unreliable (eg 'hearsay' evidence: see **Chapters 11–13**, and the requirement that an individual is proven to be an expert in the relevant field before expert opinion evidence can be given: see **Chapter 17**).

We shall see that some of these rules aim to prevent parties from wasting the time and resources of the court with facts that have little value in deciding the issues in the case (eg rules that limit the extent to which parties can prove that the opposing party or his witnesses are of bad character: see **Chapters 8–10**). Other rules seek to prevent the court from being distracted from deciding the real issues of the case. There is therefore a process of filtering out some facts from cases. This is more frequently the case in criminal trials than in civil trials.

At the heart of this filtering process is the concept of 'weight' (see **1.3.2**), which is simply a way of evaluating the capacity of some evidence, or combinations of evidence and argument, to prove conclusions. The weight to be attached to any fact is significant in two ways. First, it often determines whether the court will admit evidence of the fact at all (eg where the fact is adduced to prove the bad character of a criminal defendant: see **Chapter 9**). Second, it is used to decide whether the evidence in support of a fact in issue is sufficient to reach a particular standard of proof (ie to prove a particular conclusion: see **Chapter 2**).

1.1.2.4 The tribunal of fact and the tribunal of law

A general term for the person or persons who must decide whether the facts in question are proven is 'the tribunal of fact' or the 'fact-finder'. Quite who this is depends on in which court a party is appearing. The tribunal of fact in a Crown Court trial is the jury. In the Crown Court the jury is responsible for reaching factual decisions and the judge for deciding legal issues. This raises an important distinction that we will return to later (see **1.8**). The 'law-decider' is generally referred to as the 'tribunal of law'. The legal decisions include matters such as the appropriate sentence for a person who has been found guilty of an offence, or the effect of the frustration of a contract. However, legal decisions also include decisions such as whether particular evidence should be put in front of a tribunal of fact at all. Therefore, the tribunal of law may occasionally have to examine the facts (and particularly the weight to be attached to the facts) to decide legal issues. For example, a judge deciding whether a confession was obtained unlawfully would have to decide the *factual* questions surrounding the circumstances in which it was obtained in order to reach a *legal* conclusion as to the admissibility of the confession.

The tribunal of fact and the tribunal of law are often the same person or persons. Most civil cases are heard by a single judge who determines both the facts of the case and the legal issues. This is also so with criminal cases heard in the magistrates' court. Although the fact-finder and the tribunal of law are the same in many cases, the distinction between tribunals of fact and law is important.

1.1.3 Evidence

Facts and arguments combine to prove conclusions and this is so in cases brought before the courts as much as anywhere else. However, not all things asserted as 'facts' are accepted as such by other people. The term 'fact' is slightly misleading. The meaning given to the word by the ***Oxford English Dictionary*** is '*Something that has really occurred or is actually the case; … hence, a particular truth known by actual observation or authentic testimony, as opposed to what is merely inferred*'. Although there is no formal definition of the term in law, the word is most correctly used to describe matters that are accepted by the tribunal of fact to have occurred. The tribunal of fact will consider various matters put before it and decide whether the alleged thing is true or not (ie whether the alleged thing is established as a 'fact'). The matters it receives to reach that decision are 'evidence of that fact'. Looking again at the definition given above, a tribunal of fact will not be relying on 'actual observation' and so will have to rely on 'authentic testimony' to reach its conclusions. We shall see that testimony is given a particular meaning at law but for the time being we can take testimony to mean evidence and note that evidence establishes facts.

It is worth noting at this point that evidence will not only prove a fact but that a proven fact may combine with other evidence (or proven facts) to prove some other fact. In other words, a fact may be evidence of another fact.

In essence, evidence is that which proves facts and 'proof' is the process of converting evidence into facts.

1.2 Facts in issue

It was noted earlier that all issues in a case must be proven. These are often termed the 'facts in issue'. Identifying the facts in issue is not as straightforward as it might first appear. First, what the facts in issue are in a particular case depends on the relevant law. Second, because of the adversarial nature of litigation in England and Wales, the parties to a case will make allegations and counter-allegations. A defendant may either challenge the allegations of the prosecution (in criminal cases) or claimant (in civil cases) or may raise some entirely different legal defence. Clearly, these counter-allegations have to be resolved. Finally, quite what the facts in issue are at trial is affected by rules of procedure (ie rules dictating how the trial process will run). This means that there are differences between civil and criminal cases.

1.2.1 Criminal cases: general principle

In criminal cases, whether in the Crown Court or a magistrates' court, a trial starts with a process of arraignment or plea. The defendant is accused formally of the commission of an offence and asked to plead to it. If the plea is 'not guilty', *all* of the elements of the offence are put in issue (ie the defendant has required the prosecution to prove them all). Furthermore, the defendant may raise defences during trial which will also be put in issue.

Therefore, every element of the offence for which a defendant is being tried must be established in criminal cases. In addition, any defence alleged and for which some evidence is admitted (see the 'evidential burden' in **Chapter 2**) will become a fact in issue. In *R v Sims* [1946] KB 531, CCA, Lord Goddard CJ said (at p 539):

> The prosecution has to prove the whole of their case including the identity of the accused, the nature of the act and the existence of any necessary knowledge or intent.

Therefore, the facts in issue in a criminal case are:

- the identity of the culprit;
- the *actus reus* of the offence (which will have several elements);
- the *mens rea* of the offence; and
- any defences raised at trial.

1.2.2 Civil cases: general principle

In civil cases, the process of making allegations begins much earlier and is more sophisticated than in criminal cases. Cases are initiated by the 'statement of case' process (see Sime, ***A Practical Approach to Civil Procedure*** or the ***White Book***). The claimant will make detailed allegations of some particular civil wrong (such as a breach of contract) in his or her 'particulars of claim' as required by the Civil Procedure Rules 1998 (CPR), r 16.4. The defendant will respond by way of a defence (assuming the defendant does not fully admit liability at this point). The defence will respond to each particular allegation made by the claimant.

CPR, r 16.5(1), provides:

In his defence, the defendant must state—

(a) which of the allegations ... he denies;

(b) which allegations he is unable to admit or deny, but which he requires the claimant to prove; and

(c) which allegations he admits.

Denial of an allegation puts the denying party under an obligation to state reasons for denial (CPR, r 16.5(2)). The requirement to prove an allegation as stated in paragraph (b) recognises that there may be allegations made by a claimant that a defendant is simply not able to form a judgement upon (particularly matters such as loss and damage that may be within the personal knowledge of the claimant).

In so far as a party admits an allegation made by another party, it ceases to be a fact in issue. Where the defendant fails to deal with an allegation made by another party, they are taken to have admitted it (CPR, r 16.5(5)). Otherwise the allegation remains a fact in issue (paragraphs (a) and (b)).

In addition to responding to the case alleged by a claimant, a defendant may raise new issues which would constitute a defence. For example, even if a defendant admits to having entered into a contract with the claimant, he might allege the existence of a frustrating event (ie raise the defence of frustration). This would be done in his defence and would raise new facts in issue.

There is therefore much more flexibility as to what may or may not be a fact in issue in a civil case. First of all, the parties have far more control over what might be a fact in issue before trial. Second, there is a greater variety of subject matter being litigated in civil courts. While all criminal cases are composed of an *actus reus* and a *mens rea*, civil cases are not so strictly categorised. Each area of substantive civil law will have different potential facts in issue.

1.2.3 Significance of facts in issue

It might be wondered why a lawyer will bother to identify the facts in issue in a case. In fact, many lawyers who have experience in particular areas probably identify the facts in issue by instinct. The phrase 'facts in issue' is not used widely in the courts. However, it is useful in understanding how evidence proves cases. By identifying the facts in issue in a case, three things are achieved, as follows:

(a) A list of issues is identified so that it is possible to go on to determine *who* it is that must prove which issue. In other words, identifying the facts in issue is the first step in determining who bears the various *burdens of proof* in a case. This is dealt with in more detail in **Chapter 2**.

(b) This list places limits on the evidence that should and can be admitted at trial. The courts will not entertain evidence that does not assist in resolving the matters in dispute (ie the facts in issue). In other words, the facts in issue determine the *relevance* of evidence. Relevance in turn is one of the factors that determines the *admissibility* of evidence: evidence which is not relevant to one or more facts in issue is inadmissible at trial.

(c) A lawyer is thereby better able to analyse the case, to identify evidence to be admitted, and to formulate arguments about evidence.

1.3 Proof concepts

The rules of evidence are based on four very important concepts: relevance, weight, probative value, and prejudicial effect. One or more of these concepts underpins every rule of evidence.

1.3.1 Relevance

As noted in **1.2.3**, the concept of relevance is fundamental to all evidence. Evidence must be relevant for it to be admissible in both civil and criminal cases. Furthermore, a clear understanding of the relevance of a particular piece of evidence is necessary in applying other rules of admissibility such as the rule against hearsay.

1.3.1.1 Definition

There have been a number of attempts to define relevance. In *DPP v Kilbourne* [1973] AC 729, Lord Simon said (at p 756):

> Evidence is relevant if it is logically probative or disprobative of some matter which requires proof. It is sufficient to say ... that relevant (ie logically probative or disprobative) evidence is evidence which makes the matter ... more or less probable.

Note the stress upon logic in the above excerpt. Relevance does not stem from intuition or feelings about a particular piece of evidence but from how one might rationalise and explain it. An advocate will often highlight the relevance of particular pieces of evidence in his or her closing speech in order to persuade the court to reach a particular conclusion.

A slightly more complicated definition is given at Article 1 of Stephen's ***Digest of the Law of Evidence*** (12th edn, 1936), where it was said:

> Any two facts to which it was applied are so related to each other that according to the common course of events one either taken by itself or in connection with other facts proves or renders probable the ... existence or non-existence of the other.

It follows that evidence does not have to *prove* a matter to be relevant. Rather, it has to *assist* in proving a matter. One fact (the item of evidence) has a relationship with another fact (the conclusion from the item of evidence) because it at least renders probable the conclusion.

In *R v Randall* [2004] 1 WLR 56, Lord Steyn noted that a judge, in determining the issue of relevance, '*has to decide whether the evidence is capable of increasing or decreasing the existence of a fact in issue*'. Lord Steyn also adopted the observation in Keane, ***The Modern Law of Evidence***, that the question of relevance '*is typically a matter of degree to be determined, for the most part by common sense and experience*'. Relevance is therefore not a rule of law. There are no cases that set precedents for what will or will not be relevant in any particular situation.

1.3.1.2 Direct and circumstantial evidence

Relevant facts may tend to prove or disprove a fact in issue either directly or indirectly. Classic examples of direct evidence include:

(a) testimony by a witness about his or her own perception of a fact in issue, for example, that he saw the accused stab the deceased to prove directly that a stabbing took place;

(b) the production to the court of some object the existence of which is in issue, for example, a lease to prove the existence of the lease.

Circumstantial evidence does not involve the immediate perception of a fact in issue, but is evidence from which the existence or non-existence of a fact in issue can be inferred. Circumstantial evidence works cumulatively (*R v Taylor, Weaver and Donovan* (1928) 21 Cr App R 20, CA); one piece of circumstantial evidence may be insufficient to prove a fact in issue, but circumstantial evidence may be particularly powerful when it demonstrates a variety of different facts all pointing to the same logical conclusion. Examples include:

(a) evidence of opportunity, ie evidence of presence at the time and place of the act in question;

(b) certain types of evidence of identity, for example, that DNA samples taken from the accused match those found at the scene of the crime;

(c) evidence of facts providing a motive for a person to have done a particular act;

(d) lies told by the accused (discussed further at **Chapter 15**).

In none of these situations does the evidence prove the defendant's commission of the offence alone; it will only do so when combined with other evidence.

1.3.1.3 Sufficiency of relevance

It is sometimes said that a fact is 'not very relevant' or 'of marginal relevance' or that one fact is 'more' relevant than another. On the other hand, if relevance is determined by a strictly logical test of whether something makes a '*matter ... more or less probable*' (*per* Lord Simon in *DPP v Kilbourne* [1973] AC 729), then relevance is a quality which a piece of evidence either does or does not have.

Consider an example in a civil case: Arthur is being sued for negligence and breach of contract in respect of building works he has carried out for Amy. Amy wishes to show that he has been successfully sued in respect of a road accident in which he was alleged to have driven carelessly.

If we were to adopt a literal approach to Lord Simon's test, we might say that the driving case is relevant to the building works case. Our argument would be that the previous case shows that Arthur has previously been less than careful. We would say that Arthur is therefore a relatively careless person and that this would show, to some small extent, that he may have been careless when carrying out work for Amy. By a very small degree it renders more probable the conclusion that Arthur was negligent on this occasion.

In fact, a court would probably be unwilling to accept this evidence and this would be on the grounds that it is not relevant. It would therefore appear that the courts have qualified the strictness of the test for relevance by introducing the concept of 'sufficiency of relevance', ie that evidence must display a sufficient degree of relevance before it will be admitted.

Consider the following examples:

- In *R v Whitehead* (1848) 3 Car & Kir 202, a doctor was tried for manslaughter of one patient. Evidence that the doctor had treated other patients skilfully was held to be irrelevant. Only evidence of the skill used in treating the patient who died was held to be relevant.

- In *Hart v Lancashire and Yorkshire Railway Co* (1869) 21 LT 261, the defendant was sued for negligently causing an accident. It was alleged that the accident had been caused by the changing of railway points. Evidence that the defendant company had altered its practice in changing railway points after an accident was held to be irrelevant.
- *Hollingham v Head* (1858) 27 LJ CP 241 was a breach of contract case in which the defendant sought to prove certain terms of the contract that would excuse him from liability. To prove that those terms were incorporated into the contract with the defendant, he sought to adduce evidence that the plaintiff had entered into contracts with other persons on those same terms. The Court of Common Pleas held that evidence of contracting behaviour with other parties was irrelevant.
- *R v Blastland* [1986] AC 41 concerned the murder and buggery of a boy. The defendant wished to adduce evidence which showed that, before the victim's body had been found, another person, M, had spoken about the murder of a boy. The House of Lords held that evidence which showed that M knew of the murder was irrelevant to the issue in the case, namely whether the defendant was the murderer.
- In *R v T (AB)* [2007] 1 Cr App R 43, a 7-year-old child made statements accusing her uncle, grandfather, and step-grandfather of sexual abuse. Her grandfather admitted the allegations to the police, and her step-grandfather pleaded guilty to four counts of indecent assault based on the child's accusations. It was held that evidence of her accusations against her grandfather and step-grandfather could not possibly be relevant to the issue of whether she had been abused by her uncle. The mere fact that she had told the truth about the other incidents was not logically probative of the facts alleged against the uncle.

In these cases, the courts often justified the conclusion that there was no relevance to the evidence by identifying or describing a test that is slightly different to that identified in *Kilbourne*. In *Hollingham v Head* the court said that the previous contracting behaviour was not relevant because it supported no *reasonable* inference as to how the parties had contracted. This stricter test may be compared with Stephen's use of the phrase 'renders probable' noted earlier. The evidence does not simply have to be relevant, but it has to be sufficiently relevant to permit the tribunal of fact reasonably to draw an inference as to the existence of the term in the contract. In cases such as *Blastland* it is not difficult to formulate arguments on the relevance of the evidence as follows:

- M said that the boy had been murdered before this was generally known.
- Therefore, M had some peculiar knowledge of the death of the boy.
- Therefore, M may have murdered the boy.
- Therefore, the defendant may not have murdered the boy.

While this argument is not without its flaws, it is logical and it is sustainable. Nonetheless, the House of Lords concluded that the evidence represented by the first bullet point was not relevant to the conclusion in the final bullet point. This must be because the logic is *insufficiently* strong or, in evidential terms, the evidence is *insufficiently* relevant.

The rationale for the restriction of evidence of marginal relevance is that it would increase the issues that have to be litigated, with a resulting increase in cost and complexity of the trial process (see *R v Patel* [1951] 2 All ER 29).

Thus, the test for relevance is not simply whether the evidence might tend to prove or disprove a fact in issue. Evidence must be capable of proving or disproving it to a sufficient degree. There is no clear statement of *how* relevant evidence has to be. In part this is because relevance is, as Lord Steyn affirmed in *R v Randall* [2004] 1 WLR 56, not an issue of law but a matter of logic, common sense, or experience. This means that relevance cannot be assessed by reference to precedent but only on the basis of the facts of each case.

1.3.1.4 Conditional relevance

We have seen that some evidence does not have relevance on its own. Rather, its relevance depends on its relationship to other evidence in the case. As a result, the court may admit evidence conditionally upon the proof of such facts as render that evidence relevant. If the other evidence is not adduced, the judge will have to direct the jury to ignore the evidence that was conditionally admitted (or a civil judge or magistrate would have to disregard it). In extreme cases (where it will not be possible for the tribunal of fact to ignore it) the trial may have to be discontinued.

1.3.1.5 Importance of argument

To recap, the relevance of evidence is a matter of logic or of common sense. Relevance is a filter upon evidence: no evidence which is deemed irrelevant will be admitted. The test is whether the evidence will increase or decrease the probability of a fact in issue being proved (or possibly whether it is sufficiently likely to do so or likely to do so to a sufficient extent). This will be a matter of argument or explanation. In many cases the relevance of direct evidence or circumstantial evidence will be so clear that the argument does not need to be stated. Generally, however, some argument will have to be made at some point during the course of the trial. Given that relevance is not a matter of law but a matter of logic, it is not possible to lay down any rules about such arguments. However, the following points should be borne in mind:

(a) Evidence is not simply 'relevant'. Rather, it is relevant to something. Identifying to which facts in issue evidence is relevant is necessary to constructing convincing arguments.

(b) Evidence need not be directly relevant to a fact in issue. Instead, the evidence may be relevant to a fact that, in turn, is relevant to a fact in issue.

(c) It is not only necessary to identify *what* evidence is relevant to; it is necessary to identify *how* or *why* that evidence is relevant to that issue. This requires drawing on logic or common sense to construct generalisations about human behaviour.

(d) Finally, and most importantly, evidence is relevant if it is *capable* of leading to a particular conclusion, not if it *will* necessarily lead to that conclusion.

1.3.2 Weight

We have seen in the preceding section that the *relevance* of evidence concerns what conclusions the evidence is capable of proving or disproving. The *weight* of the evidence concerns the extent to which the evidence does prove or disprove the conclusion. While it is still possible to disagree about what something is capable of proving, this is not likely in most cases and, even where it is, the disagreement is usually based on logical analysis or 'common sense'. Weight is far more subjective. Among 12 jurors, some may be inclined to reach a particular conclusion from a particular piece of evidence, and others may not. There might be difficulty articulating why they do or do not do so. In so far as they can, they might draw on concepts such as 'belief' or 'feelings' or 'instinct'. However, they may also draw on 'logic' and 'common sense'.

1.3.2.1 Importance of weight at trial

Weight is generally a matter for the tribunal of fact. Once the tribunal of law decides to admit evidence, it is a matter for the tribunal of fact to decide how much weight to attach to it.

There are a number of ways in which weight will influence what a lawyer does, as follows:

(a) A lawyer may seek to *influence* the weight to be attached to evidence by the tribunal of fact. An advocate cross-examining a witness is generally seeking to reduce the weight to be attached to the evidence of that witness. An advocate must therefore be aware of how particular evidence or questions might affect the weight that might be attached to other evidence in the case.

(b) Lawyers do not only fight cases at trial. Many cases are settled before trial. Defendants in criminal proceedings plead guilty in the face of strong evidence and civil litigants compromise their claims in the face of strong opposition. Therefore, lawyers must be able to *assess* the weight of evidence for both parties so that they can give clear advice about the prospects of success.

(c) Lawyers will often have to *argue* about the weight to be attached to evidence. This arises in a number of different ways:

   (i) In both civil and criminal cases advocates will make submissions or speeches to the tribunal of fact. In doing so, they seek to persuade the tribunal to reach the desired conclusions by emphasising the weight of favourable evidence and attacking the apparent weight of less favourable evidence. This is only possible if the advocate understands the strengths and weaknesses of the evidence as presented.

   (ii) As will be seen in later chapters of this manual (such as **Chapter 9** on character evidence, and later in this chapter), some evidence is excluded in part because of its lack of weight. To conduct arguments about the probative force of evidence, the weight of that evidence must be understood and explained.

   (iii) The failure to call sufficient evidence (ie evidence of sufficient weight) on a particular issue or as a whole has procedural consequences. The most dramatic is the submission of no case to answer (see the ***Criminal Litigation and Sentencing*** manual or ***Blackstone's Criminal Practice***). Furthermore, as will be seen in **Chapter 2**, a party is only required to disprove an issue once the opposing party has called evidence of sufficient weight to put the matter in issue.

1.3.2.2 Challenges to the weight of evidence

A distinction may be drawn between evidence which is relevant to the facts in issue and evidence which is relevant to the credibility of a witness. For example, where an eyewitness to a criminal offence is shown to have poor eyesight and a grudge against the defendant, these would be matters going, not to the facts in issue, but to the credibility of the witness. Evidence affecting credibility is also known as collateral evidence and includes:

(a) challenges to the truthfulness of particular witnesses;

(b) challenges to the ability of the particular witnesses to give an accurate account;

(c) challenges to the strength or validity of the arguments or generalisations made about the evidence; and

(d) alternative explanations about the evidence.

Guidance on the weight to be attached to evidence is occasionally given in case law (eg *R v Turnbull* [1977] QB 224 on identification, see **Chapter 16**) or by statute law (eg Civil Evidence Act 1995, see **Chapter 12**) on what might influence the weight to be attached to the evidence.

1.3.2.3 Collateral evidence

Both civil and criminal courts seek to limit the extent to which collateral evidence will be admitted. Collateral evidence does not prove or disprove the facts in issue at trial but it may affect the reception or admissibility of other evidence tendered to prove a fact in issue. Collateral facts are those facts affecting the competence or credibility of a witness, and preliminary facts which must be proved as a condition precedent to the admission of certain items of evidence (for which see **1.5.1**). While clearly of use to the tribunal of fact, to allow collateral facts to be admitted on all occasions could lead to a great deal of evidence being admitted which does not directly bear on the issues in the case. This concern about keeping cases focused on the factual disputes has led to a general rule restricting collateral evidence, namely the rule of finality. This will be examined in detail at **7.10**.

1.3.3 Probative value and prejudicial effect

Probative value and prejudicial effect are often balanced one against the other. As will be seen at **1.6.2**, in a criminal case where the probative value of evidence is outweighed by its prejudicial effect, that evidence may be excluded (ie it will never go before the jury). What, then, do these two concepts mean?

Probative value is a combination of relevance (what something might prove) and weight (whether it does prove it). Probative value is essentially an evaluation of the extent to which an item of evidence proves a case in a rational way.

Prejudicial effect is an evaluation of the *risk* that the evidence in question will be used by the tribunal in an inappropriate way, for example, becoming distracted from deciding the case to the requisite standard of proof or taking into consideration irrelevant or immaterial matters. Prejudicial effect includes an over-willingness on the part of the tribunal of fact to convict (or make some other adverse finding) contrary either to the relevance or the weight that ought to be attached to the evidence before it.

In so far as these concepts are to be compared and balanced, no real guidance has been provided on when one outweighs the other. As will be seen at **1.6.2**, the balance is exercised as a judicial discretion and therefore rules about how the test ought to be applied have been avoided.

1.4 Proof of facts without evidence

One party or another must prove each and every fact in issue. This is usually done by adducing evidence at court. Most of this manual concerns the restrictions on the admissibility of that evidence. However, before examining such matters, it should be recognised that there are rules of practice and procedure which allow the court to reach conclusions on some facts in issue (or even on some very small details of a case) without calling evidence. Two of these will be examined: formal admissions and judicial notice. This section will also deal with the question of the extent to which the tribunal of fact or law can rely upon its own personal knowledge to fill evidential gaps in the case. Presumptions, another means by which a party may prove a fact without adducing evidence, will be considered in **Chapter 3**.

1.4.1 Formal admissions

Both the civil and criminal courts have rules of procedure which allow the parties to reduce the number of facts in issue in a case which have to be proved by evidence. These rules allow a party formally to admit a fact in issue or a fact that might assist in proving a fact in issue. A formal admission of this sort determines that particular matter: it is proved and no further evidence will be admitted to prove or disprove it.

Formal admissions are often made to enable cases to be disposed of more quickly and efficiently where there is no serious dispute on the matters admitted. Occasionally, however, a party might see a tactical advantage in admitting a particular fact, rather than running extra risks in requiring the other side to call damaging evidence to prove it.

Note the distinction between formal and informal admissions:

(a) A *formal* admission is the result of a rule of procedure. The effect of the formal admission is that the particular issue is finally resolved: the admission is conclusive of that fact. Following a formal admission, evidence that proves or disproves that issue alone ceases to be relevant and will not be admitted.

(b) In contrast, a party may make an *informal* admission, for example, by admitting to another person (including a police officer in a police station) particular relevant facts. This latter type of admission, commonly known as a confession, is only evidence of that particular fact. It is still possible for the tribunal of fact to disregard it. For detailed analysis of the rules of evidence concerning informal admissions, see **Chapter 14**.

1.4.1.1 Criminal cases

Formal admissions are governed by the Criminal Justice Act 1967. Section 10(1) provides:

> *Subject to the provisions of this section, any fact of which oral evidence may be given ... may be admitted ... and the admission by any party of any such fact under this section shall, as against that party, be conclusive evidence ... of the fact admitted.*

Section 10(2) sets out how such formal admissions are made. In essence, the section provides that formal admissions:

- can be made by or on behalf of the defendant or the prosecutor (s 10(1));
- can be made at trial or before trial (s 10(2)(a));
- can be made orally in court. If made on behalf of the defendant, they must be made by the defendant's solicitor or barrister (s 10(2)(b) and (d));
- can be made in writing either in court or outside of court. The written formal admission must be signed either by the defendant (or prosecutor) in person or, if the party making the admission is a company, by an appropriate officer of that company (s 10(2)(c)).

A formal admission may be withdrawn with leave of the court (s 10(4)). *R v Kolton* [2000] Crim LR 761 suggests that this will only happen rarely. The court will expect cogent evidence from both the party making the admission and that party's legal representatives which shows the admission to have been made by mistake or misunderstanding.

The Criminal Procedure Rules 2015 (Crim PR), r 24.6 and r 25.13 provide that in proceedings before the magistrates' court and before the Crown Court respectively a written record must be made of the admission unless the court directs otherwise.

1.4.1.2 Civil cases

Statements of case may formally admit facts in issue. However, the CPR also provide for situations in which parties may wish to admit facts once the statement of case process has ended. CPR, r 14.1, allows a party to admit the truth of the whole or any part of another party's case by giving notice in writing (such as in a statement of case or by letter). Such admissions can be made voluntarily by a party, usually to save costs and time. The court may also allow a party to amend or withdraw an admission. Furthermore, there are various provisions of the CPR that allow one party to request or demand of another party admissions on particular points or issues, such as the 'notice to admit facts' (r 32.18) and the rules relating to written requests or court orders to provide additional information (r 18.1).

1.4.2 Judicial notice

In some cases, a judge may take judicial notice of a fact. Where this happens, there is no longer any requirement to prove the fact in question. The matter is accepted by the court without evidence being adduced.

1.4.2.1 Judicial notice without enquiry

There are some matters which are so obvious or so far beyond dispute that it would be a waste of court resources for them to have to be proved every time a case is litigated. In such situations it is possible for a judge to 'take notice' of the fact and to dispense with any requirement that it be proved.

Where a fact is so commonly agreed as to be beyond serious dispute, a judge may take notice of it without hearing any evidence. Famous examples include:

- *R v Luffe* (1807) 8 East 193 (two weeks is too short a period for human gestation);
- *Dennis v A J White and Co* [1916] 2 KB 1 (that the streets of London are full of traffic);
- *Nye v Niblett* [1918] 1 KB 23 (cats are ordinarily kept for domestic purposes); and
- *Green v Bannister* [2003] EWCA Civ 1819 (the existence of a 'blind spot' that cannot be observed in a car's wing mirror).

Some matters are taken on judicial notice by virtue of legislation. For example:

- Acts of Parliament do not have to be proved by evidence. It is not necessary to prove an Act's content or that it was passed by both Houses of Parliament (Interpretation Act 1978, ss 3 and 22(1)); and
- European Union Treaties, the Official Journal of the Communities, and decisions of the European Court of Justice (ECJ) are taken on judicial notice (European Communities Act 1972, s 3(2)).

1.4.2.2 Judicial notice after enquiry

Where a fact is not quite so widely known, it is still possible for judicial notice of that fact to be taken. However, in such cases, the judge will conduct an investigation. This will happen when the matter is one that is easily resolved by reference to sources of great reliability (such as ministerial certificates or learned works, etc).

This enquiry is not a trial on the matter. The rules of evidence do not regulate what the judge may consult and it is not possible to call evidence to rebut the judge's findings. Furthermore, the conclusions of the judge in a particular case constitute a binding legal precedent on the point.

This form of judicial notice will take place in relation to the following types of information:

(a) facts of a general nature which can be readily demonstrated by reference to authoritative extraneous sources, such as diaries, atlases, encyclopaedias, etc. In

McQuaker v Goddard [1940] 1 KB 687, a judge resolved that a camel was a domestic creature by consulting books and hearing expert evidence;

(b) facts of a political nature, for example relations between the UK Government and a foreign state or the status of a foreign sovereign or government. Judicial notice can be taken of these matters following enquiry of political sources. In *R v Bottrill, ex p Kuechenmeister* [1947] 1 KB 41, judicial notice was taken of the fact that the country was still at war with Germany after examining a certificate from the Foreign Secretary to that effect; and

(c) customs and professional practices following consultation of suitably qualified experts in that field or area. For example, in *Heather v P-E Consulting Group Ltd* [1973] Ch 189, judicial notice was taken of accountancy practices.

1.4.3 Personal knowledge

To what extent can a judge take judicial notice of something within his own personal knowledge? May a juror or a magistrate do so? The general rule is that neither a judge nor the jurors may apply their personal knowledge of facts in issue or relevant to the issue (*Palmer v Crone* [1927] 1 KB 804) and jurors should be warned not to take steps to acquire such knowledge during the trial (eg by visiting the scene of an alleged crime) (*R v Oliver* [1996] 2 Cr App R 514). In *Bowman v DPP* [1991] RTR 263, the use of personal knowledge was distinguished from judicial notice. It was also stated that any personal knowledge ought to be identified, so as to allow comment by parties to the case.

However, the courts have allowed judges to use their general knowledge and magistrates may use their local knowledge in reaching decisions (eg *Paul v DPP* (1989) 90 Cr App R 173). In *Wetherhall v Harrison* [1976] QB 773, the Divisional Court drew a distinction between judges, on the one hand, and jurors and magistrates, on the other. It said that the former ought not to use their personal knowledge but the latter could do so in the interpretation and evaluation of evidence heard at trial. The rationale was in part to facilitate the sharing of their personal experiences and local knowledge. This does not extend to allowing a juror or magistrate to give evidence of matters within their personal knowledge.

There are no clear rules on the extent to which personal knowledge of matters not established by evidence can be used. In part, this is due to the difficulty of separating the personal knowledge of a judge from judicial notice in many cases. So far as personal knowledge of jurors and lay magistrates is concerned, as their deliberations take place away from the public gaze it will rarely be apparent that they have not resorted to personal knowledge or experience.

In *Hammington v Berker Sportcraft Ltd* [1980] ICR 248, it was stated that the tribunal of fact should only be able to rely on personal knowledge if the parties had been given the opportunity to deal with the evidence during the trial.

1.5 Admissibility

So far, we have considered how evidence proves cases. However, we shall see in the rest of this manual that many of the rules of evidence are concerned with whether evidence that could prove a relevant fact will be admitted. The starting point is that any item of evidence, if sufficiently relevant, is admissible unless there is a specific rule that it is not admissible. In other words, the vast majority of the rules of evidence are about the *inadmissibility* of evidence: the rules of evidence are a series of filters keeping evidence out of court rather than a series of principles letting it in.

For example, an item of evidence might be relevant in a particular criminal case but because it is given by an incompetent witness it is *inadmissible*.

1.5.1 Preliminary facts

Some rules of evidence simply state that evidence of a particular class is admissible or inadmissible as a matter of law or logic. The court can determine the admissibility of this evidence without, for example, having to determine whether the evidence was obtained in a particular way and without hearing evidence on this point.

However, some rules of evidence state that evidence will not be admissible if it was obtained in particular circumstances (such as the exclusion of confession evidence obtained by oppression under s 76(2)(a) of the Police and Criminal Evidence Act 1984), or that evidence will only be admitted if certain matters are proved (eg a witness cannot give expert opinion evidence until he or she is accepted as an expert). Therefore, admissibility depends on proof of particular collateral facts known as preliminary facts. The facts that lead to the admission or exclusion of evidence are not ordinary facts in the case. They do not go to prove the facts in issue themselves. They are a necessary step for the admission of other evidence. They are called *preliminary facts* because they have to be proved *before* the evidence to which they relate can be admitted. The process used in court for determining these factual disputes is called a 'trial within a trial' or a *voir dire*.

1.6 Exclusion

There is no general judicial discretion to *include* evidence which is rendered inadmissible by a rule of evidence (see *Sparks v R* [1964] AC 964, PC and *Myers v DPP* [1965] AC 1001, HL). However, there is a power to exclude otherwise admissible evidence in both civil and criminal cases.

1.6.1 Civil cases

The general exclusionary discretion is contained in CPR, r 32.1, which provides:

> *(1) The court may control the evidence by giving directions as to—*
> *(a) the issues on which it requires evidence;*
> *(b) the nature of the evidence which it requires to decide those issues; and*
> *(c) the way in which the evidence is to be placed before the court.*
> *(2) The court may use its power under this rule to exclude evidence that would otherwise be admissible.*
> *(3) The court may limit cross examination.*

This power should be exercised to give effect to the 'overriding objective' of enabling the court to deal with cases justly and at proportionate cost (see CPR, r 1.1; Sime, ***A Practical Approach to Civil Procedure***, or the ***White Book***).

1.6.2 Criminal cases

There are important discretions to exclude evidence in criminal cases. There are two types of discretion which must be considered:

- discretion to exclude prejudicial evidence; and
- discretion to exclude evidence obtained unfairly.

1.6.2.1 Discretion to exclude prejudicial evidence

In *R v Sang* [1980] AC 402, it was held that a trial judge had a common law discretion to exclude evidence tendered by the prosecution if its prejudicial effect outweighed its probative value. This discretion was an aspect of the judge's duty to regulate the trial process. It is important to be clear about the two important concepts: probative value and prejudicial effect. These have already been referred to at **1.3.3**.

- *Probative value* This is the likely effect of the evidence on the minds of a tribunal of fact which is acting rationally.
- *Prejudicial effect* This is the use of evidence in an irrational way. The prejudicial effect could either be the capacity of the evidence to tempt the tribunal of fact to convict on inadequate evidence (eg because the evidence causes the jury to be disgusted with the defendant's alleged conduct), or to reach false conclusions on the evidence in question (eg evidence that the defendant has committed offences in the past might be given too much weight in deciding his or her guilt for the present offence).

The discretion to exclude prejudicial evidence is useful in situations in which evidence might prove more than one thing. On the one hand, it will have probative value but, on the other, it will have one or more prejudicial effects.

Note that this principle does not oblige the judge to exclude such evidence; it is a matter of judicial discretion. The judge has to weigh up the probative value of the evidence and compare it to the risk of prejudice.

The exclusionary discretion only applies to evidence tendered by the prosecution, not evidence tendered by a co-accused (*R v Lobban* [1995] 2 All ER 602). The discretion exists to protect the accused from wrongful conviction. Thus, where a defendant seeks to exclude evidence adduced by a co-defendant, the judge would not be able to act without potentially increasing the risk of the wrongful conviction of the co-defendant. Therefore, the judge has no discretion to intervene in such a situation.

This discretion applies to any prosecution evidence which may lead the jury to follow an impermissible line of reasoning. *R v Lobban*, for example, concerned prejudice deriving from the admissibility of statements made in confessions, whereas another application may be for evidence of previous bad character by a defendant.

1.6.2.2 Discretion to exclude unfairly obtained evidence

There is a statutory discretion under s 78 of the Police and Criminal Evidence Act 1984 (PACE 1984) to exclude evidence as follows:

> *(1) In any proceedings the court may refuse to allow evidence on which the prosecution proposes to rely to be given if it appears to the court that, having regard to all the circumstances, including the circumstances in which the evidence was obtained, the admission of the evidence would have such an adverse effect on the fairness of the proceedings that the court ought not to admit it.*

The detail of this discretion will be considered in **Chapter 14**. However, some preliminary points are worth noting:

(a) There is some overlap between this statutory power and the common law power noted earlier. However, the main difference is that the common law discretion is limited to balancing the probative value of the evidence and the irrational ways in which a jury may evaluate that same evidence. In exercising its discretion under s 78, both the probative value and the way in which the evidence might be misused may be taken into consideration, but s 78 goes much further. The court is required to consider the effect on the fairness of the proceedings and to examine how the evidence was obtained. This means that potentially probative evidence that would not lead to prejudicial thinking on the part of the jury could be excluded if it would have an adverse effect on the fairness of proceedings for other reasons. Examples of such exclusion include tricks played on the accused and/or his legal advisers with a view to obtaining confessions (*R v Mason* [1988] 1 WLR 139); denial of the accused's right to legal advice (*R v Samuel* [1988] QB 615); and the improper use of undercover surveillance (*R v Loosely* [2001] 1 WLR 2060).

(b) This discretion only applies before evidence is admitted. Once it has been admitted, the defence will have to rely on the common law discretion to exclude the evidence that is preserved by s 82(3) (see *R v Sat-Bhambra* (1989) 88 Cr App R 55).

1.6.2.3 Appealing a refusal to exercise a discretion to exclude

As the exclusion of the evidence both at common law and under PACE 1984, s 78 is discretionary, it will be very difficult to overturn a judge's decision on such a matter on appeal. In such situations the court will not intervene unless the discretion was exercised perversely by either refusing to exercise a discretion or erring in principle: see *R v Cook* [1959] 2 QB 340 and *R v Uniacke* [2003] EWCA Crim 30. However, the failure by a judge to apply (or show the application of) the concepts of relevance and weight or other matters relevant to the discretion in question may lead to his or her exercise of discretion being overturned.

1.6.2.4 Other discretions

Various statutes have created discretions to exclude particular classes of otherwise admissible evidence. For example, the Criminal Justice Act 2003 (CJA 2003), s 101(3) allows the judge to exclude evidence of the defendant's bad character, while s 126 of the same Act provides the court with a discretion to exclude hearsay evidence. These provisions are considered further in **Chapters 9** and **13** respectively.

1.7 Adducing evidence

An advocate can only advance arguments based on evidence which has been presented to the court by legitimate means. The three bases of putting evidence before the court ('adducing evidence') are:

- testimony;
- documentary evidence; and
- real evidence.

1.7.1 Testimony

This is evidence that is given by a witness. Usually the witness will attend court, swear an oath or affirm, stand in the witness box and give his or her evidence orally. Each statement of fact by the witness is evidence of that fact. Having been given by a witness, the evidence becomes 'testimony'.

There are rules of procedure which allow parties to rely on written witness statements in place of calling the witness. In criminal cases this is, for example, by virtue of s 9 of the Criminal Justice Act 1967 (see **4.4.1.1**). In civil cases, CPR, r 32.5(2) permits a witness's statement to stand as his or her evidence-in-chief unless the court orders otherwise (see **4.5.1**).

1.7.2 Documentary evidence

Documentary evidence is evidence which is contained in a document. The contents of the documents are not treated as the testimony of the maker.

Like oral statements, the content of a document is subject to the general rules of evidence on admissibility but, in addition, documentary evidence must be 'proved' by a witness. This means that the origin and relevance of the document must be established. It does not mean that the author of the document must in all cases be established. An anonymous note found lying at the scene of a crime might be admissible to prove certain facts without actually establishing who wrote it (although such proof may often be necessary to establish the relevance of the document to the proceedings in question). What proof in this sense requires is that it is established that the document has some bearing on the case in question.

1.7.3 Real evidence

Real evidence derives its evidential value from the physical nature of an object. The item is produced in court (as an exhibit) or the court will go on a site visit, for example, when the court goes to the place where an incident took place (often referred to as the *locus in quo*) to view it. The significance of real evidence is that the tribunal of fact can reach conclusions based on the physical characteristics of the item or place rather than any words narrated. Therefore, a book could be both documentary evidence (by reading and interpreting it) and real evidence (by examining its physical characteristics). Furthermore, a witness in court would be giving testimonial evidence but the witness would also be real evidence himself or herself in so far as the tribunal of fact evaluates him or her as a person while giving evidence to determine, for example, whether he or she appears to be telling the truth or whether (where relevant to an issue in the case) he or she has particular physical characteristics.

1.8 Tribunals of fact and law

1.8.1 General rule: the distinction between the tribunal of law and the tribunal of fact

The general rule is that the tribunal of fact in any given case will decide the facts and that the tribunal of law will decide the law. In the Crown Court, this distinction is clear to see. The judge, as the tribunal of law, deals with legal issues and will often do so in the absence of the jury. The jury deals with factual issues and the judge is under a duty to remind jurors that this is their function, not his (*R v Jackson* [1992] Crim LR 214). The Crown Court Compendium 2017, Part 1 (Functions of judge and jury), gives judges guidance on the directions that juries should receive in respect of the different functions of the judge and jury. These include:

(1) The judge and the jury play different parts in a criminal trial.

(2) The judge alone is responsible for legal matters. When summing up the judge will tell the jury about the law which is relevant to the case, and the jury must follow and apply what the judge says about the law.

(3) The jury alone are responsible for weighing up the evidence, deciding what has or has not been proved, and returning a verdict/verdicts based on their view of the facts and what the judge has told them about the law.

1.8.2 Exceptions to the general rule

The tribunal of law will decide factual matters in the following cases.

1.8.2.1 Summing up to the jury

The judge is not completely barred from considering and commenting upon the evidence in a case. As noted in **1.8.1**, it was said in *R v Jackson* [1992] Crim LR 214 that the judge should direct the jury on its respective functions. However, the judge should remind the jury of the evidence and review it. Clearly, this will involve some evaluation and consideration of the evidence. A judge may comment on the weight of evidence, plausibility, and credibility of a witness provided that he also makes clear that the jury are not bound by his views on the evidence. It is probably true to say, however, that the judge is not in fact *deciding* factual issues.

Where the judge strays too far in commenting or sifting the facts of a case, there may be a ground for appeal (see the ***Criminal Litigation and Sentencing*** manual or ***Blackstone's Criminal Practice***).

1.8.2.2 Preliminary facts and the *voir dire*

As noted at **1.5.1**, some questions as to the admissibility of evidence must be resolved by the proof of particular facts ('preliminary facts'). As the issue of admissibility is a matter of law, the tribunal of law must determine it and will therefore have to decide whether the facts relevant to admissibility have been established. For example, by virtue of s 76(2)(a) of PACE 1984, a confession is only admissible if the prosecution proves that it was not obtained by oppression. As the consequence of proving this issue is the admissibility or inadmissibility of a confession, it must be resolved by the judge and it is therefore the judge who will have to decide whether there was in fact oppressive conduct that led to the confession.

Generally, the process of establishing the admissibility of evidence should be something of which the jury is unaware as its awareness of such evidence could lead to prejudice against a party if the evidence were subsequently excluded. Therefore, the determination of admissibility is achieved by a 'trial within a trial' or *voir dire*, which takes place in the absence of the jury. As its name suggests, this is a trial to resolve a preliminary issue during or at the start of the main trial to which it relates. Both parties can call witnesses on the matter in question and make submissions. The judge will then decide the issue and give reasons for the conclusion reached. In this respect, the judge is clearly exercising the role of a fact-finder. For further details of the *voir dire* process, see the ***Criminal Litigation and Sentencing*** manual and ***Blackstone's Criminal Practice***.

Not all determinations of preliminary issues take place in the absence of the jury. Many matters (such as whether a witness is qualified to give expert evidence) are conducted in the presence of the jury. This is generally the case where the matter would not take long to resolve and where the jury would not be likely to reach prejudicial conclusions from knowing of the existence of the evidence.

1.8.2.3 Sufficiency of evidence

As will be seen in **Chapter 2**, one party or another must call sufficient evidence to put a matter in dispute at trial ('discharging the evidential burden'). This is a question of law that must be resolved by analysis of the evidence.

In criminal cases the prosecution has to prove that there is a case for the defence to meet on all of the elements of the offence. In the Crown Court, the test is that set out in *R v Galbraith* [1981] 1 WLR 1039, CA:

> (1) If there is no evidence that the crime alleged has been committed by the defendant, there is no difficulty—the judge will stop the case.
>
> (2) The difficulty arises where there is some evidence but it is of a tenuous character, for example, because of inherent weakness or vagueness or because it is inconsistent with other

> evidence ... where the judge concludes that the prosecution evidence, taken at its highest is such that a jury properly directed could not properly convict on it, it is his duty on a submission being made to stop the case.

In a magistrates' court, Crim PR, r 24.3(3) provides as follows:

> *(3) ...*
>
> ...
>
> *(d) at the conclusion of the prosecution case, on the defendant's application or on its own initiative, the court—*
>
> *(i) may acquit on the ground that the prosecution evidence is insufficient for any reasonable court properly to convict, but*
>
> *(ii) must not do so unless the prosecutor has had an opportunity to make representations.*

A submission that there is no case for the defence to meet is known as a submission of no case to answer. The trial judge may only entertain such a submission at the close of the prosecution case. The reason for the jurisdiction to entertain such a submission to be exercised at that stage of the trial is that it is only then that it is known for certain what the evidence actually is. Until then, the most that can be known is what it is expected to be. It may sometimes be helpful for the parties to agree to ask the judge to rule as a matter of law whether on agreed or admitted facts the offence charged is made out. This may be done before evidence is called, for example, with a view to the prosecution accepting that it may offer no evidence if the ruling is against it, or with a view to a defendant considering whether to plead guilty if the ruling is otherwise. Similarly, a ruling may be sought part way through the prosecution case where the outstanding evidence is not disputed but has not yet been adduced. However, in such a case, any direction to the jury to return a verdict of 'Not guilty' ought ordinarily to await the end of the prosecution case, unless the prosecution bows to the ruling and offers no further evidence (*R v N Ltd* [2009] 1 Cr App R 3, CA). The submission must be made in the absence of the jury, who should not be told that the submission took place (*R v Smith* (1987) 85 Cr App R 197, CA). For further details on submissions of no case to answer, see the ***Criminal Litigation and Sentencing*** manual or ***Blackstone's Criminal Practice***.

In civil cases, the judge has a discretion whether to allow a party to make a submission of no case to answer, and a further discretion whether to put the party making the submission to its election whether it will call any evidence if the submission is unsuccessful (see Sime, ***A Practical Approach to Civil Procedure*** or the ***White Book***).

1.8.2.4 The meaning of words

In *Brutus v Cozens* [1973] AC 854, HL, it was stated that, generally, the meaning of words is a question of fact for the jury to determine. However, Lord Reid envisaged that words might require judicial interpretation if it is shown that they are being used in an unusual way in the statute in question or if there is an issue as to whether the jury reached a perverse interpretation of the word in question.

1.8.2.5 Other special cases

There are particular situations in which the law has given the judge the responsibility of determining questions of fact. For example:

(a) in libel cases it is for the judge to determine whether a document is *capable* of bearing a defamatory meaning. It is then a matter for the jury whether the document does bear the defamatory meaning (*Nevill v Fine Arts and General Insurance Co Ltd* [1897] AC 68 and *Jameel v Wall Street Journal Europe* [2004] EMLR 6);

(b) under the Perjury Act 1911, s 1(1), a person commits perjury if he or she makes a false statement that is 'material' to a proceeding. It is a question of law whether a statement was in fact material (s 11(6)); and

(c) questions of foreign law are questions of fact to be determined after consideration of evidence. However, in criminal cases under s 15 of the Administration of Justice Act 1920 and in civil cases under s 69(5) of the Senior Courts Act 1981 and s 68 of the County Courts Act 1984, it is for the judge rather than the jury to decide this issue.

1.8.3 When the same person or persons exercise the role of the tribunal of law and the tribunal of fact

In a magistrates' court and in civil courts where a jury is not used, the functions of the tribunal of law and the tribunal of fact are exercised by the same person or persons. Therefore, a county court judge or a magistrate will determine both legal and factual issues. This often makes the process much simpler and more efficient but it also poses two practical difficulties for a lawyer.

(a) It can be difficult to determine the basis upon which a decision has been reached. In jury trials, while the same difficulty can arise, the appellate courts will consider the way in which the jury was directed by the judge to determine how it might have reached its decisions and to decide whether there is a valid basis of appeal due to an error. Where the same person or persons are both tribunal of law and tribunal of fact, there is no practical requirement for the tribunal of law to tell the tribunal of fact how to apply legal concepts. Therefore, there is nothing upon which to base an appeal. To solve this difficulty, the rules of procedure for various courts lay down rules requiring the court to give reasons for its decisions. Quite how much reasoning is required varies, depending on the type of court. See the ***Criminal Litigation and Sentencing*** manual; ***Blackstone's Criminal Practice***; Sime, ***A Practical Approach to Civil Procedure***, or the ***White Book*** for detail on the giving of reasons.

(b) The same person or persons will both determine that evidence is inadmissible and will, at some later point, decide the factual issues in the case. In jury trials, where evidence is to be excluded, the decision to exclude will be made in the absence of the jury. If the application succeeds, the jury will not have heard the evidence and will not have to discount it. Where there is no jury, this is not usually possible. Magistrates, for example, may decide to exclude a confession under s 78 of PACE 1984, and will then have to proceed on the assumption that they never heard it. Clearly, there is a risk that the bench will not be able to disregard that evidence completely. However, it is an implicit feature of these court processes that the magistrates, or the judge in a civil court, will be able to ignore evidence in such circumstances. Where magistrates exclude evidence of a defendant's pre-trial statements, the correct approach is for the magistrates to seek the views of the parties and then consider whether the substantive hearing should be dealt with by a differently constituted bench (*DPP v Lawrence* [2008] 1 Cr App R 147).

2

Burden and standard of proof

2.1 Introduction

2.1.1 Burden of proof

The law of evidence recognises two principal burdens:

- the legal burden; and
- the evidential burden.

2.1.1.1 The legal burden

The legal burden is the obligation placed on a party to prove a fact in issue to the required standard. The legal burden is also known as the 'persuasive burden' and the 'burden of proof'. Whether a party has discharged the legal burden to the required standard of proof is a question to be determined by the tribunal of fact at the end of the trial. Where the tribunal of fact finds that a party has discharged the legal burden in respect of a particular fact in issue, that fact in issue has been proved. By contrast, where a party fails to discharge a legal burden, they will lose on the issue in question.

2.1.1.2 Evidential burden

The evidential burden is the obligation on a party to adduce sufficient evidence to raise a fact in issue, that is, to make a particular issue a 'live' issue at trial. Whether a party has discharged the evidential burden is a question of law for the judge. The judge will assess whether the amount and quality of the evidence adduced by a party in respect of a fact in issue is sufficient to leave the issue with the tribunal of fact for deliberation. If the judge decides that the amount and quality of the evidence is not sufficient, the party has failed to raise the fact in issue. The consequence is that the fact in issue may not be put before the fact-finding tribunal. For this reason, the evidential burden is sometimes known as 'passing the judge'.

2.1.2 Standard of proof

The standard of proof is the degree of cogency or persuasiveness required of the evidence in order to discharge a burden of proof.

2.2 Burden and standard of proof in criminal proceedings

The presumption of innocence in criminal law means that the legal burden in criminal cases properly lies with the prosecution, and that a high standard of proof is required.

2.2.1 Incidence of the legal burden

2.2.1.1 General rule

The general rule is that the prosecution bears the legal burden to prove all elements of the offence(s) on which the defendant is tried. The classic exposition of this rule was provided in *Woolmington v DPP* [1935] AC 462 by Viscount Sankey LC at pp 481–2:

> Throughout the web of the English criminal law one golden thread is always to be seen, that it is the duty of the prosecution to prove the prisoner's guilt subject to what I have already said as to the defence of insanity and subject also to any statutory exception ... No matter what the charge or where the trial, the principle that the prosecution must prove the guilt of the prisoner is part of the common law of England and no attempt to whittle it down can be entertained.

2.2.1.2 Exceptions to the general rule

2.2.1.2.1 Defence of insanity

The only common law exception to the general rule that the prosecution bears the burden of proof is the defence of insanity. Where this defence is raised, the legal burden of proving that the defendant was insane is borne by the defence (*M'Naghten's Case* (1843) 10 Cl & F 200; *R v Smith* (1910) 6 Cr App R 19; *Sodeman v The King* [1936] 2 All ER 1138). See *Criminal Liability: Insanity and Automatism, A Discussion Paper*, 23 July 2013, for the Law Commission's proposals for reform (http://www.lawcom.gov.uk/wp-content/uploads/2015/06/insanity_discussion_summary.pdf). For all other common law defences only an evidential burden is borne by the defence (see **2.2.2**).

2.2.1.2.2 Express statutory exceptions

A number of statutory defences purport to place a legal burden on the defence, commonly referred to as a 'reverse burden'. Where this is the case, the legal burden in respect of all other facts in issue remains with the prosecution. For example, the Homicide Act 1957, s 2 (as amended by the Coroners and Justice Act 2009 (CAJA 2009)) makes it a defence to murder for the defendant to prove that he or she was suffering from an abnormality of the mind, which substantially impaired his or her mental responsibility for acts or omissions in doing or being a party to the killing. See also *R v Wilcocks* [2017] Cr App R which expressly states that the legal burden lies with of this defence the accused.

2.2.1.2.3 Implied statutory exceptions

Reverse burdens may also be implied by statute, ie on its true construction. The Magistrates' Courts Act 1980, s 101 provides:

> *Where the defendant ... relies for his defence on any exception, exemption, proviso, excuse, or qualification, whether or not it accompanies the description of the offence or matter of complaint in the enactment creating the offence or on which the complaint is founded, the burden of proving the exception, exemption, proviso, excuse or qualification shall be on him: and this notwithstanding that the information or complaint contains an allegation negativing the exception, exemption, proviso, excuse, or qualification.*

An example of an implied statutory exception arises in respect of an offence of driving otherwise than in accordance with a licence under the Road Traffic Act 1988, s 87(1). The prosecution is only required to prove that the driver was driving a motor vehicle on a road and the driver must then prove that he or she held a valid licence (see *John v Humphreys* [1955] 1 WLR 325).

On its wording, s 101 of the 1980 Act is confined to summary trials. The position in trials on indictment was set out in *R v Edwards* [1975] QB 27 where the Court of Appeal held that a similar principle operated at common law that provided an exception to the general rule that the prosecution must prove every element of the offence charged. This was confirmed in *R v Hunt* [1987] AC 353 in which the Court of Appeal made it clear that when, in the case of *Woolmington v DPP* [1935] AC 462, Viscount Sankey referred to 'any statutory exceptions' he was referring to statutory exceptions in which the legal burden was borne by the accused either expressly or by implication (ie on its true construction).

The exception is limited to offences arising under enactments which prohibit the doing of an act save in specified circumstances, or by persons of specified classes or with specified qualifications, or with the licence or permission of specified authorities. These specified circumstances are categorised as provisos, exemptions, excuses, or qualifications and where an accused seeks to rely on them he will bear the legal burden. Whether a statutory provision impliedly places the legal burden of proof on the accused is a question of statutory construction for the court. Such questions are not always easy to resolve. For example, it was an offence under s 155(1) of the Factories Act 1961 not to comply with s 29(1) (now repealed) of the Act, which required that any workplace '*shall, so far as is reasonably practicable be made and kept safe for any person working therein*'. In *Nimmo v Alexander Cowan and Sons Ltd* [1968] AC 107, HL, the question arose as to whether the phrase '*so far as is reasonably practicable*' placed a legal burden on the defendant or the plaintiff in the case of proceedings brought for a statutory tort under the Factories Act 1961, s 29(1). It was held, by a majority, that it was for the plaintiff to prove that the workplace was not safe and for the defendant to prove that it was not reasonably practicable for him to do more in keeping his workplace safe than he had done.

In *R v Hunt* [1987] AC 352, the defendant was prosecuted for possession of morphine under the Misuse of Drugs Act 1971, s 5. The Misuse of Drugs Regulations 1973, Sch 1, para 3, provides that s 5 shall have no effect in relation to any preparation of morphine containing not more than 0.2 per cent of morphine. The House of Lords held that on its proper construction the statute required the prosecution to prove that the substance in question contained more than 0.2 per cent of morphine. Lord Griffiths made the following observation on the question of whether an implied statutory exception places a legal burden on an accused:

> if the linguistic construction of the statute did not clearly indicate on whom the burden should lie the court should look to other considerations to determine the intention of Parliament, such as the mischief at which the Act was aimed and practical considerations affecting the burden of proof and, in particular, the ease or difficulty that the respective parties would encounter in discharging the burden.

2.2.1.2.4 *Compatibility of reverse burdens with the presumption of innocence*

The imposition of the legal burden on the defence is open to challenge on the basis that is it incompatible with the presumption of innocence under Article 6(2) of the European Convention on Human Rights (ECHR), which provides that:

> *Everyone charged with a criminal offence shall be presumed innocent until proved guilty according to law.*

Imposing the legal burden on the defence does not inevitably give rise to a declaration of incompatibility but where the courts find that a reverse burden does infringe Article 6(2), an issue will arise as to whether the statute should be 'read down'. Where a statute is read down, only the evidential burden is borne by the accused; the prosecution bear the legal burden of proof.

The question of whether a legal burden on the defence is compatible with the presumption of innocence under the ECHR, Article 6(2) has been considered in a number of decisions by the House of Lords and the Court of Appeal. The leading authority is *Attorney-General's Reference (No 4 of 2002)* [2005] 1 AC 264, from which the following principles may be distilled:

(a) The defendant has a right to a fair trial.

(b) The presumption of innocence is an important, but not an absolute right and so derogations from the principle are permitted.

(c) The ECHR requires a balance to be struck between the rights of the individual and the wider interests of the community.

(d) There is an obligation on the state to justify any derogation from the presumption of innocence.

(e) For a reverse burden of proof to be legitimate, there must be a compelling reason justifying why it is fair and reasonable to deny the accused person the protection normally guaranteed to everyone by the presumption of innocence.

(f) In determining whether the imposition of a reverse burden is justified, the courts should have regard to:

   (i) the seriousness of the punishment that may flow from conviction;

   (ii) the extent and nature of the factual matters required to be proved by the accused, and their importance relative to the matters required to be proved by the prosecution;

   (iii) the extent to which the burden on the accused relates to facts that, if they exist, are readily provable by him as matters within his own knowledge or to which he has ready access; and

   (iv) the particular social problem or mischief that the measure has been enacted to address.

(g) Where a reverse burden infringes Article 6(2), the courts should, where possible, 'read down' the offending provision under the Human Rights Act 1998, s 3 so that it imposes only an evidential burden on the defendant. The obligation to interpret reverse burdens in this way so as to comply with s 3 of the 1998 Act is a strong one; it places a duty on the court to strive to find a possible interpretation compatible with the ECHR. It applies even if there is no ambiguity in the language of the provision and it will sometimes be necessary to adopt an interpretation that linguistically may appear strained.

(h) Where it is not possible to read down the provision, the court should make a declaration of incompatibility. However, this is a measure of last resort.

2.2.1.2.5 *Examples of statutory defences imposing a legal burden on the accused*

(a) *Road Traffic Act 1988, s 5(2)*: Where an accused is charged with an offence of being in charge of a motor vehicle on a road or other public place with an excess alcohol level under s 5(1)(b) of the Act, the defence provided by s 5(2) is that there was no likelihood of him driving (*Attorney-General's Reference (No 4 of 2002)* [2005] 1 AC 264).

(b) *Criminal Justice Act 1988, s 139(4)*: Where an accused is charged with possession of a bladed article in a public place under s 139, the defence provided by s 139(4) is that the accused had a good reason or lawful authority for being in possession of the article (*L v DPP* [2003] QB 137; *R v Matthews* [2004] QB 690).

(c) *Trademarks Act 1994, s 92(5)*: Where an accused is charged with unauthorised use of a trademark under s 92, the defence provided by s 92(5) is that the accused believed on reasonable grounds that his or her use of a sign was not infringing a trademark (*R v Johnston* [2003] 1 WLR 1736, HL).

(d) *Insolvency Act 1986, s 352*: Where an accused is bankrupt and is charged under s 353(1) with failing to inform the official receiver that property belonging to his or her estate has been disposed of, the defence provided by s 352 is that he or she had no intention to defraud or conceal the state of his or her affairs (*Attorney-General's Reference (No 1 of 2004)* [2004] 1 WLR 2111).

(e) *Protection from Eviction Act 1977, s 1(2)*: Where an accused is a landlord charged with unlawful eviction, the defence provided by s 1(2) is that he believed the occupier had ceased to reside at the premises (*Attorney-General's Reference (No 1 of 2004)* [2004] 1 WLR 2111).

(f) *Homicide Act 1957, s 4(1)*: Where an accused is charged with murder, the defence provided by s 4(1) of the Homicide Act 1957 is that the accused survived a suicide pact (*Attorney-General's Reference (No 1 of 2004)* [2004] 1 WLR 2111).

(g) *Criminal Justice and Public Order Act 1994, s 51(7)*: Where an accused is charged with witness intimidation under s 51(1), the defence is that this was not done with the relevant intention (*Attorney-General's Reference (No 1 of 2004)* [2004] 1 WLR 2111).

(h) *Immigration and Asylum Act 1999, s 84*: Where an accused is charged with providing legal services without being qualified to do so under s 91, the defence provided is that the accused must prove that he possesses the relevant qualification (*R v Clarke* [2008] EWCA 893).

2.2.1.2.6 Examples of statutory defences read down so as to impose an evidential burden on the accused

(a) *Misuse of Drugs Act 1971, s 5(3)*: Where an accused is charged with possession of drugs with intent to supply under s 5(3), the defence under s 28(2) and (3) is that the accused neither believed, suspected, nor had reason to suspect that the substance he or she had was a controlled drug (*R v Lambert* [2001] 3 All ER 547).

(b) *Terrorism Act 2000, s 11(1)*: Where an accused is charged with membership of a proscribed organisation under s 11(1), the defence provided by s 11(2) is that the organisation was not proscribed on the last time the accused was or professed to be a member and he or she had not taken part in any of its activities while it was proscribed (*Attorney-General's Reference (No 4 of 2002)* [2005] 1 AC 264).

(c) *Official Secrets Act 1989, ss 2 and 3*: Where an accused is charged with disclosing official information or material relating to defence or international relations, the defence is that the accused did not do so knowingly or had no reasonable cause to believe that it would be damaging (*R v Keogh* [2007] 1 WLR 1500).

(d) *Hunting Act 2004, s 1*: Where an accused is charged with hunting a wild mammal with a dog, the defence is that the hunting may be exempt under s 2 if, on its facts, it comes within one of the exemptions set out in Sch 1 of the 2004 Act *(R (Scott) v Taunton Deane Magistrates' Court* [2009] EWHC 105 (Admin); see also, *DPP v Wright* [2009] 3 All ER 726, DC).

(e) *Firearms Act 1982, s 1:* Where an accused is charged with control of imitation firearms readily convertible into firearms, the defence under s 1(5) is that the accused did not know and had no reason to suspect that an imitation firearm was so constructed or adapted as to be readily convertible into a firearm (*R v Williams* [2013] 1 WLR 1200).

2.2.2 Incidence of the evidential burden

The evidential burden may be described as the obligation to adduce sufficient evidence which, if believed and left uncontradicted, would justify as a possibility a finding by the jury in favour of the party bearing the burden (*Jayasena v R* [1970] AC 618).

Generally, the party who bears the legal burden on a particular issue will also bear the evidential burden on that issue. However, in some situations a party will bear only an evidential burden.

Certain common law and statutory criminal defences place an evidential burden, but not a legal burden, on the accused. Where the defendant bears only an evidential burden, the defendant must adduce such evidence as would, if believed and left uncontradicted, induce a reasonable doubt in the mind of the jury as to whether his version might not be true (*Bratty v Attorney-General for Northern Ireland* [1963] AC 386, HL). Once the accused has adduced sufficient evidence to discharge the evidential burden, the legal burden of disproving the defence then falls to the prosecution. This will be the case even if, in the judge's opinion, the defence evidence is unlikely to be of sufficient cogency or strength to be accepted by the jury. Whatever the judge thinks of the merits of the defence on the facts, it is nevertheless incumbent upon him not to withdraw the defence from the jury by impermissibly reaching his own conclusions on the facts (*R v Hammond* [2013] EWCA 2709).

While the evidential burden is most commonly discharged by the defendant adducing evidence, it will also be discharged if the defendant can point to evidence to the same effect that has been adduced by another party. Even where a defence is not specifically raised, if there is sufficient evidence of such a defence, whether adduced by the prosecution or the accused, then the judge must allow the defence to be considered by the jury (*Palmer v R* [1971] AC 814) and the legal burden to disprove the defence will be on the prosecution (*Bullard v R* [1957] AC 635, PC). This remains the case even if the defence in question has been expressly disclaimed by the accused (*R v Kachikwu* (1968) 52 Cr App R 538, CA) or is inconsistent with the defence that the accused has in fact raised (*R v Newell* [1989] Crim LR 906).

Examples of common law defences imposing an evidential burden only include:

- self-defence (*R v Lobell* [1957] 1 QB 547, CCA);
- duress (*R v Gill* (1963) 47 Cr App R 166, CCA);
- non-insane automatism (*Bratty v Attorney-General for Northern Ireland* [1963] AC 386, HL); and
- intoxication (*R v Foote* [1964] Crim LR 405).

Examples of statutory defences imposing an evidential burden only include the following:

- *Criminal Law Act 1967, s 3*, which permits the use of reasonable force to prevent the commission of a crime or effect or assist in the lawful arrest of offenders, suspected offenders, or those unlawfully at large.

- *Sexual Offences Act 2003, s 75*, which requires an accused charged with certain sexual offences to adduce (or point to) some evidence that the complainant consented where one or more of the circumstances set out in s 75(2)(a)–(f) are present. If the defendant fails to adduce (or point to) any such evidence, then the jury must presume that the complainant did not consent. The evidential burden placed on an accused relying on the defence of consent may also be seen in terms of a burden to rebut an evidential presumption that consent was not present (see **3.4.6**).
- *Coroners and Justice Act 2009, s 54*, which creates the defence of loss of self-control. This defence replaces the common law defence of provocation and, by virtue of s 54(6), is available where sufficient evidence is adduced upon which, in the opinion of the trial judge, a jury, properly directed, could reasonably conclude that the defence might apply. Where the defence is available, it will succeed unless the prosecution disproves it beyond a reasonable doubt (s 54(4)). See *R v Gurpinar* [2015] 1 WLR 3442 for the evidential implications of s 54 of the CAJA 2009.
- *Various terrorism offences*: see the Terrorism Act 2000, ss 12(4), 39(5)(a), 54, 57, 58, 77, and 118. Where an accused is charged under s 58 with collecting information likely to be useful to a terrorist, the defence that the accused had a reasonable excuse under s 118 imposes an evidential burden only (see *R v G; R v J* [2009] 2 WLR 724). See also the Northern Ireland (Emergency Provisions) Act 1996, ss 13, 32, and 33 (possession of information offences).

These statutory defences expressly state that they impose only an evidential burden on the accused and are in addition to defences which purport to place a legal burden on the accused but have been 'read down' to impose an evidential burden only (see **2.2.1.2.6**).

2.2.3 The standard of proof

2.2.3.1 The standard of proof borne by the prosecution in a criminal case

In the past, the standard of proof that the prosecution must meet in a criminal case has been described as *'beyond reasonable doubt'* (*Woolmington v DPP* [1935] AC 462, HL), *'making the jury sure'* (*R v Kritz* [1950] 1 KB 82), *'satisfied beyond a reasonable doubt so that [the jury] feel sure of the defendant's guilt'* (*Ferguson v R* [1979] 1 WLR 94 at 99, PC). In *Miller v Minister of Pensions* [1947] 2 All ER 372, Denning J, although he was dealing with a civil case, described the concept in the following terms:

> It need not reach certainty, but it must carry a high degree of probability. Proof beyond reasonable doubt does not mean proof beyond the shadow of doubt. The law would fail to protect the community if it admitted fanciful possibilities to deflect the course of justice. If the evidence is so strong against a man as to leave only a remote possibility in his favour which can be dismissed with the sentence 'of course it is possible, but not in the least probable', the case is proved beyond reasonable doubt, but nothing short of that will suffice.

However, juries have found the concept of 'reasonable doubt' difficult to apply, particularly in relation to the degree of doubt required to constitute 'reasonable doubt'. Consequently, in *R v Majid* [2009] EWCA Crim 2563, the Court of Appeal made it clear that the direction on the criminal standard of proof must avoid referring to 'beyond reasonable doubt' and should instead refer only to the standard of 'sure'. For the avoidance of doubt, this does not change the standard of proof borne by the prosecution, merely the terminology used to describe it. The Crown Court Compendium 2017,

Part 1 (burden and standard of proof) gives guidance to judges on how to direct juries in relation to the standard of proof. The Compendium gives the following advice:

> The prosecution must prove that D is guilty. D does not have to prove anything to you. He does not have to prove that he is innocent. The prosecution will only succeed in proving that D is guilty if you have been made sure of his guilt. If, after considering all of the evidence, you are sure that D is guilty, your verdict must be 'Guilty'. If you are not sure that he is guilty, or sure that he is innocent, your verdict must be 'Not Guilty'. If reference has been made to 'beyond reasonable doubt' by any advocate, the following may be added: You have heard reference to the phrase 'beyond reasonable doubt'. This means the same as being sure.

Where an issue is raised by a jury about how 'sure' they must be, they should be directed simply that fanciful possibilities may be discounted. Great care must be taken to ensure that the correct standard of proof is applied. In *JS (A Child) v DPP* [2017] EWHC 1162 (Admin), the use of the word 'viable' by a magistrates' court in finding a minor guilty of an offence under s 25 of the Road Traffic Act 1988 was found on appeal to have created the impression that the magistrates might not have applied the correct standard of proof.

2.2.3.2 The standard of proof borne by the defence in a criminal case

Where the defence bears a legal burden in relation to a fact in issue in a criminal trial, the standard of proof is the balance of probabilities (*R v Carr-Briant* [1943] KB 607).

2.2.4 The burden and standard of proof on 'preliminary facts' in a criminal case

Where the admissibility of evidence, such as a confession alleged to have been obtained by oppression, depends on the proof of particular facts, these facts are known as preliminary facts (see **1.5.1**). Generally, the party seeking to have the evidence admitted will have the burden of proving the preliminary facts in accordance with the standard imposed by the relevant rules of evidence (*R v Sartori* [1961] Crim LR 397; *R v Yacoob* (1981) 72 Cr App R 313). Thus, where the prosecution seeks to adduce evidence of a confession challenged on the basis that it was obtained by oppression, then PACE 1984, s 76(2) requires the prosecution to prove beyond reasonable doubt that it was not so obtained. Where a defendant seeks to adduce the confession of a co-defendant, and oppression is raised, then the defendant is required by PACE 1984, s 76A to disprove oppression on the balance of probabilities (see **Chapter 14**).

2.3 Civil proceedings

2.3.1 Incidence of the legal burden

2.3.1.1 Common law

In civil cases, the general rule at common law is that the legal burden on any fact in issue is borne by the party asserting and not denying: '*he who asserts must prove not he who denies*' (*Joseph Constantine Steamship Line Ltd v Imperial Smelting Corporation Ltd* [1942] AC 154; *Re H (Minors) (Sexual Abuse: Standard of Proof)* [1996] AC 563, HL). Accordingly, the claimant usually bears the legal (and evidential) burden of proving all the elements of his claim. Similarly, the defendant bears the legal (and evidential) burden of proving any defence and/or counterclaim against the claimant. This general rule includes negative assertions: '*if the assertion of a negative is an essential part of the plaintiff's case, the proof of the assertion still rests upon the plaintiff*' (*per* Bowen LJ, *Abrath v North Eastern Railway Company* (1883) 11 QBD 440, CA, at 457). So, for example, where a builder alleges breach of contract because he has not been paid for building works, he must prove not only that there was a contract for building works that were performed (positive assertions), but also that he has not been paid (a negative assertion).

The incidence of the legal burden is usually apparent from the statements of case (*BHP Billiton Petroleum Ltd v Dalmine SpA* [2003] BLR 271). However, sometimes a party may try to avoid a legal burden by drafting the statement of case in such a way that his own assertions necessarily involve contrary assertions by his opponent. *Soward v Leggatt* (1856) 7 C & P 613 provides an example. A landlord claimed that his tenant 'did not repair' the premises. The tenant claimed that he 'did well and sufficiently repair'. Although in one sense the landlord's claim that the tenant did not repair required the tenant to assert that he did repair, regardless of how the landlord drafted his statement of case, the burden remained with the landlord. It was held that he could as easily have pleaded that the defendant tenant 'allowed the house to become dilapidated'. The reality was that it was the landlord who was alleging breach of covenant and, therefore, it was for him to prove it, not for the defendant tenant to prove that there had been no breach.

However, difficulties arise when it is unclear whether a particular fact in issue is properly classified as a part of the claimant's cause in action or the defendant's defence. Where this situation arises, it is for the court to determine who bears the burden of proof. In such cases the courts will determine the issue by reference to policy considerations and, in particular, the ease or difficulty that the respective parties would encounter in discharging the burden. Thus, in *Joseph Constantine Steamship Line Ltd v Imperial Smelting Corporation Ltd* [1942] AC 154, HL, the plaintiffs were charterers of a ship who claimed damages from the owners for failure to load. However, the ship had exploded before it could be loaded and the defendant owners relied on the defence of frustration. The defence of frustration is not available where the frustrating event was the fault of the party seeking to rely on it. Therefore, the charterers argued that the defendant owners could not rely on frustration unless they proved that the explosion was not their fault. The House of Lords held that once the defence of frustration was raised, the burden of proving that the frustration was due to the negligence of the defendant owners was on the charterers.

In bailment cases it has been held that once the bailor has proved bailment, the bailee has the burden of proving that the goods were lost or damaged without fault on his or her part (*Coldman v Hill* [1919] 1 KB 443; *Levison v Patent Steam Carpet Cleaning Ltd* [1978] QB 69). The rationale for this is that it would be too onerous for the bailor to prove fault on the part of the bailee.

2.3.1.2 Agreement

In contract cases, which party bears the legal burden on a certain issue may be fixed by the express terms of the contract. Where the terms of the contract are silent as to who bears the burden on a particular issue, it is a matter of construction for the courts. In *Munro, Brice and Co v War Risks Association Ltd* [1918] 2 KB 78, a marine insurance policy against loss by perils of the sea contained an exemption clause excepting loss by capture, seizure, and consequences of hostilities. The insured ship left port and was never heard of again. It was held that it was for the claimant to show the loss was by the perils of the sea and for the defendant underwriters to show that the loss came within an exception, ie was by capture, seizure, or consequences of hostilities.

However, contrast *Munro, Brice and Co* with *Hurst v Evans* [1917] 1 KB 352, which concerned a policy of insurance against loss of or damage to jewellery unless caused by breakage or by theft or dishonesty committed by any servant of the assured. A robbery occurred during which jewellery was taken and damaged. The plaintiff claimed under the policy of insurance and, when this was refused, brought an action for damages. The defendant insurance company relied on the exemption clause arguing that the loss was caused by the theft or dishonesty of one of the plaintiff's employees. It was held that the plaintiff bore the legal burden of proving that the jewellery was not stolen or damaged by his servants or agents. This decision was clearly influenced by policy considerations, the judge stating that to hold that the burden was on the defendant, on the facts of the case, would 'produce absurd results'.

Where the claimant relies upon a proviso to an exemption clause, the courts have held that it is for the claimant to prove that the facts of the case bring it within the proviso. In *The Glendarroch* [1894] P 226, the plaintiffs sued for damage to goods shipped on *The Glendarroch*. The defendant carriers alleged that the claim fell within an exemption clause excepting liability for damage caused by perils of the sea. The plaintiffs argued that the loss did not come within the exemption clause as it was due to the fault of negligent navigation by the defendant carriers. The Court of Appeal held that it was for the plaintiffs to prove the contract and non-delivery; for the defendants to bring the case within the exemption clause (perils of the sea); but for the plaintiffs to bring the case within the proviso to the exemption clause (defendants' negligence).

2.3.1.3 Statute

The incidence of the legal burden may be fixed by statute. For example, if, in proceedings referred to in the Consumer Credit Act 1974, s 140A the debtor or any surety alleges that the credit relationship is an unfair one within the meaning of s 140A(1) then, under s 140B(9), it is for the creditor to prove the contrary.

2.3.2 Incidence of the evidential burden

The general rule in civil proceedings is that the party bearing the legal burden on a particular issue will also bear the evidential burden on that issue. In civil proceedings the judge will decide that the evidential burden has been discharged if evidence is adduced sufficient to justify the possibility of a finding that the legal burden on that issue has been discharged.

2.3.3 Standard of proof

In *Miller v Minister of Pensions* [1947] 2 All ER 372, at 374, Denning J described the standard of proof in civil cases as follows:

> If the evidence is such that the tribunal can say; 'We think it more probable than not', the burden is discharged, but, if the probabilities are equal, it is not.

There are, however, some exceptional cases where a higher, criminal standard of proof is required, for example:

(a) committal proceedings for civil contempt of court (*Re Bramblevale Ltd* [1970] Ch 128, CA; *Dean v Dean* [1987] 1 FLR 517, CA; *Re A (A Child) (Abduction: Contempt)* [2009] 1 FLR 1, HL);

(b) binding over for breach of the peace (*Percy v DPP* [1995] 1 WLR 1382, DC);

(c) where a person's livelihood is at stake (*R v Milk Marketing Board, ex p Austin*, The Times, 21 March 1983);

(d) allegations of misconduct amounting to a criminal offence in disciplinary hearings (*Re A Solicitor* [1993] QB 69, DC; *R (S) v Governing Body of YP School* [2003] EWCA Civ 1306);

(e) where an application is made for a football banning order under s 14B of the Football Spectators Act 1989 (see *Gough v Chief Constable of Derbyshire Constabulary* [2002] QC 1213, CA, where it was held that the standard of proof required was virtually indistinguishable from the criminal standard);

(f) where statute requires the criminal standard of proof (*Judd v Minister of Pensions and National Insurance* [1966] 2 QB 580).

In civil cases where allegations are made of misconduct so serious that it could form the basis of a criminal prosecution (eg allegations of child abuse in care proceedings), the standard remains the balance of probabilities. In such cases, it has been held that when applying the civil standard of proof, the courts should have regard to the seriousness of the allegation and the probability of what was alleged actually occurring. The more serious the allegation, the lower the probability of its being true and so the stronger should be the evidence in order for the court to find that the allegation is proved on the balance of probabilities (*Hornal v Neuberger Products Ltd* [1957] 1 QB 247; *R v Home Secretary, ex p Khawaja* [1984] AC 74, HL; *Re H (Minors) (Sexual Abuse: Standard of Proof)* [1996] AC 563, HL). Such an approach however was rejected by the House of Lords in *Re B (Children) (Care Proceedings: Standard of Proof)* [2009] 1 AC 11, HL. It was held that there was 'no necessary connection' between the seriousness of an allegation and the probability that it occurred. Therefore, the standard of proof that applied when deciding whether an allegation occurred, regardless of its seriousness, was the simple balance of probabilities (see also *Re D (Children)* [2009] EWCA Civ 472). According to the Supreme Court in *Re S-B (Children) (Care Proceedings: Standard of Proof)* [2010] 1 AC 678, SC, it is now settled law that there is only one single civil standard of proof, namely proof on the balance of probabilities.

3

Presumptions

3.1 Introduction

There are two types of presumption:

- presumptions with proof of basic facts; and
- presumptions without proof of basic facts.

3.2 Presumptions with proof of basic facts

This type of presumption is an evidential device that permits a court to conclude the existence of a fact ('the presumed fact') on the proof of a preliminary fact ('the basic fact'). For example, where it is proved that two persons went through a marriage ceremony with the intention to marry ('the basic fact'), the court may presume that all the formalities required for a valid marriage were complied with ('the presumed fact'). This type of presumption operates as an evidential shortcut enabling a party to prove a fact in issue without having to call any further evidence on the point.

Presumptions with proof of basic facts may be subdivided into three categories:

(a) irrebuttable presumptions of law;

(b) rebuttable presumptions of law; and

(c) presumptions of fact.

3.3 Irrebuttable presumptions of law

Definition Upon proof of the preliminary fact, the court *must* conclude the existence of the presumed fact, and no evidence may be adduced to the contrary. Thus, the presumption is said to be irrebuttable. In practice, irrebuttable presumptions are simply rules of substantive law. The following examples may be given:

3.3.1 Civil Evidence Act 1968, s 13(1)

Section 13(1) of the Civil Evidence Act 1968 provides:

In an action for libel or slander in which the question whether a person did or did not commit a criminal offence is relevant to an issue arising in the action, proof that at the time when that issue falls to be determined, that person stands convicted of that offence shall be conclusive evidence that he committed that offence; and his conviction thereof shall be admissible in evidence accordingly.

3.3.2 Children and Young Persons Act 1933, s 50

Section 50 of the Children and Young Persons Act 1933 provides:

It shall be conclusively presumed that no child under the age of 10 years can be guilty of an offence.

3.3.3 Sexual Offences Act 2003, s 76

Section 76 of the Sexual Offences Act 2003 provides:

(1) *If in proceedings for an offence to which this section applies it is proved that the defendant did the relevant act and that any of the circumstances specified in subsection (2) existed, it is to be conclusively presumed—*

  (a) *that the complainant did not consent to the relevant act, and*

  (b) *that the defendant did not believe that the complainant consented to the relevant act.*

(2) *The circumstances are that—*

  (a) *the defendant intentionally deceived the complainant as to the nature or purpose of the relevant act;*

  (b) *the defendant intentionally induced the complainant to consent to the relevant act by impersonating a person known personally to the complainant.*

Section 76 of the Sexual Offences Act 2003 applies to offences under ss 1–4 of that Act. Commentators have argued that this provision might contravene the ECHR, Article 6(2) as it deprives the defendant of the opportunity to put forward a defence, namely that the victim was aware of the deception but consented nonetheless. However, the point has yet to be tested on appeal.

3.4 Rebuttable presumptions of law

Definition Upon proof of the preliminary fact the court must conclude the existence of the presumed fact, unless sufficient evidence to the contrary is adduced. For this reason, the presumption is said to be rebuttable.

3.4.1 Civil proceedings

In civil proceedings rebuttable presumptions of law may be further divided into the following two categories:

(a) *Evidential presumptions* An evidential presumption places only an evidential burden on the party against whom it operates. Thus, in order to rebut the existence of the presumed fact, the party disputing it need only adduce some evidence on the point.

(b) *Persuasive presumptions* A persuasive presumption places a persuasive, or legal, burden on the party against whom it operates. Thus, in order to rebut the existence of the presumed fact, the party disputing it must disprove it.

3.4.2 Criminal proceedings

In criminal proceedings the position is slightly different. As noted in **Chapter 2**, the prosecution bears the burden of proving the accused's guilt. As a result, where the prosecution relies on a common law rebuttable presumption, only an evidential burden can be placed on the defendant. Similarly, where the defendant relies upon a common law rebuttable presumption, a legal burden must be placed on the prosecution. Statutory presumptions, on the other hand, may operate so as to place a legal burden on the accused.

The prosecution is further restricted in the use of presumptions in that it cannot rely on a presumption to prove facts that are central to an offence (*Dillon v R* [1982] AC 484, PC).

3.4.3 Presumption of marriage

There are two presumptions of marriage, as follows:

3.4.3.1 Formal validity

Where it is proved that the parties to the marriage went through a marriage ceremony with the intention to marry, it is presumed that the marriage complied with the formalities required for a valid marriage (*Piers v Piers* (1849) 2 HL Cas 331; *Mahadervan v Mahadervan* [1964] P 233; *Hayaleth v Modfy* [2017] EWCA Civ 70). There is little authority on the point but it is thought that this presumption applies to both civil and criminal proceedings. In civil proceedings it operates as a persuasive presumption.

3.4.3.2 Essential validity

Where it is proved that a formally valid marriage ceremony was conducted, it is presumed that the parties to the marriage had the requisite capacity and gave their consent. Again, it is thought that this presumption applies to both civil and criminal proceedings. In so far as it applies to civil proceedings, it is probably a persuasive presumption although the authorities are not entirely clear on the point (*Re Peete* [1952] 2 All ER 599; *Taylor v Taylor* [1967] P 25).

3.4.4 Presumption of legitimacy

Where paternity is in dispute, and it is proved that a child was either conceived while the mother was married (*Maturin v Attorney-General* [1938] 2 All ER 214) or born to her while she was lawfully married (*The Poulett Peerage Case* [1903] AC 395), it is presumed that the child is the legitimate offspring of the parties to the marriage. This presumption applies to civil proceedings only. It is expressly made a persuasive presumption by the Family Law Reform Act 1969, s 26. DNA evidence is likely to be sufficiently cogent to rebut the presumption (*Re Baronetcy of Pringle of Stichill* [2016] UKPC 16).

3.4.5 Presumption of death

3.4.5.1 Presumption of Death Act 2013

Pursuant to s 2 of the Presumption of Death Act 2013, if the High Court is satisfied that a missing person has not been known to be alive for a period of at least seven years, it may declare that the person is presumed to be dead. Such a declaration is 'effective against all persons and for all purposes, including the acquisition of an interest in any property, and the ending of a civil marriage or civil partnership to which the missing person is a party' (s 3(2)).

The common law on the presumption of death remains relevant as to how the court might satisfy itself that the person has not been known to be alive for the relevant period. In *Chard v Chard* [1956] P 259, it was held that the court must presume a person's death where it is proved that:

(a) there is no acceptable affirmative evidence that the person was alive during a seven-year period;

(b) there are several people who would be expected to have heard from the person during that seven-year period;

(c) those people have not heard from that person; and

(d) all due enquiries that are appropriate have been made in respect of the person.

The continued relevance of *Chard v Chard* is clear from s 12(1) of the Presumption of Death Act 2013, which provides that the High Court:

may by order at any stage require a person who is not a party to the proceedings to provide it with specified information that it considers relevant to the question of whether the missing person is alive or dead.

If the court is satisfied that the person has not been known to be alive for a period of at least seven years then the court will presume that the person died 'at the end of the period of 7 years beginning with the day after the day on which he or she was last known to be alive' (s 2(4)).

The presumption is only an evidential presumption (*A v H* [2016] EWHC 762 (Fam); *Greathead v Greathead* [2017] EWHC 1154 (Ch)). This is also implicit from the first of the basic facts identified in *Chard v Chard*.

3.4.5.2 Law of Property Act 1925, s 184

Section 184 of the Law of Property Act 1925 provides:

In all cases where ... two or more persons have died in circumstances rendering it uncertain which of them survived the other or others, such deaths shall (subject to any order of the court) ... be presumed to have occurred in order of seniority, and accordingly the younger shall be deemed to have survived the elder.

This is a persuasive presumption that applies in any civil proceedings concerning claims to property. An example of its application may be found in *Hickman v Peacey* [1945] AC 304, where the residents of a house were all killed by a bomb explosion.

3.4.6 Presumption under Sexual Offences Act 2003, s 75

Section 75 of the Sexual Offences Act 2003 provides:

(1) If in proceedings for an offence to which this section applies it is proved—

(a) that the defendant did the relevant act,

(b) that any of the circumstances specified in subsection (2) existed, and

(c) that the defendant knew that those circumstances existed,

the complainant is to be taken not to have consented to the relevant act unless sufficient evidence is adduced to raise an issue as to whether he consented, and the defendant is to be taken not to have reasonably believed that the complainant consented unless sufficient evidence is adduced to raise an issue as to whether he reasonably believed it.

The circumstances set out in s 75(2) include:

- the use of violence against the complainant at, or immediately before, the commission of the relevant act (s 75(2)(a));
- the complainant's inability to communicate consent to the defendant owing to his or her physical disability (s 75(2)(e)); and
- the administration of a substance to the complainant that was capable of causing or enabling the complainant to be stupefied or overpowered at the time of the relevant act (s 75(2)(f)).

The wording of the provision (*'unless sufficient evidence is produced'*) and the fact that the burden is borne by the defence clearly make this an evidential presumption. As a result, it is thought that this provision is compatible with the Human Rights Act 1998. This provision only applies to offences under ss 1–4 of the 2003 Act.

3.4.7 Presumption of official regularity

Where it is proved that a person has acted in a judicial, official, or public capacity, it will be presumed that the person had been properly appointed and that the act complied with all necessary formalities. This presumption applies in both civil and criminal proceedings. In civil proceedings it operates as a persuasive presumption. Two examples may be given. In *R v Cresswell* (1873) 1 QBD 446, it was proved that a building had been used for marriage ceremonies, and so it was presumed that the building had been duly consecrated. In *R v Roberts* (1878) 14 Cox CC 101, CCR, it was proved that a person had acted as a deputy county court judge, and so it was presumed that that person had been properly appointed.

3.5 Presumptions of fact

Definition Upon proof of the preliminary fact, the court may conclude the existence of the presumed fact. Presumptions of fact are no more than commonly occurring examples of inferences that may be drawn on the basis of circumstantial evidence.

There are two key differences between presumptions of law and presumptions of fact. First of all, a presumption of fact does not require the court to conclude the existence of the presumed fact; rather, it simply permits it to do so. Second, a presumption of fact has no effect on the burden of proof; instead, it places a 'tactical' burden on the party against whom it operates. In other words, because the presumption permits the tribunal of fact to find in favour of one party on a certain issue, it places a tactical obligation on the other party to call evidence on that point, because if it fails to do so, there is a danger that it may lose on that issue.

3.5.1 Presumption of intention

Section 8 of the Criminal Justice Act 1967 provides:

A court or jury, in determining whether a person has committed an offence—

(a) shall not be bound in law to infer that he intended or foresaw a result of his actions by reason only of its being a natural and probable consequence of those actions; but

(b) *shall decide whether he did intend or foresee that result by reference to all the evidence, drawing such inferences from the evidence as appear proper in the circumstances.*

The effect of this provision is that the tribunal of fact is not obliged to conclude that a defendant intended or foresaw the natural and probable consequence of his or her actions, but is permitted to infer that the defendant did so in the light of all the evidence. This presumption obviously only applies in criminal proceedings.

3.5.2 Presumption of guilty knowledge

This presumption applies where a person is charged with theft, handling stolen goods, or an offence that has theft as an ingredient, such as burglary. Where evidence is given that the accused was found in possession of the property soon after it had been stolen, and the accused either offered no explanation as to how it came to be in his or her possession, or offered an explanation that the tribunal of fact finds to be untrue, then the tribunal of fact may infer that the accused was either the thief, a handler of stolen goods, or the burglar. This presumption is more commonly known by practitioners as the doctrine of recent possession.

3.5.3 Presumption of continuance of life

Where a person is proved to have been alive on a particular date, that person may be presumed to have been alive on a subsequent date. Whether the presumption will be made in a particular case depends on factors such as the age and health of the person and the circumstances in which he or she was last seen. Clearly, the longer it is since the person was seen, the less likely it is that the tribunal of fact will reach the conclusion that he or she is still alive. This presumption applies in both civil and criminal proceedings.

3.6 *Res ipsa loquitur*

In *Scott v London and St Katherine Docks Co* (1865) 3 Hurl & C 596, it was held, *per* Erle CJ, that:

> where the thing is shown to be under the management of the defendant or his servants, and the accident is such as in the ordinary course of things does not happen if those who have management use proper care, it affords reasonable evidence, in the absence of explanation by the defendants, that the accident arose from want of care.

Thus, in a claim for negligence, where it is shown that:

(a) something is under the control of the defendant;

(b) that thing caused an accident; and

(c) the accident would not have happened if the thing had been properly managed,

then it may be presumed that the accident arose due to the negligence of the defendant. There is contradictory authority as to whether the doctrine of *res ipsa loquitur* is properly classified as a presumption of fact (see, eg, *Ng Chun Pui v Lee Chuen Tat* [1988] RTR 298, PC), a persuasive presumption (see, eg, *Woods v Duncan* [1946] AC 401), or an evidential presumption (see, eg, *The Kite* [1933] P 154). It has been argued that this presumption defies classification; the strength of the inference of negligence that may be drawn in a particular case will differ depending on the facts, and so the presumption can operate so as to place either a tactical, evidential, or legal burden on the other party.

3.7 Conflicting presumptions

Where two presumptions of equal strength apply to the facts of a case, the one leading to a conclusion that conflicts with that of the other, the authorities are unclear as to the approach that the court should adopt. *Monckton v Tarr* (1930) 2 BWCC 504, CA is authority for the view that conflicting presumptions of equal strength should cancel out each other. However, *Taylor v Taylor* [1967] P 25 suggests that the court may choose between the different presumed facts by a comparison of their likelihood, or even on the basis of policy considerations.

3.8 Presumptions without proof of basic facts

This type of presumption, in contrast to those examined so far, is not a 'true' presumption in that it does not require that a basic, or preliminary, fact be proved before the presumption can be made. It is simply a way of stating where the burden of proof lies in certain situations. The most common examples of this type of presumption are as follows:

3.8.1 Presumption of innocence

The presumption of innocence requires that in a criminal trial the court must conclude that the defendant is innocent unless the contrary is proved. It is simply a way of expressing the common law rule that the prosecution bears the legal burden of proving the accused's guilt beyond reasonable doubt.

3.8.2 Presumption of sanity

The presumption of sanity requires that in a criminal trial the court must conclude that the defendant is sane until the contrary is proved. It is simply a way of expressing the common law rule that where the defence of insanity has been raised, the accused bears the legal burden of proving it.

3.8.3 Presumption of mechanical regularity

Where a mechanical device is of a type that is ordinarily in working order, the court must conclude that it was working on the particular instance in question. A party wishing to prove that such a device was not working properly bears an evidential burden. This presumption has been used to prove that mechanical devices such as traffic lights (*Tingle Jacobs and Co v Kennedy* [1964] 1 WLR 638) and speedometers (*Nicholas v Penny* [1950] 2 KB 466) were operating properly. This presumption applies to both civil and criminal proceedings.

4 Witnesses

4.1 Introduction

The most common way for evidence to be adduced is through the testimony of a witness. In this chapter we will consider the rules that determine which persons may give evidence, when a person may be compelled to give evidence, and how a person's evidence may be given.

4.2 Competence and compellability

A witness is said to be 'competent' if he or she can as a matter of law be called by a party to give evidence. A witness is said to be 'compellable' if, being competent, he or she can as a matter of law be compelled by the court to give evidence.

A compellable witness who, having been ordered to attend court, refuses to do so, or on attending court refuses to give sworn evidence, is liable to be fined and/or imprisoned for contempt of court (in proceedings before the High Court or the Crown Court), fined and/or committed to prison (in proceedings before a magistrates' court), or fined up to £1,000 (in proceedings before a county court).

4.2.1 General rule

The general rule at common law has two limbs:

- all persons are competent; and
- all competent persons are compellable.

In criminal proceedings the first limb of the general rule has been put on a statutory footing in the Youth Justice and Criminal Evidence Act 1999 (the YJCEA 1999), s 53(1), which provides:

At every stage in criminal proceedings all persons are (whatever their age) competent to give evidence.

The rule that all persons are competent and that all competent witnesses are compellable is subject to a number of statutory and common law exceptions in both criminal and civil proceedings. We shall consider each in turn.

4.2.2 Exceptions in criminal proceedings

4.2.2.1 Children and persons of unsound mind

As noted at **4.2.1**, all persons, whatever their age, are competent to give evidence in criminal proceedings. Thus, a child witness is not prevented from giving evidence by virtue of his or her age. However, the YJCEA 1999, s 53(3) provides:

A person is not competent to give evidence in criminal proceedings if it appears to the court that he is not a person who is able to—

(a) understand questions put to him, and

(b) give answers to them which can be understood.

This exception applies to all witnesses but will most commonly affect children and persons of unsound mind. In *R v Sed* [2005] 1 Cr App R 4, a case concerning a witness suffering from Alzheimer's disease, the Court of Appeal rejected the argument that unless the witness understood all the material questions put to her and all her material answers were understandable, she could not qualify as competent within the terms of s 53. Depending on the length and the nature of the questioning and the complexity of the subject of it, 100 per cent mutual understanding between questioner and questioned is not always required as a precondition of competence. Allowance should also be made for the fact that the witness's performance and command of detail may vary according to the importance to him or her of the subject matter, how recent it was, and any strong feelings that it may have engendered. *R v MacPherson* [2006] 1 Cr App R 30 concerned a complainant who was about 4½ years old at the time of the offence, the trial taking place six months later. It was held that the test is simply one of understanding. A child should not be found incompetent on the basis of age alone. Moreover, questions of credibility, reliability, and the child's awareness of their status as a witness are not relevant to competence. See also *R v B* [2010] EWCA Crim 4, in which a child aged 4 gave evidence about offences committed when she was aged 2. It was held that under s 53(1) a witness need not understand the special importance that the truth should be told in court, nor understand every single question or give a readily understood answer to every question. Provided the witness can understand the questions put to him and can also provide understandable answers, he is competent. However, the question of a child's competence should be kept under review throughout the trial.

4.2.2.2 The accused

4.2.2.2.1 For the prosecution

Section 53(4) of the YJCEA 1999 provides:

A person charged in criminal proceedings is not competent to give evidence in the proceedings for the prosecution (whether he is the only person charged, or is one of two or more persons charged in the proceedings).

However, s 53(5) states that '*a person charged in criminal proceedings*' does not include a person who is not, or is no longer, liable to be convicted of any offence in the proceedings. An accused is thus competent to give evidence for the prosecution:

- on pleading guilty;
- on acquittal;
- where separate trials are ordered; or
- where a *nolle prosequi* has been entered on the direction of the Attorney-General.

Where the accused pleads guilty and intends to give evidence for the prosecution against his or her former co-accused, there is a danger that he or she may tailor his or her evidence in the hope of receiving a more lenient sentence. Thus, the court has a discretion to sentence him or her before evidence is given (*R v Palmer* (1993) 99 Cr App R 83). A similar situation arises where the prosecution wishes to call an accomplice against whom proceedings are pending. There is a rule of practice, but not law, that the prosecution should only be allowed to call such witnesses where it has given an undertaking either to discontinue proceedings or not to prosecute him or her (*R v Pipe* (1966) 51 Cr App R 17; *R v Turner* (1975) 61 Cr App R 67). As it is only a rule of practice, it is ultimately a matter of judicial discretion whether or not to allow the accomplice to be called.

4.2.2.2.2 *For the accused*

By virtue of the YJCEA 1999, s 53(1), the accused is competent to give evidence on his or her own behalf. However, he or she is not compellable. Section 1(1) of the Criminal Evidence Act 1898 provides:

> *A person charged in criminal proceedings shall not be called as a witness in the proceedings except upon his own application.*

Where the accused does elect to give evidence, two important consequences follow. First, any evidence that the accused may give is admissible against any co-accused (*R v Rudd* (1948) 32 Cr App R 138). Second, he is open to cross-examination by both the prosecution and any co-accused. Thus, while an accused is neither competent nor compellable for the prosecution when appearing in his or her own defence, he or she may be cross-examined by the prosecution about his own guilt and the guilt of a co-accused (*R v Paul* [1920] 2 KB 183).

If an accused decides not to testify the tribunal of fact may draw an inference against him under s 35 of the Criminal Justice and Public Order Act 1994 (considered in more detail at **15.4.5**). Consequently, counsel should record the decision and require the accused to sign the record, giving a clear indication that he or she has by their own will decided not to testify bearing in mind the advice, if any, given to him or her by their counsel (*R v Bevan* (1993) 98 Cr App R 354, CA; *R v Chatroodi* [2001] All ER (D) 259 (Feb)). In practice, this is done by endorsing the decision on the brief itself.

4.2.2.2.3 *For the co-accused*

The accused is competent as a witness for a co-accused (YJCEA 1999, s 53(1)) but is not compellable (Criminal Evidence Act 1898, s 1(1)). Once the accused is no longer a '*person charged*' in the proceedings, he or she will become compellable. An accused ceases to be a person charged:

- on pleading guilty;
- on acquittal;
- where separate trials are ordered; or
- where a *nolle prosequi* has been entered on the direction of the Attorney-General.

4.2.2.3 Spouse or civil partner of the accused

4.2.2.3.1 *Competence*

A spouse or civil partner of an accused is competent for any party in criminal proceedings (YJCEA 1999, s 53(1)) unless also a person charged in the same criminal proceedings (s 54(4)). It follows that where the accused and their spouse or civil partner are both charged in the proceedings, neither will be competent for the prosecution (s 53(4)).

4.2.2.3.2 *Compellability*

The compellability of the spouse or civil partner of the accused is governed by the Police and Criminal Evidence Act 1984 (PACE 1984), s 80:

> ...
>
> (2) *In any proceedings the spouse or civil partner of a person charged in the proceedings shall, subject to subsection (4) below, be compellable to give evidence on behalf of that person.*

(2A) In any proceedings the spouse or civil partner of a person charged in the proceedings shall, subject to subsection (4) below, be compellable—

(a) to give evidence on behalf of any other person charged in the proceedings but only in respect of any specified offence with which that other person is charged; or

(b) to give evidence for the prosecution but only in respect of any specified offence with which any person is charged in the proceedings.

(3) In relation to the spouse or civil partner of a person charged in any proceedings, an offence is a specified offence for the purposes of subsection (2A) above if—

(a) it involves an assault on, or injury or a threat of injury to, the spouse or civil partner or a person who was at the material time under the age of 16;

(b) it is a sexual offence alleged to have been committed in respect of a person who was at the material time under that age; or

(c) it consists of attempting or conspiring to commit, or of aiding, abetting, counselling, procuring or inciting the commission of, an offence falling within paragraph (a) or (b) above.

(4) No person who is charged in any proceedings shall be compellable by virtue of subsection (2) or (2A) above to give evidence in the proceedings.

(4A) References in this section to a person charged in any proceedings do not include a person who is not, or is no longer, liable to be convicted of any offence in the proceedings (whether as a result of pleading guilty or for any other reason).

(5) In any proceedings a person who has been but is no longer married to the accused shall be compellable to give evidence as if that person and the accused had never been married.

(5A) In any proceedings a person who has been but is no longer the civil partner of the accused shall be compellable to give evidence as if that person and the accused had never been civil partners.

(6) Where in any proceedings the age of any person at any time is material for the purposes of subsection (3) above, his age at the material time shall for the purposes of that provision be deemed to be or to have been that which appears to the court to be or to have been his age at that time.

(7) In subsection (3)(b) above 'sexual offence' means an offence under the Protection of Children Act 1978 or Part 1 of the Sexual Offences Act 2003, or an offence under section 2 of the Modern Slavery Act 2015 (human trafficking) committed with a view to exploitation that consists of or includes behaviour within section 3(3) of that Act (sexual exploitation).

The common law offence of incitement was abolished by the Serious Crime Act 2007, s 59 and the reference to incitement in PACE 1984, s 80(3)(c) has effect as a reference to (or to conduct amounting to) the offences of encouraging or assisting crime under Part 2 of the Serious Crime Act 2007 (s 63(1) and Sch 6, para 9 of the 2007 Act).

4.2.2.3.3 *For the prosecution*

A spouse or civil partner is only compellable to give evidence on behalf of the prosecution against the accused or any co-accused, in respect of a specified offence (PACE 1984, s 80(2A)(b)). Section 80(3)(a)–(c) provides that an offence is a specified offence if:

- it involves an assault on, or injury or threat of injury to, the spouse or civil partner (s 80(3)(a));
- it involves an assault on, or injury or threat of injury to, a person under the age of 16 (s 80(3)(a));
- it is a sexual offence committed in relation to a person under the age of 16 (s 80(3)(b)); or
- it is an offence that consists of attempting or conspiring to commit, or of aiding, abetting, counselling, procuring, or inciting the commission of any of the above offences (s 80(3)(c)).

However, where the spouse or civil partner is charged in the same proceedings, he or she is not compellable at all unless he or she is no longer liable to be convicted of any offence in the proceedings (s 80(4), (4A)).

In *R v L* [2009] 1 WLR 626, CA, it was held that the policy that prevents a spouse or civil partner from giving evidence does not extend to requiring that the police tell them that they are not a compellable witness against the accused before interviewing them about the offence. However, it may be advisable to do so because if it is clear that the evidence was given voluntarily, the court will be more inclined to admit it as hearsay in the interests of justice should an application be made (see **13.6**). See also *Horsnell* [2012] EWCA Crim 277.

The drafting of s 80 gave rise to an apparent problem which stemmed from the use of the word 'involves' in s 80(3)(a). The question arose as to whether the test was legal (ie whether s 80(3) referred to those offences that include assault, injury, or threat of injury as an element of the offence) or factual (ie whether it also includes those offences that involve assault, injury, or threat of injury, on the facts alone). The question was resolved in the case of *BA* [2013] Crim LR 168 in which the Court of Appeal held that for the purposes of s 80(3) 'involvement' must be legal. The offence need not have 'an assault on or injury or threat of injury' as an element of the offence itself as long as it encompasses a real possibility of an assault. *BA* considered a charge of threatening to destroy or damage property under s 2(a) of the Criminal Damage Act 1972, an offence directed at property. It was the prosecution case that the accused had threatened to burn down their home with their children inside it. It was held that the accused's wife was not a compellable witness for the prosecution as the offence itself did not encompass the real possibility of an assault.

4.2.2.3.4 For the accused

The spouse or civil partner of the accused is generally compellable for the accused (PACE 1984, s 80(2)). The only exception is that where the spouse or civil partner is charged in the same proceedings, he or she is not compellable unless they are no longer liable to be convicted (s 80(4), (4A)).

4.2.2.3.5 For the co-accused

A spouse or civil partner of an accused is compellable to give evidence on behalf of any other person charged in the proceedings, but only in respect of specified offences (PACE 1984, s 80(2A)(a) and s 80(3)(a)–(c)). Where the spouse or civil partner is charged in the same proceedings, he or she is not compellable unless they are no longer liable to be convicted (s 80(4), (4A)).

4.2.2.3.6 Former spouse or civil partner

PACE 1984, s 80(5) and (5A) provide that the exceptions to the general rule of compellability in s 80 do not apply where the spouse is no longer married to the accused or the civil partnership has ended. If a marriage is void *ab initio*, there never was a spouse. The marriage or civil partnership must be recognised in English law for the provisions under s 80 to apply. See *Bala* [2016] EWCA Crim 560. Thus, in *R v Khan* (1987) 84 Cr App R 44, CA, it was held that a woman with whom a man had gone through a bigamous ceremony of marriage was a competent witness against him for the prosecution. (This case was decided at a time when s 80(5) governed competence as well as compellability.) On the other hand, parties who are married remain married where they are judicially separated, or simply not cohabiting (whether by reason of an informal arrangement, a separation agreement, or a non-cohabitation order).

4.2.2.3.7 Cohabitees

In *R v Pearce* [2002] 1 WLR 1553, it was held that PACE 1984, s 80 does not cover the cohabitee of an accused who is not married to the accused.

4.2.2.4 Heads of state

The Sovereign and the sovereign or head of foreign states are competent (YJCEA 1999, s 53(1)) but not compellable witnesses. Furthermore, diplomats and consular officials, and their staff, have immunity from compellability pursuant to a wide variety of statutory provisions.

4.2.2.5 Bankers

Bankers and bank officials are competent (YJCEA 1999, s 53(1)). Their compellability is governed by the Bankers' Books Evidence Act 1879. Section 6 of that Act provides that bankers and bank officials shall not be compellable, in legal proceedings to which the bank is not a party, to produce any banker's book the contents of which may be proved under the Act, or to appear as witnesses to prove the matters recorded therein, unless by order of a judge.

4.2.2.6 Judges

Judges and masters are competent (YJCEA 1999, s 53(1)) but cannot be compelled to give evidence relating to judicial function (*Warren v Warren* [1997] QB 488).

4.2.3 Procedure

An issue regarding the competence of a witness should be determined at the beginning of the trial (*R v Yacoob* (1981) 72 Cr App R 313, CA) and in the absence of the jury (YJCEA 1999, ss 53(3) and 54(4)). Competence may be raised either by a party to the proceedings or by the court of its own motion (s 54(1)). The party calling the witness must satisfy the court, on the balance of probabilities, that the witness is competent to give evidence in criminal proceedings (s 54(2)). Any questioning of the witness is conducted by the court in the presence of the parties (s 54(6)).

The parties may call expert evidence (s 54(5)). Under different provisions of the YJCEA 1999 the court has the power to make special measures directions to facilitate the giving of evidence by a vulnerable or incapacitated witness (see **4.11**). The court, in determining competence under s 53(3), is required to treat the witness as if they have the benefit of any special measures directions that the court would make if the witness were to give evidence at trial (s 54(3)).

4.2.4 Exceptions in civil proceedings

The basic test for competence in civil cases is whether the witness is capable of understanding the nature of an oath and of giving rational testimony. The general rule in civil proceedings is that all persons are competent and that all competent persons are compellable. The only exceptions to this rule are children, persons of unsound mind, the Sovereign, foreign heads of state, diplomats, bankers, and judges.

4.2.4.1 Children

Section 96 of the Children Act 1989 provides:

> *(1) Subsection (2) applies where a child who is called as a witness in any civil proceedings does not, in the opinion of the court, understand the nature of an oath.*
>
> *(2) The child's evidence may be heard by the court if, in its opinion—*
>
> *(a) he understands that it is his duty to speak the truth; and*
>
> *(b) he has sufficient understanding to justify his evidence being heard.*

A 'child', for these purposes, is a person under the age of 18 (s 105). The court must first determine whether or not a child witness understands the oath (s 96(1)). In deciding this issue, the courts are likely to be guided by the decision of the Court of Appeal in *R v Hayes* [1977] 1 WLR 238. *Hayes* is a criminal case that was decided at a time when the position in criminal proceedings was similar to that provided by s 96. The test laid down in *Hayes* was:

> Whether the child has a sufficient appreciation of the solemnity of the occasion and the added responsibility to tell the truth, which is involved in taking an oath, over and above the duty to tell the truth which is an ordinary duty of normal social conduct.

In civil proceedings, if a child understands the nature of the oath, they may give sworn oral evidence. If, however, a child fails the test set out in *Hayes*, he or she may only give evidence if the conditions in s 96(2) are satisfied and any evidence must be given unsworn.

On matters of procedure, the courts are also likely to draw on previous criminal authority. As the competence of the witness is a matter for the judge, he should put to the child preliminary questions so as to be able to form an opinion on a child's competence as a witness (*R v Surgenor* (1940) 27 Cr App R 175). Whether a child is sufficiently young to warrant examination to see whether he or she can give sworn evidence is a matter for the judge to decide on the particular facts of the case. However, in *R v Khan* (1981) 73 Cr App R 190, CA it was held that although much depends on the type of child before the court, as a general working rule inquiry is necessary in the case of a child under the age of 14.

4.2.4.2 Persons of unsound mind

In civil cases the competence of a person of unsound mind is determined by his or her ability to understand the nature and sanction of the oath. If such a witness does not understand the nature of the oath, then he or she cannot testify (*R v Hill* (1851) 2 Den 254). In determining whether such a witness understands the nature of the oath, the courts have adopted the test in *R v Hayes* [1977] 1 WLR 238 (see **4.2.4.1**). If the witness understands the nature of the oath, and is therefore competent to testify, it is a matter for the tribunal of fact to decide how much weight should be attached to his or her evidence (*R v Hill* (1851) 2 Den 254).

4.2.4.3 Heads of state, bankers, and judges

The rules concerning the competence and compellability of the Sovereign, foreign heads of state, diplomats, bankers, and judges in criminal proceedings (see **4.2.2.4–4.2.2.6**) apply equally to civil proceedings with one exception, namely that in civil proceedings competence is determined by the common law and not the YJCEA 1999.

4.3 Oaths and affirmations

4.3.1 Sworn evidence

Generally, evidence given by a witness in both civil and criminal proceedings will be given on oath. Evidence given on oath is known as sworn evidence. The present law is governed by the Oaths Act 1978.

Section 1(1) of the 1978 Act directs the form and manner in which oaths are to be administered and taken by Christians and Jews. It provides as follows:

> *(1) Any oath may be administered and taken in England, Wales or Northern Ireland in the following form and manner:—*

> *The person taking the oath shall hold the New Testament, or, in the case of a Jew, the Old Testament, in his uplifted hand, and shall say or repeat after the officer administering the oath the words 'I swear by Almighty God that ...', followed by the words of the oath prescribed by law.*

In *R v Chapman* [1980] Crim LR 42, it was held that failure to comply with s 1(1), which was directory only, did not necessarily invalidate the whole taking of the oath. The oath was valid if taken in a way binding and intended to be binding upon the conscience of the witness.

Section 1(3) of the 1978 Act provides that for those of other religious beliefs the oath shall be administered '*in any lawful manner*'. An oath is lawfully administered where:

- it appears to the court that the oath is binding on the conscience of the witness; and
- the witness considers the oath to be binding on his or her conscience.

In *R v Kemble* [1990] 1 WLR 1111, CA, the evidence of a Muslim witness was held to have been lawfully administered even though it had been administered on the New Testament, whereas Islam requires that a binding oath must be made on a copy of the Quran that is written in Arabic.

To prevent persons with no religious belief from taking an oath and later alleging that, because of their beliefs, the oath was of no effect, s 4(2) of the 1978 Act provides that the fact that a person taking an oath has no religious belief does not prevent it from being binding on that person. Section 5(1) permits any person who objects to being sworn to make a solemn affirmation instead of taking an oath. A solemn affirmation is of the same force and effect as an oath (s 5(4)). It was held in *R v Majid* [2009] EWCA Crim 2563 that where a religious person chooses to affirm rather than take an oath, he may not be cross-examined on this fact unless there is a good reason to suggest that he feels less bound to tell the truth and the judge has given permission. In *Majid*, the Court of Appeal held that it was unnecessary and improper to have cross-examined a religious Muslim on the fact that he had affirmed rather than sworn upon the Quran (see also *R v Mehrban* [2001] EWCA Crim 2627).

4.3.2 Criminal proceedings

The ability to give sworn evidence is governed by the YJCEA 1999, s 55. Section 55(2) provides:

> *The witness may not be sworn ... unless—*
>
> *(a) he has attained the age of 14, and*
>
> *(b) he has sufficient appreciation of the solemnity of the occasion and of the particular responsibility to tell the truth which is involved in taking the oath.*

Under the YJCEA 1999, s 55(3), a person who is able to give intelligible testimony—that is, someone who is able to understand questions put to him or her and able to give answers that can be understood—is presumed to have sufficient appreciation of the solemnity of the occasion and of the responsibility to tell the truth. It is a rebuttable presumption. If evidence to the contrary is adduced, it is for the party seeking to have the witness sworn to prove, on a balance of probabilities, that the witness has attained the age of 14 and has a sufficient appreciation of the matters mentioned (s 55(4)). The preliminary facts required to trigger the presumption in s 55(3) are the same as the requirements of the test for competence in s 53(3) (see **4.2.2.1**). Thus, the combined effect of ss 53(3) and 55(3) is that a competent witness who is at least 14 years of age will be presumed capable of giving sworn evidence.

Section 55 of the YJCEA 1999 provides that the determination of whether a witness may be sworn (which can be raised by either party or the court) must take place in the absence of the jury (s 55(5)), but in the presence of the parties (s 55(7)). Expert evidence can be received (s 55(6)).

A witness who is not permitted to give sworn evidence by virtue of the YJCEA 1999, s 55(2) must give his or her evidence unsworn (s 56(2)) and a court may properly receive unsworn evidence in such circumstances (s 56(4)).

Children and persons of unsound mind are the two categories of witness who most commonly give evidence unsworn. The amount of weight to be attached to the evidence of such a witness is a matter for the jury. In *R v Hill* (1851) 2 Den 254, it was held that if the evidence is so tainted with insanity as to be unworthy of credit, the jury will properly disregard it. Equally, however, a person suffering from a mental illness may be a perfectly reliable witness. In *R v Barratt* [1996] Crim LR 495, CA, the witness was suffering from fixed belief paranoia and held bizarre beliefs about certain aspects of her private life, but the court could see no reason to suppose that on matters not affected by her condition, her evidence was not as reliable as that of any other witness.

Where, under a special measures direction, a child or person of unsound mind is supported by a registered intermediary when giving evidence, the intermediary is required to make an 'intermediary's declaration' (an oath for intermediaries) just before the child or person of unsound mind gives evidence (see the Criminal Practice Directions [2015] EWCA Crim 1567, para 3E.2). Special measures directions are considered further at **4.11**.

4.3.3 Civil proceedings

The general rule is that a witness who is not sworn cannot give evidence at all and a judgment based on such evidence will be set aside as a nullity (*R v Marsham, ex p Lawrence* [1912] 2 KB 362). However, a person may give unsworn evidence if:

- the case is brought on the small claims track and the court does not require evidence on oath (CPR, r 27.8(4));
- the witness is producing a document that can be identified by another witness on oath (*Perry v Gibson* (1834) 1 Ad & El 48);
- the evidence is of the terms of an agreement between parties and the witness is counsel for one of the parties (*Hickman v Berens* [1895] 2 Ch 638); or
- the witness is a child and is not competent to give sworn testimony (Children Act 1989, s 96, for which see **4.2.4.1**).

Unlike criminal cases, there is no general power on the part of the civil courts to accept the unsworn testimony of a person suffering from a mental illness or other mental disability.

4.4 Form of witness evidence

The general rule is that a witness's evidence must be given orally by the witness in court. However, there are a number of important exceptions to this rule.

4.4.1 Criminal proceedings

In criminal proceedings the exceptions are that:

- evidence may be read with the agreement of both parties (Criminal Justice Act 1967, s 9);

- evidence may be read where it is admitted under the hearsay provisions of the Criminal Justice Act 2003, ss 114–126 (see **Chapter 13**);
- evidence may be given through a live link (Criminal Justice Act 2003, s 51; YJCEA 1999, ss 24 and 33A; Criminal Justice Act 1988, s 32); and
- evidence may be given by a pre-recorded video (Criminal Justice Act 2003, s 137; YJCEA 1999, ss 27 and 28).

4.4.1.1 Evidence read by agreement

By virtue of the Criminal Justice Act 1967, s 9, a written statement shall be admissible to the same extent as oral evidence by the maker of the statement where:

(a) the statement purports to be signed by the maker (s 9(2)(a));

(b) the statement contains a declaration by that person to the effect that it is true to the best of his or her knowledge and belief and that he or she made the statement knowing that if it were tendered in evidence, he or she would be liable to prosecution if he or she wilfully stated in it anything that he or she knew to be false or did not believe to be true (s 9(2)(b));

(c) a copy of the statement has been served on each of the other parties (s 9(2)(c));

(d) none of the parties have served a notice objecting to the statement being tendered in evidence (s 9(2)(d)).

This provision is commonly relied upon where a witness does not give controversial evidence.

4.4.1.2 Evidence admitted under the hearsay provisions of the Criminal Justice Act 2003

This subject is dealt with separately in **Chapter 13.**

4.4.1.3 Evidence through a live link

4.4.1.3.1 *Criminal Justice Act 2003, s 51*

Under the Criminal Justice Act 2003, s 51, the court has a general power to direct that a witness, other than the defendant, give evidence through a live link. This enables a witness to give their evidence from a place other than within the court in which the proceedings are being held. The live link will usually be a closed-circuit television link, but could be any technology with the same effect, such as video-conferencing facilities or the internet, as long as the witness is able to see and hear the proceedings in court and so that they can be seen and heard within the court by the defendant(s), the judge or justices and the jury, the legal representatives acting in the proceedings, and any interpreter or other person appointed by the court to assist the witness (s 56(3)). The witness must be in the United Kingdom at the time when the evidence is given (s 56(2)); there is no provision for a witness to give evidence from abroad by telephone (*R v Diane* [2010] 2 Cr App R 1, CA), even where the parties give consent to a witness giving evidence by telephone (*R v Hampson* [2014] 1 Cr App R 28). Evidence may only be given through a live link where it is in the interests of the efficient or effective administration of justice for the witness to do so (s 51(4)(a)). In deciding whether to make a direction the court must consider all the circumstances in the case, including:

(a) the availability of the witness;

(b) the need for the witness to attend in person;

(c) the importance of the witness's evidence to the proceedings;

(d) the views of the witness;

(e) the suitability of the facilities at the place where the witness would give evidence through a live link; and

(f) whether a direction might tend to inhibit any party to the proceedings from effectively testing the witness's evidence.

Where a direction for a live link is given, the witness may not give evidence other than via live link (s 52(2)) unless the direction is rescinded (s 52(3)). Where a witness gives evidence via a live link, the judge may give such direction as necessary to ensure that the jury gives the same weight to that evidence as if it were given by a witness within the court room (s 54).

4.4.1.3.2 *Criminal Justice Act 1988, s 32*

Under the Criminal Justice Act 1988, s 32, a witness other than the accused who is outside the United Kingdom may, with the leave of the court, give his or her evidence by live television link but only in the following proceedings:

- trials on indictment;
- appeals to the Court of Appeal Criminal Division;
- references by the Criminal Cases Review Commission;
- proceedings in youth courts; and
- appeals to the Crown Court arising out of proceedings in the youth court.

4.4.1.3.3 *Special measures directions*

Under the YJCEA 1999, s 19, the court has the power to make a 'special measures direction' in respect of certain types of vulnerable witness. Where the court makes a special measures direction, it may order that the witness may give evidence by live link (YJCEA 1999, s 24). Special measures directions will be considered in more detail at **4.11**.

4.4.1.3.4 *Vulnerable accused*

Under the YJCEA 1999, s 33A a vulnerable accused may be permitted to give evidence via a live link. (This power will be considered in greater detail at **4.13.2**.)

4.4.1.4 Pre-recorded video evidence

4.4.1.4.1 *Criminal Justice Act 2003, s 137*

Should this section be brought into force, s 137 of the Criminal Justice Act 2003 will give the court a general power to direct that all, or part, of the pre-recorded video evidence of a witness, other than the defendant, shall stand as a witness's evidence-in-chief where:

(a) a person is called as a witness in proceedings for an offence that is either triable on indictment only or is a prescribed either-way offence (s 137(1)(a));

(b) that person witnessed the offence, part of the offence, or events closely connected with the offence (s 137(1)(b));

(c) the witness has given a video-recorded account of those events at a time when they were still fresh in their memory (s 137(1)(c)–(e));

(d) the witness's recollection of the events in question is likely to have been significantly better when he or she gave that account (s 137(3)(b)(i));

(e) the witness in oral evidence in the proceedings asserts the truth of the statements made by him or her in the recorded account (s 137(2)); and

(f) it is in the interests of justice for the recording to be admitted (s 137(3)(b)(ii)) having regard to:

(i) the interval between the time of the events in question and the time when the recorded account was made (s 137(4)(a));

(ii) any factors that might affect the reliability of what the witness said in that account (s 137(4)(b));

(iii) the quality of the recording (s 137(4)(c)); and

(iv) any views of the witness as to whether his or her evidence-in-chief should be given orally or by means of the recording (s 137(4)(d)).

It will not matter if the statements in the recorded account were not made on oath (s 137(5)).

4.4.1.4.2 Special measures directions

When making a special measures direction under the YJCEA 1999, s 19, the court may direct that a pre-recorded video interview with a witness stands as his or her evidence-in-chief (YJCEA 1999, s 27) (see also the Criminal Procedure Rules 2015 (Crim PR), Part 18 and the Criminal Practice Directions [2015] EWCA Crim 1567, para 16B)) and that cross-examination or re-examination be pre-recorded (YJCEA 1999, s 28). See **4.11**.

Where the prosecution relies on a pre-recorded video of a child's evidence-in-chief, the judge may allow the jury to have transcripts of the recording if this would assist it in following the recording. The judge should make it clear that the transcript is only for that limited purpose and should give the jury directions both at the time, and during summing-up, so as to safeguard against the risk of disproportionate weight being given to the transcript (*R v Welstead* [1996] 1 Cr App R 59). The judge has a discretion to permit a jury to view a video of a child's evidence again in court (*R v Rawlings* [1995] 1 WLR 178). However, the judge must always warn the jury not to attach disproportionate weight to the evidence and remind it of the cross-examination and re-examination of the witness. It is submitted that these principles will also apply to evidence adduced under s 137 of the Criminal Justice Act 2003 if it is brought into force.

4.4.2 Civil proceedings

Under CPR, r 32.2(1), the general rule is that any fact that needs to be established by the evidence of a witness is to be proved:

(a) at trial, by his oral evidence given in public; and

(b) at any other hearing, by his evidence in writing.

However, this provision is subject to any provision to the contrary contained in the CPR or elsewhere, or to any order of the court (CPR, r 32.2(2)). For example, under CPR, r 32.3, the court may allow a witness to give evidence through a video link or by other means. In *Polanski v Condé Nast Publications Ltd* [2005] 1 WLR 637, Lord Nicholls observed that video-conferencing orders were now readily available to all litigants.

4.5 The content of witness evidence

The general rule in civil proceedings is that the statement of a witness must be served in advance of the trial. In criminal proceedings the prosecution must also serve the statements of any witness on whom it proposes to rely.

4.5.1 Civil proceedings

Under CPR, r 32.5(1), where a party has served a witness statement, and wishes to rely at trial on the evidence of the witness who made the statement, the witness must be called to give oral evidence unless the court orders otherwise or the statement is put in as hearsay evidence. By r 32.5(2), where a witness is called to give oral evidence under r 32.5(1), his or her witness statement shall stand as their evidence-in-chief unless the court orders otherwise. However, the court may permit a witness to amplify his or her witness statement and give evidence in relation to new matters that have arisen since the witness statement was served if it considers that there is a good reason for not confining the evidence of the witness to the contents of his or her statement (r 32.5(3), (4)).

For details of the formal requirements of witness statements and discussion of other procedural issues such as disclosure, see Sime, ***A Practical Approach to Civil Procedure*** or the ***White Book***.

4.5.2 Criminal proceedings

The requirement on the prosecution is to reveal its case in sufficient detail to enable the defendant properly to prepare his defence for trial. Supplementary questions can be asked, and areas can be explored in greater detail than revealed in the disclosed material, so long as the fair trial and natural justice requirements of the case are not breached. In *Filmer v DPP* [2007] RTR 28, DC, it was held that whether the trial is in the Crown Court or the magistrates' court, the prosecution is not limited in either the questions it asks of its witnesses or the evidence it introduces by the precise wording or content of the disclosed statements, exhibits, or other documentation.

4.6 Power of a party to choose its witnesses

4.6.1 No property in a witness

In both criminal and civil proceedings, a party may call any witness even if the witness has previously agreed to give evidence for the opposing party. In *Harmony Shipping Co SA v Saudi Europe Line Ltd* [1979] 1 WLR 1380, CA, a handwriting expert was approached by the plaintiffs to authenticate a particular document. The expert's view was that it was a forgery (which was unfavourable to the plaintiffs' case). Later, the defendants asked him to advise on the same issue and, forgetting his previous involvement in the case, he expressed the same view as before. On discovering that the plaintiffs had already retained him, the expert refused to accept any further instructions from the defendants. The defendants then issued a subpoena against him. The Court of Appeal held that, as there is no property in a witness, the expert witness was compellable on behalf of the defendants. It should be noted that any communications between the expert and the plaintiffs might have been protected by legal professional privilege (see **Chapter 19**). However, in *Harmony Shipping*, it was not the communications that were in issue but the evidence.

4.6.2 Criminal proceedings

4.6.2.1 The accused

The accused may call such witnesses to support his or her case as they think fit (subject to the rules of competence and compellability). However, once a witness has given evidence for the prosecution, he or she cannot be called to give evidence for the defence (*R v Kelly*, The Times, 27 July 1985, CA).

4.6.2.2 The prosecution

As for the prosecution, the relevant rules for trials on indictment were set out in *R v Russell-Jones* [1995] 3 All ER 239, CA, as follows:

(a) The prosecution must bring to court all the witnesses whose statements have been served as witnesses on whom the prosecution intends to rely, if the defence wants them to attend. (In deciding which statements to serve, the prosecution has an unfettered discretion, but must normally disclose material statements not served.)

(b) The prosecution enjoys a discretion, which must be exercised in the interests of justice to promote a fair trial, whether to call, or tender for cross-examination, any witnesses it requires to attend.

(c) The prosecution ought normally to call, or offer to call, all the witnesses who give direct evidence of the primary facts of the case, even if there are inconsistencies between one witness and another, unless for good reason the prosecutor regards the witnesses' evidence as unworthy of belief.

(d) It is for the prosecution to decide which witnesses can give direct evidence of the primary facts.

(e) The prosecutor is also the primary judge of whether or not a witness is unworthy of belief.

(f) The prosecutor is not obliged to proffer a witness merely in order to give the defence material to attack the credit of other prosecution witnesses.

In *R v Haringey Justices, ex p DPP* [1996] QB 351, DC, it was held that the principles set out in *Russell-Jones* also apply to criminal trials in magistrates' courts. However, a question arose as to the point at which the procedure in a magistrates' court is equivalent to the service of statements in proceedings on indictment (see (a) above). The court concluded that, in the case of an offence triable either way, that point was reached when the prosecution served copies of witness statements by way of advanced information, but that in other cases the prosecutor should retain an unfettered discretion until the case starts. Following the incorporation of the ECHR into domestic law by the Human Rights Act 1998, the Attorney-General issued guidelines entitled 'Disclosure of Information in Criminal Proceedings'. The guidelines are persuasive authority but do not have the force of law. One of the principal aims of the guidelines is to ensure that defendants receive a fair trial within the meaning of Article 6(1) of the ECHR. Paragraph 57 of the guidelines provides:

> The prosecutor should ... provide to the defence all evidence upon which the Crown proposes to rely in a summary trial. Such provision should allow the accused and their legal advisers sufficient time properly to consider the evidence before it is called.

There is conflicting authority as to whether the trial judge has the power to direct the prosecution to call a witness. In *R v Sterk* [1972] Crim LR 391, prosecution counsel referred to a witness in opening but later formed the view that he was unreliable and declined to call him. The Court of Appeal held that the judge should have ordered the prosecution at least to tender the witness for cross-examination. However, in *R v Oliva* [1965] 1 WLR 1028, it was held that the judge has a discretion to invite the prosecution to call a witness, but that if it refuses, the ultimate sanction is for the judge to call the witness himself. This approach was followed in *R v Haringey Justices, ex p DPP* [1996] QB 351, DC.

4.6.3 Civil proceedings

Prior to the implementation of the CPR, parties to civil proceedings had an unfettered choice as to which witnesses they would call (*Briscoe v Briscoe* [1968] P 501). However, CPR, r 32.1 provides that:

> *(1) The court may control the evidence by giving direction as to—*
>
> *(a) the issues on which it requires evidence;*
>
> *(b) the nature of the evidence which it requires to decide those issues;*
>
> *(c) the way in which the evidence is to be placed before the court.*
>
> *(2) The court may use its power under this rule to exclude evidence that would otherwise be admissible.*

Under CPR, r 32.5(1), where a party has served a witness statement, and wishes to rely at trial on the evidence of the witness who made the statement, the witness must be called to give oral evidence unless the court orders otherwise or the statement is put in as hearsay evidence. Although there are conflicting authorities on the point, it would appear that currently the trial judge has no power to order a party to call a particular witness (*Society of Lloyd's v Jaffray*, The Times, 3 August 2000).

4.7 Order of witnesses

Parties are generally free to call witnesses in the order of their choice. The only major restriction concerns the order of defence witnesses in criminal trials. PACE 1984, s 79 provides that:

> *If at the trial of any person for an offence—*
>
> *(a) the defence intends to call two or more witnesses to the facts of the case; and*
>
> *(b) those witnesses include the accused,*
>
> *the accused shall be called before the other witness or witnesses unless the court in its discretion otherwise directs.*

The court may exercise its discretion to permit the defence to call a witness to fact other than the defendant first where, for example:

(a) the witness's evidence relates to some formal or uncontroversial matter; or

(b) the witness's evidence concerns events that occurred before the time of the events about which the accused will give evidence and the defence case will be more readily understood if told in chronological order.

Section 79 of PACE 1984 is of no application to persons who are not witnesses to fact, for example, expert witnesses.

4.8 Calling a witness after the close of the case

The general rule is that a party must adduce all of its evidence before the close of its case. Thus, a party will generally not be allowed at some later stage to remedy defects in its case, or contradict the evidence of the other party, by adducing additional evidence.

4.8.1 Criminal proceedings

4.8.1.1 Prosecution evidence

There are two well-established exceptions to this general rule.

(a) *Matters arising ex improviso* Where a matter arises that could not reasonably have been foreseen, then the judge has a discretion to allow a party who has already closed its case to call evidence in rebuttal (*R v Scott* (1984) 79 Cr App R 49; *R v Hutchinson* (1985) 82 Cr App R 51, CA).

(b) *Formal evidence omitted through inadvertence or oversight* The court will normally allow evidence in rebuttal to be called in order to make good a purely formal omission. For example, in *Price v Humphries* [1958] 2 QB 353, DC, the prosecutor failed to prove that the Director of Public Prosecutions had given leave to bring the proceedings.

However, the discretion of the trial judge to permit the prosecution to call evidence after the close of its case is not restricted to the above exceptions. It has been held that the judge has a wider discretion, the limits of which should not be precisely defined, but which should be exercised only rarely outside the two established exceptions, especially when the evidence is tendered after the case for the accused has begun (*R v Francis* [1991] 1 WLR 1264, CA and *R v Munnery* [1990] 94 Cr App R 164, CA). In *Francis*, evidence having been given that at a group identification the man standing at position number 20 was identified, the prosecution was allowed to recall the inspector in charge of the identification procedure to say that it was the appellant who was standing at position number 20. Counsel for the prosecution was under the impression that the name of the person standing in that position was not in issue. In *Jolly v DPP* [2000] Crim LR 471, DC, the Divisional Court held that it was now 'beyond argument' that there was a general discretion to permit the calling of evidence after the close of the prosecution case that must be exercised having regard to the interests of justice and to any possible prejudice to the defendant. The court stated that the discretion would be sparingly exercised but it doubted whether it assisted the court any longer to speak in terms of exceptional circumstances. Each case had to be considered on its own facts.

4.8.1.2 Defence evidence

The judge has a discretionary power to allow the recall of a defendant at any stage of the trial subsequent to his initial evidence and prior to the summing up for the putting of such questions as the exigencies of justice require. However, a judge will permit a defendant to be recalled only to deal with matters that have arisen since he gave evidence if he could not reasonably have anticipated them (*R v Cook* [2005] EWCA Crim 2011). In *R v Ikram* [2009] 1 WLR 1419, CA, it was held that a judge had a discretion to allow a defendant to be recalled to clarify some feature of his evidence or to address a possible source of misunderstanding, or to answer new allegations by the co-defendant that were not put to the defendant in cross-examination. However, for the defendant to seek to be recalled in order to give evidence in support of a new defence that contradicts the evidence he has already given would normally constitute an abuse of process.

4.8.1.3 Evidence after the retirement of the tribunal of fact

In the Crown Court, there is a rule that once the jury has retired to consider its verdict, no witnesses may be called or recalled (*R v Owen* [1952] 2 QB 362), although the judge has a discretion to permit witnesses to be called up to that point and witnesses have even been called while the judge is summing up the case (*R v Sanderson* [1953] 1 WLR 392). In recent years, the Court of Appeal has relaxed this rule and allowed evidence to be placed before the jury after retirement where the request was made by the defendant on the basis that it advanced or purported to advance his case (see *R v Karayaka* [2005] EWCA Crim 346; *R v Hallam* [2007] EWCA Crim 1495; and *R v Khan* [2008] EWCA Crim 1112).

In the magistrates' courts special circumstances may arise permitting the prosecution to reopen its case even after the magistrates have retired, for example where the defence has ambushed the prosecution by failing to identify the issues in the trial until closing speeches in breach of its duty under Crim PR, r 3.3(a) (*Malcolm v DPP* [2007] 2 Cr App R 1). However, in no circumstances can evidence be called after the court has announced its verdict (Crim PR, r 24.3(4)(b)).

4.8.2 Civil proceedings

In civil cases the claimant may be permitted to adduce further evidence after the close of the trial but before judgment has been handed down where to ignore the evidence would neither be just nor in accordance with the overriding objective (*Stocznia Gdanska SA v Latvian Shipping Co* (2000) LTL 19/10/2000).

4.9 Judges' powers to call and examine witnesses

4.9.1 Criminal proceedings

In criminal proceedings in the Crown Court, the judge, without the consent of either party, may call and examine any witnesses not called by the parties (*R v Chapman* (1838) 8 Car & P 558; *R v Harris* [1927] 2 KB 587). Magistrates have a similar power (*R v Haringey Justices, ex p DPP* [1996] QB 351, DC).

4.9.2 Civil proceedings

Prior to the implementation of the CPR, apart from cases for civil contempt, the judge could not call a witness without the consent of the parties (*Re Enoch and Zaretsky, Bock and Co's Arbitration* [1910] 1 KB 327, CA). Under CPR, r 32.1, the court now has the power to direct the nature of the evidence that it requires to decide an issue and the way in which such evidence is to be placed before the court. Thus, it appears, the judge has the power to direct that a witness give evidence without the consent of either party. See *Kesse v Secretary of State for the Home Department* [2001] EWCA Civ 177, *Jaffray v Society of Lloyd's* [2002] EWCA Civ 1101, *Tarajan Overseas Ltd v Kaye* [2001] EWCA Civ 1859, and *Lissack v Manhattan Loft Corporation Ltd* [2013] EWHC 128 (Ch).

4.10 Securing the attendance of witnesses

4.10.1 Criminal proceedings

Where the prosecution or defence anticipates that a witness will not attend the Crown Court voluntarily, it may apply for a witness summons under the Criminal Procedure (Attendance of Witnesses) Act 1965, s 2. The party seeking the summons must show that the witness is likely to be able to give material evidence, or produce a material exhibit, but will not voluntarily attend as a witness or will not voluntarily produce the exhibit and that it would be in the interests of justice for a summons to be issued. Failure to comply with a witness summons may be summarily punished as contempt of court by up to three months' imprisonment (s 3).

In a magistrates' court the attendance of witnesses may be secured by a witness summons or a warrant under the Magistrates' Court Act 1980, s 97. A witness summons may be issued where the witness is likely to be able to give material evidence, or produce a material exhibit, but will not voluntarily attend as a witness or will not voluntarily produce the exhibit and it is in the interests of justice to issue a summons to secure that witness's attendance to give evidence or produce the exhibit. However, should the witness fail to attend court in answer to the summons or should they attend but fail to testify or produce the exhibit, the court may issue a warrant for his or her arrest (s 97(3)). Refusal to be sworn or give evidence may be punished by up to one month's imprisonment and/or a fine of up to £2,500 (s 97(4)).

4.10.2 Civil proceedings

The attendance of a witness in a civil case is secured by the issuing of a witness summons under CPR, r 34. A civil witness summons may similarly require a witness to attend court to give oral evidence or to produce a document. Failure to obey a witness summons issued by the High Court is contempt of court and the contemnor may be committed to prison for up to two years and/or fined (*Wyatt v Wingford* (1729) 2 Ld Raym 1528; Contempt of Court Act 1981, s 14(1)). Refusal to be sworn or give evidence also amounts to contempt of court (*R v Daye* [1908] 2 KB 333). A person failing to answer to a witness summons issued by a county court may be fined up to £1,000 (County Courts Act 1984, s 55(1) and (2)). Refusal to be sworn or give evidence may also be punished by a fine (s 55(1)).

4.11 Special measures directions

The YJCEA 1999 introduced in criminal proceedings a statutory regime of 'special measures directions'. A special measures direction is an order that may be made by the court, either of its own motion or on application by either party, which is intended to protect vulnerable and intimidated witnesses and facilitate the giving of their evidence. The YJCEA 1999 ss 16–30 modify the orthodox trial process for children, those in fear, those suffering from a physical or mental disability, and the alleged victims of sexual assault so as to enable them to give their best evidence. While the statutory regime offers witnesses a broad range of special measures, the court retains its responsibility for the fairness of a trial. It may therefore exercise its residual inherent jurisdiction to modify court procedures on an ad hoc basis for witnesses who are not eligible for special measures under the statutory regime, where to do so is in the interests of justice (YJCEA 1999, s 19(6) and Crim PR, r 3.5(1)).

4.11.1 Eligibility

Under the YJCEA 1999, a witness will be eligible in principle for a special measures direction if he or she comes within any of the following categories:

(a) he or she is under the age of 18 at the time of the hearing (s 16(1)(a));

(b) the court considers that the quality of evidence given by the witness is likely to be diminished because the witness:

   (i) suffers from a mental disorder within the meaning of the Mental Health Act 1983;

(ii) has a significant impairment of intelligence and social functioning; or

(iii) has a physical disability or is suffering from a physical disorder (s 16(1)(b));

(c) the court considers that the quality of evidence given by the witness is likely to be diminished by reason of fear or distress on the part of the witness in connection with testifying in the proceedings (s 17(1)). In determining this issue, s 17(2) and (3) requires the court to take into account factors such as:

(i) the nature and alleged circumstances of the offence;

(ii) the age of the witness;

(iii) the social and cultural background and ethnic origins of the witness;

(iv) the witness's domestic and employment circumstances;

(v) the religious beliefs and political opinions of the witness;

(vi) the behaviour of the accused, his or her family, or associates towards the witness; and

(vii) any views expressed by the witness;

(d) the witness is an adult complainant in respect of a sexual offence or an offence under the Modern Slavery Act 2015, ss 1 and 2 (unless the witness informs the court of his wish not to be so eligible) (s 17(4));

(e) the witness is a witness to an offence involving the use or possession of a knife or a firearm which is specified in Sch 1A of the YJCEA 1999 (s 17(5)).

The accused is not eligible for a special measures direction (YJCEA 1999, ss 16(1) and 17(1)). However, under the YJCEA 1999, s 33A, a vulnerable accused may be eligible to give evidence through a live link (see **4.13.2**) or through a registered intermediary (see **4.13.3**).

4.11.2 Special measures available for witnesses

Witnesses who are eligible for a special measures direction by virtue of their age (s 16(1)(a)) or physical or mental incapacity (s 16(1)(b)) may be assisted by any of the special measures directions available under ss 23–30. Witnesses who are eligible by virtue of their fear or distress (s 17(1)) may be assisted by any of the special measures directions available under ss 23–28. See **Table 4.1**.

Where the court determines that a witness is eligible for special measures it must make a declaration of eligibility and must then go on to consider:

(a) whether any of the special measures available (or any combination of them) would be likely to improve the quality of evidence given by the witness (s 19(2)(a)); and, if so,

(b) which of those special measures (or any combination of them) would be likely to maximise so far as practicable the quality of the witness's evidence (s 19(2)(b)).

The court must have regard to all the circumstances of the case and, in particular, the views of the witness and the extent to which any special measure might tend to inhibit the witness's evidence being effectively tested by a party to the proceedings (s 19(3)).

4.11.3 Child witnesses

Section 100 of the Coroners and Justice Act 2009 amends the YJCEA 1999, s 21, so that all witnesses under the age of 18 at the time of the hearing (or if over 18 at the time of trial, who were under the age of 18 when a video-recorded interview took place) are

Table 4.1 **Special measures directions**

Section authorising direction	Special measures direction available	Available		Limits
		s 16	s 17	
23	Witness prevented from seeing accused by screen or other means	Yes	Yes	The witness must still be visible to the judge and jury or justices, the legal representatives in the case, and any interpreter or other person appointed by the court to assist the witness (s 23(2)).
24	Evidence given by live link	Yes	Yes	
25	Exclusion of specified person from court	Yes	Yes	Only if: • proceedings relate to an offence under s 1 or 2 of the Modern Slavery Act 2015 or to a sexual offence; or • there are reasonable grounds for believing that person other than accused has sought or will seek to intimidate the witness about testifying. The accused, legal representatives, and any interpreter or other person appointed to assist the witness cannot be excluded from the court. The court must also provide for a nominated representative of a news gathering or reporting organisation to attend.
26	Wigs and gowns not worn	Yes	Yes	
27	Pre-recorded video interview with witness taken by a police officer or social worker to stand as evidence-in-chief	Yes	Yes	The witness must be available for cross-examination at trial unless s 28 applies.
28	Cross-examination or re-examination to be pre-recorded	Yes	Yes	Only if a s 27 direction has been made. Following a successful pilot scheme trialling the use of pre-recorded cross-examination and re-examination in the Crown Courts at Kingston-upon-Thames, Leeds, and Liverpool, s 28 was formally brought into force on 2 January 2017 but only for proceedings brought in the three pilot areas and only for witnesses under 16 years of age or witnesses eligible on the grounds of incapacity. Section 28 will be introduced nationwide on an incremental basis. The three pilot courts will also commence pilots of pre-trial cross-examination and re-examination of adult complainants of sexual offences.
29	Examination of witness through interpreter or court-approved intermediary	Yes	No	The intermediary's role is to assist the witness with communication; not to provide expert testimony or an opinion on the witness's reliability or fitness to plead.
30	Use of devices to enable communication between witness and others during examination	Yes	No	Usually ordered in conjunction with an intermediary to ensure accurate communication with the court.

'child witnesses' and are automatically eligible for special measures regardless of the offence to which the proceedings relate. Section 21(3) of the YJCEA 1999 provides that, in relation to a child witness, the court must make a special measures direction that:

(a) provides for any video-recorded interview to stand as evidence-in-chief under s 27 of the YJCEA 1999 (s 21(3)(a)); and

(b) provides for any evidence that is not given by means of a video recording (whether in-chief or otherwise) to be given by means of a live link under s 24 of the YJCEA 1999 (s 21(3)(b)) (see also the Criminal Practice Directions [2015] EWCA Crim 1567, para 16B).

However, the court need not make such a special measures direction where:

(a) having regard to all the circumstances it is in the interests of justice not to admit a video recording of the witness's evidence-in-chief (s 21(4)(b)); or

(b) the court is satisfied that neither direction would be likely to maximise the quality of the witness's evidence so far as is practicable (eg where some other special measures available would have that effect) (s 21(4)(c)).

This is known as the 'primary rule'. Section 100 of the Coroners and Justice Act 2009 modifies the 'primary rule' by permitting a child witness to opt out of giving evidence either by video-recorded evidence-in-chief and live link, or both, provided the court is satisfied, after taking into account certain factors, that not giving evidence in that way will not diminish the quality of the child's evidence. If as a result of 'opting out', the child witness would fall to give evidence in court (and not by way of a live link), a secondary requirement will apply. This obliges the child witness to give evidence in court in accordance with the special measure in s 23 of the 1999 Act, that is, from behind a screen that shields him or her from viewing the defendant. The secondary requirement does not apply if the court considers it would not maximise the quality of the child's evidence. The child may also opt out of this secondary requirement, subject to the agreement of the court. The court will only agree to the child opting out where it is satisfied that doing so would not diminish the quality of the child's evidence.

Once the court has applied the primary rule, the court must then consider whether any other special measures would be likely to improve the quality of the child witness's evidence and, if so, determine which measures would be likely to maximise the quality of that witness's evidence, as per s 19(2).

In addition to the special measures regime under the YJCEA 1999, advocates must consider that a child witness's individual needs must be evaluated at an early stage in any investigation using the guidance in *Achieving Best Evidence (2011)* and the Advocate's Gateway Toolkits (see 7.3.2.1).

4.11.4 Adult complainants of sexual offences and offences under ss 1 and 2 of the Modern Slavery Act 2015

Adult complainants in sexual offence cases are automatically eligible for special measures (s 17(4)); they are presumed to be in fear or distress about testifying. Therefore, they are not subject to any additional eligibility criteria. Section 101 of the Coroners and Justice Act 2009 inserts s 22A into the YJCEA 1999, permitting an adult complainant in a sexual offence case tried in the Crown Court to apply for his or her evidence-in-chief to be given by a video recording under s 27 of the 1999 Act. Upon making an application, the witness is automatically eligible for this special measure and the court must make a direction for the admission of video-recorded evidence-in-chief unless it is satisfied that this would not maximise the quality of the complainant's evidence. The court will then consider whether any additional special measures would be likely to maximise the quality of the witness's evidence in accordance with the YJCEA 1999, s 19(2).

Adult complainants to offences under ss 1 and 2 of the Modern Slavery Act 2015 (slavery, servitude, forced or compulsory labour, and human trafficking) are automatically eligible for special measures unless they decline to be so considered (YJCEA 1999 s 17(4)). The court will determine appropriate special measures using the test set out at the YJCEA 1999, s 19(2) as described above at **4.11.2**.

4.11.5 Offences involving weapons

Section 99 of the Coroners and Justice Act 2009 amends the YJCEA 1999, s 17, so that a witness to certain specified offences involving firearms, knives, or bladed or pointed articles is automatically eligible for special measures unless the witness informs the court that he does not wish to be eligible. The offences are set out in the Coroners and Justice Act 2009, Sch 14, which inserts Sch 1A into the YJCEA 1999. What measures, if any, may be appropriate in individual cases, will be determined by the court in accordance with s 19(2). Note that, unless they decline, all witnesses to such cases, including police officers, are automatically eligible for special measures. There is no need for proof of intimidation or other ground for concern as to their ability to give their best evidence.

4.11.6 Procedure

The procedure for applying for a special measures direction is set out in the Crim PR, r 18 and the Criminal Practice Directions [2015] EWCA Crim 1567, para 18A–18E. In the case of an application to a magistrates' court, the application must be made in writing within 28 days of the defendant entering a not guilty plea. In the case of an application to the Crown Court, the application must be made in writing within 14 days after the defendant enters a not guilty plea. The application must be sent to the court and a copy sent to every other party to the proceedings. If a party wishes to oppose the application, that party must give written notice to the applicant and the court within 14 days of the date on which the party was served with the application.

Where a party applies for special measures in respect of a witness, the party must inform the witness of the court's decision in relation to the application as soon as is reasonably practicable, and explain to the witness what arrangements will be made for him or her to give evidence.

4.11.7 Warning to jury

On a trial on indictment where evidence has been given in accordance with a special measures direction, the judge must give the jury such warning (if any) as the judge considers necessary to ensure that the direction given in relation to the witness does not prejudice the accused (YJCEA 1999, s 32).

4.12 Witness anonymity

4.12.1 Common law

In particularly serious trials where the witnesses were in such fear of reprisals from the defendant, or the defendant's associates, that they were unwilling to give evidence even with the benefit of a special measures direction, a practice arose of permitting witnesses to give evidence anonymously. This practice was challenged in *R v Davis* [2008] 1 AC 1128, in which the House of Lords held that it was a long-established principle of the English common law that, subject to certain exceptions and statutory qualifications, defendants in a criminal trial should be confronted by their accusers in order that they may cross-examine them and challenge their evidence. While the problem of witness intimidation was not new, the common law had never permitted witnesses to give their evidence under conditions of anonymity and the House of Lords stated that it was unable to set a precedent that would so gravely compromise the ability of defence counsel to properly cross-examine a decisive witness. Their Lordships added that it was not for the House of Lords, in its judicial capacity, to allow such a far-reaching inroad into the common law rights of a defendant. Consideration was also given to the question of whether the use of anonymous evidence was compatible with the defendant's right to a fair trial under the ECHR, Article 6. They concluded that while such evidence was not always incompatible with Article 6, where a conviction was based solely or to a decisive extent on the testimony of anonymous witnesses, the trial could not be regarded as fair.

4.12.2 Witness anonymity orders

Parliament responded swiftly to the decision in *Davis* with the introduction of the Criminal Evidence (Witness Anonymity) Act 2008. The Act created a new power to make a witness anonymity order. The relevant provisions are now contained in the Coroners and Justice Act 2009. In *R v Mayers* [2009] 1 Cr App R 30, the Court of Appeal stated that such orders may fairly be regarded as a new statutory special measure: the special measure of last practicable resort. This point was reiterated in respect of the 2009 Act in *Donovan* [2012] EWCA Crim 2749.

Section 86(1) of the 2009 Act provides that a witness anonymity order is an order made by a court that requires such specified measures to be taken in relation to a witness in criminal proceedings as the court considers appropriate to ensure that the identity of the witness is not disclosed in, or in connection with, the proceedings. Section 86(2) provides that the kinds of measures that may be required to be taken in relation to a witness include measures for securing one or more of the following:

(a) *that the witness's name and other identifying details may be:*
  (i) *withheld;*
  (ii) *removed from materials disclosed to any party to the proceedings;*
(b) *that the witness may use a pseudonym;*
(c) *that the witness is not asked questions of any specified description that might lead to the identification of the witness;*
(d) *that the witness is screened to any specified extent;*
(e) *that the witness's voice is subjected to modulation to any specified extent.*

Section 88(3)–(5) provides that a witness anonymity order may only be made if conditions A, B, and C are met and are met to the highest standard (*Mayers* [2009] 1 Cr App R 30 2 at [37]):

(3) *Condition A: the measures to be specified in the order are necessary—*
  (i) *in order to protect the safety of the witness or another person or to prevent any serious damage to property, or*
  (ii) *in order to prevent real harm to the public interest (whether affecting the carrying on of any activities in the public interest or the safety of a person involved in carrying on such activities, or otherwise).*

(4) *Condition B: having regard to all the circumstances, the effect of the proposed order would be consistent with the defendant receiving a fair trial.*

(5) *Condition C: the importance of the witness's testimony is such that in the interests of justice the witness ought to testify and*

(i) *the witness would not testify if the proposed order were not made, or*

(ii) *there would be real harm to the public interest if the witness were to testify without the proposed order being made.*

In determining whether the conditions are met, s 89(1) and (2) provides that the court must have regard to:

(a) the general right of a defendant in criminal proceedings to know the identity of a witness in the proceedings;

(b) the extent to which the credibility of the witness concerned would be a relevant factor when the weight of his or her evidence comes to be assessed;

(c) whether evidence given by the witness might be the sole or decisive evidence implicating the defendant;

(d) whether the witness's evidence could be properly tested (whether on grounds of credibility or otherwise) without his or her identity being disclosed;

(e) whether there is any reason to believe that the witness—

(i) has a tendency to be dishonest, or

(ii) has any motive to be dishonest in the circumstances of the case,

having regard (in particular) to any previous convictions of the witness and to any relationship between the witness and the defendant or any associates of the defendant;

(f) whether it would be reasonably practicable to protect the witness by any means other than by making a witness anonymity order specifying the measures that are under consideration by the court; and

(g) such other matters as the court considers relevant.

Applications may be made by either the prosecution or the defence (s 87(1)). Applications may be made *ex parte* if it is appropriate to do so (s 87(7)).

If the trial takes place in the Crown Court, the judge must give the jury such warning as he or she considers appropriate to ensure that the fact that the order was made in relation to the witness does not prejudice the defendant (s 90(2)).

Guidance on applying for a witness anonymity order is provided in the Attorney-General's 'Guidelines on Witness Anonymity Orders'. Detailed guidance on how the making of witness anonymity orders should be approached was given by the Court of Appeal in *R v Mayers* [2009] 1 Cr App R 30.

The procedure for applying for a witness anonymity order is set out in the Crim PR, Part 18 and in the Criminal Practice Directions [2015] EWCA Crim 1567, para 18D.

4.13 The vulnerable accused

4.13.1 The Criminal Practice Directions

The Criminal Practice Directions [2015] EWCA Crim 1567, paras 3D and 3G specify how the needs of vulnerable defendants should be addressed when making arrangements for trial. The Directions require that all reasonable steps be taken to help a vulnerable defendant to understand and participate in criminal proceedings. The ordinary trial process should, so far as necessary, be adapted to meet those ends. Principally, a vulnerable accused should be enabled to give his or her best evidence and to comprehend the proceedings and engage fully with his or her defence. A defendant may be classified as vulnerable because he or she is under 18 years, because they have a mental disorder or learning disability or a physical disorder or disability or because they are likely to suffer fear or distress in giving evidence because of their own circumstances or those relating to the case. The Directions apply to both magistrates' courts and the Crown Court.

The Criminal Practice Directions [2015] EWCA Crim 1567, para 3G, cover general matters in relation to the arrangements which should be made for a vulnerable accused before trial, including familiarisation with the court, use of intermediaries, and live links.

4.13.2 Live link

The YJCEA 1999 expressly excludes the accused from access to special measures available to all other witnesses at trial. The resultant disparity in treatment between child or vulnerable defendants and other witnesses was such that Parliament came under increasing pressure from the House of Lords and the European Court of Human Rights to give some limited access to special measures to vulnerable defendants (*Camberwell Green Youth Court ex p D* [2005] 1 All ER 999; *SC v UK* (2005) 40 EHRR 226).

Under s 33A of the YJCEA 1999, inserted by s 47 of the Police and Justice Act 2006, the court may now direct that any evidence given by the accused should be given over a live video link where it is satisfied:

(a) that it would be in the interests of justice; and
(b) where the accused is under the age of 18:
   (i) that his ability to participate effectively as a witness is compromised by his level of intelligence or social functioning; and
   (ii) that his ability to participate effectively would be improved by giving evidence over a live link; or
(c) where the accused is aged 18 or over:
   (i) that he is unable to participate in the proceedings effectively because he has a mental disorder or a significant impairment of intelligence or social function; and
   (ii) that his ability to participate effectively would be improved by giving evidence over a live link.

The test for eligibility for a juvenile is less strict than for an adult. Section 33A of the YJCEA 1999 was inserted by the Police and Justice Act 2006. The Explanatory Notes to the 2006 Act state that the lower threshold recognises that it may be more common for juveniles to experience difficulties during the trial through limited intelligence and social development than it may be for adults. However, the provision is aimed at juvenile defendants with a low level of intelligence or a particular problem in dealing with social situations, and is not intended to operate merely because an accused is a juvenile and is nervous, for example. Once a direction has been made, the accused must give all his evidence through a live link, unless the court exercises its discretion to discharge the direction where it is in the interests of justice to do so (s 33A(7)). Where a vulnerable defendant is to give evidence by live link, he should have an opportunity to practise using the live link as part of a pre-trial familiarisation visit to court (see the Criminal Practice Directions [2015] EWCA Crim 1567, para 3G.4).

The Court of Appeal has held that there is no residual common law power to allow an accused who falls outside the statutory code to give evidence via live link (*Ukpabio* [2008] 1 Cr App R 6 and *Hamberger* [2017] EWCA Crim 273).

4.13.3 Intermediaries

At present, the Crown Court and magistrates' courts may use their inherent powers to direct that the defendant be assisted by a registered intermediary in giving his evidence (*R (C) v Sevenoaks Youth Court* [2010] 1 All ER 735; *Head* [2009] EWCA Crim 1401; *R (P) v West London Youth Court* [2006] 1 All ER 477). A vulnerable accused is entitled, like other vulnerable witnesses, to give his best evidence. Where necessary this may require the assistance of a registered intermediary even where an accused's communication difficulties do not render him wholly incapable of communicating his testimony (*R (AS) v Great Yarmouth Youth Court* [2011] EWHC 2059 (Admin)).

Section 104 of the Coroners and Justice Act 2009 inserts new ss 33BA and 33BB into the YJCEA 1999. If brought into force they will provide statutory authorisation for the use of an intermediary by vulnerable accused. At present, these provisions are not in force and it seems unlikely that they will be brought into force as currently drafted. The Law Commission has urged that these provisions are not implemented in their current form, arguing that the provisions do not adequately protect child and vulnerable defendants' right to participate effectively at trial (Unfitness to Plead, Law Commission Report No 364 (January 2016) vol 1 at para 2.65).

Under s 33BA, where the accused is aged under 18, he will only be eligible to be assisted by an intermediary if his ability to participate effectively in the proceedings as a witness giving oral evidence in court is compromised by his level of intellectual ability or social functioning (s 33BA(5)). Where the accused has attained the age of 18 he will only be eligible if he:

(a) suffers from a mental disorder (within the meaning of the Mental Health Act 1983) or otherwise has a significant impairment of intelligence and social function; and

(b) is for that reason unable to participate effectively in the proceedings as a witness giving oral evidence in court.

In all cases, the court must additionally be satisfied that making the direction is necessary in order to ensure that the accused receives a fair trial (s 33BA(2)(b)). See also the Criminal Practice Directions [2015] EWCA Crim 1567, para 3G.3.

5 Corroboration and care warnings

5.1 Introduction

The general rule is that there is no need for evidence to be corroborated. A court's decision may properly be based on the evidence of a single witness and the tribunal of fact need not be warned of the danger of uncorroborated evidence. However, in criminal proceedings there are certain offences which require corroboration before a conviction can be secured, and, where certain 'unreliable' witnesses give unsupported evidence, the jury may need to be given a care warning before relying on these witnesses' testimonies.

There are other circumstances that give rise to a special need for caution before acting on unsupported evidence: a confession by a mentally handicapped accused; identification evidence; sudden unexplained infant death; and unconvincing hearsay evidence. The first three of these will be considered in this chapter. The rules relating to unconvincing hearsay are governed by s 125 of the Criminal Justice Act 2003 and are considered in **Chapter 13**.

5.2 Offences requiring corroboration

Corroboration is required before a person can be convicted of the following offences:

5.2.1 Perjury

Section 13 of the Perjury Act 1911 provides:

> *A person shall not be liable to be convicted of any offence against this Act, or of any offence declared by any other Act to be perjury or subornation of perjury, or to be punishable as perjury or subornation of perjury, solely upon the evidence of one witness as to the falsity of any statement alleged to be false.*

In the case of perjury, for evidence to be capable of amounting to corroboration it must be:

(a) relevant and admissible (*Scarrott* [1978] QB 1016, CA at p 1021);

(b) credible (*DPP v Kilbourne* [1973] AC 729 at p 746 and *DPP v Hester* [1973] AC 296 at p 315);

(c) independent (*Whitehead* [1929] 1 KB 99; *Cooper* 1 WLR 2390); and

(d) implicate the accused.

Corroboration need not be by the testimony of another witness and may take the form of documentary evidence. However, if the evidence proposed as corroboration is in the form of documents, the documents must come from a source other than a sole witness who is giving evidence. If a sole witness giving evidence is the single source of the documents, those documents will not qualify as corroboration for the purposes of the Perjury Act 1911, s 13 (*R v Cooper* [2010] 1 WLR 2390).

The jury must be directed by the judge to look for evidence that is capable of corroborating the evidence given by the main witness as to the falsity of the statement made by the accused; if it can find none, the jury should acquit the accused (*R v Rider* (1986) 83 Cr App R 207).

5.2.2 Speeding

Section 89(1) of the Road Traffic Regulation Act 1984 creates the offence of speeding. Subsection (2) provides:

> *A person prosecuted for such an offence shall not be liable to be convicted solely on the evidence of one witness to the effect that, in the opinion of that witness, the person prosecuted was driving the vehicle at a speed exceeding a specified limit.*

The need for corroboration arises from the possible inaccuracy of a witness's evidence as to the speed of the vehicle. The evidence of at least two witnesses that a vehicle was travelling at excessive speed is required to successfully convict an accused, as long as the evidence relates to the speed of the vehicle at the same place and time (*Brighty v Pearson* [1938] 4 All ER 127). However, in most cases evidence of the vehicle's speed comes from a reading taken by an automatic camera or radar gun. As this is factual evidence, rather than opinion evidence, s 89(2) of the 1984 Act will not apply.

5.2.3 Treason

The Treason Act 1795, s 1 provides that a person charged with an offence of treason by compassing the death or restraint of the Queen or her heirs shall not be convicted except on the oaths of two lawful and credible witnesses.

5.2.4 Attempt

Where an accused is charged with attempting to commit the preceding offences, the same requirement for corroboration applies to the trial for the attempt as it would in a trial for the completed offence (Criminal Attempts Act 1981, s 2(1) and (2)(g)).

5.2.5 Corroboration direction

Where a judge directs the jury on corroboration, he should explain what corroboration means, taking care to clearly set out the requirements of credibility, independence, and implication (*R v Fallon* [1993] Crim LR 591). The judge must also clearly indicate what evidence is capable of amounting to corroboration (*Charles* (1976) 68 Cr App R 334n; *Cullinane* [1984] *Crim* LR 420; *Webber* [1987] Crim LR 412), and, where evidence is *capable* of being corroboration, explain that it is for the jury to decide whether or not it *does* in fact constitute corroboration (*Tragen* [1956] *Crim* LR 332).

5.3 Care warnings

Where certain types of witness give unsupported evidence, the jury should, in appropriate circumstances, be given a warning to exercise caution before relying on that witness's testimony. Whether, and in what terms, the warning is given is a matter of judicial discretion and will depend on the facts and circumstances of a case. There are several categories of witness for whom consideration should be given as to whether a care warning may be appropriate. These include:

(i) accomplices giving evidence for the prosecution and complainants (whether male or female) in sexual cases;

(ii) witnesses whose evidence may be unreliable or tainted by improper motive; and

(iii) children.

5.3.1 Accomplices giving evidence for the prosecution and complainants in sexual cases

Historically, the common law required, subject to very limited exceptions, that judges warn the jury of the danger of convicting an accused on the basis of such a witness's uncorroborated evidence. The warning was required to be a 'full' warning composed of:

(1) a warning to the jury that it was dangerous to convict on the uncorroborated evidence of the witness but that they could do so if satisfied of the truth of such evidence;

(2) an explanation of the meaning of corroboration;

(3) an indication of what evidence was (and was not) capable of amounting to corroboration; and

(4) an explanation that it was for the jury to decide whether evidence did in fact constitute corroboration.

The requirement for the judge to give such warnings to the jury was abrogated by the Criminal Justice and Public Order Act 1994, s 32. Although full warnings are no longer required, the judge retains a discretion to warn the jury to exercise caution when he considers appropriate to do so, whether in respect of uncorroborated evidence given by an accomplice, a complainant in a sexual offence case, or for any other witness.

Following the abrogation of the requirement to give care warnings for complainants in sexual offences and accomplices, the Court of Appeal gave guidance on how the court should approach the evidence of unreliable witnesses in *R v Makanjuola* [1995] 2 Cr App R 469. Lord Taylor of Gosforth CJ summarised the new position in eight points:

> (1) Section 32(1) [of the Criminal Justice and Public Order Act 1994] abrogated the requirement to give a corroboration direction in respect of an alleged accomplice or a complainant of a sexual offence, simply because a witness falls into one of those categories.
>
> (2) It is a matter for the judge's discretion what, if any, warning he or she considers appropriate in respect of such a witness as indeed in respect of any other witness in whatever type of case. Whether the judge chooses to give a warning and in what terms will depend on the circumstances of the case, the issues raised and the content and quality of the witness's evidence.
>
> (3) In some cases, it may be appropriate for the judge to warn the jury to exercise some caution before acting upon the unsupported evidence of a witness. This will not be so simply because the witness is a complainant of a sexual offence nor will it necessarily be so because the witness is alleged to be an accomplice. There will need to be an evidential basis for

suggesting that the evidence of the witness may be unreliable. An evidential basis does not include mere suggestion by cross-examining counsel.

(4) If any question arises as to whether the judge should give a special warning in respect of a witness, it is desirable that the question be resolved by discussion with counsel in the absence of the jury before final speeches.

(5) Where the judge does decide to give some warning in respect of a witness, it will be appropriate to do so as part of the judge's review of the evidence and his comments as to how the jury should evaluate it rather than as a set-piece legal direction.

(6) Where some warning is required, it will be for the judge to decide the strength and terms of the warning. It does not have to be invested with the whole florid regime of the old corroboration rules.

(7) It follows that we emphatically disagree with the tentative suggestion [that if a judge does give a warning, he should give a full warning and should tell the jury what corroboration is in the technical sense and identify the evidence capable of being corroborative]. Attempts to re-impose the straitjacket of the old corroboration rules are strongly to be deprecated.

(8) Finally, [the Court of Appeal] will be disinclined to interfere with a trial judge's exercise of his or her discretion save in a case where that exercise is unreasonable in the *Wednesbury* sense.

Lord Taylor gave further guidance as follows (at p 732):

The judge will often consider that no special warning is required at all. Where, however, the witness has been shown to be unreliable, he or she may consider it necessary to urge caution. In a more extreme case, if the witness is shown to have lied, to have made previous false complaints, or to bear the defendant some grudge, a stronger warning may be thought appropriate and the judge may suggest it would be wise to look for some supporting material before acting on the impugned witness's evidence. We stress that these observations are merely illustrative of some, not all, of the factors which the judges may take into account in measuring where a witness stands in the scale of reliability and what response they should make at that level in their directions to the jury.

The crucial factor is that the judge always has a wide discretion whether to warn or not. He has to decide whether any warning is appropriate and what form the warning should take. There is no set form of words for the warning (*Blasiak* [2010] EWCA Crim 2620). The decision will depend on the issues raised in the trial, the circumstances of the case, and the judge's view of the content and quality of the witness's evidence. In those cases where the judge suggests that the jury might look for supporting material, the judge ought to identify for the jury any evidence that is capable of being supporting evidence and also any evidence which a jury might think offers support but which in law cannot do so (*R v B (MT)* [2000] Crim LR 181).

5.3.2 Witnesses whose evidence may be tainted by an improper motive

The common law also recognised several further categories of witness that, while not requiring a full corroboration warning from the judge, nevertheless required a warning as to a special need for caution. They became known collectively as the 'analogous cases' and included categories such as co-defendants and other witnesses whose evidence may be tainted by an improper motive. In *R v Muncaster* [1999] Crim LR 409, CA, it was held that the guidance in *R v Makanjuola* applied equally to these cases.

5.3.2.1 Co-defendants

There is a danger that a co-defendant who gives incriminating evidence against his co-accused has a purpose of his own to serve. Following *Makanjuola* and *Muncaster*, whether any warning is given, and the terms of any warning, are at the discretion of the judge. However, it has been held that it is desirable, as a matter of practice, for the jury to be warned of the need to have caution when relying on such unsupported evidence (*R v Knowlden* (1983) 77 Cr App R 94; *R v Cheema* [1994] 1 WLR 147, CA). In *Jones* [2004] 1 Cr App R 5, CA, it was suggested that the direction should consist of four parts:

(a) the jury should consider the case for and against each defendant separately;

(b) the jury should decide the case on all the evidence, including the evidence of each defendant's co-defendant;

(c) when considering the evidence of co-defendants, the jury should bear in mind that they may have an interest to serve or, as it is often put, an axe to grind; and

(d) the jury should assess the evidence of co-defendants in the same way as the evidence of any other witness.

In *R v Petkar* [2004] 1 Cr App R 270, CA, the court followed *Jones* but raised concerns that such a direction might devalue the testimony of both defendants. In that case, the failure of the trial judge to give any form of warning was not fatal to the safety of the conviction, because it was obvious that both of the accused had axes to grind.

5.3.2.2 Other witnesses with an improper motive

A judge should warn a jury to treat with caution the evidence of any other witness where there is material to suggest that a witness's evidence may be tainted by improper motive or his own purpose to serve (*R v Beck* [1982] 1 WLR 461). Where there is evidence to suggest that a witness is acting out of spite, or that they have some financial or other personal interest in the outcome of a trial, or that they are biased or partial, a warning may be appropriate where that witness's evidence is unsupported. For example, where an offender is awaiting sentence and gives evidence for the prosecution in another case, knowing that by doing so there is a chance this might help to reduce any sentence he will receive, the jury should be made aware of the potential for unreliability of his evidence (*Chan Wai-Keung v R* [1995] 2 All ER 438).

It has been held that evidence given by a fellow prisoner of a cell confession allegedly made by the accused is inherently unreliable and, while it is undesirable to restrict the circumstances in which a judge might warn the jury to exercise caution in regard to a particular witness's evidence and the terms in which any such warning might be given, the judge in such a case ought to draw the attention of the jury to any indications that the evidence might be tainted by an improper motive and its possible significance. The judge should then advise the jury to be cautious before accepting the evidence (*Pringle v The Queen* [2003] UKPC9 and *Benedetto v R* [2003] 1 WLR 1545, PC). However, the Court of Appeal in *R v Stone* [2005] Crim LR 569 held that not every case requires such a detailed direction. It was held that any case involving a cell confession requires the most careful consideration by the judge but the judge's consideration is not trammelled by fixed rules. In the case of a standard two-line cell confession, there will generally be a need for the judge to point out to the jury that such confessions are often easy to concoct and difficult to prove and that experience has shown that prisoners may have many motives to lie. If the prison informant has a significant criminal record or a history of lying, then usually the judge should point this out to the jury and explain that it gives rise to a need for great care and why. The trial judge will be best placed to decide the strength of such warnings and the necessary extent of the accompanying analysis. But not every case requires such a warning. A summing-up should be tailored by the judge to the circumstances of the particular case. For example, if an alleged confession would not have been easy to invent, it would be absurd to require the judge to tell the jury that confessions are often easy to concoct. Further, there are cases where a prisoner has witnessed acts constituting the offence in which it will be appropriate to treat him as a normal witness about whose evidence nothing out of the ordinary needs to be said. Any indications that the prison informant's evidence may be tainted by an improper motive must be found in the evidence.

5.3.3 Children

Under the Children and Young Persons Act 1933 (CYPA 1933), s 38(1), an accused could not be convicted on the unsworn evidence of a child appearing on behalf of the prosecution unless the child's evidence was corroborated; and at common law, a corroboration warning was required in respect of a child's sworn evidence. The rationale for s 38(1) and the common law rule was the danger that a child's evidence may be unreliable because of childish imagination, suggestibility, or fallibility of memory. Section 38(1) of CYPA 1933 was repealed by the Criminal Justice Act (CJA) 1991, s 101(2), and s 34(2) of CJA 1988 now provides that 'Any requirement whereby at a trial on indictment it is obligatory for the court to give the jury a warning about convicting the accused on the uncorroborated evidence of a child is abrogated'. Despite these reforms, the underlying dangers remain and following *Makanjuola* [1995] 3 All ER 730 it is clear that judges retain a discretion as to whether, and in what terms, to give a care warning in respect of the unsupported evidence of a child. Whether judges give such a direction will depend on the circumstances of the case (*L* [1999] Crim LR 489 and *Barker* [2010] EWCA Crim 4). Relevant factors include the age and intelligence of the child, whether the evidence is sworn, or, if unsworn, the extent to which the child understands the duty of speaking the truth.

5.4 Identification witnesses

The Court of Appeal has recognised that identification evidence is also potentially unreliable and has taken a similar approach to that taken in relation to unreliable witnesses. Whenever the prosecution case rests wholly or substantially on the correctness of one or more identifications of the accused, which the defence alleges to be mistaken, the judge should warn the jury of the special need for caution. Where the quality of the identifying evidence is poor, the judge should withdraw the case from the jury unless there is evidence to support the reliability of the identification. The judge should identify to the jury the evidence that he or she adjudges to be capable of being supporting evidence and any evidence that the jury might think was supporting but which does not have that quality (*R v Turnbull* [1977] QB 224). Identification evidence will be considered further at **Chapter 16**.

5.5 Confessions by mentally handicapped defendants

Where the prosecution seek to rely on a confession made by a mentally handicapped person, the fact that the confession was made by someone suffering from a mental handicap is something that may be taken into consideration by the judge in determining whether to exclude that confession as a matter of law under s 76 of the Police and Criminal Evidence Act 1984 (PACE 1984), or to exercise his discretion to exclude it under s 78 or 82(3) of that Act.

Where the confession is admitted, s 77(1) of PACE 1984 requires the trial judge to warn the jury of the special need for caution before convicting a defendant where the prosecution evidence depends wholly or substantially on a confession by a defendant suffering from a mental handicap and the confession was not made in the presence of an independent person. The requirement applies to summary trials (s 77(2)) and trials on indictment without a jury (s 77(2A)); here the court shall treat the case as one in which there is a special need for caution before convicting the accused on his confession. 'Independent person' does not include a police officer or a person employed for or engaged on police purposes (s 77(3)). 'Mentally handicapped' is defined under the Act to mean a state of arrested or incomplete development of mind, which includes significant impairment of intelligence and social functioning (s 77(3)).

The warning should be given by the trial judge when summing up the case. However, where the prosecution case depends wholly upon confession evidence, the accused suffers from a significant degree of mental handicap, and, in the opinion of the judge, the confession evidence is unconvincing to a point where the jury, properly directed by the judge, could not properly convict on reliance of that evidence, then the judge should withdraw the case from the jury (*R v Mackenzie* (1993) 96 Cr App R 98).

5.6 Sudden unexplained infant deaths

Sudden Infant Death Syndrome (SIDS) is the term given to the death of an infant, the cause or causes of which, although natural, is or are as yet unknown. In *R v Cannings* [2004] 1 WLR 2607, the prosecution case was that the defendant had smothered three of her children. The defence case was that they had died from SIDS. The defendant was convicted of murder but successfully appealed to the Court of Appeal. At the conclusion of its judgment the Court of Appeal held, *per curiam*, that where a full investigation into two or more sudden unexplained infant deaths in the same family is followed by a serious disagreement between reputable experts about the cause of death, and natural causes cannot be excluded as a reasonable possibility, a prosecution for murder should not be started, or continued, unless there is additional cogent evidence, extraneous to the expert evidence, that tends to support the conclusion that the infant was deliberately harmed.

Cannings was distinguished in *Kai-Whitewind* [2005] 2 Cr App R 457. In *Cannings*, the case concerned inferences drawn on the basis of the unlikelihood of two or more infant deaths in the same family. In *Kai-Whitewind*, the court held that it did not follow that there should always be a need for additional independent evidence for a case to succeed whenever there was a conflict between expert witnesses; that situation would only apply when the prosecution case relied solely on inferences based on the coincidence of multiple infant deaths.

6

Examination-in-chief

6.1 Introduction

Examination-in-chief is the questioning of a witness by the party calling him or her with the object of eliciting evidence supportive of the party's case. This chapter considers the rules governing how examination-in-chief may be conducted.

6.2 Leading questions

6.2.1 General rule

Leading questions are those questions that either suggest the answer sought or assume the existence of a fact not yet established. For example, where the prosecution case is that A stole money from B, a question that suggests the answer sought would be:

Did you see A taking money from B's wallet?

A question that assumes the existence of a fact not yet established would be:

How much money did you see A take from B?

The general rule is that a witness may not be asked leading questions during examination-in-chief. The rationale of this rule is to prevent the witness from being led into giving answers that are favourable only to the party calling the witness and thereby giving a distorted account of the events. If evidence is elicited by leading questions, it remains admissible, but the weight to be attached to it may be reduced (*Moor v Moor* [1954] 1 WLR 927).

6.2.2 Exceptions to the rule

There are three main exceptions to the rule, as follows.

(a) *Introductory matters* Leading questions may be asked in relation to matters that are introductory, such as the witness's name and occupation.

(b) *Undisputed matters* Where a matter is not in dispute, leading questions may be asked.

(c) *Hostile witnesses* Where the court has given leave for the party to treat its own witness as hostile, leading questions may be put (see **6.6.2**).

6.3 Refreshing memory before giving evidence

Witnesses may struggle to recall events to which their evidence relates, especially when these events took place some time ago. To help witnesses to give their evidence, common law rules evolved to allow witnesses to refresh their memory. The rules regarding the circumstances in which a witness is permitted to refresh his or her memory out of court apply to both civil and criminal proceedings.

In *R v Richardson* [1971] 2 QB 484, the Court of Appeal approved the practice of permitting witnesses to refresh their memory from a copy of their witness statements before giving evidence. The court recognised that requiring witnesses to give evidence without the opportunity to do so would reduce their testimony in the witness box to more of a test of memory than of truthfulness. It would tend to create difficulties for the honest witness but would be likely to do little to hamper dishonest witnesses. The court warned that it would be wrong for several witnesses to be handed their statements in circumstances that enabled one to compare with another what each had said. Likewise, such statements should not be read to witnesses in each other's presence (*R v Skinner* (1993) 99 Cr App R 212, CA).

Where prosecution witnesses in a criminal trial have refreshed their memory before giving evidence, it is desirable that the defence should be informed (*Worley v Bentley* [1976] 2 All ER 449). However, a failure to do so will not, by itself, be a ground for acquittal (*R v Westwell* [1976] 2 All ER 812). The defence is entitled to inspect and cross-examine the witness on a document used to refresh his or her memory. Where such cross-examination extends to matters contained in the document to which the witness has not referred, then the party calling the witness is entitled to put the whole of the document in evidence so that the court may see the document on which the witness has been cross-examined.

6.4 Refreshing memory while giving evidence in court

6.4.1 Civil proceedings

In the vast majority of cases a witness's witness statement will stand as his or her evidence-in-chief (CPR, r 32.5(2)). However, a witness may nevertheless benefit from being able to refresh his or her memory while giving evidence. At common law, which applies both in the civil and criminal courts, a witness may be permitted to refresh their memory from a document if they meet certain criteria (*R v Da Silva* [1990] 1 All ER 29). The witness will be permitted to refresh his or her memory from any document where:

(a) the document was made or verified at the time of the events in question or so shortly thereafter that the facts were still fresh in the witness's memory;

(b) the document is produced in court for inspection by the court and any other party; and

(c) that, in cases where the witness has no recollection of the events in question but simply swears to the accuracy of the contents of the document, it is the original or, if the original is not available, an accurate copy.

6.4.2 Criminal proceedings

Although the common law rule has not been repealed, in criminal proceedings it has been relaxed and largely superseded by the CJA 2003, s 139. This section provides:

> *(1) A person giving oral evidence in criminal proceedings about any matter may, at any stage in the course of doing so, refresh his memory of it from a document made or verified by him at an earlier time if—*
>
> *(a) he states in his oral evidence that the document records his recollection of the matter at that earlier time; and*
>
> *(b) his recollection of the matter is likely to have been significantly better at that time than it is at the time of his oral evidence.*

This provision applies to any person giving oral evidence, including the accused (*Britton* (1987) 2 All ER 412, a case decided under the common law). An application to refresh a witness's memory is normally made by an advocate, but where the interests of justice demand it, the judge may suggest that a witness refresh his or her memory from a document (*Tyagi* (1986) The Times, 21 July 1986, CA). Whether s 139(1)(b) is met is matter for the judge to determine, whatever the witness's view of the matter (*Mangena* (2010) 174 JP 67) Once the matters under s 139 are proved there is a presumption that the witness will be permitted to refresh his or her memory from the document.

The witness will normally remain in the witness box while they refresh their memory from a document but, in some cases, it may be appropriate for the witness to withdraw from the witness box to review the document in private (*Da Silva* [1990] 1 All ER 29). Once the witness has refreshed their memory and resumes giving his or her evidence, the document must be removed from them.

6.4.3 Stage of proceedings

A witness may be allowed to refresh his or her memory at any stage of the proceedings, even in re-examination (*R v Sutton* [1991] Crim LR 836, CA; CJA 2003, s 139(1)).

6.4.4 Present recollection revived and past recollection recorded

The common law rule has been held to apply both in cases of 'present recollection revived' and 'past recollection recorded'. 'Present recollection revived' describes the situation where a witness uses a document to refresh an existing memory. 'Past recollection recorded' refers to the situation where the witness has no actual recollection of the past event and simply swears to the accuracy of a record in made in a document. An example of 'past recollection recorded' may be found in *Maugham v Hubbard* (1828) 8 B & C 14, where an issue arose as to whether a sum of money had been paid. A witness was permitted to prove receipt of the money by looking at a written acknowledgement initialled by himself and stating in evidence that, on the basis of seeing his initials, he was sure that he had received the money, although he had no actual recollection of doing so.

Section 139 of the CJA 2003 applies only to 'present recollection revived'. Where a witness has no recollection of an event (in cases of 'past recollection recorded'), documents that would formerly have been reviewed by the witness under the common law memory refreshing rules may now be admissible under s 120(1), (4), and (6) of the 2003 Act:

> *(1) This section applies where a person (the witness) is called to give evidence in criminal proceedings.*
>
> ...

> *(4) A previous statement by the witness is admissible as evidence of any matter stated of which oral evidence by him would be admissible, if—*
>
> *(a) any of the following conditions is satisfied, and*
>
> *(b) while giving evidence the witness indicates that to the best of his knowledge and belief he made the statement, and that to the best of his belief it states the truth.*
>
> ...
>
> *(6) The second condition is that the statement was made by the witness when the matters stated were fresh in his memory but he does not remember them, and cannot reasonably be expected to remember them, well enough to give oral evidence of them in the proceedings.*

Concerning s 120(4) and (6), the following principles apply by virtue of *R v Chinn* [2012] 2 Cr App R 39:

1. Section 120(4) and (6) is not restricted to evidence of 'routine' matters which is recorded in previous statements.
2. Where there is a dispute about matters in s 120(6), it is for the judge to decide.
3. If there is a dispute as to whether the witness could in fact be reasonably expected to remember matters sufficiently well to give oral evidence, then the judge should decide objectively having regard to the characteristics of the witness, the circumstances in which he witnessed matters recorded, the time that has passed and anything that might have happened to the witness since witnessing the matters recorded.
4. Where it is disputed that a witness satisfies the conditions in s 120(6), the witness may be asked, in the absence of the jury, why he does not remember matters and may be cross-examined. Any issues as to the exclusion of the previous statement under PACE 1984, s 78, should be considered at this point.
5. Where a previous statement is admissible under s 120, the judge should direct the jury during his summing up (i) that they may take it into consideration because the witness could not reasonably be expected to remember what was recorded in the statement sufficiently well to give oral evidence; (ii) that they should consider the reliability of the witness's recollection of matters contained in the previous statement; and (iii) that it is for them to decide what weight to give the evidence.

6.4.5 Making and verifying a document

CJA 2003, s 140 defines a document for the purpose of s 139 as anything in which information is recorded but not including recordings of sound or moving images. At common law and under s 139 of the 2003 Act a memory-refreshing document must either be made by the witness or made by another and verified by the witness. The witness must have verified the accuracy of the contents of the document when the facts were still fresh in his memory (*Eleftheriou v Eleftheriou* [1993] Crim LR 947).

Verification may be visual or aural. In *Anderson v Whalley* (1852) 3 Car & Kir 54, it was held that entries in a ship's log made by the mate and inspected by the captain could be used by the latter to refresh his memory. In *R v Kelsey* (1982) 74 Cr App R 213, it was held that a witness could refresh his memory from a note dictated to a police officer and read back to the witness where the police officer was called to prove that the note was the one he had taken down and read back. *Kelsey* was followed in *Cummings v CPS* (Unreported, 15 December 2016).

6.4.6 Contemporaneity

At common law, the memory-refreshing document must have been made at the time of the events recorded or so shortly after that those events were still fresh in the witness's memory. The Court of Appeal has stated that the concept of contemporaneity contains *'a measure of elasticity and should not be taken to confine a witness to an over-short period'* (*R v Richardson* [1971] 2 QB 484).

Section 139 of the 2003 Act contains no requirement that the memory-refreshing document be made contemporaneously or while the events were still fresh in the memory.

6.4.7 Originals and copies

At common law and under the CJA 2003, s 139, there is no requirement that the memory-refreshing document be the original. A witness may refresh his or her memory from a copy of the original document. Thus, in *Topham v McGregor* (1844) Car & K 320, a witness was permitted to refresh his memory from an accurate copy of a newspaper article, the original having been destroyed. In *R v Chisnell* [1992] Crim LR 507, an officer was allowed to refresh his memory from a statement made nine months after the events it recorded, where the court was satisfied that it was an accurate transcription of a contemporaneous note that had subsequently been lost.

Similarly, a witness may be permitted to refresh his or her memory from a document based on an original note and containing substantially what was in it. In *R v Cheng* (1976) 63 Cr App R 20, a police officer made a statement based upon notes that he had made shortly after the defendant's arrest. By the time of the trial the original notes had been lost but the officer was permitted to refresh his memory from the statement because the statement substantially reproduced what was in the original notes, even if it was not an exact copy. In *Attorney-General's Reference (No 3 of 1979)* (1979) 69 Cr App R 411, the court allowed a witness to refresh his memory from a document that he had compiled from jottings taken during the course of an interview, the events being fresh in his mind at the time he made the note, even though he was unable to decipher the jottings at trial and the note was not a complete record of the interview.

6.4.8 Inspection of a document

A memory-refreshing document must be made available for inspection by any other parties to the proceedings, who may then cross-examine the witness on its contents. A memory-refreshing document may go before the jury if it would assist it in determining an issue at the trial. In *R v Bass* [1953] 1 QB 680, two police officers read identical accounts of a confession allegedly made by the defendant. The defendant disputed making the confession. The officers denied that they had collaborated in preparing their notes of the interview. It was held that the jury should have been allowed to inspect the officers' notebooks as it may have assisted the jury in evaluating the credibility and accuracy of the officers' evidence. It should be noted that the practice of officers pooling their recollections, while introducing risks of innocent contamination and deliberate collusion, is nevertheless permitted. The Divisional Court has observed that the practice can improve the accuracy of an officer's notes, for example, by reminding him of something which he had forgotten, correcting something that he had misstated, or helping him to make sense of confused recollections, and can also have significant operational advantages (*R (Saunders) v Independent Police Complaints Commission* [2009] 1 All ER 379).

In *R v Sekhon* (1987) 85 Cr App R 19, the Court of Appeal identified two other circumstances in which a memory-refreshing document may go before a jury:

(a) where it is difficult for the jury to follow the cross-examination of the witness who has refreshed his memory, without having the record before it; and

(b) where it is convenient to use the record as an aide-memoire as to the witness's evidence where that evidence is long and involved.

6.4.9 Cross-examination on the document

A party to the proceedings may cross-examine a witness on the contents of a document he or she has used to refresh his or her memory. However, where cross-examination goes beyond those parts used by the witness to refresh his or her memory, the party calling the witness is entitled to put the document in evidence (*Gregory v Tavernor* (1833) 6 Car & P 280; *Senat v Senat* [1965] P 172). Similarly, where the document is inconsistent with the witness's testimony, the document is admissible as evidence of the inconsistency. Also, where cross-examination involves a suggestion that the witness has fabricated his or her evidence, which will usually involve, either expressly or impliedly, an allegation that the memory-refreshing document is concocted, the memory-refreshing document may then be admissible as evidence to rebut this suggestion and to show whether or not it is a genuine contemporaneous record that has not subsequently been altered (*R v Sekhon* (1987) 85 Cr App R 19).

Where a memory-refreshing document is put in evidence following cross-examination it is evidence of consistency and/or the truth of the matters stated in it (Civil Evidence Act 1995, ss 1, 6(4), and (5); CJA 2003, s 120(3)). The CJA 2003, s 120 provides:

> *(1) This section applies where a person (the witness) is called to give evidence in criminal proceedings.*
>
> ...
>
> *(3) A statement made by the witness in a document—*
>
> *(a) which is used by him to refresh his memory while giving evidence.*
>
> *(b) on which he is cross-examined, and*
>
> *(c) which as a consequence is received in evidence in the proceedings,*
>
> *is admissible of any matter stated of which oral evidence by him would be admissible.*

Section 120(3) does not create an exception to the rule against hearsay (see **Chapter 11**) but simply regulates the purposes for which a memory-refreshing document may be used once it has been admitted in evidence under the common law principles (*R v Pashmfouroush* [2006] EWCA Crim 2330). Where the witness is unable to refresh his or her memory from his or her statement in the document, the statement may be admissible under s 120(4) and (6) as evidence of the matters stated in it (*R v Chinn* [2012] 2 Cr App R 39).

6.4.10 Use of memory-refreshing documents as exhibits

Where a document is admitted into evidence under s 120(3) and the document is produced as an exhibit, then it should not accompany the jury when they retire to consider their verdict unless the court considers it appropriate or all parties to the proceedings agree (s 122). It is normally sufficient for the judge to remind the jury when summing up the case of the contents of the document and anything said by the witness about the document and the circumstances in which it was made. This helps to reduce the risk of the jury placing disproportionate weight on the document as compared with oral evidence.

6.5 Previous consistent statements

The general rule, in both civil and criminal proceedings, is that a witness may not be asked in examination-in-chief about a previous oral or written statement, consistent with his testimony, in order to show his consistency (*R v Gregson* [2003] 2 Cr App R 34). Nor may a party seek to adduce evidence of such a statement through another witness. The rationale for the rule is that such evidence is too easy for a witness to fabricate. It has also been suggested that such evidence is, in any event, superfluous as a witness's evidence should be taken as true until there is a reason for impeaching it.

Two examples may be given. In *Corke v Corke* [1958] P 93, the Court of Appeal held that a wife, whose husband had accused her of having committed adultery with a lodger, should not have been permitted to adduce evidence that she had telephoned her doctor immediately after the accusation had been made, requesting him to come at once and examine both her and the lodger, with a view to establishing their innocence of misconduct. In *R v Roberts* [1942] 1 All ER 187, the accused was charged with the murder of a girl by shooting her. At the trial he gave evidence that the gun went off accidentally while he was trying to make up a quarrel with the girl. Two days after the alleged offence, the accused had told his father that his defence would be one of accident. The Court of Appeal held that proof of this conversation was not permissible if tendered to bolster the credibility of the accused by showing his consistency.

There are a number of exceptions to the rule in both civil and criminal proceedings.

6.5.1 Exceptions in civil proceedings

Section 6 of the Civil Evidence Act 1995 provides:

...

(2) A party who has called or intends to call a person as a witness in civil proceedings may not in those proceedings adduce evidence of a previous statement made by that person except—

(a) with leave of the court, or

(b) for the purpose of rebutting a suggestion that his evidence has been fabricated.

...

(4) Nothing in this Act affects any of the rules of law as to the circumstances in which, where a person called as a witness in civil proceedings is cross-examined on a document used by him to refresh his memory, that document may be made evidence in the proceedings.

Therefore, there are three exceptions to the general rule in civil proceedings:

- the statement is admissible with the leave of the court (s 6(2)(a));
- the statement is admissible to rebut an allegation of recent fabrication (s 6(2)(b)); and
- the statement is admissible as a memory-refreshing document (s 6(4)).

6.5.1.1 Leave of the court

Under the CEA 1995, s 6(2)(a), the court has a wide discretion to admit previous consistent statements where it would be just to do so. In *Morris v Stratford-upon-Avon Rural District Council* [1973] 1 WLR 1059, a decision under the equivalent provision in the Civil Evidence Act 1968, the trial was held five years after the accident that gave rise to the action. A witness whose recollection of the facts was hazy was allowed to adduce in his evidence-in-chief a statement that he had made to an insurance company nine months after the accident.

6.5.1.2 Evidence in rebuttal of an allegation of recent fabrication

The mere fact that the cross-examination of a witness suggests that the witness is not worthy of belief does not allow the proof of a previous statement by the witness to reinforce his credibility. This is so even if the cross-examination exposes a previous inconsistency or contradiction between his evidence and a statement made on a previous occasion (*R v Coll* (1889) 25 LR Ir 522; *R v Beattie* (1998) 89 Cr App R 302). However, where it is suggested that the witness has recently fabricated his or her evidence, evidence is admissible in rebuttal to show that on an earlier occasion the witness made a statement consistent with that testimony (*R v Oyesiku* (1971) 56 Cr App R 240, CA; *Fox v General Medical Council* [1960] 1 WLR 1017). For example, in *Flanaghan v Fahy* [1918] 2 IR 361, it was put to a witness, who had testified that a certain document was a forgery, that he had invented his evidence because of the hostility that existed between him and the defendant. The witness was then allowed to call evidence to show that he had told someone else that it was a forgery before the cause of the hostility between him and the defendant arose. In *R v Athwal* [2009] 1 WLR 2430, the Court of Appeal held that 'recent' in this context should not be confined within a temporal straitjacket but should be understood as an 'elastic' description which should allow for the admission of a previous consistent statement where there is a rational and cogent basis on which it could assist the tribunal of fact in determining where the truth lies.

In *R v Oyesiku* (1971) 56 Cr App R 240, the Court of Appeal approved the judgment of Dixon CJ in the Australian case *Nominal Defendant v Clement* (1961) 104 CLR 476, in which he held that:

(a) where it is suggested that the witness's account is a recent invention or reconstruction, even though not with conscious dishonesty, a previous consistent statement is admissible;
(b) the previous statement must have been made either contemporaneously with the event or at a time sufficiently early to be inconsistent with the suggestion that his evidence is a recent invention or reconstruction;
(c) the judge must exercise great care in determining whether a previous statement is admissible. In particular, he must be satisfied that:
    (i) the account given by the witness has been attacked on the ground of recent invention or reconstruction or that foundation for such an attack has been laid;
    (ii) the contents of the previous statement are in fact to the like effect as the account given by the witness in evidence; and
    (iii) having regard to the time and circumstances in which it was made, it rationally tends to answer the attack.

The facts in *R v Oyesiku* were as follows. After the defendant had been arrested, and while he was still in custody, his wife made a written statement to his solicitor. At trial, prosecution counsel suggested in cross-examination that she had made up her evidence to help her husband. The Court of Appeal held that in re-examination she had properly been permitted to adduce evidence of her previous consistent statement. However, the conviction was quashed as the trial judge had not allowed the document to go before the jury, which would have assisted it in determining the extent to which the previous statement answered the attack.

A previous consistent statement can be proved either during the re-examination of the witness or by calling the other person to whom the statement was made (*R v Wilmot* (1989) 89 Cr App R 341).

6.5.1.3 Memory-refreshing document

See **6.4.1**.

6.5.1.4 Evidential status of a previous consistent statement

A previous consistent statement admissible under the CEA 1995, s 6 is admissible as evidence of consistency and of the truth of the matters stated (ss 1 and 6(5)).

6.5.2 Exceptions in criminal proceedings

6.5.2.1 Memory-refreshing documents

See **6.4.4** and **6.4.9**.

6.5.2.2 Previous identifications

At common law, evidence of a previous identification of the accused by a witness out of court is permissible (*R v Christie* [1914] AC 545). However, the common law rules have been superseded by the CJA 2003, s 120, which provides:

> *(1) This section applies where a person (the witness) is called to give evidence in criminal proceedings.*
>
> ...
>
> *(4) A previous statement by the witness is admissible as evidence of any matter stated of which oral evidence by him would be admissible, if—*
>
> *(a) any of the following conditions is satisfied, and*
>
> *(b) while giving evidence the witness indicates that to the best of his knowledge and belief he made the statement, and that to the best of his belief it states the truth.*
>
> ...
>
> *(5) the first condition is that the statement identifies or describes a person, object or place.*

In relation to s 120(5), it was held in *R v Chinn* [2012] 2 Cr App R 39 that, although its precise scope was unclear, the provision should be construed broadly because 'a [bare] description of a person, object or place in a vacuum is of no use in criminal proceedings'. Accordingly, evidence admissible under s 120(5) is not restricted to evidence which is bare identification information. The section allows evidence to be admitted which contains not only a description of 'a person, object or place, but also puts that description in the relevant context'.

6.5.2.3 Previous complaint

For a long time, it was a part of the common law that where a complainant, in the case of a sexual offence, made a voluntary complaint shortly after the alleged incident, then evidence could be given of the complaint. Such evidence was not evidence of the matters stated, but evidence of consistency between the complainant's conduct and his testimony, and could be used to disprove consent (*R v Lillyman* [1896] 2 QB 167, CCR). Again, the common law has been superseded by the CJA 2003, s 120, which provides:

> *(1) This section applies where a person (the witness) is called to give evidence in criminal proceedings.*
>
> ...
>
> *(4) A previous statement by the witness is admissible as evidence of any matter stated of which oral evidence by him would be admissible, if—*
>
> *(a) any of the following conditions is satisfied, and*
>
> *(b) while giving evidence the witness indicates that to the best of his knowledge and belief he made the statement, and that to the best of his belief it states the truth.*
>
> ...
>
> *(7) The third condition is that—*
>
> *(a) the witness claims to be a person against whom an offence has been committed,*

> (b) *the offence is one to which the proceedings relate,*
>
> (c) *the statement consists of a complaint made by the witness (whether to a person in authority or not) about conduct which would, if proved, constitute the offence or part of the offence,*
>
> ...
>
> (e) *the complaint was not made as a result of a threat or a promise, and*
>
> (f) *before the statement is adduced the witness gives oral evidence in connection with its subject matter.*
>
> (8) *For the purpose of subsection (7) the fact that the complaint was elicited (for example, by a leading question) is irrelevant unless a threat or promise was involved.*

Section 120(7) broadens the previous common law exception so as to permit evidence of a previous complaint in relation to any offence, not just a sexual offence. At common law, evidence of a complaint elicited as the result of a leading question was inadmissible (*R v Osborne* [1905] 1 KB 551). However, the CJA 2003 expressly permits the admission of complaints made in answer to such questions as long as no threat or promise was involved (s 120(8)). Of course, such questioning may nevertheless affect the weight that the tribunal of fact attaches to the evidence.

Previously, s 120(7)(d) had imposed an additional requirement, namely that the complaint be made as soon as could reasonably be expected. However, this provision was repealed by the Coroners and Justice Act 2009, s 112.

It is essential that the complainant states in his or her evidence that, to the best of their knowledge and belief, he or she made the complaint and to the best of his or her belief it was true. Failure to do so will render the complaint inadmissible (*Avery* [2007] EWCA Crim 1830).

For the purposes of s 120(7)(a) and (b) the 'offence' must be one with which the defendant is charged in the present proceedings (*R v T* [2008] EWCA Crim 484).

A previous complaint is evidence of the truth of the matters stated, consistency between a complainant's conduct and his or her evidence at trial and, where consent is in issue, lack of consent (s 120(4)).

6.5.2.4 Statements in rebuttal of recent fabrication

Section 120 provides:

> (1) *This section applies where a person (the witness) is called to give evidence in criminal proceedings.*
>
> (2) *If a previous statement by the witness is admitted as evidence to rebut a suggestion that his oral evidence has been fabricated, that statement is admissible as evidence of any matter stated of which oral evidence by the witness would be admissible.*

In *R v T* [2008] EWCA Crim 484, the Court of Appeal stressed that s 120(2) does not govern *admissibility* but merely regulates the use to which such evidence, once admitted, may be put and its evidential value (its evidential value is that it becomes evidence of matters stated). Accordingly, the *admissibility* of evidence to rebut fabrication must be considered by reference to the principles that have governed this question in the past, ie the common law principles. It is submitted that the decision in *R v T* is consistent with the intention of the statute, namely that s 120 should govern the use and evidential value of previous statements once admitted, rather than their admissibility into evidence in the first place. Therefore, the common law rules that govern the admissibility of statements in rebuttal of recent fabrication in civil proceedings apply equally to criminal proceedings (see **6.5.1.2**). It follows that, although s 120(2) omits any reference to the recency of the fabrication, this does not mean that it is no longer a requirement for admissibility (see R Pattenden, *R v Athwal* (Case Comment) (2009) 13 E & P 342 but cf D Ormerod, *R v Athwal* (Case Comment) [2009] Crim LR 726). In relation to the evidential value of a previous statement once it has been admitted in criminal proceedings, it can be put forward as evidence of the witness's consistency and as evidence of any matter stated of which oral evidence by that witness would be admissible (CJA 2003, s 120(2)).

In *R v A* (2011) 175 JP 437, CA, it was held that where a witness's previous statement is admitted to rebut a suggestion of fabrication, the judge must give a specific direction to the jury that the evidence is not evidence which is independent of the complainant and the direction recommended in *R v AA* [2007] EWCA Crim 1779, CA, should be followed routinely. In *R v AA,* the Court of Appeal made the following recommendation concerning how a jury should be directed:

> In our judgment ... juries should be directed that ... a previous consistent statement or recent complaint is, if the jury accepts it was given or made and the conditions specified in section 120 are fulfilled, evidence of the truth of what was stated: but in deciding what weight such a statement should bear, the jury should have in mind the fact that it comes from the same person who now makes the complaint in the witness box and not from some independent source.

6.5.2.5 Statements upon accusation

An accusation of involvement in a criminal offence will most often be made by police officers in an informal conversation with the suspect, or on arrest or in an interview under caution. The law of evidence recognises three types of statement that could be made by a person when confronted by such an accusation:

- an admission;
- an exculpatory statement;
- a mixed statement.

6.5.2.5.1 Admissions

A statement that contains an admission is admissible as a confession under PACE 1984, s 76(1) as evidence of the facts stated. Confessions will be considered further in **Chapter 14**.

6.5.2.5.2 Exculpatory statements

An exculpatory statement is a statement denying any involvement in the offence. It is admissible as evidence of the attitude and reaction of the accused when taxed with incriminating facts and, thus, evidence of the consistency of the accused's defence, but it is not evidence of the truth of the matters stated (*R v Storey* (1968) 52 Cr App R 334).

In *R v Storey*, the prosecution adduced evidence-in-chief that when a quantity of cannabis had been found in the accused's flat, she had explained that it belonged to a man who had brought it there against her will. The defence relied on this statement in a submission of no case to answer. The Court of Appeal upheld the judge's ruling that the statement was not evidence of the facts stated; it was evidence of the reaction of the accused that formed part of the general picture to be considered by the jury.

In *R v Pearce* (1979) 69 Cr App R 365, it was held that this exception to the rule against previous consistent statements is not limited to statements made on the first encounter with the police. However, the longer the time that has elapsed after the first encounter, the less weight will be attached to the denial.

Where a previous exculpatory statement adds nothing to the evidence already before the court it may be excluded on the basis that it is not relevant and is, therefore, inadmissible. This was the reasoning of the Court of Appeal in *R v Tooke* (1989) 90 Cr App R 417, when upholding the trial judge's decision to exclude a spontaneous written statement made to the police within an hour of the incident because, during the course of the trial, a statement made at the scene to the same effect had already been admitted. The court recognised that in such a case it is not an easy task for the judge to decide, in his discretion, where the dividing line falls.

6.5.2.5.3 *Mixed statements*

A mixed statement is one that is partly incriminatory and partly exculpatory. For example: 'I hit W, but only because I was trying to defend myself.' The whole of a mixed statement is admissible because it would obviously be unfair for the prosecution to exclude those parts that are favourable to the accused, while relying on those parts favourable to the prosecution (*R v Storey* (1968) 52 Cr App R 334). Moreover, the whole statement is to be taken into consideration in determining where the truth lies. While it could be argued that the exculpatory parts should be admitted as evidence of reaction only, and not as evidence of the truth of the matters stated, it is considered too difficult to explain this legal nicety to a jury. However, the judge may point out that the incriminating parts are likely to be true (otherwise why say them?), whereas excuses do not have the same weight (*R v Sharp* [1988] 1 WLR 7, HL; *R v Aziz* [1996] AC 41, HL).

In *R v Garrod* [1997] Crim LR 445, the Court of Appeal addressed the question of how to identify when a statement contained enough in the nature of admissions to justify calling it 'mixed'. The court, acknowledging that many statements could be said to contain some admissions of relevant fact, as well as a statement of innocence and a denial of guilt, held that a statement should be regarded as mixed if it contained an admission of fact that was significant to any issue in the case, ie capable of adding some degree of weight to the prosecution case on an issue that was relevant to guilt. The correctness of this approach was confirmed in *R v Papworth* [2008] 1 Cr App R 439, in which the Court of Appeal held that an admission by the defendant during a police interview of an ingredient of the offence will often, but not always, constitute a significant admission. Further, the determination of whether a mixed statement is 'significant' in relation to an issue in the case can only be determined by reference to what happens at trial and, therefore, can only be finally resolved at the close of the evidence. The greater the prosecution's reliance on the inculpatory parts of the statement at the conclusion of the trial, the more likely it is that the jury should be told that the exculpatory parts are also evidence in the case.

In *R v Aziz* [1996] AC 41, HL, it was held that mixed statements are only admissible as evidence of the truth of the matters stated if tendered by the prosecution. However, where the prosecution tenders a mixed statement but does not rely on it as proof of any part of its case against the accused, the accused may rely upon it for the truth of its contents (*Western v DPP* [1997] 1 Cr App R 474, DC).

6.5.2.6 *Res gestae* statements

Under the doctrine of *res gestae*, evidence is admissible of any act or statement so closely associated in time, place, and circumstances with some matter in issue that it can be said to be a part of the same transaction. A *res gestae* statement may be admitted as evidence of consistency and for the truth of its contents. In *R v Fowkes*, The Times, 8 March 1856, the defendant was charged with murder. The son of the victim and another person present at the scene were permitted to give evidence that on seeing a face at the window through which a shot was fired, the son had said, 'There's Butcher' (a name by which the defendant was known). The doctrine of *res gestae* is preserved by the CJA 2003, s 118, para 4 and will be considered in greater detail at **13.4.3**.

6.5.2.7 Documents produced as exhibits

See **6.4.10**. In a Crown Court trial where a statement made in a document is admitted in evidence under s 120 and the document or a copy of it is produced as an exhibit, the exhibit must not accompany the jury when they retire to consider their verdict unless the court considers it appropriate, or all the parties to the proceedings agree (CJA 2003, s 122).

6.6 Unfavourable and hostile witnesses

A party may not impeach the credibility of its own witness, whether by:

- asking leading questions; or
- asking about or calling evidence to prove prior inconsistent statements, prior discreditable conduct, bad character, previous convictions, or bias.

However, evidence of a witness's prior discreditable conduct may be adduced in circumstances where it is relevant, not to impeach that witness's credibility, but for some other purpose (*R v Ross* [2008] Crim LR 306).

6.6.1 Unfavourable witnesses

An unfavourable witness is one who either fails to prove that which he or she was expected to prove ('fails to come up to proof') or who gives evidence unfavourable to the party by whom he or she has been called. In accordance with the general rule, the party calling the witness may not impeach his or her credibility but may only call other witnesses to prove the matters that the unfavourable witness failed to prove (*Ewer v Ambrose* (1825) 3 B & C 746).

6.6.2 Hostile witnesses

A hostile witness is one who, in the opinion of the judge, '*is not desirous of telling the truth to the court at the instance of the party calling him*' (***Stephen's Digest of the Law of Evidence***, 12th edn, 1936, Article 147). When a witness is declared to be hostile, the party calling the witness may cross-examine him or her by asking leading questions and may, with the leave of the judge, prove prior inconsistent statements made by that witness.

In criminal proceedings, the prosecution may call a person even if he or she has shown that he or she is likely to be a hostile witness, for example, by retracting an earlier statement and/or making a second statement (*R v Mann* (1972) 56 Cr App R 750, CA). Similarly, there is no barrier to calling a witness in civil proceedings who has shown signs of hostility, for example by refusing to provide a statement (see CPR, r 32.9).

An application for leave to treat a witness as hostile must be made to the judge and, in criminal proceedings, should generally be made in the presence of the jury (*R v Darby* [1989] Crim LR 817, CA; *R v Khan* [2003] Crim LR 428 CA).

An application for leave to treat a witness as hostile can be made at any time during the witness's evidence. It should be made when the witness first shows signs of unmistakable hostility (*Pestano* [1981] Crim LR 397); normally this will be during examination-in-chief. However, in rare cases in which a witness shows hostility in re-examination, an application can be made at this later stage (*R v Powell* [1985] 1 WLR 1364). Where a witness gives evidence contrary to an earlier statement or fails to give the evidence expected, the party calling the witness and the trial judge should not immediately proceed to treat him or her as hostile, unless that is the only appropriate course given of the degree of hostility, but should consider first inviting the witness to refresh his or her memory from appropriate material (*R v Maw* [1994] Crim LR 841, CA).

In determining an application to treat a witness as hostile, the judge should have regard to the demeanour of the witness, the evidence the witness gives, the evidence the witness does not give, and the witness's willingness to cooperate.

Where the judge grants leave to treat a witness as hostile, the party calling the witness may, at common law, ask leading questions (*R v Thompson* (1976) 64 Cr App R 96, CA).

The Criminal Procedure Act 1865, s 3, which applies in both civil and criminal proceedings, makes provision for the party calling a hostile witness to prove previous inconsistent statements made by that witness. Section 3 provides that:

> *A party producing a witness shall not be allowed to impeach his credit by general evidence of bad character, but he may, in case the witness shall in the opinion of the judge prove adverse, contradict him by other evidence, or, by leave of the judge, prove that he has made at other times a statement inconsistent with his present testimony; but before such last-mentioned proof can be given the circumstances of the supposed statement, sufficient to designate the particular occasion, must be mentioned to the witness, and he must be asked whether or not he has made such a statement.*

The first part of s 3 of the 1865 Act merely restates the common law rule that a party cannot impeach its own witness. The remainder of the provision applies only to adverse witnesses. In *Greenough v Eccles* (1859) 5 CB NS 786, it was held that 'adverse' means hostile. Thus, the section allows a party calling a hostile witness:

- to contradict the witness, in the same manner as an unfavourable witness, by calling other evidence; or
- to prove a previous inconsistent statement against the witness.

If the witness, under cross-examination on a previous inconsistent statement, admits that he or she made the statement and confirms its contents, then that will stand as his or her evidence and can be accepted by the tribunal of fact subject to assessment of the witness's credibility (*R v Maw* [1994] Crim LR 841, CA). Where the witness does not admit the truth of the previous statement, the statement is admissible as evidence of the matters stated in both civil proceedings (Civil Evidence Act 1995, ss 1, 6(3) and (5)) and criminal proceedings (CJA 2003, s 119(1)). Thus, where a witness does not admit making the previous inconsistent statement, and it is proved against him or her, it will be open to the tribunal of fact to accept either the present testimony of the witness or the previous inconsistent statement and to determine the weight to be attached (*R v Joyce (RJ) and Joyce (JP)* [2005] EWCA Crim 1785). In *R v Billingham* [2009] 2 Cr App R 20, the Court of Appeal held that in criminal proceedings the jury must be sure that a witness's evidence or prior statement is true before they may rely on it as evidence of truth supporting the prosecution case. However, where it is exculpatory of the accused, it is sufficient if they are persuaded that it may be true. Moreover, the jury should not be directed that a previous statement is just as much evidence as the witness's testimony in court because the jury may take the direction to mean that they are obliged to give both the same evidential weight. Save possibly in the most exceptional cases, once a witness has been treated as hostile some warning should be given to the jury about approaching his or her evidence with caution; the nature of the warning will obviously be dependent on the particular facts of the case (see **Chapter 5**).

A statement admissible under s 119 may be excluded under PACE 1984, s 78 where the admission of the evidence would adversely affect the fairness of the proceedings. The defence may also make a submission of no case to answer or an application under the CJA 2003, s 125 (see **13.9.3**) at the close of the Crown's case, on the grounds of the unreliability of the prosecution evidence (*R v Joyce (RJ) and Joyce (JP)* [2005] EWCA Crim 1785; *R v Bennett* [2008] EWCA Crim 248 and *R v Gibbons* [2009] Crim LR 197, CA).

In a Crown Court trial where a previous inconsistent statement is contained in a document and during the trial that document is admitted as an exhibit, the CJA 2003, s 122 provides that the document should not be taken to the jury room when the jury retires unless either the court considers it appropriate or all the parties in the case agree (see *R v Hulme* [2007] 1 Cr App R 334).

7

Cross-examination and re-examination

7.1 Cross-examination

Cross-examination is the questioning of a witness by any party to the proceedings other than the party calling him. The judge may also ask a witness questions, typically to clarify matters that he or she does not understand or fears that the jury may not understand, and, in particular, where the accused is unrepresented, the court may ask a witness any questions necessary in the interests of the accused (Crim PR, r 24.4(6) for magistrates' courts and r 25.11(6) for the Crown Court). The purpose of cross-examination is:

- to elicit evidence favourable to the cross-examining party's case;
- to qualify, weaken, or cast doubt upon evidence unfavourable to the cross-examining party's case; and
- in appropriate circumstances, to impeach the witness's credibility.

Questions in cross-examination may relate to any relevant fact or any fact in issue or to the credibility of the witness; cross-examination is not limited to those matters raised in evidence-in-chief. A witness may be asked leading questions during cross-examination, ie questions that either suggest the answer sought or assume the existence of a fact not yet established.

7.2 Liability to cross-examination

All witnesses who have been called by a party and taken the oath are liable to cross-examination except:

- those who produce documents without being sworn (*Summers v Mosely* (1834) 2 Cr & M 477);
- those called by mistake who cannot give material evidence (*Wood v Mackinson* (1840) 2 Mood & R 273); and
- those who have been called by the judge, unless the judge grants leave (*Coulson v Disborough* [1894] 2 QB 316).

If a witness dies before being cross-examined his or her evidence-in-chief is still admissible (*R v Doolin* (1832) 1 Jebb CC 123, IR). Where a witness, in cross-examination, becomes incapable of giving further evidence while giving evidence, the witness's evidence up to that point is admissible and the trial may continue but the judge should warn the jury that if it feels unable to assess that witness's credibility because cross-examination was incomplete, then it should acquit the defendant (*R v Stretton* (1986) 86 Cr App R 7, CA; *R v Wyatt* [1990] Crim LR 343). In contrast, it was doubted whether a judicial direction could counteract the prejudice to the defendant who was deprived of the opportunity to test the evidence in cross-examination in the case of a witness who was unable to continue to give evidence after his examination-in-chief, and who gave the only direct evidence on an important part of the prosecution case (*R v Lawless* (1993) 98 Cr App R 342). In determining whether the accused can have a fair trial if the complainant's evidence is incomplete, the court can have regard to the extent to which the defence has been explored with the complainant, whether previous inconsistent statements can be reduced to agreed facts in writing and put before the jury, and whether there is other evidence against the accused (*Pipe* [2014] EWCA Crim 2570).

In criminal proceedings, a witness is normally examined-in-chief before being cross-examined. However, sometimes a witness will simply be tendered by the prosecution for cross-examination. This typically happens where a police officer gives evidence of observations he or she made with a second officer, and the second officer's witness statement does no more than confirm the first officer's evidence in all material details. The prosecution would call the second officer, after the first has given evidence in full, ask the officer sufficient questions to identify him or her, and permit the officer to use any memory-refreshing document, before leaving the witness to be cross-examined by the defence.

In civil proceedings, as the witness statement will usually stand as a witness's evidence-in-chief (CPR, r 32.5(2)), evidence-in-chief may consist simply of the witness identifying the witness statement and confirming his or her belief in the truth of its contents. Cross-examination follows immediately after.

7.3 Restrictions on cross-examination

7.3.1 Restrictions on cross-examination by the accused in person in criminal proceedings

Generally, a witness called by one party to the proceedings, and liable to cross-examination, may be cross-examined by the accused in person. However, there are a number of restrictions placed upon cross-examination by the accused.

7.3.1.1 Common law

At common law, the judge can restrict both the length of the cross-examination and the issues to which it relates (*R v Brown* [1998] 2 Cr App R 364).

7.3.1.2 The complainant in sexual offences

The YJCEA 1999 places significant restrictions on the accused's ability to cross-examine certain witnesses in person. Section 34 of the YJCEA 1999 provides:

> *(1) No person charged with a sexual offence may in any criminal proceedings cross-examine in person a witness who is the complainant, either—*
>
> *(a) in connection with that offence, or*
>
> *(b) in connection with any other offence (of whatever nature) with which that person is charged in the proceedings.*

'Sexual offence' is defined in the YJCEA 1999, s 62 as any offence under the Sexual Offences Act 2003, Part 1; an offence of human trafficking committed with a view to sexual exploitation under the Modern Slavery Act 2015, s 2; or any relevant superseded offence. 'Relevant superseded offence' includes the following: rape or burglary with intent to rape; an offence under the Sexual Offences Act 1956, ss 2–12 and 14–17; an offence under the Mental Health Act 1959, s 128 (unlawful intercourse with a person receiving treatment for mental disorder by member of hospital staff); an offence under the Indecency with Children Act 1960, s 1 (indecent conduct towards a child under 14 years of age); and an offence under the Criminal Law Act 1977, s 54 (incitement of child under 16 to commit incest).

7.3.1.3 Protected witnesses

Section 35 of the YJCEA 1999 provides:

> *(1) No person charged with an offence to which this section applies may in any criminal proceedings cross-examine in person a protected witness, either—*
>
> *(a) in connection with that offence, or*
>
> *(b) in connection with any other offence (of whatever nature) with which that person is charged in the proceedings.*

A 'protected witness' is a witness who:

(a) is either the complainant or a witness (s 35(2)(a)) to one or more of the offences specified in the YJCEA 1999, s 35(3), namely:

- (i) sexual offences under the Sexual Offences Act 1956, ss 33–36, the Protection of Children Act 1978, Part 1 of the Sexual Offences Act 2003 or any relevant superseded enactment (s 35(3)(a)). 'Relevant superseded enactment' means an offence under the Sexual Offences Act 1956, ss 1–32; the Indecency with Children Act 1960; the Sexual Offences Act 1967; and the Criminal Law Act 1977, s 54;
- (ii) slavery or human trafficking offences under the Modern Slavery Act 2015, ss 1 and 2 (s 35(3)(a));
- (iii) kidnapping, false imprisonment, or child abduction (s 35(3)(b));
- (iv) child cruelty (s 35(3)(c)); or
- (v) any other offence involving an assault on, or injury, or threat of injury to any person (s 35(3)(d));

and

(b) either

- (i) where the offence is a sexual offence or a slavery or human trafficking case, the witness is under the age of 18 or falls to be cross-examined having given evidence-in-chief when under that age (s 35(2)(b) as amended by the Coroners and Justice Act 2009, s 105); or
- (ii) in the case of any other specified offence, the witness is under the age of 14 or falls to be cross-examined having given evidence-in-chief when under that age (s 35(2)(b)).

7.3.1.4 General discretion

Section 36 of the YJCEA 1999 permits the court to make a direction prohibiting the accused from cross-examining a witness in person where neither the YJCEA 1999, s 34 nor 35 operate if:

> ...
>
> *(2) ... it appears to the court—*

(a) that the quality of evidence given by the witness on cross-examination—

(i) is likely to be diminished if the cross-examination ... is conducted by the accused in person, and

(ii) would be likely to be improved if a direction were given under this section, and

(b) that it would not be contrary to the interests of justice to give such a direction.

In determining whether the YJCEA 1999, s 36(2)(a) applies, the court must take into account the various factors set out in s 35(3), including any views expressed by the witness, the nature of the questions likely to be asked, and the behaviour of the accused both towards the witness and generally. 'Witness' for the purposes of this section does not include a co-accused (s 36(4)(a)).

7.3.1.5 Procedure

In cases where cross-examination by the accused is prevented under any of the provisions just noted, the YJCEA 1999, s 38 requires that the court must invite the accused to arrange for a legal representative to act for him or her for the purposes of cross-examination, and requires the accused to notify the court whether such a person is to act. If the accused fails to arrange for a legal representative or, failing notification, it appears that there will be no such representative, the court must consider whether it is necessary in the interests of justice for the witness to be cross-examined by a legal representative appointed to represent the accused's interests. If so, the court must appoint a qualified legal representative to cross-examine the witness in the interests of the accused.

Under the YJCEA 1999, s 39, a judge is required to give such warning as is necessary (if any) to the jury, in a case where cross-examination in person has been prevented, to ensure that the accused is not prejudiced by any inferences that might be drawn from the fact that he or she has been prevented from cross-examining, and, where there is a court-appointed legal representative acting, that that person was not acting as the accused's own legal representative.

7.3.2 Judicial power to restrain unnecessary or improper questions and to impose time limits

The judge has a common law discretion to prevent counsel from conducting unnecessary or improper cross-examination. Counsel should not waste time with protracted and irrelevant cross-examination but should cross-examine with restraint and the courtesy and consideration that witnesses are entitled to expect (*Mechanical and General Inventions Co Ltd v Austin* [1935] AC 346, HL; *R v Kalia* (1974) 60 Cr App R 200).

As part of their case management powers, judges in the criminal courts may limit the duration of any stage of the hearing including the cross-examination of a witness. While judges are entitled to impose time limits, this should not be a routine feature of trial management but proper judicial management of court time is not inconsistent with the entitlement to a fair trial (*B* [2005] EWCA Crim 805).

In civil proceedings, the court has an additional power to limit cross-examination under CPR, r 32.1(3) (see **1.6.1**).

7.3.2.1 Cross-examination of vulnerable witnesses and defendants in criminal cases

Whenever a vulnerable witness or defendant is to be questioned at trial, advocates should have regard to the Advocacy Training Council's Advocacy Toolkits. These toolkits represent best practice and should be consulted and followed by advocates whenever they prepare to question a young or otherwise vulnerable witness or defendant. See Criminal

Practice Direction I, para 3D.7. Further, where a vulnerable witness or defendant is to be cross-examined during a criminal trial, the scope and nature of the cross-examination should be determined by the judge in advance, applying the guidance in the 'Judicial College Bench Checklist: Young Witness Cases' and the directions in the Criminal Practice Directions [2015] EWCA Crim 1567, para 3E.

The aim of the Judicial College's 'checklist' for young witness cases is to enable a young witness to give his or her 'best evidence'. Before any questioning of a young witness may take place, a checklist of issues should be considered and directions given to advocates by the judge in a 'ground rules' discussion. The checklist covers questioning in examination-in-chief, cross-examination, and re-examination. In respect of cross-examination, examples of directions which can be given include:

- Avoid questions which could produce unreliable answers, such as questions with a 'tag' (eg 'He did not touch you like that, *did he*?'), since the tag might cause the young witness to give an unreliable answer. The child may agree simply in order to please, to relieve stress, or to bring questioning to an end as quickly as possible. Instead, the question should be expressed in a more 'immediate' way, without a tag and using a name rather than a pronoun (eg 'Did Andy touch you?' and if the answer is 'yes', 'How did Andy touch you?')
- Avoid suggesting wrongdoing to a young witness without reasonable grounds, because the witness may respond with an unreliable answer. The witness may agree with what is put, again, to relieve stress or to bring the experience of being cross-examined to an end as quickly as possible.
- Do not necessarily put the defence case to the young witness in a detailed way so that, for example, evidence highlighting inconsistencies should be adduced but assertions as to how the inconsistencies might undermine credibility are saved for a closing speech to the jury.

The checklist is supplemented by the Criminal Practice Directions [2015] EWCA Crim 1567. Paragraph 3E of the Criminal Practice Directions sets out the following key directions in relation to the questioning of vulnerable witnesses and defendants:

- The judiciary is responsible for controlling questioning by advocates and an over-rigorous or repetitive cross-examination of a child or vulnerable witness must be stopped. To avoid intervention by the judge, the magistrate, or an intermediary (where one attends to support the witness), questioning should be discussed in advance and ground rules should be agreed and adhered to. See para 3E.1.
- A ground rules discussion must take place in all trials in which an intermediary is involved before the witness gives evidence. The intermediary should be present but is not required to take the oath (although an intermediary's declaration will be made just before the witness is due to give evidence). See para 3E.2.
- A ground rules discussion is good practice in all young witnesses' cases and in all cases where the witness or defendant has communication needs, whether or not an intermediary is to be used. The discussion should take place preferably before the day of the trial, to give advocates sufficient time to prepare questioning in accordance with what is agreed. It might be helpful for the trial judge to prepare a 'trial practice note' of the limits of questioning, which can be referred to in order to ensure that what was agreed at the discussion is adhered to. See para 3E.3.
- Vulnerable witnesses and defendants should be able to give the best evidence they can and this may require departing radically from traditional cross-examination.

The court may dispense with the normal practice of the advocate being permitted to 'put his case' where the vulnerable witness might not understand or become distressed or compliant with leading questions. See para 3E.4.

- Any limitations on questioning must be clearly defined by the judge, and enforced, and the reasons for them explained to the jury. Where an advocate does not comply, the judge should intervene to ensure compliance and should direct the jury where non-compliance occurs. See para 3E.4.
- Inconsistencies should not be highlighted during cross-examination itself; rather, they should be brought to the jury's attention by the advocate or the judge following a discussion *after* the cross-examination. The judge should also remind the jury of these inconsistencies during summing up and should be vigilant about inconsistencies put forward by the advocate which are trivial or which are not actually inconsistencies. See para 3E.4.
- In 'multi-handed' cases, where there is more than one defendant, the judge should not permit advocates to repeat questioning of the vulnerable witness. In the ground rules discussion, advocates should divide issues between them, with the advocate for the first defendant taking the lead in questioning and the other advocates only asking questions about issues which have not already been covered and which relate to their defendant's defence. See para 3E.5.
- Where the trial involves a sexual offence, 'body maps' should be provided to assist the witness to give his or her best evidence. If the witness needs to give evidence about a part of the body, the advocate should ask the witness to point it out on the body map and the judge should not permit the advocate to ask the witness to point to a part of the witness's own body. Photographs of the witness's own body should not be shown in court when the witness is giving evidence. See para 3E.6.

The extent to which advocates may now be limited in the conduct of cross-examination was illustrated in *R v Edwards* [2011] EWCA Crim 3028. In *Edwards*, the accused was convicted of cruelty to a person under 16, the prosecution case having been that he punched the child complainant in the stomach and caused injuries. The child was 5 years old at the time of the offence and 6½ years old at the time of the trial. At the trial, the judge made directions that the accused's counsel could, during cross-examination of the child, ask any questions to which he wanted answers but, due to the child's age and the difficulty she would have in remembering an event which took place over a year-and-a-half before, counsel should not put the defence case or challenge the child about what she had said before. The judge informed the jury of this direction and during the cross-examination intervened to stop counsel putting points and to request that counsel's questions be 'a little bit open'. On appeal, it was argued that the accused's right to a fair trial had been infringed because the judge had given the impression to the jury that the child's rights outweighed the accused's, and because defence counsel was so severely restricted in his ability to cross-examine. Restrictions included being unable to put to the child that the accused had not punched her and that she had lied about being punched in the stomach. The latter could not be put even though there was evidence from the child herself that she had fallen out of bed and that on another occasion she had been thrown to the floor by another girl, and evidence from a neighbour that the child had fallen down some steps. Dismissing the appeal, the Court of Appeal held that the jury would not have been given the impression that the child's rights superseded the accused, so that the trial was one-sided. The jury were given appropriate directions in which the judge explained his decision on the approach to be taken to cross-examination and told the jury to 'make proper fair allowances for the difficulties faced by the defence'.

See also *R v Lubemba* [2014] EWCA 2064 in which the Court of Appeal rejected complaints that the trial judge had excessively restricted the scope and length of a child witness's cross-examination. On appeal the court saw nothing inappropriate in how the trial judge had imposed certain restrictions on counsel's questioning, limited cross-examination of the complainant to 45 minutes, or interrupted when he felt that counsel's questions were inappropriate, or in his directions to counsel not to put her case on a number of occasions. The Court of Appeal held that the judge is responsible for controlling questioning and ensuring that vulnerable witnesses and defendants are able to give their best evidence. As such the judge has a duty to intervene where an advocate's questioning is inappropriate. It was held that, save in very exceptional cases, a 'ground rules' hearing should take place in every case involving a vulnerable witness and that the hearing should cover, *inter alia*, the length of questioning, the frequency of breaks, and the nature of questions that may be asked.

In *SG* [2017] EWCA Crim 617, the Court of Appeal set out principles to be applied when a complainant becomes distressed. In particular, it was noted in that case that a witness exhibiting signs of distress is not necessarily a vulnerable witness.

Further guidance for advocates on the approach to cross-examination of vulnerable witnesses may be found in the Advocacy Training Council Report, *Raising the Bar: The handling of vulnerable witnesses, victims and defendants in court.*

7.3.3 The Conduct Rules for the Bar

There are also a number of rules to be observed that are set out in the Code of Conduct in Part 2 of the Bar Standards Board Handbook, 3rd Edition, including in particular, the following paragraphs of Section C, 'The Conduct Rules':

C3

You owe a duty to the court to act with independence in the interests of justice. This duty overrides any inconsistent obligations which you may have (other than obligations under the criminal law). It includes the following specific obligations which apply whether you are acting as an advocate or are otherwise involved in the conduct of litigation in whatever role (with the exception of Rule C3.1 below, which applies when acting as an advocate):

1. You must not knowingly or recklessly mislead or attempt to mislead the court;
2. You must not abuse your role as an advocate;
3. You must take reasonable steps to avoid wasting the *court's* time;
4. You must take reasonable steps to ensure that the court has before it all relevant decisions and legislative provisions;
5. You must ensure that your ability to act independently is not compromised.

C7

Where you are acting as an advocate, your duty not to abuse your role includes the following obligations:

1. You must not make statements or ask questions merely to insult, humiliate, or annoy a witness or any other person;
2. You must not make a serious allegation against a witness whom you have had an opportunity to cross-examine unless you have given that witness a chance to answer the allegation in cross-examination;
3. You must not make a serious allegation against any person, or suggest that a person is guilty of a crime with which your client is charged unless:
   (a) You have reasonable grounds for the allegation; and

(b) The allegation is relevant to your *client's* case or the credibility of a witness; and

(c) Where the allegation relates to a third party, you avoid naming them in open court unless this is reasonably necessary.

4. You must not put forward to the court a personal opinion of the facts or the law unless you are invited or required to do so by the court or by law.

While the Conduct Rules are not binding on the court, they do have persuasive force (*R v McFadden* (1975) 62 Cr App R 187, a case concerning the Bar Council Rules that the Code of Conduct replaced).

7.4 Consequences of failing to cross-examine

In *R v Wood Green Crown Court, ex p Taylor* [1995] Crim LR 879, it was held that a party who fails to cross-examine a witness on a fact is deemed to have tacitly accepted what the witness says on that fact and therefore cannot invite the tribunal of fact to disbelieve him or her on that matter. Therefore, counsel is under a duty to put their case; this is a fundamental requirement of cross-examination.

However, if it is proposed to invite the jury to disbelieve a witness on a particular matter, it does not follow that it is always necessary to put to the witness explicitly that he or she is lying, provided that the overall tenor of the cross-examination is designed to show that his or her account is incapable of belief (*R v Lovelock* [1997] Crim LR 821, CA). In *O'Connell v Adams* [1973] CMMLR 3B it was held that the rule in *ex p Taylor* does not apply to proceedings before lay justices, although as that case concerned a police officer conducting a prosecution, not a professional advocate, it is submitted that it ought not to be regarded as authority displacing counsel's duty to put his case in the magistrates' court. If counsel omits to cross-examine on a particular point by reason of inadvertence, the judge has a discretion to allow the witness to be recalled (*R v Wilson* [1977] Crim LR 553, CA).

Where a witness is young or otherwise vulnerable, the court may impose restrictions on an advocate's cross-examination including a restriction on 'putting his case'. See **7.3.2.1**.

7.5 Cross-examination and inadmissible evidence

The rules governing the admissibility of evidence apply equally to cross-examination and examination-in-chief. Therefore, questions seeking to elicit evidence that would not be admissible in examination-in-chief cannot be put to a witness in cross-examination. For example, it has been held to be improper for a cross-examining party to attempt to elicit hearsay evidence (*R v Thomson* [1912] 3 KB 19).

Many of the cases in this area concern the use to which admissions and confessions may be put. In *R v Treacy* [1944] 2 All ER 229, it was held that the prosecution should not have been permitted to cross-examine the accused so as to reveal that he had made a confession that had been ruled inadmissible as part of the prosecution case. This rule also obtains in favour of any co-accused of the maker of a confession (*R v Rice* [1963] 1 QB 857). However, where an accused's inadmissible confession is relevant to the defence of the co-accused, and the accused gives evidence inconsistent with it, the co-accused can cross-examine him or her on it, provided that the judge makes clear to the jury that it is not evidence of the accused's guilt (*R v Rowson* [1986] QB 174, CA; *Lui Mei Lin v R* [1989] 1 All ER 359, PC).

7.6 Cross-examination on documents

Where the content of a document is inadmissible, that content does not become admissible by being put to a witness in cross-examination (*Treacy* [1944] 2 All ER 229). Counsel may, however, show a document to a witness during cross-examination, ask the witness to read it silently to him or herself, and then ask the witness if the contents are true. If the witness admits that they are and he or she would have been permitted to give oral evidence of the matters stated, then they become part of the witness's evidence and can be revealed (*R v Gillespie* (1967) 51 Cr App R 172; *R v Cooper* (1985) 82 Cr App R 74). For cross-examination of a witness on a previous inconsistent statement see **7.7**.

Where a document is used by a witness to refresh their memory, this document may be examined by the cross-examining party without the document being put into evidence (*Gregory v Turner* (1833) 6 C&P 280).

7.7 Previous inconsistent statements

A previous inconsistent statement is any statement made by the witness prior to giving evidence that is inconsistent with their testimony. Cross-examination on inconsistencies in a witness's previous statements can be a persuasive means of discrediting that witness by implying their unreliability or untruthfulness.

7.7.1 Criminal Procedure Act 1865, ss 4 and 5

Where a previous inconsistent statement is put to the witness and he or she admits to having made it, then it becomes part of the witness's evidence and no further proof of the statement is required (*R v P (GR)* [1998] Crim LR 663). Where the witness does not admit making the previous statement, then it may be proved. Proof of previous inconsistent statements is governed, in both criminal and civil proceedings, by the Criminal Procedure Act 1865, ss 4 and 5. Section 4 provides:

If a witness, upon cross-examination as to a former statement made by him relative to the subject matter of the indictment or proceeding, and inconsistent with his present testimony, does not distinctly admit that he has made such statement, proof may be given that he did in fact make it; but before such proof can be given the circumstances of the supposed statement, sufficient to designate the particular occasion, must be mentioned to the witness, and he must be asked whether or not he has made such statement.

In *R v Derby Magistrates' Court, ex p B* [1996] AC 487, HL, Lord Taylor of Gosforth CJ confirmed that s 4 of the 1865 Act applies to both oral and written statements and s 5 of the Act is confined to written statements.

The phrase '*relative to the subject matter of the indictment or proceeding*', which is used in ss 4 and 5 of the 1865 Act, means relevant to the facts in issue as opposed to some collateral matter such as, for example, matters going solely to the credit of the witness (*R v Funderburk* [1990] 1 WLR 587). Thus, where the previous inconsistent statement is relevant only to the credibility of the witness, the 1865 Act does not apply. However, it is not always easy to determine whether an issue is relevant to a fact in issue or merely credibility. This is particularly true where the disputed issue is a sexual one between two persons in private as, in those circumstances, the difference between questions going to credit and questions going to the issue is reduced almost to vanishing point. Whether a matter is 'relative to the subject matter of the indictment or proceeding' is a matter of judicial discretion (*Bashir* [1969] 3 All ER 692).

Section 5 of the Criminal Procure Act 1865 provides:

A witness may be cross-examined as to previous statements made by him in writing, or reduced into writing, relative to the subject matter of the indictment or proceeding, without such writing being shown to him; but if it is intended to contradict such witness by the writing, his attention must, before such contradictory proof can be given, be called to those parts of the writing which are to be used for the purpose of so contradicting him: Provided always, that it shall be competent for the judge, at any time during the trial, to require the production of the writing for his inspection, and he may thereupon make such use of it for the purposes of the trial as he may think fit.

Under s 5 of the 1865 Act, counsel can cross-examine a witness on a document without showing it to the witness. However, even if counsel does not intend to contradict the witness with the document, counsel must have the document in court because the judge may require the document to be produced (*R v Anderson* (1929) 21 Cr App R 178).

Where a document contains a previous statement that is inconsistent with the witness's oral testimony at trial, the usual practice is for counsel to first hand the document to the witness and ask the witness to read the relevant part to him or herself. This does not make the document an exhibit. Counsel will then ask the witness whether he or she still stands by the evidence given to the court. If the witness accepts that the previous inconsistent statement is true, then that becomes part of his or her evidence. If the witness stands by his or her evidence given to the court, then counsel can choose whether or not to prove the previous statement. If counsel wishes to do so he or she may prove it by reading, or asking the witness to read, the relevant part to the court. It is then open to the court to examine the document to see the extent of the inconsistency. There is no obligation on the cross-examining party to prove the previous inconsistent statement and put the document into evidence. Indeed, counsel may choose not to do so where the inconsistency is a minor one or the document, taken as a whole, is largely consistent with the witness's testimony.

Where a witness has been cross-examined on a previous inconsistent statement, then, because s 5 of the 1865 Act allows the judge to make such use of it for the purposes of the trial as he or she may think fit, it is open to the judge to allow the whole of the statement to go before the jury, but the judge has a discretion to allow the jury to see only those parts on which cross-examination was based.

A previous inconsistent statement is admissible, in both criminal proceedings (CJA 2003, s 119(1)) and civil proceedings (CEA 1995, ss 1, 6(3) and (5)), as evidence of the truth of that statement and as evidence affecting credibility. It follows that the court or jury may accept as true either the present testimony or the previous statement, or may reject both. In *R v Billingham* [2009] 2 Cr App R 20, the Court of Appeal held that the jury must be sure that a witness's evidence or prior statement is true before they may rely on it as evidence of truth supporting the prosecution case. However, where it is exculpatory of the accused, it is sufficient if they are persuaded that it may be true. Additional protection for the defendant is afforded by virtue of the judge's power under PACE 1984, s 78, to rule that the previous inconsistent statement is not admissible for the truth of the matters stated where its admission would have an adverse effect on the fairness of the proceedings (*R v Coates* (2008) 1 Cr App 3). Alternatively, the judge may exclude the evidence in its entirety. Further safeguards are to be found in a submission of no case to answer, an application under the CJA 2003, s 125 (see 13.9.3) at the close of the Crown's case on the grounds of the unreliability of the prosecution evidence, and judicial directions to the jury in the summing up (see *R v Joyce (RJ) and Joyce (JP)* [2005] EWCA Crim 1798 and *R v Bennett* [2008] EWCA Crim 248).

Where, in a Crown Court trial, a previous inconsistent statement is contained in a document and during the trial that document is admitted as an exhibit, the CJA 2003, s 122 provides that the document should not be taken to the jury room when the jury retires unless either the court considers it appropriate or all the parties in the case agree (see *R v Hulme* [2007] 1 Cr App R 334).

7.8 Cross-examination as to credit

There are numerous different types of question that can be put in cross-examination with a view to attacking the credit of the witness called for the other side. For example, one may ask questions to show that the witness's testimony has errors or omissions, inconsistencies, exaggerations, or improbabilities. One may ask questions about the witness's means of knowledge, their opportunity for observing what they purport to have observed, their reasons for remembering or believing something, their experience, and their powers of memory and perception. Subject to the strict limitations on cross-examination in criminal proceedings imposed by the CJA 2003, in relation to bad character, and the YJCEA 1999, s 41, in respect of questioning a complainant to sexual offences as to their previous sexual history (which are considered in detail in **Chapters 9** and **10** and **7.9** respectively), one can also ask questions in cross-examination on previous convictions, bias, corruption, and discreditable conduct.

The limits to cross-examination in civil cases on the character of one's opponent's witnesses are best summarised by Sankey LJ in *Hobbs v Tinling & Co Ltd* [1929] 2 KB 1, CA at 51:

(1) Such questions are proper if they are of such a nature that the truth of the imputation conveyed by them would seriously affect the opinion of the court as to the credibility of the witness on the matter to which he testifies.
(2) Such questions are improper if the imputation which they convey relates to matters so remote in time, or of such a character that the truth of the imputation would not affect, or would affect to a slight degree, the opinion of the court as to the credibility of the witness on the matter to which he testifies.
(3) Such questions are improper if there is a great disproportion between the importance of the imputation made against the witness's character and the importance of his evidence.

Further guidance was given by the Court of Appeal in *R v Sweet-Escott* (1971) 55 Cr App R 316, CA. The question before the court was how far back is it permissible to delve into a witness's past when cross-examining as to credit? The answer given, *per* Lawton LJ, was:

> Since the purpose of cross-examination as to credit is to show that the witness ought not to be believed on oath, the matters about which he is questioned must relate to his likely standing after cross-examination with the tribunal which is trying him or listening to his evidence.

The guidance in *Hobbs v Tinling & Co Ltd* and *R v Sweet-Escott* only applies to criminal proceedings in so far as the cross-examination relates to conduct outside the statutory definition of bad character as defined by the CJA 2003, s 98, for which see **Chapters 9** and **10**.

7.9 Complainants in sexual cases

7.9.1 General restriction

Section 41 of the YJCEA 1999 places restrictions on the extent to which complainants to sexual offences may be cross-examined about their sexual history. The provisions recognise that questioning a victim of sexual offences as to their previous sexual history is unfair to them and may deter victims from making a complaint. The intention of the restriction on questioning a complainant as to their previous sexual history was to counter the suggestions that 'unchaste women were more likely to consent to intercourse and are in any event less worthy of belief'. See *Seaboyer* [1991] 2 SCR 577 at 604 *per* McLachlin J. Section 41 provides:

> (1) *If at a trial a person is charged with a sexual offence, then, except with the leave of the court—*
>
> (a) *no evidence may be adduced, and*
>
> (b) *no question may be asked in cross-examination,*
>
> *by or on behalf of any accused at the trial, about any sexual behaviour of the complainant.*
>
> (2) *The court may give leave in relation to any evidence or question only on an application made by or on behalf of an accused, and may not give such leave unless it is satisfied—*
>
> (a) *that subsection (3) or (5) applies, and*
>
> (b) *that a refusal of leave might have the result of rendering unsafe a conclusion of the jury or (as the case may be) the court on any relevant issue in the case.*
>
> (3) *This subsection applies if the evidence or question relates to a relevant issue in the case and either—*
>
> (a) *that issue is not an issue of consent; or*
>
> (b) *it is an issue of consent and the sexual behaviour of the complainant to which the evidence or question relates is alleged to have taken place at or about the same time as the event which is the subject matter of the charge against the accused; or*
>
> (c) *it is an issue of consent and the sexual behaviour of the complainant to which the evidence or question relates is alleged to have been, in any respect, so similar—*
>
> (i) *to any sexual behaviour of the complainant which (according to evidence adduced or to be adduced by or on behalf of the accused) took place as part of the event which is the subject matter of the charge against the accused, or*
>
> (ii) *to any other sexual behaviour of the complainant which (according to such evidence) took place at or about the same time as that event,*
>
> *that the similarity cannot reasonably be explained as a coincidence.*
>
> (4) *For the purposes of subsection (3) no evidence or question shall be regarded as relating to a relevant issue in the case if it appears to the court to be reasonable to assume that the purpose (or main purpose) for which it would be adduced or asked is to establish or elicit material for impugning the credibility of the complainant as a witness.*
>
> (5) *This subsection applies if the evidence or question—*
>
> (a) *relates to any evidence adduced by the prosecution about any sexual behaviour of the complainant; and*
>
> (b) *in the opinion of the court, would go no further than is necessary to enable the evidence adduced by the prosecution to be rebutted or explained by or on behalf of the accused.*
>
> (6) *For the purposes of subsections (3) and (5) the evidence or question must relate to a specific instance (or specific instances) of alleged sexual behaviour on the part of the complainant (and accordingly nothing in those subsections is capable of applying in relation to the evidence or question to the extent that it does not so relate).*

(7) Where this section applies in relation to a trial by virtue of the fact that one or more of a number of persons charged in the proceedings is or are charged with a sexual offence—

(a) it shall cease to apply in relation to the trial if the prosecutor decides not to proceed with the case against that person or those persons in respect of that charge; but

(b) it shall not cease to do so in the event of that person or those persons pleading guilty to, or being convicted of, that charge.

(8) Nothing in this section authorises any evidence to be adduced or any question to be asked which cannot be adduced or asked apart from this section.

'Sexual offence' is defined in the YJCEA 1999, s 62 as any offence under the Sexual Offences Act 2003, Part 1, or any relevant superseded offence. 'Relevant superseded offence' includes the following: rape or burglary with intent to rape; an offence of human trafficking committed with a view to sexual exploitation under the Modern Slavery Act 2015, s 2; an offence under the Sexual Offences Act 1956, ss 2–12 and 14–17; an offence under the Mental Health Act 1959, s 128; an offence under the Indecency with Children Act 1960, s 1; and an offence under the Criminal Law Act 1977, s 54 (incitement of child under 16 to commit incest).

7.9.2 Extent of the restriction

Section 42 of the YJCEA 1999 provides:

...

(c) 'sexual behaviour' means any sexual behaviour or other sexual experience, whether or not involving any accused or other person, but excluding (except in section 41(3)(c)(i) and (5)(a)) anything alleged to have taken place as part of the event which is the subject matter of the charge against the accused;

...

The restriction imposed by s 41 therefore only relates to questions or evidence about other sexual behaviour; it does not prohibit questions or evidence about the sexual behaviour that is part of the incident or incidents for which the accused is being tried. In *R v Mukadi* [2004] Crim LR 373, the Court of Appeal stated that it was not possible to define sexual behaviour. Rather, what was meant by the term was a matter of 'impression and common sense'. The behaviour in question in that case was the act of getting into a car driven by an unknown man who had pulled up alongside the complainant and the exchange of telephone numbers in the car. In allowing the defendant's appeal, the Court of Appeal concluded that in the circumstances such conduct could be sexual behaviour within the meaning of the Act.

If s 41 is restricted to questions or evidence about sexual behaviour, what approach should the court take when the proposed cross-examination or evidence relates to a false allegation that the complainant has made about alleged sexual assaults in the past? In *R v T* [2002] 1 WLR 632, the Court of Appeal held that normally questions or evidence concerning false statements about sexual assaults made in the past by a complainant are not ones 'about' any sexual behaviour of the complainant. They relate not to his or her sexual behaviour but to his or her statements in the past or to his or her failure to complain. However, the defence, wishing to put questions about alleged previous false complaints, must seek a ruling from the judge that s 41 does not exclude them. It would be professionally improper for those representing the defendant to put such questions in order to elicit evidence about the complainant's past sexual behaviour under the guise of previous false complaints. But, in any case, the defence must have a proper evidential basis for asserting that any such previous statement was (a) made and (b) untrue. If those requirements are not met, then the questions would not be about lies but would be 'about [the] sexual behaviour of the complainant' within the meaning of s 41(1). Whether there is a proper evidential basis is fact sensitive; determination of this issue is a matter of judgement rather than discretion (*R v All-Hilly* [2014] 2 Cr App R 530 (33)).

In *R v M* [2009] EWCA Crim 618, the question of what constitutes a proper evidential basis fell to be considered. It was held that a strong factual foundation for concluding that the previous complaint was false is not required but there must be some material from which it could properly be concluded that the complaint was false. The trial judge must ask himself on the material before him, depending on the answers given by the complainant, whether the jury could have been satisfied that the previous complaint was false. Each case must turn on its own facts. The facts of *R v M* provide a useful illustration. The accused alleged that the complainant had lied about a previous allegation of rape. A sufficient evidential basis to warrant cross-examination by the accused was established through: (1) an interval of four months between the date of that alleged rape and the date when the complainant reported it to the police; (2) aspects of the complaint that were puzzling and that caused the investigating police to be sceptical; (3) the complainant's failure to follow through with her complaint and to allow the police to pursue an investigation; (4) the complainant's willingness to give the police only sufficient information to enable her to achieve her goal of being rehoused.

However, in *R v D* [2009] EWCA Crim 2137, Keene LJ observed that authorities such as *R v M* should not be regarded as 'authorising the use of a trial as a vehicle for investigating the truth or falsity of an earlier allegation merely because there is some material which could be used to try and persuade a jury that it was in fact false'. In *D*, it was held that the trial judge was correct to disallow, under s 41, cross-examination about the complainant's previous allegation of rape against a third party that had not resulted in prosecution. The mere fact that the allegation had not been prosecuted did not mean that it was false and did not provide the defence with an evidential basis for asserting that it was false. See also *R v All-Hilly* [2014] 2 Cr App R 530 (33).

Where it is alleged that the complainant has made a false denial about previous sexual behaviour, then any questions or evidence on the issue will be prohibited by s 41 as one could only prove the denial to be false by adducing evidence of the previous sexual behaviour (*R v Winter* [2008] Crim LR 971).

A different example of questioning which was not questioning about 'sexual behaviour' is provided by *R v P (RP)* [2013] EWCA Crim 2331, where the accused sought to question the complainant about his having provided her with financial and emotional support following her abortion. Although in other cases, questioning a complainant about an abortion might have been aimed at her sexual behaviour, in this case, evidence that the accused had supported the complainant after her abortion was intended to undermine her evidence that she regarded him with 'distaste'. The questions were not about her 'sexual behaviour' and so not caught by the restriction in s 41.

7.9.3 Restriction on cross-examination

Under s 41, questions or evidence about the complainant's sexual behaviour will only be permitted if the court grants leave (s 41(1)). Leave can only be granted if:

- one of the four qualifying circumstances apply (s 41(2)(a)); *and*
- refusal to grant leave might render a conviction unsafe (s 41(2)(b)).

7.9.3.1 Qualifying circumstances

The four qualifying circumstances, one of which is required before questions or evidence about other sexual behaviour will be permitted, are as follows:

(a) The cross-examination or evidence relates to an issue other than consent (s 41(3)(a)).
   (i) Belief in consent is an issue 'other than consent' and therefore if the issue is reasonable *belief* in consent cross-examination may be permitted (subject to the other elements of the test) under this section (s 41(1)(b)).
   (ii) This exception would also include cases in which the accused puts forward an alternative explanation for the physical conditions on which the Crown relies to establish that intercourse took place, for example, the defence that no sexual act took place between the accused and the complainant and the accused seeks to show that the complainant had had sexual intercourse with another person at the material time.
   (iii) This exception would likewise include an allegation that the complainant was biased against the accused or had a motive to fabricate the evidence.

(b) The cross-examination or evidence relates to the issue of consent and the previous sexual behaviour took place 'at or about the same time' as the offence (s 41(3)(b)), but this behaviour must not include anything alleged to have taken place as part of the event which is the subject matter of the alleged offence (s 42(1)(c)).
   (i) The explanatory note to the Act expected that this would be interpreted as no more than 24 hours. In *A (No 2)* [2002] 1 AC 45 at [9], [40], [82], and [132], it was observed that at or about the same time meant a matter of hours rather than days.
   (ii) It would appear that this category of permissible questioning is aimed at defences using evidence of the complainant's promiscuity to prove that at the time of the alleged offence he or she is likely to have consented to the sexual act in question.

(c) The cross-examination or evidence relates to the issue of consent and the previous sexual behaviour in question is very similar either to the alleged offence or other sexual behaviour at about the same time as the alleged offence (s 41(3)(c)).
   (i) The exact phrase used by the Act is '*so similar ... that the similarity cannot reasonably be explained as a coincidence*'.
   (ii) This is potentially quite complicated but appears to be aimed at evidence of previous consensual sexual behaviour of a distinctive nature that bears such a strong similarity to what appears to have taken place during the offence that this similarity may raise a reasonable doubt as to the complainant's lack of consent.
   (iii) For example, evidence that the complainant regularly had consensual sexual intercourse in a particularly distinctive way with the accused on previous occasions might be admissible under this circumstance if there was evidence that the sexual act forming the charge had very similar characteristics.
   (iv) It is submitted that if the sexual behaviour on the previous and current occasions were, due to their nature, incapable of being consensual acts, then such previous behaviour would not be admissible under s 41.
   (v) Note that s 41(3)(c) relates to a similarity between a previous incident and the alleged offence where the nature of the two incidents could prove the existence of consent (s 41(3)(c)(i)) and also to a similarity between the alleged offence and sexual behaviour which took place 'at or about the same time' (see s

41(3)(c)(ii): evidence of previous sexual behaviour that is similar to behaviour 'at or about the same time' as the alleged offence may also be admitted). In *R v T* [2004] 2 Cr App R 551, where the alleged rape took place within a particular climbing frame at a public park, the conviction was set aside because the trial judge had not allowed cross-examination concerning a similar (consensual) sexual encounter within the same climbing frame three weeks earlier. The trial judge had considered the defendant's application to cross-examine the complainant by reference to s 41(3)(c)(ii) and had neglected to properly consider s 41(3)(c)(i). As a result, he had misled himself into believing that a temporal constraint applied to the defendant's application when it did not. However, the similarity test was not met in *G* [2016] EWCA Crim 1633 where the Court of Appeal relied on the absence of a 'sufficient chronological nexus' in circumstances where the alleged consensual intercourse had taken place about one year before the offence and also several weeks afterwards.

(vi) In *R v Richardson* [2003] EWCA Crim 2754, the Court of Appeal concluded that evidence of a previous relationship and of a relationship after an alleged rape would not be permitted under s 41(3)(c) as the sexual behaviour in question (the relationship in general) would not bear sufficient similarity to the alleged offence. See also *C* [2016] EWCA Crim 1631 where alleged consensual sexual activity with the accused occurred nine months after the offence. The court was of the view that admitting the evidence would risk reinforcing the stereotypical and potentially false view that, in a complex relationship, no victim of a sexual offence would subsequently engage in consensual sexual activity with the accused.

(d) The cross-examination or evidence relates to evidence adduced by the prosecution about the complainant's previous sexual behaviour and would go no further than is necessary to rebut or explain that evidence (s 41(5)).

(i) This exception is not restricted to situations in which the defence is consent.

(ii) Section 41(5) would apply, for example, where the complainant attributes her pregnancy to the accused in a case in which the accused denies sexual activity with the complainant. The accused would be permitted under this section to adduce evidence in rebuttal that the complainant had previously attributed her pregnancy to another (*F* [2008] EWCA Crim 2859).

(iii) In *R v Hamadi* [2008] Crim LR 635, the Court of Appeal stated that where the complainant gives evidence in cross-examination which was not deliberately elicited by defence counsel and is potentially damaging to the defence case, then it could be treated as *'evidence adduced by the prosecution'* for the purposes of s 41(5).

7.9.3.2 Questioning or evidence going only to credibility

No cross-examination or evidence will be permitted if its sole purpose is to undermine the credibility of the complainant (s 41(4)).

In *R v M* [2004] 2 Cr App R 22, the Court of Appeal stated that where cross-examination would have the effect of undermining the complainant's credibility *and* of supporting the defendant's denial of the complainant's allegations, then such evidence would not be excluded under s 41(4).

Section 41(4) applies only to questions or evidence allowed under s 41(3) but not under s 41(5). Thus, in *R v F* [2008] EWCA Crim 2859, the Court of Appeal held that the accused ought to have been permitted to ask questions about a reference to a 'condom accident' in the complainant's medical notes in order to undermine the credibility of the complainant's assertion that when she was raped and made pregnant by the defendant, she was not otherwise sexually active.

7.9.3.3 Questioning or evidence must relate to specific incidents

Even if the alleged sexual behaviour falls within one or more of the four categories of exception set out in s 41(3)–(5), such behaviour cannot be admitted unless it relates to specific incidents (s 41(6)). Therefore, in *R v White* [2004] EWCA Crim 946, evidence of previous convictions of the complainant for prostitution was held to have rightly been excluded as such convictions would be too general.

7.9.3.4 Risk of unsafe conviction

The effect of s 41 is that the defence will have to persuade the court to grant leave to question about or adduce evidence of the sexual behaviour of the complainant. The court cannot grant leave unless persuaded, first, that the evidence or questioning comes within one or more of the qualifying circumstances set out earlier and, second, that the accused would be left at risk of an unsafe conviction unless leave is granted.

7.9.3.5 Section 41 and Article 6 of the ECHR

In *R v A* [2001] 3 All ER 1, HL, the House of Lords considered s 41 in light of the right to a fair trial under Article 6 of the ECHR. It recognised that the right to a fair trial included the ability to put forward a full defence and that the restrictions imposed by s 41 of the 1999 Act created a risk that this would not be possible. It therefore invoked s 3 of the Human Rights Act 1998 to interpret s 41 to require that judges should consider the extent to which an accused would be deprived of a material defence and therefore a fair trial as a result of a refusal to grant leave. It was held *per* Lord Steyn at [45] that:

> Section 3 of the 1998 Act requires the court to subordinate the niceties of the language of s 41(3)(c) of the 1999 Act, and in particular the touchstone of coincidence, to broader considerations of relevance judged by logical and common sense criteria of time and circumstances. After all, it is realistic to proceed on the basis that the legislature would not, if alerted to the problem, have wished to deny the right to an accused to put forward a full and complete defence by advancing truly probative material. It is therefore possible under s 3 of the 1998 Act to read s 41 of the 1999 Act, and in particular s 41(3)(c), as subject to the implied provision that evidence or questioning which is required to ensure a fair trial under Art 6 of the convention should not be treated as inadmissible. The result of such a reading would be that sometimes logically relevant sexual experiences between a complainant and an accused may be admitted under s 41(3)(c). On the other hand, there will be cases where previous sexual experience between a complainant and an accused will be irrelevant, eg an isolated episode distant in time and circumstances. Where the line is to be drawn must be left to the judgment of trial judges.

Thus, where there is evidence of a sexual relationship between the complainant and the defendant that does not satisfy the provisions of s 41(3) or (5), the judge may still admit the evidence where to do so is necessary to ensure that the defendant receives a fair trial within the meaning of Article 6 of the ECHR.

In *R v Richardson* (discussed earlier), the Court of Appeal concluded that the strict interpretation of s 41(3)(c) that excluded cross-examination about ongoing sexual relationships between the complainant and the defendant was unfair within the meaning of *R v A* and therefore quashed a conviction where the trial judge, applying s 41(3)(c), had not permitted such cross-examination.

In *R v Mukadi* (discussed earlier), the issue was whether the complainant had consented to sexual intercourse. The complainant's evidence was that she had gone to the defendant's flat with him, not intending any sexual acts to take place, but that she had allowed him to carry out various sexual acts short of intercourse in the hope that he would then not have full intercourse with her, but that he had subsequently carried out sexual intercourse without her consent. The case for the defendant was that the complainant had willingly consented to all the sexual acts that took place. The Court of Appeal held the behaviour of getting into a car with an unknown person and exchanging telephone numbers a matter of hours before the events alleged would be sufficiently relevant and probative to prove that she may have intended, in going to the defendant's flat, to carry out sexual acts. It was noted that if her evidence had been that she had gone to the defendant's flat willing to engage in sexual activity short of full sexual intercourse, the previous event would not have been particularly probative and therefore probably not admissible. However, as she had stated in evidence that she had not intended to engage in any sexual acts, the previous event was probative not only in proving that she may have been willing to consent but also that her denial of consent was probably untrue. As such, the previous event should have been admitted. *R v Mukadi* therefore illustrates that any analysis of the probative value and therefore of the fairness of refusing to allow questioning will depend on detailed analysis of the issues raised by the evidence of the parties and cannot be determined by simple categorisation of the evidence. See also *Andrade* [2015] EWCA Crim 1722.

7.9.4 Rules of procedure

Section 43(3) of the YJCEA 1999 allows the creation of rules of court concerning the admission of the evidence of the complainant's sexual behaviour. The complete rules are set out in Crim PR, r 22. The main provisions are as follows:

Application for permission to introduce evidence or cross-examine

22.2 The defendant must apply for permission to do so—

- *(a) in writing; and*
- *(b) not more than 28 days after the prosecutor has complied or purported to comply with section 3 of the Criminal Procedure and Investigations Act 1996 (disclosure by prosecutor).*

Content of application

22.3 The application must—

- *(a) identify the issue to which the defendant says the complainant's sexual behaviour is relevant;*
- *(b) give particulars of—*
  - *(i) any evidence that the defendant wants to introduce, and*
  - *(ii) any questions that the defendant wants to ask;*
- *(c) identify the exception to the prohibition in section 41 of the Youth Justice and Criminal Evidence Act 1999 on which the defendant relies; and*
- *(d) give the name and date of birth of any witness whose evidence about the complainant's sexual behaviour the defendant wants to introduce.*

Reply to application

22.5 A party who wants to make representations about an application under rule 22.2 must—

- *(a) do so in writing not more than 14 days after receiving it; and*
- *(b) serve those representations on the court officer and all other parties.*

An application to lift the restriction under s 41 must be heard in private in the absence of the complainant (s 43(1)). Once the application is determined, the court must state its reasons for the decision in open court (but in the absence of the jury) and, if leave is given, the extent to which the evidence may be adduced or questions asked (s 43(2)).

7.10 The rule of finality

7.10.1 General rule

A witness's answer to a question concerning a collateral issue is final in that the cross-examining party cannot attempt to call any further evidence to prove the contrary (*Harris v Tippett* (1811) 2 Camp 637). However, the tribunal of fact is under no obligation to accept the answer given by the witness as true. A collateral issue is one that goes merely to credibility but is not otherwise directly relevant to the facts in issue in the case. The classic, if somewhat circular, test for identifying a collateral issue was given in *Attorney-General v Hitchcock* (1847) 1 Exch 91 by Pollock CB:

> The test whether a matter is collateral or not is this: if the answer of a witness is a matter which you would be allowed on your own part to prove in evidence—if it have such a connection with the issues, that you would be allowed to give it in evidence—then it is a matter on which you may contradict him.

For example, in *R v Burke* (1858) 8 Cox CC 44, in order to undermine the credibility of an Irish witness who was giving evidence through an interpreter, it was suggested in cross-examination that the witness had spoken to two people in English in the court building prior to giving evidence. It was held that the witness's ability to speak English was a collateral issue and, as the witness denied it, evidence to the contrary could not be called. In *R v Marsh* (1985) 83 Cr App R 165, by contrast, a witness's denial that he had threatened the accused was not treated as a collateral issue, part of the defence being that the accused believed that the witness had intended to attack him.

The principal rationale for the rule is that it prevents a proliferation of the issues at trial. However, the rule also recognises that it would be unfair to ambush a witness with questioning on issues that he had not anticipated.

Determining whether a particular issue is relevant to a fact in issue or is a collateral issue can be very difficult and may require the court to draw some very fine distinctions. In *R v Funderburk* [1990] 1 WLR 587 (citing ***Cross on Evidence***, 7th edn, 1990), the Court of Appeal urged a flexible, rather than an overly pedantic, approach to such questions, even recognising that the test may be instinctive and depend upon the prosecutor's and the court's sense of fair play. Where the disputed issue is a sexual one between two persons in private, the difference between questions going to credit and questions going to the issue is reduced almost to vanishing point. This is because sexual intercourse, whether or not consensual, usually takes place in private and leaves few visible traces of having occurred, so that the evidence is often limited to that of the parties and much is likely to turn on the balance of credibility between them.

Whether an issue is collateral or not is a decision to be made by the judge, and it is a decision with which the Court of Appeal will only interfere if it is wrong in principle or clearly wrong on the facts of the case (*R v Somers* [1999] Crim LR 744).

7.10.2 Exceptions

The general rule is subject to three exceptions:

- previous convictions;
- bias; and
- disability affecting reliability.

Where a question concerning any one of the above issues is put to the witness and answered in the negative, the cross-examining party will be permitted to call evidence in rebuttal.

7.10.2.1 Previous convictions

Section 6 of the Criminal Procedure Act 1865, which applies to both civil and criminal proceedings, provides:

> *If, upon a witness being lawfully questioned as to whether he has been convicted of any offence, he either denies or does not admit the fact, or refuses to answer, it shall be lawful for the cross-examining party to prove such a conviction.*

In criminal proceedings, the admissibility of evidence of a witness's previous convictions is governed by the CJA 2003. Thus, the questioning of a witness about a previous conviction is only 'lawful' where the provisions of the CJA 2003 regarding bad character have been satisfied. Section 100 governs the admissibility of the bad character of a witness other than the defendant and s 101 the bad character of the defendant. These provisions will be considered in detail in **Chapters 9** and **10**. As will be seen, once the requirements of ss 100 and 101 are satisfied, evidence of bad character is admissible even where it is collateral because it is only relevant to the witness's credit. For this reason, it is thought that in criminal proceedings this exception to the rule of finality is now of less significance than it has been in the past. In civil proceedings, cross-examination on 'spent convictions' is not permitted unless justice cannot be done in the case except by admitting or requiring such evidence (Rehabilitation of Offenders Act 1974, ss 4(1) and 7(3)). The 1974 Act does not prohibit cross-examination on spent convictions in criminal proceedings; however, the Criminal Practice Directions [2015] EWCA Crim 1567, Part 21A, recommends that where bad character evidence is sought to be admitted under the bad character provisions of the CJA 2003, both the court and advocates should have regard for the general principles of the Rehabilitation of Offenders Act 1974.

7.10.2.2 Bias

Where a witness denies a suggestion of bias or partiality in cross-examination, then evidence to contradict the witness may be called in rebuttal in order to show that the witness is prejudiced. For example, in *R v Shaw* (1888) 16 Cox CC 503, the accused was permitted to call evidence to contradict a prosecution witness who denied having threatened to take revenge upon the accused. In *R v Mendy* (1976) 64 Cr App 4, the accused's husband gave evidence on her behalf. The common practice in criminal trials is that witnesses are not allowed into the courtroom until they give their evidence. In cross-examination he denied having spoken to a man who had been seen in the public gallery taking notes of the evidence during the prosecution case. The prosecution was permitted to call evidence in rebuttal. Following *Thomas v David* (1836) 7 Car & P 350, where a witness denies being the kept mistress of the claimant, the defendant will be permitted to call evidence to prove the nature of their relationship.

It is submitted that in criminal proceedings, following the enactment of the CJA 2003, the exception of bias is only concerned with evidence of bias that falls short of a criminal offence or reprehensible behaviour. Section 99 of the 2003 Act abolished the common law rules governing the admissibility of evidence of bad character in criminal proceedings. As the exception of bias is a common law rule, to the extent that it admitted evidence of bad character it has now been abolished. However, the exception will continue to apply to evidence of bias that does not amount to bad character. The 2003 Act defines bad character as evidence relating to the commission of an offence or other reprehensible behaviour. Thus, the rule now only operates in relation to evidence of bias falling short of this definition.

7.10.2.3 Evidence of disability affecting reliability

Medical evidence is admissible to show that a witness suffers from a physical or mental disability that affects the reliability of his or her evidence (*Toohey v Metropolitan Police Commissioner* [1965] AC 595, HL). Such evidence is not restricted to a general opinion of the unreliability of the witness, but may include evidence of the foundations of, and reasons for, the diagnosis and the extent to which the credibility of the witness is affected.

For example, in *R v Eades* [1972] Crim LR 99, the prosecution was properly allowed to call a consultant psychiatrist to contradict the accused's account of how he had recovered his memory after an accident and prove that it was not consistent with current medical knowledge.

7.11 Re-examination

After cross-examination a witness may be re-examined by the party calling him or her. This is so even in the case of a hostile witness. The aim of re-examination is, broadly, to repair damage done to the witness's evidence during cross-examination. This is done by clarifying matters that arose in cross-examination. Re-examination is subject to the same rules as evidence-in-chief so the witness may not be asked leading questions. Except with leave of the judge, re-examination must be restricted to the matters that arose in cross-examination (*Prince v Samo* (1838) 7 Ad & El 627).

In *R v Beattie* (1989) 89 Cr App R 302, CA, it was held that a party is not entitled, merely by reason of cross-examination on a previous inconsistent statement, to re-examine the witness on a previous statement consistent with the witness's testimony. However, in *R v Ali* [2004] 1 Cr App R 501, the Court of Appeal recognised that the court does have a residual discretion to allow re-examination on a previous consistent statement, to prevent the jury from being positively misled as to the existence of some fact or the terms of an earlier statement.

8

Character evidence: civil proceedings

8.1 Introduction

Character evidence may be defined as evidence of a person's reputation or their disposition to behave in a particular way. It includes evidence of good as well as bad character.

8.2 The relevance of character evidence

Character evidence may be relevant in the following ways.

(a) *Character as a fact issue* The character of a party might itself be a fact in issue in the proceedings. For example, in a defamation claim in which the defence is justification, the defendant's character will be a fact in issue.

(b) *Character relevant to a fact in issue* The character of a person, although not a fact in issue, may be probative of one or more facts in issue. For example, where a claimant in civil proceedings alleges that he suffered food poisoning at the defendant's restaurant due to poor food hygiene, evidence from other parties who suffered food poisoning having eaten at the defendant's restaurant might be admissible to prove that the defendant prepared food unhygienically.

(c) *Character relevant to credit* The character of a party or witness may be relevant to their credibility; for example, where a witness in civil proceedings has a previous conviction for perjury, the previous conviction is relevant to whether their evidence is worthy of belief.

8.3 Character of parties

In civil proceedings different rules apply depending on whether the character evidence relates to a party in the proceedings or a person who is not a party.

8.3.1 The character of parties in proceedings

8.3.1.1 Character as a fact in issue

The character of a party to a case is admissible if it is a fact in issue in the case. Defamation proceedings provide a good example of when a party's character may, itself, be a fact in issue (see also **8.2**). Where the defendant pleads justification, the claimant's character is in issue and both parties are permitted to call evidence relevant to that issue (*Maisel v Financial Times Ltd* (1915) 84 LJKB 2145). Evidence of the claimant's character is also admissible in defamation proceedings on the issue of the quantum of damages (see, generally, *Scott v Sampson* (1882) 8 QBD 491).

8.3.1.2 Character relevant to a fact in issue

8.3.1.2.1 Good character

The good character of a party may not be adduced. The rationale for this rule was given by Martin B in *Attorney-General v Bowman* (1791) 2 Bos & P 532n, in which he explained that in criminal proceedings a defendant's good character is admissible because there is a fair and just presumption that a person of good character would not commit a crime, whereas no presumption that the defendant did not commit the civil wrong alleged would fairly arise from his good character in the majority of civil cases. The same principle applies to the evidence of the good character of the claimant (*Cornwell v Richardson* (1825) 1 Ry & M 305). Although these authorities are old, the case of *Cooper v Hatton* [2001] EWCA Civ 623 suggests that the principle remains of general applicability. In the context of road traffic collision cases, Jonathan Parker LJ held that evidence of a party's previous exemplary driving history is 'completely worthless', observing that 'every driver is a careful driver until he makes a careless mistake'.

8.3.1.2.2 Bad character

The character of the defendant, while not itself a fact in issue, may nevertheless be probative of one or more of the facts in issue in the case. For example, in *Hales v Kerr* [1908] 2 KB 601, the plaintiff in an action for negligence alleged that he had contracted an infectious disease through the negligence of the defendant, a barber, in using razors and other appliances in a dirty and unsanitary condition. In support of his case he tendered the evidence of two witnesses who had contracted a similar disease in the defendant's shop.

The character of the claimant may be admitted on the same basis. So, for example, where an application is made in family proceedings for a residence order to recover custody of a child, evidence that the applicant has previously assaulted the child and is therefore not a suitable custodian would be admissible. This type of character evidence is sometimes known as 'similar fact evidence'. However, this phrase can be misleading to the extent that it may give the impression that the previous misconduct must be factually similar in order to be admissible. While in many cases there is factual similarity between the bad character evidence and the issue to which it is relevant, such similarity is not a *requirement* for admissibility. The test for admissibility was laid down in *Mood Music Publishing Co Ltd v De Wolfe Ltd* [1976] Ch 119, CA and did not include the presence of a factual similarity: evidence of bad character was admissible simply if it was logically probative. Character evidence would be admissible if it was logically relevant in determining the matter that is in issue, provided that it is not oppressive or unfair to the other side, and also provided that the other side has fair notice of it and is able to deal with it.

In *Mood Music*, the plaintiffs were music publishers who sought damages for the infringement of their copyright on a piece of music, 'Sogno Nostalgico'. They alleged that the defendants, another music publishing company, had copied 'Sogno Nostalgico' in producing a piece of their own music called 'Girl in the Dark'. In their defence, the defendants claimed that any similarity was coincidental. In order to rebut this defence, the plaintiffs were permitted to adduce three more scores by the defendants each of which bore a remarkable similarity to music owned by the plaintiffs. The Court of Appeal held that such evidence was admissible as logically probative to disprove the defence of coincidence: it tended to show that the similarities were due to copying and were not merely coincidental. Whereas it was possible for there to be one case of coincidental similarity, it was very unlikely that there would be four such coincidences.

This decision was approved by the House of Lords in *O'Brien v Chief Constable of South Wales Police* [2005] 2 AC 534, where it was stated *per* Lord Philips of Worth Matravers:

> I would simply apply the test of relevance as the test of admissibility of similar fact evidence in a civil suit. Such evidence is admissible if it is potentially probative of an issue in the action.

Their Lordships held that admissibility of this type of character evidence is a two-stage process. First, the judge must decide if the evidence is relevant. Second, if he decides that it is, he then has a discretion (under CPR, r 32.1) to refuse to admit it. *Per* Lord Philips of Worth Matravers:

> Evidence of impropriety which reflects adversely on the character of a party may risk causing prejudice that is disproportionate to its relevance, particularly where the trial is taking place before a jury. In such a case the judge will be astute to see that the probative cogency of the evidence justifies the risk of prejudice in the interests of a fair trial. Equally, when considering whether to admit evidence, or permit cross-examination, on matters that are collateral to the central issues, the judge will have regard to the need for proportionality and expedition. He will consider whether the evidence in question is likely to be relatively uncontroversial, or whether its admission is likely to create side issues which will unbalance the trial and make it harder to see the wood from the trees.

8.3.1.3 Evidence of character relevant to credibility

8.3.1.3.1 Good character

Where a party gives evidence in the proceedings his credibility will be in issue but evidence of his good character cannot be admitted simply in order to bolster his credibility. However, where the other side has attacked his credibility, then he may be permitted to call evidence of his good character in rebuttal.

8.3.1.3.2 Bad character

As noted at **7.8**, a party may discredit an opponent's witnesses by cross-examining him on his bad character as long as the questioning is relevant. Where a party to the proceedings gives evidence, then he may be subject to such cross-examination. However, the judge has a duty to prevent questioning that is improper or oppressive and a general discretion to limit cross-examination under CPR, r 32.1(3). In *Hobbs v CT Tinling & Co Ltd* [1929] 2 KB 1, the Court of Appeal gave guidance as to the limits of cross-examination going to the credit of a witness:

> (1) Such questions are proper if they are of such a nature that the truth of the imputation conveyed by them would seriously affect the opinion of the court as to the credibility of the witness on the matter to which he testifies.
>
> (2) Such questions are improper if the imputation which they convey relates to matters so remote in time, or of such a character that the truth of the imputation would not affect, or would affect in a slight degree, the opinion of the court as to the credibility of the witness on the matter to which he testifies.
>
> (3) Such questions are improper if there is a great disproportion between the importance of the imputation made against the witness's character and the importance of his evidence.

Further guidance was given by the Court of Appeal in *R v Sweet-Escott* (1971) 55 Cr App R 316. The question before the court was: how far back is it permissible to delve into a witness's past when cross-examining as to credit? The answer given, *per* Lawton LJ, was in the form of a general approach to be applied:

> Since the purpose of cross-examination as to credit is to show that the witness ought not to be believed on oath, the matters about which he is questioned must relate to his likely standing after cross-examination with the tribunal which is trying him or listening to his evidence.

8.4 Persons other than parties to the proceedings

8.4.1 Evidence of character relevant to a fact in issue

8.4.1.1 Good character

Evidence of the good character of a person who is not a party in the proceedings is rarely, if ever, relevant to a fact in issue. In any event, were it to be relevant it would not be admissible by analogy with the rule in *Attorney-General v Bowman* (1791) 2 Bos & P 532n and *Cornwell v Richardson* (1825) 1 Ry & M 305 (see **8.3.1.2.1**).

8.4.1.2 Bad character

Evidence of the bad character of a third party may be relevant to a fact in issue in the proceedings. Where it is, the test laid down in *Mood Music Publishing Co Ltd v De Wolfe Ltd* [1976] Ch 119, CA and *O'Brien v Chief Constable of South Wales Police* [2005] 2 WLR 1061, HL will apply. An example of how the character of a third party may be relevant to a fact in issue in the proceedings arose in *Joy v Philips, Mills & Co Ltd* [1916] 1 KB 849. That case involved a claim for compensation by a deceased workman's dependent father. The deceased, who had been employed as a stable boy by the respondents, was found in their stable clutching a halter, suffering from a kick behind the ear from one of their horses. In order to rebut the claim that the accident had happened in the course of the deceased's employment, the defendant adduced evidence that the deceased had previously hit the horses with a halter and teased them.

8.4.2 Evidence of character relevant to credibility

In most cases, the only persons, other than the parties, whose credibility will be of concern to the court will be witnesses.

8.4.2.1 Good character

A party calling a witness may wish to adduce evidence of that witness's good character in order to boost the credibility of their testimony. However, in civil proceedings, a party is not permitted to call evidence of the good character of its own witness. In *R v Turner* [1975] QB 834, CA, it was stated *per* Lawton LJ:

> in general evidence can be called to impugn the credibility of a witness but not led in chief to bolster it up.

However, in practice, it is not uncommon for the party calling a witness to seek to bolster their evidence by adducing evidence of their employment, their marital status, and even, on occasion, their lack of previous convictions.

8.4.2.2 Bad character

A witness in civil proceedings is treated in the same way as a party who gives evidence (see **8.3.1.3**) and so may be subject to cross-examination on his bad character as long as the questioning is relevant. The judge has a duty to prevent questioning that is improper or oppressive and a general discretion to limit cross-examination under CPR, r 32.1(3). The principles set out in *Hobbs v CT Tinling & Co Ltd* [1929] 2 KB 1, CA and *R v Sweet-Escott* (1971) 55 Cr App R 316, CA apply.

8.4.2.3 The rule of finality

As the credibility of a witness is not a fact in issue, or of direct relevance to a fact in issue, it is a collateral issue. As a result, the rule of finality applies (see **7.10.1**) and answers given by a witness during cross-examination as to credit cannot be contradicted by the cross-examining party. However, the rule is subject to four exceptions:

- previous convictions;
- evidence of bias;
- evidence of reputation for untruthfulness; and
- evidence of disability affecting reliability.

For further details on the exceptions to the rule of finality, see **7.10.2**.

9 Character evidence: the defendant in criminal proceedings

9.1 Introduction

This chapter considers the admissibility in criminal proceedings of evidence of the defendant's character. The rules governing the admissibility of evidence of the character of persons other than the defendant will be considered in the following chapter.

9.2 The defendant's good character

9.2.1 The nature of a good character direction

In *R v Vye* [1993] 1 WLR 471, CA, it was held that evidence of good character may be relevant to either the defendant's guilt and/or their credibility. According to *Vye*, good character is relevant to guilt because a defendant with a propensity to good behaviour is less likely to have engaged in criminal conduct. It is relevant to credibility because a defendant who is shown to be honest is less likely to give false evidence. In *Vye*, therefore, it was held that a character direction should consist of two limbs:

(1) a direction as to the relevance of the defendant's good character to a defendant's credibility. This direction must be given when the defendant has testified or made pre-trial answers or statements. Conventionally, this is known as the 'first limb' of a character direction; and

(2) a direction as to the relevance of his good character to the likelihood of his having committed the offence charged. Such a direction is to be given, whether or not the defendant has testified, or made pre-trial answers or statements. This is known as the 'second limb' of a character direction.

Reflecting the *Vye* principles, the Crown Court Compendium suggests a standard direction (Part 1, 11-5, example 1):

Good character is not a defence to the charges but it is relevant to your consideration of the case in two ways. First, the defendant has given evidence. His good character is a positive feature of the defendant which you should take into account when considering whether you accept what he told you. Secondly, the fact that the defendant has not offended in the past may make it less likely that he acted as is now alleged against him.

In cases of historic sexual abuse where a defendant is of good character, a full good character direction requires an additional element, sometimes referred to as a 'third limb'. In addition to the two limbs above, the jury should be directed that because so much time has passed between the alleged offences and the present time without the defendant having committed any offence, it is less likely that he committed the offences alleged. It was held in *R v GJB* [2011] EWCA Crim 867 that this limb was, in effect, an extrapolation of the second limb in *Vye* and was required in cases of this nature because the defendant's defence is usually a straightforward denial and he will have little else to fall back on apart from his good character.

The meaning of the phrase 'pre-trial statement and answers' in the first limb of the direction was clarified in *R v Aziz* [1995] 3 All ER 149, where their Lordships held that it referred only to mixed statements, ie statements that are both inculpatory *and* exculpatory and which are admissible on that basis as evidence of the facts they contain (see **6.5.2.5**). This means that where a defendant who is of good character does not give evidence, but evidence is admitted of pre-trial mixed statements, he will be entitled to both limbs of the direction, the first limb being in respect of the credibility of the pre-trial mixed statements. This principle was applied in *R v Patel* [2010] EWCA Crim 272, where the Court of Appeal held that the judge was wrong to withhold the first limb of a good character direction where the defendant had not given evidence but had made mixed statements in interview which were admitted in evidence during his trial. By contrast, a defendant who does not give evidence and relies only on wholly exculpatory pre-trial statements is not entitled to a first limb direction because such statements would not be admissible as evidence of the facts they contain and therefore there is nothing for the jury to assess in terms of credibility.

9.2.2 Effective good character

A defendant who has previous convictions cannot be said to be of 'absolute good character'. However, that defendant is not necessarily disqualified from a *Vye* direction. This may be the case, for example if the defendant's previous convictions are old, minor, or irrelevant to the charge. It is a matter for the judge to determine whether to treat the defendant as being of 'effective good character'. The judge should consider all the circumstances of the past offending and the offender and then decide what is required in order to be fair to all. If the judge decides to treat the accused as being of effective good character, both limbs of the direction must be given, but modified as necessary to take into account other matters and ensure the jury is not misled. The judge therefore enjoys an 'open textured' discretion as to whether to give any part of a good character direction and if so on what terms (*R v Hunter* [2015] EWCA Crim 631).

In *R v Styles* [2015] EWCA Crim 2015, the defendant was convicted of one count of making a threat to kill and one count of possessing a firearm with intent to commit an indictable offence, namely murder. The Court of Appeal held that the Recorder was wrong to withhold a good character direction where the defendant adduced a reprimand for common assault given to the defendant when he was 13 (described as a 'bit of bullying against another child at school'), a caution for stealing lead from a derelict building at 14, a caution for the use of cannabis, an admission that he had once driven without a licence unsupervised, and contravention of the conditions of a gun licence. The Court of Appeal reasoned that the earlier acts of criminality were essentially minor in nature and they were of a wholly different kind to the grave allegations he now faced. He should therefore have received a good character direction.

9.2.3 Situations in which a good character direction may be inappropriate

Where the defendant has no previous convictions or cautions, but evidence of other misconduct is admitted and relied upon by the Crown, the judge is obliged to give a 'bad character' direction. However, the judge should consider whether fairness requires that a modified 'good character' direction should be weaved into the summing up, unless it would be absurd or meaningless to do so (*R v Hunter* [2015] EWCA Crim 631). It is arguable that in many cases the giving of directions relating to both bad character and good character together would render such directions absurd or meaningless. If a judge declines to give a good character direction in these circumstances the Court of Appeal should have proper regard to the exercise of discretion by the judge who has presided over the trial (*R v Hunter* [2015] EWCA Crim 631).

If a defendant pleads guilty to an offence that is an alternative to that on which he is being tried, he ceases to be a person of good character and a good character direction becomes inappropriate (*R v Hunter* [2015] EWCA Crim 631, endorsing *R v Challenger* [1994] Crim LR 202 over the contradictory approach in *R v Teasdale* [1994] 99 Cr App R 80).

9.2.4 Co-defendants

Where there are two defendants on trial but only one of them is of good character, there is a risk that a good character direction in favour of that defendant will highlight the other defendant's lack of good character. In *R v Vye* [1993] 1 WLR 471, it was held that where a defendant of good character is jointly tried with a defendant of bad character, the former is still entitled to a full *Vye* direction. If the co-defendant's bad character has not been mentioned in most cases it is appropriate for the judge to direct the jury there has been no evidence about his character and that it must not speculate (Crown Court Compendium, Part 1, 11-2). However, any proposed direction should be discussed with the advocate for the co-defendant. Whilst such a direction may be appropriate, it is often the preferred option that no direction be given at all, so as not to draw attention to the issue (Crown Court Compendium, Part 1, 11-2).

9.2.5 Proving good character

In *R v Rowton* (1865) Le & CA 520, CCR, it was held that evidence of the defendant's good character must be limited to evidence of his general reputation among those to whom he is known; evidence of particular creditable acts and of a witness's opinion as to his good character is inadmissible. This rule has been heavily criticised and in practice has been significantly relaxed. However, *Rowton* has never been overruled and it has been held that the rule in *Rowton* still operates to exclude evidence of previous creditable acts (*R v Redgrave* (1974) Cr App R 10, CA).

9.2.6 Procedure

Part 21 of the Crim PR relates to bad character applications. The Crim PR do not deal specifically with good character. However, the Court of Appeal in *R v Hunter* [2015] EWCA Crim 631 stated expressly that a failure to give any notice to the judge is arguably a breach of the bad character procedure rules. In any event, it laid down clear guidance for good practice which should be followed when a defendant seeks to adduce evidence of good character. Defendants should put the court on notice as early as possible that character and character directions are an issue that may need to be resolved. The judge can then decide whether a good character direction would be given and if so the precise terms. This discussion should take place before the evidence is adduced. This has advantages for the court and for the parties: the defence will be better informed before the decision is made whether to adduce the evidence, the Crown can conduct any necessary checks, and the judge will have the fullest possible information upon which to rule. The judge should then ensure that the directions given accord precisely with their ruling.

9.3 The defendant's bad character

As in civil proceedings, evidence of bad character may be relevant in the following ways:

(a) *Character as a fact issue* The character of the defendant may itself be a fact in issue in the proceedings. For example, the Firearms Act 1968, s 21 makes it an offence for a person who has previously been convicted of a criminal offence and sentenced to a term of imprisonment of three or more years to be in possession of a firearm. Therefore, the defendant's bad character is one of the facts in issue that the prosecution must prove in order to secure a conviction.

(b) *Character relevant to a fact in issue* The character of the defendant, while not itself an issue in the proceedings, may be probative of one or more of the facts in issue. For example, where a defendant charged with shoplifting claims he absent-mindedly left the shop having forgotten to pay, evidence that he has numerous previous convictions for the same offence may be admissible to prove that he was acting dishonestly.

(c) *Character relevant to credit* The character of the defendant may be relevant to his credibility. For example, evidence that a defendant's recent previous convictions for perjury and fraud may be admissible to prove that his oral testimony is not worthy of belief.

Prior to the implementation of the CJA 2003, the admissibility of the defendant's bad character was governed by both statute and common law. The CJA 2003 repealed the main statutory provisions governing the admissibility of evidence of bad character in criminal proceedings (most notably the Criminal Evidence Act 1898, s 1(3)) and abolished the common law rules governing the admissibility of evidence of bad character. It replaces the old regime with a new statutory framework. In *R v Platt* [2016] EWCA Crim 4, Lord Thomas CJ described this as a 'sea-change in the law' and stated that the emphasis in court should therefore be on the wording of the CJA 2003 and on authorities based upon the CJA 2003, rather than on the older law, when determining admissibility.

The CJA 2003 applies to all trials taking place on or after 15 December 2004 (*R v Bradley* [2005] 1 Cr App R 24).

9.4 Bad character under the Criminal Justice Act 2003

9.4.1 The definition of 'bad character'

Section 98 defines bad character as follows:

References in this Chapter to evidence of a person's 'bad character' are to evidence of, or of a disposition towards, misconduct on his part …

The Act also preserves the common law rule that evidence of a person's reputation is admissible for the purpose of proving his bad character (ss 99(2) and 118(1)). Therefore, bad character under the CJA 2003 may be defined as:

- evidence of misconduct (ie specific bad acts);

- evidence of disposition towards misconduct; and
- evidence of reputation for misconduct.

Misconduct is further defined by s 112 as the commission of an offence or other reprehensible behaviour. We will consider each in turn.

9.4.1.1 The commission of an offence

Evidence of the commission of an offence may take any of the following forms:

- a previous conviction;
- another count on the indictment;
- an offence for which the defendant has never been prosecuted; or
- an offence for which the defendant has been prosecuted but acquitted.

9.4.1.1.1 Previous convictions

The most common evidence of the commission of an offence by the defendant is evidence of previous convictions. Whilst the Rehabilitation of Offenders Act 1974 allows for certain convictions to be treated as 'spent', the provisions are not applicable to the determination of admissibility in criminal proceedings (s 7(2)(a)). Nevertheless, the Criminal Practice Direction V, para 21A.2 states that 'when considering bad character applications under the 2003 Act, regard should always be had to the general principles of the Rehabilitation of Offenders Act'.

9.4.1.1.2 Another count on the indictment

Where a defendant faces an indictment containing several counts, it will sometimes be argued that evidence that the defendant has committed an offence contained in one count on the indictment is admissible as evidence of bad character in relation to the offences contained in the other counts, ie evidence of bad character will be 'cross admissible' between counts (see *R v Chopra* [2007] 1 Cr App R 16). This type of evidence will usually be admitted under s 101(1)(d) and will be considered in greater detail when we consider admissibility under that gateway (see **9.8.3.2.1**).

9.4.1.1.3 An offence for which the defendant has never been prosecuted

Evidence of the commission of an offence may also be admitted where the misconduct amounts to an offence for which proceedings have never been brought. For example, in *R v J* [2007] EWCA Crim 1892, the prosecution was permitted to adduce evidence of allegations of serious sexual abuse that had been investigated, but in relation to which no proceedings had been brought. See also *R v T* [2008] EWCA Crim 484.

9.4.1.1.4 An offence for which the defendant has been prosecuted but acquitted

In certain circumstances, even where the defendant has been tried but acquitted of an offence, evidence of the offence may be adduced as evidence of his bad character (*R v Z* [2000] 3 WLR 117, HL). In *R v Boulton* [2007] EWCA 942, for example, the defendant was charged with the rape of his pregnant partner. The prosecution was permitted to call another witness to say that she had been raped by the defendant when pregnant with his child even though the defendant, when previously prosecuted for this, had been acquitted. However, the circumstances in which a previous acquittal can be adduced are very narrowly circumscribed and will be considered in detail at **9.8.3.2.3**.

Evidence that the defendant was simply charged with an offence that is relevant to the issues in the case does not, on its own, amount to evidence of bad character: bad character evidence must be evidence of something bad done by the defendant in the past, not simply evidence that he was charged with having done something bad (*R v Hussain* [2008] EWCA Crim 1117).

9.4.1.2 Other reprehensible behaviour

It is for the courts to determine whether particular conduct is 'reprehensible'. In doing so, the court is not exercising a moral judgment (*R v Fox* [2009] EWCA Crim 653). Rather, the test is whether the conduct carries with it 'some element of culpability or blameworthiness' (*R v Renda* [2005] 1 Cr App R 24). In *R v Weir* [2006] 1 Cr App R 19, a case of rape and sexual assault on a complainant of 13 years of age, it was held that evidence of a previous sexual relationship between the defendant (then aged 34) and a 16-year-old girl, and evidence that the defendant had said to a 15-year-old girl, 'Why do you think I'm still single? If only you were a bit older and I a bit younger', did not amount to reprehensible behaviour. In *R v Osbourne* [2007] Crim LR 712, CA, it was held that evidence that the defendant, who was charged with murder, had previously argued with his partner did not cross the threshold of reprehensible behaviour. Similarly, in *R v Hall-Chung* [2007] EWCA Crim 3429, it was held that taking an overdose was not reprehensible behaviour. However, in *Saleem* [2007] EWCA Crim 1923, evidence of images of violent assaults and violent rap lyrics found on the defendant's computer were, when taken together, deemed to be evidence of reprehensible behaviour in a case of assault. Perhaps more 'clear-cut' is the decision in *Lewis* [2014] EWCA Crim 48 that participation in a YouTube video which provides evidence of membership of, or association with, a criminal gang may constitute reprehensible behaviour.

Where the conduct does not amount to reprehensible behaviour, it is not 'bad character' within the meaning of ss 98 and 112 of the Act and so its admissibility will not be affected by the Act. Instead, its admissibility will be determined by reference to common law principles of relevance.

9.4.1.3 Proving bad character

Where the defendant's bad character takes the form of previous convictions it was held in *R v Humphris* (2005) 169 JP 441, CA that evidence to prove the convictions may be adduced via a police officer's statement under the CJA 2003, s 117, or under PACE 1984, ss 73 and 74 (see **18.4**). However, where the prosecution wants to adduce evidence to prove the 'methods used' in the commission of a previous offence, this may only be done by formal admission under the CJA 1967, s 10 (see **1.4.1**) or by calling the original complainant. In *R v Hanson* [2005] 21 Cr App R 21, the court stated that its expectation was that, in many cases, the relevant circumstances of previous convictions should generally be capable of agreement between the prosecution and defence, and that, subject to the trial judge's ruling as to admissibility, they will be put before the jury by way of formal admission. Where the defendant refuses to admit the details of previous convictions which are admissible under s 101 of the CJA 2003, a summary of the evidence prepared by the prosecution may be admitted under s 114(1)(d) (see *R v Steen* [2008] 2 Cr App R 26 and **13.6**).

Where previous misconduct has not resulted in a conviction, it must be proved by calling witnesses to give evidence of the misconduct, by adducing a summary of the evidence under the CJA 2003, s 114 (see **13.6**) or by admission (as noted earlier, under the CJA 1967, s 10—see **1.4.1**).

9.4.2 Bad character evidence not covered by the Criminal Justice Act 2003

The definition of bad character under s 98 of the CJA 2003 does not include evidence that:

> ...
>
> *(a) has to do with the alleged facts of the offence with which the defendant is charged, or*
>
> *(b) is evidence of misconduct in connection with the investigation or prosecution of the offence.*

Therefore, where evidence of misconduct has to do with the alleged facts of the offence or is in connection with the investigation or prosecution of the offence, it is not covered by the Act and its admissibility will be governed by common law. Whether evidence of misconduct is, by virtue of the exceptions in s 98(a) and (b), outside the scope of the definition of 'bad character' will often be the first enquiry when considering its admissibility (*R v Edwards* [2006] 1 WLR 1524). It is appropriate to consider each exception in turn.

9.4.2.1 Section 98(a), evidence that has to do with the alleged facts of the offence

Evidence that relates to the commission of the offence for which the defendant is being tried is not affected by the 2003 Act. Clearly, such evidence must be admitted despite the fact that it shows the defendant in a bad light. In cases where the bad character of the defendant is itself an issue in the proceedings, then it would be admissible under s 98(a) of the Act. The example of the Firearms Act 1968, s 21 has already been given (see **9.3**).

However, this exception is not limited to evidence of the commission of the offence and may extend to evidence of the commission of other offences or other reprehensible behaviour. For example, in *R v Edwards* [2006] 1 Cr App R 3, CA, it was observed that the term 'to do' with the facts of the offence was drawn widely enough to cover the finding of a pistol cartridge at the home of one of the defendants when it was searched in connection with drugs offences. In *R v Machado* (2006) 170 JP 400, the Court of Appeal held that the victim's consumption of an ecstasy tablet shortly before a robbery and his offer to supply the defendant drugs immediately before the attack were effectively contemporaneous and so closely connected to the facts of the offence as to come within s 98(a).

Whilst there is often only a short period of time between the past incident and the alleged offence (see, eg, *R v Lovell* [2018] EWCA Crim 19), in *R v Lunkulu* [2015] EWCA Crim 1350, the Court of Appeal held that s 98(a) includes no necessary temporal qualification: it applies to evidence of incidents whenever they occurred so long as they are to do with the alleged facts of the offence with which the defendant is charged, which is a highly fact-specific question. The Court of Appeal endorsed the decision in *R v Sule* [2012] EWCA Crim 1130, in which Stanley Burnton LJ gave examples of why a temporal requirement would be irrational: 'A man is wounded in a shooting. He is hospitalised for six months. On discharge, he is alleged to have shot the man who is alleged to have been his attacker. In another case, the reprisal is the day after the first attack. In the second case, the evidence of the first attack is not bad character for the purposes of s 98, in the first it is.' In *R v Okokono* [2014] EWCA Crim 2521, the defendant's previous conviction for possession of a knife on the day that his best friend was killed was held to be 'highly relevant' evidence in relation to a murder which took place 18 months later. That murder was said to be a revenge attack for the earlier killing. It was therefore admissible as 'having to do with the facts of the offence'. Similarly, an appearance by a defendant accused of a gang-related murder on a YouTube video made two years earlier, which was intended to 'antagonise' members of the gang to which the deceased belonged, fell within s 98. 'The fact the video had been made some two years before does not reduce its impact or diminish its relevance' (*R v Sode* [2017] EWCA Crim 705).

9.4.2.2 Section 98(b), evidence of misconduct in connection with the investigation or prosecution

The bad character provisions of the CJA 2003, similarly, do not affect the admissibility of evidence of misconduct in connection with the investigation or prosecution of the offence for which the defendant is being tried. For example, the admissibility of evidence that the police obtained the defendant's confession by force or evidence that the defendant has attempted to frighten a witness into not giving evidence would not be affected by the Act.

9.4.3 The admissibility of evidence of bad character under the Criminal Justice Act 2003

The CJA 2003 creates seven gateways through which the defendant's bad character may be admitted in evidence. Section 101 provides that:

> *(1) In criminal proceedings evidence of the defendant's bad character is admissible if, but only if—*
>
> *(a) all parties to the proceedings agree to the evidence being admissible,*
>
> *(b) the evidence is adduced by the defendant himself or is given in answer to a question by him in cross-examination and intended to elicit it,*
>
> *(c) it is important explanatory evidence,*
>
> *(d) it is relevant to an important matter in issue between the defendant and the prosecution,*
>
> *(e) it has substantial probative value in relation to an important matter in issue between the defendant and a co-defendant,*
>
> *(f) it is evidence to correct a false impression given by the defendant, or*
>
> *(g) the defendant has made an attack on another person's character.*

In *R v Highton* [2006] 1 Cr App R 7, it was held that a distinction had to be drawn between the admissibility of evidence of bad character, which depended upon it getting through one of the 'gateways' in s 101(1), and the use to which it could be put once it was admitted. The latter depended upon the matters to which the evidence was relevant rather than upon the gateway through which it was admitted. So, evidence of bad character admitted through gateway s 101(1)(g) because the defendant has made an attack on another person's character, may, once admitted, become relevant and admissible in relation to an important matter in issue between the defendant and the prosecution. This is so even though it has been admitted through s 101(1)(g) and not s 101(1)(d), the gateway through which evidence relevant to an important matter in issue is ordinarily admitted. This approach was affirmed by the Court of Appeal in *R v Campbell* [2007] 1 WLR 2798, in which it was held that once evidence of bad character has been admitted through a gateway, it is open to the jury to attach significance to it in any respect in which it is relevant. To direct the jury only to have regard to it for some purposes and to disregard its relevance in other respects would be to revert to the unsatisfactory practices that prevailed under the old law.

Even though evidence of bad character comes within one (or more) of the gateways, the court retains a discretion to exclude the evidence. The admissibility of bad character is therefore a two-stage process:

(a) whether the evidence comes within any of the gateways; and

(b) whether, once the evidence comes within a gateway, the court will exercise a discretion to exclude it.

9.5 Agreement of the parties (s 101(1)(a))

Section 101(1)(a) provides:

> *(1) In criminal proceedings evidence of the defendant's bad character is admissible if, but only if—*
>
> *(a) all parties to the proceedings agree to the evidence being admissible.*

Where the prosecution, the defendant, and any co-defendant agree, evidence of the defendant's bad character may be admitted. The judge should be informed of any such agreement in the interests of good trial management (*R v DJ* [2010] EWCA Crim 385). Both the prosecution and the defendant may use this provision to adduce evidence of the defendant's bad character.

9.6 Evidence adduced by the defendant (s 101(1)(b))

Section 101(1)(b) provides:

> (1) *In criminal proceedings evidence of the defendant's bad character is admissible if, but only if—*
>
> ...
>
> (b) *the evidence is adduced by the defendant himself or is given in answer to a question by him in cross-examination and intended to elicit it.*

Situations in which the defendant will adduce evidence of his own bad character will be uncommon. However, *R v Harper* [2007] EWCA Crim 1746 provides an example. The defendant was charged with an offence of wounding with intent and was jointly charged, together with one other, with an offence of affray arising out of the same incident. At trial, the prosecution adduced the co-defendant's previous convictions for affray and dishonesty. The defendant, who had pleaded guilty to affray only, took a tactical decision to put his convictions before the jury under s 101(1)(b) because when taken alongside his guilty plea to the affray, they could boost his credibility. Tactically, such a course would also avoid the jury speculating about his failure to assert good character.

Another example occurs where the prosecution do not seek to adduce evidence of the defendant's bad character but the defendant's defence will involve an attack on the character of another person. In such a situation, the defendant can assume that once the attack is made, the prosecution will apply to cross-examine him on his bad character under s 101(1)(g) (see **9.11**). This being so, tactically there will be an advantage in the defendant volunteering the evidence himself. The evidence will be given under the control of his own counsel in examination-in-chief and it may give the appearance to the jury that he has taken the initiative to be honest about his past.

Defendants may put forward their old or irrelevant previous convictions or cautions in the hope that they will be treated as having 'effective good character' and therefore obtain a direction that they are less likely to commit offences of the kind with which they are now charged (see, eg, *R v Styles* [2015] EWCA Crim 1619). However, following *Hunter* [2015] EWCA Crim 631, such a defendant has no entitlement to either limb of a good character direction (see **9.2.2**).

Under s 101(1)(b), evidence of bad character can be admitted either by the defendant as part of his case, or as a result of cross-examination. Where it is elicited through cross-examination, it is only admissible if the question is intended to elicit the evidence of bad character. Therefore, if a witness unexpectedly volunteers the evidence, it will not be admissible under s 101(1)(b). In such circumstances, unless the prejudice can be cured by a direction from the judge, a retrial may have to be ordered.

9.7 Important explanatory evidence (s 101(1)(c))

Section 101(1)(c) provides that:

> (1) *In criminal proceedings evidence of the defendant's bad character is admissible if, but only if—*
>
> ...
>
> (c) *it is important explanatory evidence.*

The definition of important explanatory evidence is given in s 102 of the Act, which provides that:

> *For the purposes of section 101(1)(c) evidence is important explanatory evidence if—*

(a) *without it, the court or jury would find it impossible or difficult properly to understand other evidence in the case, and*

(b) *its value for understanding the case as a whole is substantial.*

Both the prosecution and the defence may use this provision to adduce evidence of a defendant's bad character.

To be admissible, the evidence must be more than 'background' evidence *per se*; it must be necessary to adduce that background evidence because it explains other evidence in the case that would otherwise be impossible or difficult properly to understand (see the Privy Council decisions of *Myers v The Queen* [2015] UKPC 40 and *Phillip v DPP* [2017] UKPC 14 in the context of the common law test that formed the basis of s 101(1)(c)). For example, in *R v N* [2014] EWCA Crim 419, the complainant first approached the police some 30 years after she was the victim of sexual offences because she discovered that the defendant had recently been convicted of other sexual offences. The evidence of the recent conviction was therefore properly admitted to assist the jury in understanding the timing of the report to the police.

In *Chohan*, one of the appeals heard with *R v Edwards* [2006] 1 Cr App R 3, an eyewitness was permitted to say that she was able to recognise the defendant because she had purchased heroin from him over a period of approximately one year. The fact that the identification was based on recognition was relevant to the jury's assessment of its accuracy and without the background evidence it would have been impossible or difficult for the jury properly to understand it; its value for understanding the case as a whole was also substantial.

The test for admitting 'important explanatory evidence' should be applied cautiously where it could potentially be admitted under s 101(1)(d) as evidence of propensity. Accordingly, evidence admitted under s 101(1)(c) as important explanatory evidence should not readily be used for another purpose, such as propensity, to which different statutory tests had to be satisfied. It is submitted that this would be so especially where the evidence in question might not have been admissible under those statutory tests. Section 78 of PACE 1984 might require such evidence to be excluded where it effectively amounted to evidence of propensity which would not otherwise be admitted (see *R v Davis* [2008] EWCA Crim 1156).

9.7.1 Background evidence and s 98(a)

As has already been noted, under s 98(a) evidence that has to do with the alleged facts of the offence with which the defendant is charged is not evidence of bad character for the purposes of the CJA 2003 (see **9.4.2**). In *R v Edwards* [2006] 1 Cr App R 3, CA, the Court of Appeal recognised that difficult questions can arise as to whether evidence of background or motive should be admitted under s 98(a) or under s 101(1)(c). *R v McKintosh* [2006] EWCA 193 provides an illustration of how these two provisions may overlap. In *McKintosh*, it was alleged that the defendant had raped the complainant. In her statement the complainant said that while she was being raped, the defendant's accomplice had gone to look for something and she thought he was looking for a gun. This was because approximately one year previously the defendant had used a gun to threaten her. The Court of Appeal held that the evidence of the gun was admissible as evidence of misconduct which had to do with the alleged facts of the offence (s 98(a)) but that, if it was not, it was important explanatory evidence (s 101(1)(c)) because it could explain why the complainant had not run away after the incident, why she did not tell the accomplice's girlfriend about it, and why she went into the defendant's car after the incident.

9.7.2 Exclusionary discretion

9.7.2.1 Section 78 of the Police and Criminal Evidence Act 1984

Section 101(3) of the CJA 2003 provides a statutory exclusionary discretion for some bad character evidence. This does not apply to s 101(1)(c). However, the weight of case law is in favour of PACE 1984, s 78 operating to exclude evidence of bad character the prosecution seek to admit under any gateway. The discretion applies where admission of the evidence would have such an adverse effect on the fairness of the proceedings that the court ought not to admit it (see **1.6.2.2**). In *R v Highton* [2006] 1 Cr App R 7, the Court of Appeal stated that, although it had not heard full argument, its inclination was that s 78 applies generally to evidence the prosecution proposes to adduce under s 101(1). In *R v O'Dowd* [2009] 2 Cr App R 280, it was held that the courts should have regard to s 78 where s 101(3) is unavailable.

9.7.2.2 The common law discretion

Such evidence may also be excluded by the court under its common law discretion where its prejudicial effect would outweigh its probative value (*R v Sang* [1980] AC 402; see **1.6.2.1**).

9.7.2.3 The Criminal Procedure Rules

In *R v Musone* [2007] 1 WLR 2467, CA, it was held that Crim PR 2005, r 35 (now Crim PR 2015, Part 21), concerning the procedure to be followed when seeking to admit bad character evidence, confers power on a court to exclude evidence in circumstances in which there had been a breach of the prescribed notice requirements (see further **9.16**, and also *R v Jarvis* [2008] Crim LR 632 and *R v Bullen* [2008] 2 Cr App R 75). Crim PR 2015, Part 21 retains the notice requirements of Crim PR 2005, r 35, so the principle in *Musone* that judges have a discretion to exclude evidence of bad character where notice requirements have not been adhered to continues to apply.

In *R v Ramirez* [2009] EWCA Crim 2010, the Court of Appeal considered a situation where one accused gave evidence of a co-accused's bad character, without warning. The court emphasised the importance of observing the notice requirements and stated that if this were to happen in another case in the future, it could well result in the jury being discharged and a retrial being ordered (a point reiterated in *R v Mahil* [2013] EWCA Crim 673). Further, where a legal representative deliberately manipulates the rules of the court there was a possibility of severe sanctions including, at least, a wasted costs order.

9.8 Important matters in issue between the prosecution and defence (s 101(1)(d))

Section 101(1)(d) provides that:

> *(1) In criminal proceedings evidence of the defendant's bad character is admissible if, but only if—*
>
> ...
>
> *(d) it is relevant to an important matter in issue between the defendant and the prosecution.*

Unlike the gateways considered so far, only the prosecution can adduce evidence of the defendant's bad character under this provision (s 103(6)).

9.8.1 Important matters in issue

Matters in issue between the prosecution and the defence in a criminal trial will include facts in issue and any issues of credibility or, in other words, the defendant's guilt and truthfulness.

Section 112(1) defines 'important matter' as a matter of substantial importance in the context of the case as a whole. It is submitted that this definition will encompass all of the main issues between the prosecution and the defence.

9.8.2 Relevance

Evidence of bad character will be admissible under this provision where it is 'relevant' to one or more of the matters in issue. The facts in issue to which evidence of the defendant's misconduct may be relevant under s 101(1)(d) include:

- the identity of the defendant;
- the *actus reus* of the offence;
- the *mens rea* for the offence; and
- any defences.

This test for admissibility may be compared with the tests for admissibility of the bad character of a person other than the defendant (under s 100; see **10.2**) and the bad character of a co-defendant when adduced by the defendant (under s 101(1)(e); see **9.9**), both of which, by using the wording 'substantial probative value', purport to impose an enhanced relevance test.

9.8.3 Propensity to offend

Section 103(1) of the Act provides that:

> *(1) For the purposes of s 101(1)(d) the matters in issue between the defendant and the prosecution include—*
>
> *(a) the question whether the defendant has a propensity to commit offences of the kind with which he is charged, except where his having such a propensity makes it no more likely that he is guilty of the offence.*

Section 103(1) therefore permits evidence of the defendant's propensity to commit a particular kind of offence to be admitted as relevant to the question of guilt. However, it should be noted that where the prosecution adduces evidence of the defendant's propensity to offend, it may not only be relevant to the question of whether his bad character makes it more likely that he committed the offence (his guilt), but may also be relevant to the issue of whether he is telling the truth should he testify (his credibility).

The defendant's propensity to commit offences of the kind with which he is charged may be established by:

- evidence of previous convictions; and/or
- evidence of other reprehensible behaviour.

9.8.3.1 Evidence of previous convictions

Section 101(1)(d) is supplemented by s 103, which provides that:

> *(1) For the purposes of section 101(1)(d) the matters in issue between the defendant and the prosecution include—*

> (a) *the question whether the defendant has a propensity to commit offences of the kind with which he is charged, except where his having such a propensity makes it no more likely that he is guilty of the offence;*
>
> ...
>
> (2) *Where subsection (1)(a) applies, a defendant's propensity to commit offences of the kind with which he is charged may (without prejudice to any other way of doing so) be established by evidence that he has been convicted of—*
>
> (a) *an offence of the same description as the one with which he is charged, or*
>
> (b) *an offence of the same category as the one with which he is charged.*
>
> ...
>
> (4) *For the purposes of subsection (2)—*
>
> (a) *two offences are of the same description as each other if the statement of the offence in a written charge or indictment would, in each case, be in the same terms;*
>
> (b) *two offences are of the same category as each other if they belong to the same category of offences prescribed for the purposes of this section by an order made by the Secretary of State.*
>
> (5) *A category prescribed by an order under subsection (4)(b) must consist of offences of the same type.*

Section 103(2) provides that a defendant's propensity to commit offences of the kind with which he is charged may be established by evidence that he has been convicted of:

- an offence of the same description as the one with which he is charged; or
- an offence of the same category as the one with which he is charged.

An offence is of the same description where the statement of the offence in a written charge or indictment would be in the same terms (s 103(4)). An offence is of the same category where both the previous offence and the offence charged belong to the same category of offences prescribed by the Secretary of State. At the time of writing, the Secretary of State has prescribed two categories, as follows:

(a) *The Theft Category (CJA 2003 (Categories of Offences) Order 2004, SI 2004/3346, Part 1)* This category includes all the main offences under the Theft Act 1968 (theft, robbery, burglary, etc), the offence of making off without payment under the Theft Act 1978, and offences of aiding, abetting, counselling, or procuring such offences and attempting to commit any such offences.

(b) *The Sexual Offences (Persons Under the Age of 16) Category (CJA 2003 (Categories of Offences) Order 2004, SI 2004/3346, Part 2)* This category includes 36 sexual offences and offences of aiding, abetting, counselling, or procuring such offences and attempting to commit any such offences. The complainant must have been under 16 years of age at the time the offence was committed.

Section 144, Sch 17 of the Coroners and Justice Act 2009 inserts s 103(7)–(11) into the CJA 2003. The effect is that offences committed outside England and Wales are admissible as offences of the same description and category if they would constitute an offence of the same description and category in England and Wales.

Simply establishing that a conviction is of the same description or category as that charged is not necessarily sufficient in order to establish a propensity to commit the offence. Whether a conviction establishes such a propensity depends on the interrelation of a number of factors, including the exact nature of the conviction, the age of the conviction, and the offence with which the defendant is presently charged. A previous conviction will not automatically be admissible as evidence of propensity simply because it falls within the same category.

Propensity may also be established by evidence of other previous convictions. While s 103(2) permits a propensity to commit the offence to be established by evidence of a previous conviction of the same description or category, it also states that it is without prejudice to any other way of doing so. This means that it is not a requirement that a previous offence is of the same description or category before the offence can be admitted to show propensity to commit the offence charged. *R v Weir* [2006] 1 Cr App R 19 provides an example, although it concerned the admission of a previous caution which was not of the same description or in the same category as the offence charged, rather than a previous conviction. In *Weir*, the defendant was charged with an offence of sexual assault by touching a girl under the age of 13 contrary to s 7 of the Sexual Offences Act 2003. The prosecution sought to adduce a previous caution for an offence of taking an indecent photograph of a child contrary to s 1 of the Protection of Children Act 1978 as evidence of a propensity to commit offences of sexual assault on girls under the age of 13. The offence with which the defendant was charged had been categorised by order of the Secretary of State (see the Sexual Offences (Persons Under the Age of 16) Category (CJA 2003 (Categories of Offences) Order 2004, SI 2004/3346, Part 2), but the offence in respect of which the defendant had received a caution had not. The Court of Appeal held that the prosecution was allowed to rely upon the previous caution as evidence of propensity despite the fact that it was neither of the same description nor specified in the same category as the offence with which he was charged.

Therefore, the defendant's propensity may be proven by evidence of:

- previous convictions of the same description;
- previous convictions of the same category; or
- other previous convictions.

Careful consideration should be given to whether to rely simply upon the fact of conviction or also upon its circumstances. The former may be sufficient when the circumstances of the offence are sufficiently apparent from its description to justify a finding that it can establish propensity (*R v Hanson* [2005] 21 Cr App R 21, CA). For example, where the defendant is on trial for dwelling-house burglary, proof of a succession of previous convictions for dwelling-house burglaries may of itself establish propensity without the need for further proof of how the burglaries were committed.

9.8.3.2 Evidence of other reprehensible behaviour

As has already been noted, s 103(2) is expressly stated as being without prejudice to any other way of proving the defendant's propensity to commit offences of the kind with which he is charged. Therefore, not only is it possible to establish propensity by reference to previous convictions that are not of the same description or category as the offence charged, but the defendant's propensity may also be established by any evidence of misconduct or disposition towards misconduct, whether or not it resulted in a conviction. It may therefore be established by evidence of:

- misconduct that is the subject of another count on the indictment;
- misconduct for which the defendant has never been prosecuted;
- misconduct for which the defendant has been prosecuted but acquitted; or
- misconduct not amounting to the commission of a criminal offence.

9.8.3.2.1 Misconduct that is the subject of another count on the indictment

Evidence of misconduct that has not resulted in a conviction will commonly be relied upon by the prosecution where a defendant faces an indictment containing several counts and it is argued that the evidence in relation to one count is admissible as evidence of bad character in relation to the other counts (ie it is 'cross-admissible'). Section 112(2) of the CJA 2003 states:

> *Where a defendant is charged with two or more offences in the same criminal proceedings, this Chapter… has effect as if each offence were charged in separate proceedings; and reference to the offence with which the defendant is charged are to be read accordingly.*

In *R v Chopra* [2007] 1 Cr App R 16, the Court of Appeal confirmed that, pursuant to s 112(2) of the CJA 2003, where a defendant is charged upon several counts the evidence that goes to suggest that he committed one count is, so far as the other counts are concerned, bad character evidence within the Act (see also *R v Wallace* [2008] 1 WLR 572). It is therefore admissible as evidence in relation to the other counts if it passes through one of the gateways in s 101. When considering admissibility, the judge is required, under s 109, to assume that the evidence is truthful unless no jury could reasonably believe it (see **9.14**). Whether it is in fact truthful is for the jury to decide. In *Chopra*, the defendant, a dentist, was charged with three counts of indecent assault against three young female patients. In each case, it was alleged that he had touched their breast while conducting a dental examination. It was held that the evidence was cross-admissible under s 101(1)(d) as it was relevant to an important matter in issue between the defendant and the prosecution, namely a propensity in the defendant occasionally to molest young female patients in the course of dental examination.

9.8.3.2.2 *Misconduct for which the defendant has never been prosecuted*

Evidence of previous misconduct may also be admitted where the misconduct amounts to an offence for which proceedings have never been brought. *R v J* [2007] EWCA Crim 1892 has been mentioned earlier as an example where the prosecution was permitted to adduce evidence of allegations of serious sexual abuse that had been investigated, but in relation to which no proceedings had been brought. See also *R v McKenzie* [2008] RTR 22.

9.8.3.2.3 *Misconduct for which the defendant has been prosecuted but acquitted*

At common law, where a person had been tried for and acquitted of an offence on some previous occasion, that did not necessarily mean that evidence of the commission of that offence would be inadmissible to prove the commission of some other offence at a later date. In *R v Z* [2000] 3 WLR 117, HL, the defendant had been tried on three previous occasions for rape and had been acquitted having run the defence of consent. He was then tried for a fourth rape in which he also ran the defence of consent. There were similarities in his conduct on all four occasions. The House of Lords upheld the trial judge's admission of the evidence of the misconduct that gave rise to the previous charges, notwithstanding that it showed him to be guilty of offences for which he had been acquitted. It is submitted that this doctrine will continue to apply under the 2003 Act and that were *Z* to be heard now, the evidence from three previous acquittals for rape would have been admitted under s 101(1)(d) as relevant to an important matter in issue between the defendant and the prosecution. Its relevance to an important matter in issue in *Z* might include rebutting the defendant's defence of consent on the basis that in three previous trials for rape he had relied on this defence and he was now relying on it for a fourth time.

In circumstances where evidence that the defendant was simply charged with an offence may be relevant to the issues in the case, it is however not to be treated as evidence of bad character. According to *R v Hussain* [2008] EWCA Crim 1117, bad character evidence must be evidence of something 'bad' done by the defendant in the past, not simply evidence that he was charged with having done something bad. Although *Hussain* involved an application by a co-defendant to adduce the defendant's bad character under s 101(1)(e), it is submitted that the same principle can apply under s 101(1)(d).

9.8.3.2.4 *Misconduct not amounting to the commission of a criminal offence*

Occasionally, the prosecution may rely on evidence of misconduct that does not amount to the commission of an offence, but which is nevertheless evidence of bad character. In *R v Saleem* [2007] EWCA Crim 1923, mentioned earlier, the defendant was charged with an offence of causing grievous bodily harm with intent. He admitted being present at the time of the assault, but denied participation. The prosecution successfully applied to adduce images related to violent assaults found in the defendant's possession and violent rap lyrics, taken from the defendant's computer. The Court of Appeal held that the evidence taken together was relevant under s 101(1)(d) to show that the defendant's presence at the scene was not innocent.

9.8.3.2.5 *Disputed facts and propensity*

Where the evidence of misconduct has not resulted in a conviction, whether because a charge was never brought, the defendant was previously acquitted, it is the subject of another count on the present indictment, or it does not amount to the commission of an offence, evidence of the defendant's misconduct will be admissible even if the defendant disputes the facts (*R v Rance* (1976) 62 Cr App R 118). The jury must, however, be sure that propensity has been proved to the criminal standard on the basis of that admitted evidence. Where there is a single instance of unproven misconduct, the jury will therefore have to examine the facts of the previous offence and be satisfied so that they are sure that they occurred in order to prove a propensity (*R v Nguyen* (2008] EWCA Crim 585; Crown Court Compendium Part 1, 13-6, Example Direction 2). Where there are several instances of misconduct, this requirement is diluted. In *R v Mitchell* [2016] UKSC 55 (an appeal from Northern Ireland on comparable statutory provisions), it was held that where there are several instances of misconduct, all tending to show a propensity, the jury does not have to be convinced of the truth and accuracy of all aspects of each of the instances. The jury should 'consider the evidence about propensity in the round. There are two interrelated reasons for this. First the improbability of a number of similar incidents alleged against a defendant being false is a consideration which should naturally inform a jury's deliberations on whether propensity has been proved. Secondly, obvious similarities in various incidents may constitute mutual corroboration of those incidents. Each incident may thus inform another. The question impelled by the Order is whether, overall, propensity has been proved' (at [43]). Therefore, 'decisions about propensity should not be the product of a review of facts about separate episodes in hermetically sealed compartments' (at [49]). The judgment is careful to couch the admission of a number of unproved disputed allegations as balancing acts. Lord Kerr opined that 'whilst reliance on cumulative past incidents in support of a case of propensity may indeed illuminate the truth of the currently indicted allegations, [...] excessive recourse to such history may skew the trial in a way which distracts attention from the central issue' and may have an adverse effect on the fairness of the trial (at [53]).

9.8.3.3 Determining the admissibility of evidence of a propensity to commit offences

Guidance on how to approach the admissibility of evidence of a propensity to commit offences was given in *R v Hanson* [2005] 2 Cr App R 21:

(a) Where propensity to commit the offence is relied upon there are essentially three questions to be considered:
   - (i) Does the history of conviction(s) establish a propensity to commit offences of the kind charged?
   - (ii) Does that propensity make it more likely that the defendant committed the offence charged?
   - (iii) Is it unjust to rely on the conviction(s) of the same description or category; and, in any event, will the proceedings be unfair if they are admitted?

(b) There is no minimum number of events necessary to demonstrate such a propensity. The fewer the number of convictions, the weaker is likely to be the evidence of propensity. A single previous conviction for an offence of the same description or category will often not show propensity. But it may do so where, for example, it shows a tendency to unusual behaviour or where its circumstances demonstrate probative force in relation to the offence charged.

(c) Circumstances demonstrating probative force are not confined to those sharing striking similarity. So, a single conviction for shoplifting, will not, without more, be admissible to show propensity to steal. But if the *modus operandi* has significant features shared by the offence charged, it may show propensity.

(d) If there is a substantial gap between the dates of commission of and conviction for the earlier offences, the date of commission should be regarded as generally being of more significance than the date of conviction when assessing admissibility. Old convictions, with no special feature shared with the offence charged, are likely seriously to affect the fairness of proceedings adversely, unless, despite their age, it can properly be said that they show a continuing propensity.

(e) It will often be necessary, before determining admissibility and even when considering offences of the same description or category, to examine each individual conviction rather than merely to look at the name of the offence or at the defendant's record as a whole.

(f) The sentence passed will not normally be probative or admissible at the behest of the prosecution, though it may be at the behest of the defence.

(g) Where the prosecution is relying on a previous conviction to prove propensity, the prosecution needs to decide, at the time of giving notice of the application, whether it proposes to rely simply upon the fact of conviction or also upon the circumstances of it. The former may be enough when the circumstances of the conviction are sufficiently apparent from its description, to justify a finding that it can establish propensity, either to commit an offence of the kind charged or to be untruthful. For example, a succession of convictions for dwelling-house burglary, where the same offence is now charged, may well call for no further evidence than proof of the fact of the convictions.

In *R v Humphris* [2005] EWCA 2030, the Court of Appeal emphasised that if the prosecution want to adduce more than the evidence of the fact of the conviction they must ensure that they have available the necessary evidence to support what they require. That will normally require the availability of either a statement by the complainant relating to the previous convictions or the complainant to be available to give first-hand evidence of what happened.

A previous conviction for an offence may be admissible as evidence of a relevant propensity to commit offences even if it was committed after the offence for which the defendant is being tried. In *R v Adenuse* [2006] Crim LR 929, the defendant was charged with an offence of using a false instrument and an offence of attempting to obtain a money transfer by deception. The Court of Appeal upheld the trial judge's decision to admit evidence under CJA 2003, s 101(1)(d) that five days *after* the commission of those offences the defendant had committed two further offences of using a false instrument.

A number of decisions under the 2003 Act usefully illustrate the principles enunciated in *R v Hanson* [2005] 2 Cr App R 21. In *Hanson* itself, one defendant was charged with theft and the prosecution sought to adduce evidence of three previous convictions for theft as evidence of a propensity to steal. All three of the offences were committed within a six-week period, ending three months before the date of the offence charged. The Court of Appeal held that the trial judge was fully entitled to conclude that the offences showed a recent persistent propensity to steal. In another of the appeals heard with *R v Hanson* [2005] 2 Cr App R 21, CA, one defendant was charged with three counts of rape and two of indecent assault against a 9-year-old girl. The trial judge permitted the prosecution to adduce the defendant's previous conviction dating from 1993 for indecent assault against an 11-year-old girl. He concluded that the earlier offence was of the same description and the same category, within the Categories of Offences Order, as the offences charged. He expressly took into account the length of time since the previous offence and said that '*a defendant's sexual mores and motivations are not necessarily affected by the passage of time*'. The Court of Appeal upheld the judge's decision. In the later case of *R v Brima* [2007] 1 Cr App R 316, the defendant was charged with murder. It was alleged that he had stabbed the deceased with a knife. The trial judge had permitted the prosecution to adduce the defendant's recent previous convictions for assault occasioning actual bodily harm and robbery under s 101(1)(d). Although the offences were much less serious than the offence charged, on both occasions a knife was used and both were committed within the three-year period prior to the date of the murder. The Court of Appeal upheld the trial judge's ruling that the offences showed that the appellant had a propensity to commit offences of violence using knives either by inflicting or threatening injury.

However, care must be taken to ensure that the previous convictions on which the prosecution proposes to rely establish a *relevant* propensity. In *R v Highton* [2006] 1 Cr App R 7, one appellant was charged with cultivating cannabis. The defendant stated that he knew that the plants in question were a controlled substance and so the only issue at trial was whether or not he was involved in their cultivation. The Court of Appeal held that the judge had been wrong to admit evidence of the defendant's heroin addiction because it was not relevant to the issue of whether he was involved in the cultivation of cannabis. Similarly, where the issue at trial is whether a defendant charged with murder had the necessary specific intent, previous convictions for offences of violence demonstrating only basic intent were not admissible (*R v Bullen* [2008] 2 Cr App R 25).

9.8.4 Propensity to be untruthful

Section 103 of the Criminal Justice Act 2003 provides that:

> *(1) For the purposes of section 101(1)(d) the matters in issue between the defendant and the prosecution include—*
>
> ...
>
> *(b) the question whether the defendant has a propensity to be untruthful, except where it is not suggested that the defendant's case is untruthful in any respect.*

In *R v Hanson* [2005] 2 Cr App R 21, it was held that propensity to untruthfulness is not the same as propensity to dishonesty. Parliament deliberately chose the word 'untruthful' to convey a different meaning, reflecting a defendant's account of his behaviour, or lies told when committing an offence. The court concluded that previous convictions, whether for offences of dishonesty or otherwise, are therefore only likely to be capable of showing a propensity to be untruthful where, in the present case, truthfulness is an issue and, in the earlier case, either there was a plea of not guilty and the defendant gave an account, on arrest, in interview, or in evidence, which the jury must have disbelieved, or the way in which the offence was committed shows a propensity for untruthfulness, for example, by the making of false representations. As with evidence of a propensity to commit offences, there is no minimum number of events necessary to demonstrate a propensity to be untruthful. The fewer the number of convictions, the weaker is likely to be the evidence of propensity.

The approach in *R v Hanson* [2005] 2 Cr App R 21 was endorsed by the Court of Appeal in *R v N* [2014] EWCA Crim 419 and was preferred to the attempt made in *R v Campbell* [2007] 1 WLR 2798 to narrow considerably the circumstances in which evidence of a propensity to be untruthful could be admitted. In *R v Campbell*, the Court of Appeal had sought to limit admissibility of a propensity to be untruthful to cases where telling lies was an element of the offence charged.

In *R v N* [2014] EWCA Crim 419, the Court of Appeal held that the defendant's 'previous sustained lying in a court context' was admissible as evidence of a propensity to untruthfulness. The defendant had been convicted of a similar matter following a not guilty plea. This suggested that he had given false evidence which was rejected by the jury. Furthermore, he admitted to having given false instructions to his barrister at his sentencing hearing.

9.8.5 Similar fact evidence and 'coincidence'

As noted above (see **9.3**), Lord Thomas CJ expressed the view that references to case law in court should, where possible, post-date the CJA 2003 (*R v Platt* [2016] EWCA Crim 4). However, the common law principles relating to the admissibility of 'similar fact' evidence have continued to inform the courts' approach to evidence sought to be admitted under the CJA 2003, s 101(1)(d). At common law, evidence of the defendant's bad character was admissible to prove the facts in issue where it had a probative force sufficiently great to make it just to admit it notwithstanding that it is prejudicial in tending to show that the defendant was guilty of another offence (*DPP v P* [1991] 2 AC 447, HL). Such evidence was known as 'similar fact evidence'.

The operation of similar fact principles under the CJA 2003 was acknowledged in *R v Freeman* [2008] EWCA Crim 1863, in the context of cross-admissibility of allegations contained in different counts on an indictment. In *Freeman*, the Court of Appeal revisited the case of *R v Chopra* [2007] 1 Cr App R 16 and concluded that while the judgment dealt mainly with the question of whether the evidence was capable of establishing a propensity to commit such an offence, it was apparent from the way the court treated the evidence that it concluded that each of the allegations was capable of making it more likely that the other allegations were true because of the similar nature of the evidence in each case. In other words, regardless of whether or not different incidents were capable of establishing a propensity, each was admissible in itself as evidence to support truth of the other allegations. This is referred to in the Crown Court Compendium as the 'coincidence approach' to s 101(1)(d) (Part 1, 13-1):

> *The jury is not being invited to reason from propensity; they are merely being asked to recognise that the evidence in relation to a particular offence on an indictment may appear stronger and more compelling when all the evidence, including evidence relating to other offences, is looked at as a whole.*

For example, 'when independent but similar complaints of sexual offences are made against the same person, the jury may be permitted to consider the improbability that those complaints are the product of mere coincidence or malice (i.e. a complainant's evidence in support of one count is relevant to the credibility of another complainant's evidence on another count–an important matter in issue)' (*R v N(H)* [2011] EWCA Crim 730). In such 'coincidence' cross-admissibility cases, the jury need not first determine whether it is satisfied on the evidence in relation to one of the counts of the defendant's guilt before it can move on to using the evidence in relation to that count in dealing with any other count in the indictment (*R v Freeman*; see also *R v O'Leary* [2013] EWCA Crim 1371).

Similar fact evidence might also be admissible outside of cross-admissibility cases to prove the identity of the offender by demonstrating a compelling 'coincidence'. For example, in *R v McAllister* [2009] 1 Cr App R 10, the defendant was charged with a robbery in Leeds. The prosecution sought to adduce evidence of another robbery in Banff, in Scotland, that took place shortly after the robbery in Leeds. The trial judge admitted evidence in relation to the Banff robbery not to establish a propensity, but rather to demonstrate that it was not a mere coincidence that the defendant was in Leeds shortly before. However, as the Banff robbery had already been tried in Scotland and a verdict of not proven returned, the jury would only be able to use the evidence if it was sure that the Scottish jury had reached the wrong conclusion. The Court of Appeal concluded that as the evidence would have effectively involved a satellite trial, it would have had such an adverse effect on the fairness of the proceedings that it should not have been admitted. The case is nevertheless a useful illustration of a situation where similar fact evidence could potentially be admitted to prove identity. A further example is given in the Crown Court Compendium, Example Direction 4 on s 101(1)(d):

The fact that D has [eg committed burglaries in the same street] cannot prove he did so on this occasion but it is evidence you may take into account as support for the prosecution case. How far it supports the prosecution case will depend on your view of (a) how much of a coincidence it is that the person identified as the burglar in this case has [eg committed burglaries on the same street in the past] and (b) the defence point about the number of other people who have [eg committed burglaries on this street].

9.8.6 Section 101(1)(d) and discretion to exclude

9.8.6.1 Section 101(3) of the Criminal Justice Act 2003

Section 101(3) and (4) provide that:

...

(3) *The court must not admit evidence under subsection 1(d) ... if, on an application by the defendant to exclude it, it appears to the court that the admission of the evidence would have such an adverse effect on the fairness of the proceedings that the court ought not to admit it.*

(4) *On an application to exclude evidence under subsection (3) the court must have regard, in particular, to the length of time between the matters to which that evidence relates and the matters which form the subject of the offence charged.*

Where the prosecution proposes to adduce evidence of the defendant's misconduct under s 101(1)(d), the court must not do so where it appears that the admission of the evidence would have such an adverse effect on the fairness of the proceedings that the court ought not to admit it. The wording of this provision is very similar to PACE 1984, s 78 (see **1.6.2.2**). The key difference is that it is expressed in mandatory ('must not admit') rather than discretionary ('may refuse to allow') terms. It is submitted that because of the clear overlap between the two provisions, s 78 will be otiose to applications to exclude evidence the prosecution proposes to adduce under s 101(1)(d). Compare the cases cited at **9.7.2.1**. In *R v Chrysostomou* [2010] EWCA Crim 1403, the Court of Appeal held that where s 101(3) was available, the focus should be on s 101(3) rather than s 78. Although that case was in respect of gateway (g), it is submitted that the principle is applicable to gateway (d) because s 101(3) is equally applicable.

9.8.6.2 Section 103(3) of the Criminal Justice Act 2003

Where the prosecution relies on previous convictions of the same description or category to prove the defendant's propensity to commit offences of the kind with which he is charged, s 103(3) provides that s 103(2) should not apply where it would be unjust. Section 103(2) and (3) provide that:

...

(2) *Where subsection (1)(a) applies, a defendant's propensity to commit offences of the kind with which he is charged may (without prejudice to any other way of doing so) be established by evidence that he has been convicted of—*

(a) *an offence of the same description as the one with which he is charged, or*

(b) *an offence of the same category as the one with which he is charged.*

> (3) *Subsection (2) does not apply in the case of a particular defendant if the court is satisfied, by reason of the length of time since the conviction or for any other reason, that it would be unjust for it to apply in his case.*

9.8.6.3 The principles to be applied under ss 101(3) and 103(3)

In *R v Hanson* [2005] 2 Cr App R 21, it was held that in a conviction case, the decisions required of the trial judge under ss 101(3) and 103(3), although not identical, are closely related. When considering what is just under s 103(3), and the fairness of the proceedings under s 101(3), the judge may, among other factors, take into consideration the degree of similarity between the previous conviction and the offence charged, albeit they are both within the same description or prescribed category. For example, theft and assault occasioning actual bodily harm may each embrace a wide spectrum of conduct. As already noted, this does not, however, mean that what used to be referred to as striking similarity must be shown before convictions become admissible. The judge may also take into consideration the respective gravity of the past and present offences. He must always consider the strength of the prosecution case. If there is no or very little other evidence against a defendant, it is unlikely to be just to admit his previous convictions, whatever they are.

9.8.6.4 The common law discretion

It is submitted that the common law discretion will apply to exclude evidence adduced by the prosecution under s 101(1)(d) where its prejudicial effect outweighs its probative value, but in practice it will seldom be relied upon because of the breadth of the discretion under s 101(3).

9.8.6.5 The Criminal Procedure Rules 2015

As previously mentioned, in *R v Musone* [2007] 1 WLR 2467, CA, it was held that Crim PR 2005, r 35, which relates to bad character evidence, confers power on a court to exclude evidence in circumstances in which there had been a breach of the prescribed notice requirements (see further **9.16**). See also *R v Jarvis* [2008] Crim LR 632. This continues to apply to the notice requirements now contained in the Part 21 of the Crim PR 2015.

9.8.7 Directing the jury

In *R v Hanson* [2005] 2 Cr App R 21, it was held that, in any case in which evidence of bad character is admitted to show propensity, the judge in summing up should warn the jury clearly against placing undue reliance on previous convictions. Evidence of bad character cannot be used simply to bolster a weak case, or to prejudice the minds of a jury against a defendant.

In particular, the jury should be directed:

- that it should not conclude that the defendant is guilty merely because he has these convictions;
- that, although the convictions may show a propensity, this does not mean that he has committed this offence;
- that whether they in fact show a propensity is for it to decide;
- that it must take into account what the defendant has said about his previous convictions; and

- that, although it is entitled, if it finds propensity is shown, to take this into account when determining guilt, propensity is only one relevant factor and that it must assess its significance in the light of all other evidence in the case.

In *R v Edwards* [2006] 1 Cr App R 3, it was held that the guidance given in *Hanson* must not be taken as a blueprint, departure from which will result in the quashing of a conviction. What the summing-up must contain is a clear warning to the jury against placing undue reliance on previous convictions, which cannot, by themselves, prove guilt. It should be explained to the jury why it has heard the evidence and the ways in which that evidence is relevant to, and may help, its decision. Provided that the judge gives such a clear warning, explanation, and guidance as to use, the terms in which he does so can properly differ.

In *R v Campbell* [2007] 1 WLR 2798, Lord Phillips stressed that the 2003 Act should be the occasion for simplifying directions to juries. In particular, when directing a jury in relation to bad character, it is undesirable to make specific reference to the gateway through which the evidence had been admitted. Instead, the jury should be given assistance as to the relevance of the evidence of bad character tailored to the facts of the individual case and that relevance could normally be deduced by the application of common sense. The summing-up that assists the jury with the relevance of bad character evidence will accord with common sense and assist the jury to avoid prejudice.

The suggested content of a judicial direction relating to s 101(1)(d) and examples of such directions can be found in Chapter 12-6 of the ***Crown Court Compendium Part 1*** 2017, available at: <https://www.judiciary.gov.uk/wp-content/uploads/2016/06/crown-court-compendium-pt1-jury-and-trial-management-and-summing-up-nov2017-v3.pdf>

9.9 Substantial probative value to an important matter in issue between co-defendants (s 101(1)(e))

Section 101(1)(e) provides:

> (1) *In criminal proceedings evidence of the defendant's bad character is admissible if, but only if—*
>
> ...
>
> (e) *it has substantial probative value in relation to an important matter in issue between the defendant and a co-defendant.*

Section 101 is supplemented by s 104, which provides:

> ...
>
> (2) *Only evidence—*
>
> (a) *which is to be (or has been) adduced by the co-defendant, or*
>
> (b) *which a witness is to be invited to give (or has given) in cross-examination by the co-defendant, is admissible under section 101(1)(e).*

Therefore, only a co-defendant can adduce evidence of the defendant's bad character under s 101(1)(e).

In the case of *R v Platt* [2016] EWCA Crim 4, Lord Thomas CJ stated that admissibility under s 101(1)(e) should be determined solely with reference to the statutory test under the CJA 2003 (and to decisions of the courts made in connection with the CJA 2003 provisions), without regard to common law authorities which pre-date the Act.

9.9.1 Matters in issue

The matters in issue between the defendant and the co-defendant may include the facts in issue and any issues of credibility, including any propensity to be untruthful. The facts in issue will be a matter in issue where a cut-throat defence is being advanced by the defendant. Section 112(1) defines 'important matter' as a matter of substantial importance in the context of the case as a whole. See, generally, **9.8.1**.

9.9.2 The probative value required

As noted at **9.8.2**, the probative value required for the defendant's bad character to be admissible under s 101(1)(d) is mere relevance. Section 101(1)(e) gives the appearance of applying a stricter test to co-defendants. Under s 101(1)(e) the co-defendant must satisfy the court that the evidence of the defendant's bad character has substantial probative value. The difference might not be as significant as it might at first appear considering that the Explanatory Notes to the Criminal Justice Bill stated that the word 'substantial' would only operate to exclude the marginal or trivial. However, in *R v Phillips* [2012] 1 Cr App R 25, it was held that 'substantial probative value' meant enhanced capability to prove a fact in issue. The following principles may be derived from *Phillips* as to what approach should be taken when deciding whether evidence of bad character sought to be admitted under s 101(1)(e) has 'substantial probative value in relation to an important matter in issue between the defendant and co-defendant':

1. Two separate questions must be addressed—first, does the evidence have substantial probative value, and second, is the matter in respect of which the evidence is sought to be admitted, a matter of substantial importance in the context of the case as a whole?
2. Although there is an element of overlap in the questions, it is necessary to address them in turn, especially where the evidence involves a number of allegations and a number of factual issues arise between the defendant and the co-defendant.
3. In respect of the second question, where there was already probative evidence before the jury on the important matter in issue, the judge is entitled to take that into consideration when assessing whether the bad character evidence has *substantial* probative value.

   In *R v Platt* [2016] EWCA Crim 4 the Court of Appeal held that substantial is an ordinary word and needs no gloss. It should therefore be given its ordinary, unelaborated meaning.

9.9.3 Section 101(1)(e): evidence relevant to credibility and guilt

Where the issue is whether a co-defendant believed the defendant capable of a particular act rather than whether the defendant had in fact committed that act, then evidence that the co-defendant knew that the defendant had simply been charged with an offence would not be evidence of bad character. As stated earlier, bad character evidence is evidence of something 'bad' done by the defendant in the past, not simply evidence that he was charged with having done something bad (*R v Hussain* [2008] EWCA Crim 1117, CA). In *R v Hussain*, H and M were charged with attempted robbery. H's defence was duress and in support of his defence he wanted to adduce evidence that M had once been charged with murder. M had been acquitted at trial. The Court of Appeal held that the trial judge had been right to rule that evidence of an unproven charge could not on its own be evidence of bad character.

9.9.4 Sections 101(1)(e) and 104: undermining the co-defendant's defence

Section 104 provides that:

> (1) *Evidence which is relevant to the question whether the defendant has a propensity to be untruthful is admissible on that basis under section 101(1)(e) only if the nature or conduct of his defence is such as to undermine the co-defendant's defence.*

9.9.5 Section 104: propensity to be untruthful in the context of a cut-throat defence

In *R v Hanson* [2005] 2 Cr App R 21, it was held that prosecution evidence of the defendant's propensity to be untruthful is restricted to evidence of misconduct involving the making of false statements or the giving of false evidence (see **9.8.4**). However, where a co-defendant seeks to adduce evidence of a defendant's propensity to untruthfulness under s 101(1)(e) that restriction does not apply and the concept of propensity to be untruthful is approached more broadly. In *R v Lawson* [2007] 1 Cr App R 11, CA, K and L were both charged with manslaughter. It was alleged that they had encouraged a third man, who had pleaded guilty, to push a man into a lake. At trial L gave evidence that K had made an incriminating remark, which K denied. This evidence undermined K's defence. The judge ruled that, as a result, evidence of L's previous conviction for unlawful wounding was admissible in relation to his truthfulness. L appealed on the grounds that the conviction had been wrongly admitted as relevant to untruthfulness. It was held that previous convictions are capable of having substantial probative value in relation to the credibility of a defendant when he has given evidence that undermines the defence of a co-accused even where the convictions do not involve the making of false statements or the giving of false evidence. According to Hughes LJ at [34]:

> the degree of caution that is applied to a Crown application against a defendant who is on trial when considering relevance or discretion to exclude should not be applied when what is at stake is a defendant's right to deploy relevant material to defend himself against a criminal charge. A defendant who is defending himself against the evidence of a person whose history of criminal behaviour or other misconduct is such as to be capable of showing him to be unscrupulous and/or otherwise unreliable should be permitted to present that history before the jury for its evaluation of the evidence of the witness. Such suggested unreliability may be capable of being shown by conduct that does not involve an offence of untruthfulness; it may be capable of being shown by widely differing conduct, ranging from large-scale drug or people-trafficking via housebreaking to criminal violence. Whether in a particular case it is in fact capable of having substantive probative value in relation to the witness's reliability is for the trial judge to determine on all the facts of the case.

9.9.6 Section 101(1)(e) and discretion to exclude

There is no power under the 2003 Act or at common law to exclude evidence once it has been shown to satisfy the test in s 101(1)(e), even if it is prejudicial to a co-defendant (see *R v Lawson* [2007] 1 Cr App R 178; *R v Musone* [2007] 1 WLR 2467). This follows a long-standing principle of English law that the defendant should not be fettered in putting forward his defence to a criminal charge, but should be free to adduce any relevant evidence (see, eg, *Lobban v R* [1995] 1 WLR 877). *Musone* also confirmed that there was no power to exclude evidence under s 101(1)(e) on the grounds that its admission would infringe the defendant's right to a fair trial under Article 6 of the ECHR. However, where the co-defendant has breached the notice requirements of Crim PR, r 35 (now Part 21), then the court does have a power to exclude evidence of the defendant's bad character which the co-defendant proposes to adduce. In *Musone*, ten days into the trial and without giving notice as required by r 35.5 (now r 21.4), the co-defendant sought to adduce the defendant's alleged confession that he had been responsible for a murder 12 years before the trial for the instant offence. It was held that this had been a deliberate attempt to ambush the defendant and excluded the evidence. Such an ambush is inappropriate and, in *R v Ramirez* [2009] EWCA Crim 1721, Richards LJ stressed that 'the giving of bad character evidence by one defendant in relation to a co-defendant without prior notice or application could well lead to the discharge of the jury and to a retrial, with the possibility of severe sanctions in the form at least of wasted costs orders against any legal representative found to have been involved in the deliberate manipulation of the rules leading to such a consequence'.

9.10 Evidence to correct a false impression (s 101(1)(f))

Section 101(1)(f) provides:

> *(1) In criminal proceedings evidence of the defendant's bad character is admissible if but only if—*
>
> ...
>
> *(f) it is evidence to correct a false impression given by the defendant.*

Only the prosecution can adduce evidence under s 101(1)(f) to correct a false impression (s 105(7)). See *R v Assani* [2008] EWCA Crim 2563.

9.10.1 Giving a false impression

Section 101(1)(f) is supplemented by s 105, which provides:

> *(1) For the purposes of section 101(1)(f)—*
>
> *(a) the defendant gives a false impression if he is responsible for the making of an express or implied assertion which is apt to give the court or jury a false or misleading impression about the defendant;*
>
> ...
>
> *(4) Where it appears to the court that a defendant, by means of his conduct (other than the giving of evidence) in the proceedings, is seeking to give the court or jury an impression about himself that is false or misleading, the court may if it appears just to do so treat the defendant as being responsible for the making of an assertion which is apt to give that impression.*
>
> *(5) In subsection (4) 'conduct' includes appearance or dress.*

The question whether the defendant has given a '*false impression*' about himself, within s 105(1)(a), is fact specific (*R v Renda* [2006] 1 Cr App R 24).

9.10.1.1 Express and implied assertions creating a false impression

A false impression may be asserted expressly or impliedly. Implied assertions would include the conduct of the defendant, including his appearance or dress (s 105(4), (5)).

A good example of an express assertion is *R v Spartley* [2007] EWCA Crim 1789. The defendant, who was charged with possessing cannabis with intent to supply, said in his police interview that he had never been in trouble with the police in the past. The prosecution successfully applied to adduce a record of the defendant's interview with Dutch police seven years previously, in which the defendant had admitted smuggling cannabis from Holland to Spain.

9.10.1.2 Determining whether the impression given is false

A simple denial of the offence or offences alleged cannot, for the purposes of s 101(1)(f), be treated as a false impression given by the defendant (*R v Weir* [2006] 1 Cr App R 19, CA; *R v D* [2011] EWCA Crim 1474).

Unspecific and insubstantial remarks that do not amount to factual assertions will also not be treated as creating a false impression. In *R v Obva* [2015] EWCA Crim 725, the Court of Appeal quashed a conviction for assault occasioning actual bodily harm. The vague comment that the defendant was 'quite a friendly person' did not amount to an assertion that she was not the sort of person to get into fights.

Whether a false impression has been created is ultimately a matter for the judge. As long as the judge applies the correct principles and takes into account all relevant matters the Court of Appeal will not interfere with the judge's decision unless the judge was clearly wrong (*R v McLeod* [2017] EWCA Crim 800).

9.10.1.3 When the defendant is responsible for an assertion

Section 105 provides:

> ...
>
> *(2) A defendant is treated as being responsible for the making of an assertion if—*
>
> *(a) the assertion is made by the defendant in the proceedings (whether or not in evidence given by him),*
>
> *(b) the assertion was made by the defendant—*
>
> *(i) on being questioned under caution, before charge, about the offence with which he is charged, or*
>
> *(ii) on being charged with the offence or officially informed that he might be prosecuted for it, and evidence of the assertion is given in the proceedings,*
>
> *(c) the assertion is made by a witness called by the defendant,*
>
> *(d) the assertion is made by any witness in cross-examination in response to a question asked by the defendant that is intended to elicit it, or is likely to do so, or*
>
> *(e) the assertion was made by any person out of court, and the defendant adduces evidence of it in the proceedings.*
>
> *(3) A defendant who would otherwise be treated as responsible for the making of an assertion shall not be so treated if, or to the extent that, he withdraws it or disassociates himself from it.*

Therefore, a defendant is treated as being responsible for the making of an assertion where the assertion is made:

- by the defendant in the proceedings (whether or not in evidence given by him);
- by the defendant on being questioned under caution, before charge, about the offence with which he is charged and evidence of the assertion is given in the proceedings;
- by the defendant on being charged with the offence or officially informed that he might be prosecuted for it and evidence of the assertion is given in the proceedings;
- by a witness called by the defendant;
- by a witness in cross-examination in response to a question asked by the defendant that is intended to elicit it, or is likely to do so; or
- by a person out of court, and the defendant adduces evidence of it in the proceedings.

An assertion may be deemed to have been made by the defendant in the proceedings in evidence if it comes from his legal representative acting on his instructions and may also be made by his conduct or behaviour. A defendant will not be treated as being responsible for the making of an assertion if he withdraws it or disassociates himself from it (s 105(3)). A concession extracted in cross-examination that a defendant was not telling the truth in his examination-in-chief would not normally amount to a withdrawal or disassociation from the original assertion for the purposes of s 105(3) (*R v Renda* [2006] 1 Cr App R 24).

9.10.2 Correcting a false impression

Section 105 provides:

> (1) *For the purposes of section 101(1)(f)—*
>
> …
>
> (b) *evidence to correct such an impression is evidence which has probative value in correcting it.*
>
> …
>
> (6) *Evidence is admissible under section 101(1)(f) only if it goes no further than is necessary to correct the false impression.*

Thus, in order to be admissible, evidence of the defendant's bad character must, logically, be capable of rebutting the false impression. The question of whether there is evidence which may properly serve to correct a false impression within s 105(1)(b) is fact specific (*R v Renda* [2006] 1 Cr App R 24). In *R v Renda* the defendant, who was charged with robbery, sought to enhance his credibility by asserting that he had been a serving soldier in the army who had, while so employed, sustained a serious head injury. He said that at the date of his arrest he was in regular employment as a security guard. The Court of Appeal held that the prosecution had properly been permitted to cross-examine the defendant on the fact that his head injury was sustained while on holiday, that he was only temporarily employed as a security guard (and was unemployed at the time of trial), that he had previously been charged with assault occasioning actual bodily harm, and that although he was found unfit to plead, he was also found by the jury to have committed the physical act of assault.

Whether a false impression has been given will require an examination of the details and force of what has been said and, if a false impression has been given, evidence of bad character will only be admitted if it has a probative value in correcting the impression. In *R v Assani* [2008] EWCA Crim 2563, the question arose as to whether a false impression had been given as a result of evidence elicited from a prosecution witness by the defendant's counsel in cross-examination. The defendant was alleged to have stabbed another man at a party and, in cross-examination, evidence was given by the prosecution witness that the defendant was not the sort of man who would turn around and stab someone. The Court of Appeal held that the evidence from the prosecution witness had not created a false impression but that, if it had, evidence that the defendant had hit a man in the face with a shovel 'out of the blue' 14 years previously did not have probative value in correcting it.

Similarly, in *R v Stokes* [2015] EWCA Crim 1911, the Court of Appeal held that the defendant's comments about how he came to suggest a site for the cultivation of cannabis did not create a false impression that the defendant was naive about drugs. In fact, the opposite was true. In any event, convictions which were over 12 years old, when the defendant was 17, which involved simple possession of two small wraps of class A drugs, obviously for personal use only, for which the appellant received a fine, could not come 'even close to displacing a suggestion of naivety when it came to sophisticated cannabis cultivation'.

9.10.3 Issues to which evidence adduced under s 101(1)(f) is relevant

Where the prosecution adduces evidence of the defendant's bad character under s 101(1)(f) it will be relevant, in principle, to both the defendant's credibility and the facts in issue. For example, where a defendant charged with theft asserts in evidence that he is an honest man, he thereby gives the impression that he is to be believed on oath and is unlikely to have committed the offence. If the prosecution adduces evidence of his previous convictions to correct that false impression, the previous convictions may be relevant and admissible both in relation to his guilt and his credibility.

9.10.4 Section 101(1)(f) and discretion to exclude

9.10.4.1 Section 78 of the Police and Criminal Evidence Act 1984

Evidence of bad character to correct a false impression on which the prosecution proposes to rely may be excluded under PACE 1984, s 78 (see **1.6.2.2**) where the admission of the evidence would have such an adverse effect on the fairness of the proceedings that the court ought not to admit it. While there has been some doubt as to whether PACE 1984, s 78 applies to the bad character provisions of the CJA 2003, in *R v Weir* [2006] 1 Cr App R 19, the Court of Appeal said that there was no reason to doubt that PACE 1984, s 78 applied to evidence adduced under s 101(1)(f). A similar view was expressed in *R v Highton* [2006] 1 Cr App R 7, although the court acknowledged that it had not had the benefit of hearing full argument on the point. In *R v O'Dowd* [2009] 2 Cr App R 280, the Court of Appeal went further, stating that the courts should consider s 78 where s 101(3) did not apply (see also *R v Chrysostomou* [2010] EWCA Crim 1403, mentioned earlier at **9.8.6.1**).

9.10.4.2 The common law discretion

Such evidence may also be excluded by the court under its common law discretion where its prejudicial effect would outweigh its probative value (*R v Sang* [1980] AC 402; see **1.6.2.1**).

9.10.4.3 The Criminal Procedure Rules 2015

As stated previously, in *R v Musone* [2007] 1 WLR 2467, CA, it was held that Crim PR 2005, r 35, which relates to bad character evidence, confers power on a court to exclude evidence in circumstances in which there had been a breach of the prescribed notice requirements (see further **9.16**). See also *R v Jarvis* [2008] Crim LR 632. This principle will continue to apply with the new version in Part 21 of the Crim PR 2015.

9.11 A defendant's attack on the character of another person (s 101(1)(g))

Section 101(1)(g) provides:

> *(1) In criminal proceedings evidence of the defendant's bad character is admissible if, but only if—*
>
> ...
>
> *(g) the defendant has made an attack on another person's character.*

Only the prosecution can admit evidence of the defendant's bad character under this provision (s 106(3)). See *R v Assani* [2008] EWCA Crim 2563.

9.11.1 Making an attack on another person's character

Section 101(1)(g) is supplemented by s 106, which provides:

> *(1) For the purposes of section 101(1)(g) a defendant makes an attack on another person's character if—*
>
> *(a) he adduces evidence attacking the other person's character,*
>
> *(b) he ... asks questions in cross-examination that are intended to elicit such evidence or are likely to do so, or*
>
> *(c) evidence is given of an imputation about the other person made by the defendant—*

(i) on being questioned under caution, before charge, about the offence with which he is charged, or

(ii) on being charged with the offence or officially informed that he might be prosecuted for it.

(2) In subsection (1) 'evidence attacking the other person's character' means evidence to the effect that the other person—

(a) has committed an offence (whether a different offence from the one with which the defendant is charged or the same one), or

(b) has behaved, or is disposed to behave, in a reprehensible way; and 'imputation about another person' means an assertion to that effect.

A defendant will be deemed to have made an attack on another person's character in the four situations set out in s 106:

- where he adduces evidence attacking another person's character;
- where he asks questions in cross-examination that are intended to elicit such evidence or are likely to do so;
- where evidence is given of an imputation about the other person made by the defendant on being questioned under caution, before charge, about the offence with which he is charged; or
- where evidence is given of an imputation about the other person made by the defendant on being charged with the offence or officially informed that he might be prosecuted for it.

In *R v Nelson* [2007] Crim LR 709, it was held that it would be improper for the prosecution to adduce comments made by the defendant in interview attacking another's character that were not otherwise relevant to the issues in the case simply to provide a basis for satisfying s 101(1)(g) and getting the defendant's previous convictions put in evidence.

Under s 106(2), evidence attacking the other person's character means evidence to the effect that that person:

- has committed an offence; or
- has behaved, or is disposed to behave, in a reprehensible way.

An imputation about the other person means an assertion to that effect.

There is no requirement that the person on whom the attack is made is a witness in the proceedings. It will be noted that there are certain similarities between the circumstances in which a defendant will be deemed to have attacked another person's character under s 106 and those where he will be held responsible for giving a false impression under s 105. While s 106 does not expressly refer to a defendant being responsible for an attack made by a defence witness, such evidence would seem to be included as it would be evidence adduced by the defendant. It is unclear whether evidence adduced would extend to cover answers given in cross-examination by the prosecution. However, there are also marked differences between s 105 and s 106. In particular, there is no provision under s 106 which allows the defendant to withdraw or disassociate himself from an attack.

9.11.2 Attacks 'to do with' the alleged facts of the offence

Whilst the definition in s 106(2) is similar to the definition of 'bad character' under s 98 of the Act, evidence of bad character as defined under s 98 does not include evidence that has to do with the alleged facts of the offence or evidence of misconduct in connection with the investigation or prosecution of the offence. Section 106(2) does not limit attacks on character to matters outside of the alleged facts of the offence. This means that where the defendant alleges that another person committed the offence or that police have behaved improperly, for example by fabricating evidence, he will be deemed to have attacked another person's character even though it was a necessary part of his defence. In the case of *R v Lamaletie* [2008] EWCA Crim 314, the defence to assault was that the complainant was the aggressor who had started the fight. Although this was not a gratuitous attack on the character of the complainant and integral to the defence it was nevertheless an attack for the purposes of s 106(2) and s 101(1)(g) (see also *R v Matthews* [2013] EWCA Crim 2238). Similarly, accusing a complainant of deliberately concocting an allegation will amount to an attack because 'it is one thing for the applicant to deny that he had acted as alleged, but it is another thing entirely to suggest that the whole allegation against him is a deliberate and elaborate concoction on the part of the principal witness' (*R v Pedley* [2014] EWCA Crim 848; see also *R v Fitzgerald* [2017] EWCA Crim 556).

9.11.3 Relevant to credibility

Section 101(1)(g) is intended to assist the jury in determining whether the attack made by the defendant should be believed (*R v Lamaletie* [2008] EWCA Crim 314). In *R v Clarke* [2011] EWCA Crim 939, the Court of Appeal held that in light of this purpose bad character evidence admitted as to whether the defendant's attack should be believed may go beyond previous convictions involving untruthfulness because 'ordinary human experience is that a person of bad character's word may be worth less than that of those who have led exemplary lives' (*R v Singh* [2007] EWCA Crim 2140). In *R v Singh*, that evidence related to convictions for disorder, assaults on policemen, harassment, criminal damage, and driving with excess alcohol.

9.11.4 Section 101(1)(g) and discretion to exclude

9.11.4.1 Section 101(3) of the Criminal Justice Act 2003

Section 101(3) and (4) provide that:

...

> (3) *The court must not admit evidence under subsection ... 1(g) if, on an application by the defendant to exclude it, it appears to the court that the admission of the evidence would have such an adverse effect on the fairness of the proceedings that the court ought not to admit it.*
>
> (4) *On an application to exclude evidence under subsection (3) the court must have regard, in particular, to the length of time between the matters to which that evidence relates and the matters which form the subject of the offence charged.*

Where the prosecution proposes to adduce evidence of the defendant's misconduct under s 101(1)(g) the court must not do so where it appears to the court that the admission of the evidence would have such an adverse effect on the fairness of the proceedings that the court ought not to admit it. The wording of this provision is very similar to PACE 1984, s 78 (see **1.6.2.2**). The key difference is that it is expressed in mandatory ('must not admit') rather than discretionary ('may refuse to allow') terms. It is submitted that the common law discretion to exclude evidence where its prejudicial effect outweighs its probative value will also apply to evidence the prosecution proposes to adduce under s 101(1)(g).

9.11.4.1.1 Attacks necessary to the defence

Fairness does not dictate that previous convictions should be excluded from evidence merely because the attack was necessary to the defence (*R v Fitzgerald* [2017] EWCA Crim 556; *R v Pedley* [2014] EWCA Crim 848).

9.11.4.1.2 *Historic offences*

The purpose of adducing evidence of the defendant's character under s 101(1)(g) is to assist the jury in determining the credibility of their attack on the character of another. Therefore, the bad character evidence must fairly reflect the defendant's character at the time of trial. This may not be the case with historic offences (*R v Clarke* [2011] EWCA Crim 939, although on the facts of that case offences dating back until 1977 were admissible).

It may also be unfair to rely upon old convictions adduced to as to credibility which demonstrate a propensity to commit the offence (*R v Clarke*).

9.11.4.1.3 *Details of previous misconduct*

In *R v Lamaletie* [2008] EWCA Crim 314, the defendant, whose bad character had been admitted at trial under s 101(1)(g), appealed on the ground that the jury would not have been assisted on the question of his credibility by simply hearing a list of his previous convictions. It was held that a mere list of convictions was sufficient for the purposes of s 101(1)(g) of the 2003 Act, because what was relevant was 'character' in a broad general sense; detail was unnecessary and potentially distracting (see also *R v Clarke* [2011] EWCA Crim 939, in which a list of previous convictions was admissible where details of the offences were unavailable).

9.11.4.1.4 *Attacks on the character of a non-witness*

In *R v Nelson* [2007] Crim LR 709, it was held that it would be unusual for evidence of a defendant's bad character to be admitted when the only basis for so doing was an attack on the character of a non-witness who is also a non-victim. The fairness of the proceedings would normally be materially damaged by so doing.

9.11.4.2 Section 78 of the Police and Criminal Evidence Act 1984

The discretion under PACE 1984, s 78 (see **1.6.2.2**) will also apply in principle to bad character on which the prosecution proposes to rely under this gateway, but in practice it will be otiose because of the overlap with s 101(3) (see *R v Chrysostomou* [2010] EWCA Crim 1403, mentioned earlier at **9.8.6.1**).

9.11.4.3 The common law discretion

Such evidence may also be excluded by the court under its common law discretion where its prejudicial effect would outweigh its probative value (*R v Sang* [1980] AC 402; see **1.6.2.1**).

9.11.4.4 The Criminal Procedure Rules 2015

In *R v Musone* [2007] 1 WLR 2467, CA, it was held that Crim PR 2005, r 35, which relates to bad character evidence, confers power on a court to exclude evidence in circumstances in which there had been a breach of the prescribed notice requirements (see further **9.16**). See also *R v Jarvis* [2008] Crim LR 632. This principle will continue to apply in respect of breaches of the notice requirements in the new version of r 35 contained in Part 21 of the Crim PR 2015.

9.12 Stopping the case where evidence is contaminated

Section 107 provides:

> (1) *If on a defendant's trial before a judge and jury for an offence—*

(a) evidence of his bad character has been admitted under any of paragraphs (c) to (g) of section 101(1), and

(b) the court is satisfied at any time after the close of the case for the prosecution that—

(i) the evidence is contaminated, and

(ii) the contamination is such that, considering the importance of the evidence to the case against the defendant, his conviction of the offence would be unsafe, the court must either direct the jury to acquit the defendant of the offence or, if it considers that there ought to be a retrial, discharge the jury.

(2) Where—

(a) a jury is directed under subsection (1) to acquit a defendant of an offence, and

(b) the circumstances are such that, apart from this subsection, the defendant could if acquitted of that offence be found guilty of another offence, the defendant may not be found guilty of that other offence if the court is satisfied as mentioned in subsection (1)(b) in respect of it.

...

(4) This section does not prejudice any other power a court may have to direct a jury to acquit a person of the offence or to discharge a jury.

(5) For the purposes of this section a person's evidence is contaminated where—

(a) as a result of an agreement or understanding between the person and one or more others, or

(b) as a result of the person being aware of anything alleged by one or more others whose evidence may be, or has been, given in the proceedings, the evidence is false or misleading in any respect, or is different from what it would otherwise have been.

Section 107 confers on the judge a power to direct the jury to acquit the defendant or, if it considers there ought to be a retrial, to discharge the jury where the evidence of the defendant's bad character that has been adduced through gateways s 101(1)(c)–(g) is so 'contaminated' that it would render any conviction unsafe (s 107(1)). In such circumstances, the defendant cannot be convicted of a lesser alternative offence (s 107(2)).

Character evidence is contaminated if it is false or misleading either because of deliberate contamination or innocent contamination (*R v C* [2006] EWCA Crim 1079). Deliberate contamination takes the form of an understanding or agreement between witnesses in the proceedings and another person (s 107(5)(a)). Innocent contamination or unconscious influence may arise when a witness is aware of the allegations of other witnesses in the proceedings (s 107(5)(b)). For example, in *R v Lamb* [2007] EWCA Crim 1766 a discussion on a school trip between two girls resulted in each complaining to the police about sexual assault by a teacher. The Court of Appeal found that the issue of innocent contamination should have been left clearly to the jury.

As demonstrated by *R v Lamb*, applications under s 107 arise primarily where different counts in the same proceedings could be treated as cross-admissible (see **9.8.3.2.1**). A Further example includes *R v BR* [2014] EWCA Crim 1311, in which it was argued that the evidence of the three complainants was contaminated to such an extent that conviction would be unsafe.

9.12.1 Exercising judgment

In *R v C* [2006] EWCA Crim 1079, where there were two separate counts on the indictment alleging sexual assaults on two different children, the Court of Appeal noted that, unusually, s 107 requires a judge to stray into the traditional function of the jury and make findings of fact, in particular as to whether the 'evidence of a witness is false, or misleading, or different from what it would have been if it had not been contaminated'. Therefore, 'it would normally be sensible' for the judge to postpone a decision on contamination 'until the suggested contaminated evidence has been examined at trial. The judge will therefore 'not then be acting on his judgment about anticipated evidence, but making a decision based on the evidence itself'. If the judge does decide that there has been important contamination of the evidence, 'what then follows is not a matter of discretion'. The trial must be stopped and either the jury must be discharged or an acquittal must be directed.

9.13 Offences committed when the defendant was a child

Section 108 of the Act provides:

...

(2) In proceedings for an offence committed or alleged to have been committed by the defendant when aged 21 or over, evidence of his conviction for an offence when under the age of 14 is not admissible unless—

(a) both of the offences are triable only on indictment, and

(b) the court is satisfied that the interests of justice require the evidence to be admissible.

(3) Subsection (2) applies in addition to section 101.

Offences committed by the defendant as a child may include offences committed outside of England and Wales. The conduct must also constitute an offence triable only on indictment in England and Wales (s 108(2A) and (2B)).

9.14 Assumption of truth

Section 109 provides that:

(1) Subject to subsection (2), a reference in this Chapter to the relevance or probative value of evidence is a reference to its relevance or probative value on the assumption that it is true.

(2) In assessing the relevance or probative value of an item of evidence for any purpose of this Chapter, a court need not assume that the evidence is true if it appears, on the basis of any material before the court (including any evidence it decides to hear on the matter), that no court or jury could reasonably find it to be true.

Under s 109, when determining the admissibility of evidence, the judge must assess the relevance or probative value of evidence on the assumption that it is true. If the evidence takes the form of a previous conviction this provision is uncontroversial. However, where the evidence takes the form of unproven allegations of misconduct, or of allegations of misconduct of which the defendant had previously been acquitted, the court must still accept the evidence as being true. In the latter case, this means that the section creates the bizarre presumption that a person must be treated as being guilty of an offence of which he has been acquitted.

It has been held that the mere making of an allegation is capable of being 'evidence' for the purposes of s 109, at least in relation to s 101(1)(d) (*R v Edwards* [2006] 1 Cr App R 3, CA). Therefore, when a party proposes to adduce an allegation as evidence of misconduct, the court must accept it as being true for the purposes of determining its probative value and thus its admissibility. Similarly, in cross-admissibility cases where there is a risk of collusion and contamination in relation to allegations involving different complainants, the House of Lords in *R v H* [1995] 2 AC 596 held that save in exceptional cases, the court should approach the issue of *admissibility* on the basis that the allegations are true. If it becomes apparent that the admitted evidence could not be treated as free of collusion by any reasonable jury then the judge should direct the jury not to use the evidence against the defendant. If there has been important contamination of the evidence, the court must then invoke s 107 (see **9.12**).

9.15 The duty to give reasons

Section 110 provides:

> *(1) Where the court makes a relevant ruling—*
>
> *(a) it must state in open court (but in the absence of the jury, if there is one) its reasons for the ruling;*
>
> *(b) if it is a magistrates' court, it must cause the ruling and the reasons for it to be entered in the register of the court's proceedings.*
>
> *(2) In this section 'relevant ruling' means—*
>
> *(a) a ruling on whether an item of evidence is evidence of a person's bad character;*
>
> *(b) a ruling on whether an item of such evidence is admissible under section 100 or 101 (including a ruling on an application under section 101(3));*
>
> *(c) a ruling under section 107.*

9.16 Rules of procedure

Section 111 allows the creation of rules of court concerning the admission of the evidence of character. By s 111(2) and (3) these rules can (and in the case of the prosecution must) include requirements to serve notice of the intention to adduce evidence of bad character or to elicit such evidence through cross-examination. Section 111(4) provides for making rules concerning costs consequences of failure to comply with the notice requirements created under s 111(2) and (3).

As mentioned elsewhere in this text, the relevant rule for the admission of evidence of bad character is Crim PR, Part 21. The main provisions in relation to a defendant's bad character are as follows:

Content of application or notice

21.2.—*(1) A party who wants to introduce evidence of bad character must—*

> ...
>
> *(b) give notice under rule 21.4, where it is evidence of a defendant's bad character.*
>
> *(2) An application or notice must—*
>
> *(a) set out the facts of the misconduct on which that party relies,*
>
> *(b) explain how that party will prove those facts (whether by certificate of conviction, other official record, or other evidence), if another party disputes them, and*
>
> *(c) explain why the evidence is admissible.*

[Note. The Practice Direction sets out forms of application and notice for use in connection with rule ... 21.4
The fact that a person was convicted of an offence may be proved under—

> *(a) section 73 of the Police and Criminal Evidence Act 1984(2) (conviction in the United Kingdom or European Union); or*

(b) section 7 of the Evidence Act 1851(3) (conviction outside the United Kingdom).

See also sections 117 and 118 of the Criminal Justice Act 2003 (admissibility of evidence contained in business and other documents).

Under section 10 of the Criminal Justice Act 1967(4), a party may admit a matter of fact.]

Notice to introduce evidence of a defendant's bad character

***21.4.**—(1) This rule applies where a party wants to introduce evidence of a defendant's bad character.*

(2) That party must serve notice on—

(a) the court officer; and

(b) each other party.

(3) A prosecutor who wants to introduce such evidence must serve the notice not more than—

(a) 28 days after the defendant pleads not guilty, in a magistrates' court; or

(b) 14 days after the defendant pleads not guilty, in the Crown Court.

(4) A co-defendant who wants to introduce such evidence must serve the notice—

(a) as soon as reasonably practicable; and in any event

(b) not more than 14 days after the prosecutor discloses material on which the notice is based.

(5) A party who objects to the introduction of the evidence must—

(a) apply to the court to determine the objection;

(b) serve the application on—

(i) the court officer, and

(ii) each other party

not more than 14 days after service of the notice; and

(c) in the application explain, as applicable—

(i) which, if any, facts of the misconduct set out in the notice that party disputes,

(ii) what, if any, facts of the misconduct that party admits instead,

(iii) why the evidence is not admissible,

(iv) why it would be unfair to admit the evidence, and

(v) any other objection to the notice.

(6) The court—

(a) may determine an application—

(i) at a hearing, in public or in private, or

(ii) without a hearing;

(b) must not determine the application unless the party who served the notice—

(i) is present, or

(ii) has had a reasonable opportunity to respond;

(c) may adjourn the application; and

(d) may discharge or vary a determination where it can do so under—

(i) section 8B of the Magistrates' Courts Act 1980 (ruling at pre-trial hearing in a magistrates' court), or

(ii) section 9 of the Criminal Justice Act 1987, or section 31 or 40 of the Criminal Procedure and Investigations Act 1996 (ruling at preparatory or other pre-trial hearing in the Crown Court).

(7) A party entitled to receive a notice may waive that entitlement by so informing—

(a) the party who would have served it; and

(b) the court.

(8) A defendant who wants to introduce evidence of his or her own bad character must

(a) give notice, in writing or orally

(i) as soon as reasonably practicable, and in any event

(ii) before the evidence is introduced, either by the defendant or in reply to a question asked by the defendant of another party's witness in order to obtain that evidence; and

(b) in the Crown Court, at the same time give notice (in writing, or orally) of any direction about the defendant's character that the defendant wants the court to give the jury under rule 25.14 (Directions to the jury and taking the verdict).

[Note. The Practice Direction sets out a form of notice for use in connection with this rule.

See also rule 21.5 (reasons for decisions must be given in public).

If notice is not given as this rule requires, then under section 111(4) of the Criminal Justice Act 2003 the court may take the failure into account in exercising its powers to order costs]

Reasons for decisions

21.5. *The court must announce at a hearing in public (but in the absence of the jury, if there is one) the reasons for a decision—*

(a) to admit evidence as evidence of bad character, or to refuse to do so; or

(b) to direct an acquittal or a retrial under section 107 of the Criminal Justice Act 2003.

[Note. See section 110 of the Criminal Justice Act 2003]

Court's power to vary requirements under this Part

21.6.—*(1) The court may—*

(a) shorten or extend (even after it has expired) a time limit under this Part;

(b) allow an application or notice to be in a different form to one set out in the Practice Direction, or to be made or given orally;

(c) dispense with a requirement for notice to introduce evidence of a defendant's bad character.

(2) A party who wants an extension of time must—

(a) apply when serving the application or notice for which it is needed; and

(b) explain the delay.

In *R v Bovell* [2005] 2 Cr App R 27, it was held that it was necessary for all parties to have, in good time, the appropriate information in relation to previous convictions and other evidence of bad character. That could only be achieved if the rules in relation to the giving of notice were complied with. In *R v Hanson* [2005] 2 Cr App R 21, it was held that in complying with the notice requirements the prosecution should indicate whether it proposes simply to rely upon the fact of conviction or also upon the circumstances of it.

In *R (Robinson) v Sutton Coldfield Magistrates' Court* [2006] 2 Cr App R 13, the Court of Appeal stated that time limits under Crim PR, r 35 (now Crim PR, Part 21), for making an application to admit bad character must be observed. However, the court has a discretionary power to shorten a time limit or to extend it even after it has expired (r 35.8, now r 21.6). In the exercise of that discretion, the court will take account of all the relevant considerations, including the furtherance of the overriding objective of the Crim PR. Extending the time limit is not restricted to exceptional circumstances. The two principal considerations are the reason for the failure to comply with the rules and whether the opposing party was prejudiced by the failure. Failure to comply with the rules may result in the exclusion of the evidence (*R v Musone* [2007] 1 WLR 2467).

9.17 Handling stolen goods (Theft Act 1968, s 27)

Section 27(3) of the Theft Act 1968 provides:

> (3) *Where a person is being proceeded against for handling stolen goods (but not for any offence other than handling stolen goods), then at any stage in the proceedings, if evidence has been given of his having or arranging to have in his possession the goods the subject of the charge, or of his undertaking or assisting in, or arranging to undertake, or assist in, their retention, removal, disposal or realisation, the following evidence shall be admissible for the purposes of proving that he knew or believed the goods to be stolen goods—*
>
> (a) *evidence that he has had in his possession, or has undertaken or assisted in the retention, removal or disposal or realisation of, stolen goods from any theft taking place not earlier than 12 months before the offence charged; and*
>
> (b) *(provided that seven days' notice in writing has been given to him of the intention to prove the conviction) evidence that he has within the five years preceding the date of the offence charged been convicted of theft or of handling stolen goods.*

Section 27(3) allows proof of the defendant's previous convictions to prove that he knew or believed that the goods were stolen. It does not prove his dishonesty (*R v Duffas* (1994) 158 JP 224). The fact that the defendant disputes possession of the goods (or some of them) does not prevent the evidence being admitted under s 27(3) (*R v List* [1966] 1 WLR 9). However, where there are numerous charges, in some of which possession is in dispute and in some of which possession is admitted but knowledge disputed, the judge should consider whether to allow evidence of the previous convictions at all and, if it is allowed, should direct the jury that the previous convictions are only relevant to knowledge and not to any other issue in the case (*R v Wilkins* [1975] 2 All ER 734).

Where the evidence of the previous convictions is admitted, evidence of the details of previous convictions is not admissible (*R v Bradley* (1979) 70 Cr App R 200). However, in *R v Hacker* [1994] 1 WLR 1659, the House of Lords held that the proof of the previous convictions could include proof of such detail of the convictions as was included on the certificate of conviction under PACE 1984, s 73 (see **18.4.1**). The certificate of conviction would include details of the subject matter of the conviction, including the property that was handled. Previous convictions that would otherwise be admissible under s 27(3) can be excluded either at common law or under PACE 1984, s 78.

10

Character evidence: persons other than the defendant in criminal proceedings

10.1 Evidence of good character

The position with regard to evidence of the good character of a witness is the same in civil and in criminal proceedings. Thus, the rule in *R v Turner* [1975] QB 834 set out at **8.4.2.1** applies equally in criminal proceedings: a party calling a witness cannot call evidence to bolster his credibility.

10.2 Evidence of bad character

The admissibility of evidence of bad character is now governed by s 100 of the Criminal Justice Act (CJA) 2003. Section 100(1) provides:

> *(1) In criminal proceedings evidence of the bad character of a person other than the defendant is admissible if and only if—*
>
> *(a) it is important explanatory evidence,*
>
> *(b) it has substantial probative value in relation to a matter which—*
>
> *(i) is a matter in issue in the proceedings, and*
>
> *(ii) is of substantial importance in the context of the case as a whole, or*
>
> *(c) all parties to the proceedings agree to the evidence being admissible.*

The effect of s 100 is that evidence of bad character is generally inadmissible against a person other than a defendant in criminal proceedings unless it fits within the three situations provided for by s 100(1). It should also be noted that evidence under s 100(1)(a) or (b) also requires the leave of the trial judge before it will be admitted (s 100(4)).

Section 100 protects the character of prosecution witnesses, witnesses for the defence (other than the defendant) and any other persons regardless of whether they are witnesses in the case. Furthermore, the provision applies both to the party calling the witness and any party seeking to cross-examine the witness (although if a party wished to adduce the bad character of its own witness, it is submitted that this might be done by agreement using s 100(1)(c)).

Section 99(1) abolishes the common law rules governing the admissibility of evidence of bad character, as defined by s 98, with one exception, which is that evidence of the general reputation of a person proving their bad character is still admissible (s 99(2)). This means evidence of the general reputation of a person other than the defendant might be admitted at common law.

10.2.1 Meaning of 'bad character'

Section 112(1) provides that 'bad character' of persons other than the defendant has the same meaning as that provided for defendants in s 98 (see **9.4.1**). In the context of witnesses in criminal cases this means that evidence may be admissible of their previous convictions or misconduct or their disposition towards either of those things.

10.2.2 Important explanatory evidence

Section 100 provides:

> ...
>
> *(2) ... evidence is important explanatory evidence if—*
>
> *(a) without it, the court or jury would find it impossible or difficult properly to understand other evidence in the case, and*
>
> *(b) its value for understanding the case as a whole is substantial.*

The text of s 100(2) is identical to s 102, which defines important explanatory evidence admitted against a defendant (see **9.7**), and the same principles apply. An example is where an accomplice who has pleaded guilty to an offence wishes to give evidence for the prosecution. The accomplice has, by virtue of his guilty plea, become a person other than the defendant and it will clearly be necessary to adduce bad character evidence of his involvement in the commission of the offence to explain his first-hand knowledge of the matters that took place.

10.2.3 Substantial probative value to a matter in issue of substantial importance

Section 100(1)(b) allows proof of the bad character of a person where it has substantial probative value in relation to a matter of substantial importance in proceedings.

10.2.3.1 Matter in issue

'Matter in issue' includes both facts in issue and issues of credibility (*R v Weir* [2006] 1 Cr App R 19).

10.2.3.2 Substantial importance

Section 100(1)(b)(ii) has the effect of preventing gratuitous attacks, especially on witnesses.

Clearly, facts in issue are always matters in issue of substantial importance. Any allegation that a person committed the offence rather than the defendant, acted in such a way as to afford the defendant a defence such as self-defence or duress, or was in some other way complicit in either the commission of the offence or the false accusation of the defendant, will be admissible subject to the requirement of substantial probative value (see **10.2.3.3**).

In *R v Muhadeen* [2016] EWCA Crim 1, the defendant, who had been charged with wounding with intent, denied any involvement in a fight with the complainant. He denied seeing a knife at any stage. However, he suggested that if a knife was produced, it must have been produced by the complainant. He sought to introduce evidence of the complainant's four previous convictions for carrying knives or bladed articles. The Court of Appeal held that the trial judge had been correct to rule that the complainant's previous convictions for possession of a knife were not of substantial importance in the context of the case as a whole. The defence was really a denial of participation.

10.2.3.3 Substantial probative value

Evidence of bad character that has substantial importance to the proceedings as a whole will only be admissible if that evidence also has 'substantial probative value' (s 100(1)(b)(i)). The test for admissibility of evidence of bad character of a non-defendant is therefore one of 'enhanced relevance' (*R v King* [2015] EWCA Crim 1631). In assessing such relevance, a strict reading of the statutory requirements should be adopted (*R v Phillips* [2012] 1 Cr App R 332).

Section 100 provides:

...

(3) In assessing the probative value of evidence for the purposes of subsection (1)(b) the court must have regard to the following factors (and to any others it considers relevant)—

(a) the nature and number of the events, or other things, to which the evidence relates;

(b) when those events or things are alleged to have happened or existed;

(c) where—

(i) the evidence is evidence of a person's misconduct, and

(ii) it is suggested that the evidence has probative value by reason of similarity between that misconduct and other alleged misconduct, the nature and extent of the similarities and the dissimilarities between each of the alleged instances of misconduct;

(d) where—

(i) the evidence is evidence of a person's misconduct,

(ii) it is suggested that that person is also responsible for the misconduct charged, and

(iii) the identity of the person responsible for the misconduct charged is disputed, the extent to which the evidence shows or tends to show that the same person was responsible each time.

Section 100(3) then sets out factors that the court must have regard for when assessing the probative value of the evidence. As can be seen from the section, these factors include the extent to which the evidence of bad character is probative of the character of the witness by reason of the frequency of the misconduct (s 100(3)(a)), the pattern of misconduct (s 100(3)(a)), and the extent to which it is too old to be probative of the witness's current character (s 100(3)(b)). The court must have regard for these factors whatever the matter in issue is (ie relevance to a fact in issue or the credibility of the witness).

Section 100(3)(c) requires the court to consider the pattern of offending by providing that it must have regard for the propensity of the witness towards particular misconduct (whether it is the commission of the offence charged, or a tendency to lie, or a tendency to act aggressively and to cause fights). To some extent, the section reflects the common law approach to similar fact evidence. The party wishing to prove the bad character of the witness would seek to show a pattern of offending that suggests that such offending occurred on this occasion. Section 100(3)(d) deals with situations in which the defendant alleges that the witness committed the offence (s 100(3)(d)(ii)) and seeks to prove this by establishing that the offence was committed in the same way in which the offence was committed by the witness on previous occasions.

In determining the probative value of evidence, the court should treat the evidence as though it is true (s 109(1)) unless the evidence before it (possibly adduced at a *voir dire*) establishes that no reasonable tribunal could consider it true (s 109(2)). However, in *R v Bovell* [2005] 2 Cr App R 27, CA, it was doubted whether the mere making of an allegation was capable of being evidence within s 100(1) of the 2003 Act. If an allegation were admitted it would give rise to an excursion into 'satellite' matters, which was precisely the sort of excursion a trial judge should be discouraged from embarking upon. This was reinforced by the case of *Dizaei* [2013] 1 Cr App R 411, in which the Court of Appeal stated that the trial judge's consideration of what was substantial probative value might legitimately take account of the risk that satellite issues pose to the jury's grasp of the remainder of the evidence.

In *R v Braithwaite* [2010] 2 Cr App R 18, CA, it was held that allegations against a witness recorded in police Computer Record Information System (CRIS) reports would be unlikely to be admitted under s 100(1)(b) because their evidential status was hearsay. It would be rare for a judge to decide that such evidence would have the required probative value. The court noted that the fact that complainants had not been prepared to support their allegations stripped the police reports of a great deal of probative value.

10.2.3.3.1 Credibility

In *R v Stephenson* [2006] EWCA Crim 2325, the Court of Appeal, distinguishing *R v Hanson* on the basis that it applied to the admissibility of the bad character of a *defendant*, held that previous convictions may have substantial probative value in relation to the credibility of a *non-defendant* under s 100 even if they do not involve the making of false statements or the giving of false evidence. The question for the court is 'whether the evidence of [misconduct] is sufficiently persuasive to be worthy of consideration by a fair-minded tribunal upon the issue of the witness's creditworthiness' (*R v Brewster* [2010] EWCA Crim 1194). In *Brewster*, the Court of Appeal held that the judge had been wrong to prevent the accused, during his trial for kidnapping and theft over a drugs debt, from cross-examining on a witness's convictions for dwelling burglary and theft, manslaughter and possession of drugs with intent to supply, and theft by shoplifting. Although some of the convictions were old and on their own would not have been admissible, they were admissible with the other convictions to enable the accused to assert that, together, the convictions provided a more complete picture of the creditworthiness of the witness.

The same broad principle as to evidence capable of relevance as to credibility applies to both prosecution and defence witnesses: *R v Renda* [2006] 1 Cr App R 24, CA. In *Osborne*, one of the cases heard in the *Renda* appeal, the Crown had been permitted at trial to put to a defence witness his previous conviction for a single offence of serious violence, which had resulted in a two-year sentence of imprisonment. The defendant was charged with robbery committed at a public house. His defence was that the allegation was invented by the licensee, to cover deficiencies in his till and other irregularities in his conduct of the public house. The defence witness in question had given evidence to support the suggestion that the licensee was guilty of such irregularities. The Court of Appeal held that the evidence of the conviction fell within s 100. Without knowing of the witness's character, the jury would have been deprived of important evidence of substantial probative value in relation to the issue of the credibility of his evidence on the vital question whether the licensee had fabricated his complaint, or whether in truth he was rightly to be regarded as a victim.

A more restrictive approach to the admissibility of evidence of a witness's bad character in relation to the witness's credibility was taken in *R v Garnham* [2008] EWCA Crim 266. In *Garnham*, the Court of Appeal approved the trial judge's decision that the defendant, on trial for rape, should not be permitted to cross-examine the complainant on her numerous previous convictions for theft. The trial judge had decided (consistent with the reasoning in *Hanson*) that offences of dishonesty did not establish a propensity to be untruthful and that the complainant's previous convictions for theft did not have a substantial probative value on the question of her credibility. It is possible that a more restrictive approach was taken in *Garnham* because of the need to protect complainants in cases of rape, who have historically been subject to disproportionate and unfair attacks on their credibility.

A clear-cut example of credibility having substantial probative value in relation to an important matter in issue in the case is *R v Accamo* [2017] EWCA Crim 751. In that case, the defendant was identified by a witness. At the time of trial, it was thought that the witness had no previous convictions. However, it later emerged that he did have a conviction for possession of articles for use in fraud. He had also lied to police in a prepared statement about knowledge of the fraudulent equipment. In a case which effectively turned on one man's word against another, disclosure of the conviction to the jury would have cured any false impression they might have had and ensured in effect a level playing field, and so any application under s 100 would have been highly likely to succeed had the matter been known at the time of trial. Therefore, the Court of Appeal ruled that the conviction was unsafe.

10.2.3.3.2 Other important matters in issue

A recent example of an attempt to admit evidence under s 100 as having substantial probative value in relation to an important matter in issue can be seen in the case of *R v Edwards* [2018] EWCA Crim 424, where the defendant was charged with the manslaughter of H outside of a bar. The defence was that that H was being aggressive and that the defendant had used no more than reasonable force in seeking to defend a friend. H had two previous convictions. The first conviction was for GBH with intent when H was 14. The second was for battery around a year prior to the incident with which the defendant was charged. The defence sought to admit H's convictions to show that H would have had aggressive intent on the evening in question. The Court of Appeal held it was unlikely that the conviction for GBH with intent when a person was 14 could be said to be capable of showing a propensity to engage in street violence 11 years later. Even if the two convictions for violence taken together may have been regarded as showing a propensity to aggression, the CCTV evidence in the case was sufficiently clear to provide an 'obvious inference' that H had demonstrated an aggressive intent just moments before the defendant reacted. The question for the jury was simply whether, as far as the defendant was concerned, H still presented a threat in the seconds afterwards. It was therefore difficult to see how the previous convictions would have had substantial probative value in helping to answer that question.

10.2.4 Agreement of the parties

Section 100(1)(c) permits the admission of evidence of the bad character of a witness where *all* parties agree. Therefore, in a case where there was more than one defendant, all defendants would have to agree to the admission of the evidence in addition to the prosecution.

10.2.5 Requirement of leave

Section 100(4) provides that save when the parties agree to admit the evidence of bad character under s 101(1)(c), such evidence must not be admitted without leave of the court. The purpose of the leave requirement is to ensure that the judge acts as a check 'to eliminate kite-flying and innuendo against the character of a witness in favour of a concentration on the real issues in the case' (*R v Muhadeen* [2016] EWCA Crim 1, citing with approval Pitchford LJ in *Miller* [2010] 2 Cr App R 19).

10.2.6 Rules of procedure

Section 111 allows the creation of rules of court concerning the admission of the evidence of character. By s 111(2) and (3) these rules can (and in the case of the prosecution must) include requirements to serve notice of the intention to adduce evidence or cross-examine concerning bad character and any exceptions to those requirements. Section

111(4) provides for making rules concerning costs consequences of failure to comply with the notice requirements created under s 111(2) and (3).

The complete rules are set out in Crim PR 2015, Part 21. The relevant provisions are as follows:

Content of application or notice

***21.2.**—(1) A party who wants to introduce evidence of bad character must—*

(a) make an application under rule 21.3, where it is evidence of a non-defendant's bad character;

...

and

(2) An application or notice must—

(a) set out the facts of the misconduct on which that party relies,

(b) explain how that party will prove those facts (whether by certificate of conviction, other official record, or other evidence), if another party disputes them, and

(c) explain why the evidence is admissible.

[Note. The Practice Direction sets out forms of application and notice for use in connection with rules 21.3 [...].

The fact that a person was convicted of an offence may be proved under—

(a) section 73 of the Police and Criminal Evidence Act 1984(1) (conviction in the United Kingdom or European Union); or

(b) section 7 of the Evidence Act 1851(2) (conviction outside the United Kingdom).

See also sections 117 and 118 of the Criminal Justice Act 2003 (admissibility of evidence contained in business and other documents).

Under section 10 of the Criminal Justice Act 1967(3), a party may admit a matter of fact.]

Application to introduce evidence of a non-defendant's bad character

***21.3.**—(1) This rule applies where a party wants to introduce evidence of the bad character of a person other than the defendant.*

(2) That party must serve an application to do so on—

(a) the court officer; and

(b) each other party.

(3) The applicant must serve the application—

(a) as soon as reasonably practicable; and in any event

(b) not more than 14 days after the prosecutor discloses material on which the application is based (if the prosecutor is not the applicant).

(4) A party who objects to the introduction of the evidence must—

(a) serve notice on—

(i) the court officer, and

(ii) each other party

not more than 14 days after service of the application; and

(b) in the notice explain, as applicable—

(i) which, if any, facts of the misconduct set out in the application that party disputes,

(ii) what, if any, facts of the misconduct that party admits instead,

(iii) why the evidence is not admissible, and

(iv) any other objection to the application.

(5) The court—

(a) may determine an application—

(i) at a hearing, in public or in private, or

(ii) without a hearing;

(b) must not determine the application unless each party other than the applicant—

(i) is present, or

(ii) has had at least 14 days in which to serve a notice of objection;

(c) may adjourn the application; and

(d) may discharge or vary a determination where it can do so under—

(i) section 8B of the Magistrates' Courts Act 1980 (ruling at pre-trial hearing in a magistrates' court), or

(ii) section 9 of the Criminal Justice Act 1987, or section 31 or 40 of the Criminal Procedure and Investigations Act 1996 (ruling at preparatory or other pre-trial hearing in the Crown Court).

[...]

Reasons for decisions

21.5. *The court must announce at a hearing in public (but in the absence of the jury, if there is one) the reasons for a decision—*

(a) to admit evidence as evidence of bad character, or to refuse to do so; [...]

10.3 Criminal Justice Act 2003, s 100 and Youth Justice and Criminal Evidence Act 1999, s 41

There is a general prohibition on questioning or evidence relating to a complainant's sexual behaviour at the trial for a sexual offence which is imposed by s 41 of the Youth Justice and Criminal Evidence Act 1999 (YJCEA 1999) (see **7.9**). The question arises as to the relationship between s 41 of the 1999 Act and s 100 of the CJA 2003.

Section 100 of the CJA 2003 governs the admissibility of evidence of the bad character of persons other than the defendant. Section 98 of that Act defines evidence of bad character as evidence of, or of a disposition towards, misconduct on his part, other than evidence that:

(a) has to do with the alleged facts of the offence with which the defendant is charged; or

(b) is evidence of misconduct in connection with the investigation or prosecution of that offence.

It follows that the complainant's sexual behaviour that the defendant seeks leave to introduce either as evidence or by questioning may also fall within the definition of bad character under the 2003 Act. In such a situation the admission of the evidence will be governed by both the CJA 2003, s 100 and the YJCEA 1999, s 41 (for an example of an unsuccessful application under both s 100 and s 41 see *R v Smith* [2017] EWCA Crim 941). The CJA 2003, s 112(3) provides that nothing in that Act affects the exclusion of evidence under the YJCEA 1999, s 41. As s 41 involves a stricter test, evidence satisfying that test will ordinarily be admissible under s 100. This also means that evidence which satisfies s 100 of the 2003 Act but not s 41 of the 1999 Act will remain inadmissible.

11

The rule against hearsay: defining 'hearsay'

11.1 Introduction to hearsay evidence

The rule against hearsay was originally a common law rule that developed over many centuries. The rule is rooted in the concept that evidence should ordinarily be given by a witness who speaks from his or her own observations. By contrast, hearsay evidence is 'second hand'. Hearsay may arise, for example, when an account contained in a document created by an absent witness is adduced in evidence; or where a witness gives evidence of a statement originally made in his or her presence by somebody else—in other words, where he or she personally perceived the making of the statement. This can be illustrated accordingly: D is charged with assaulting V in circumstances where W1 observed the assault. In order to prove its case, the prosecution seeks to rely on the evidence of W2 who can testify that W1 told him that he (W1) had seen D punch V.

The common law rule has now been replaced by statutory schemes in both civil and criminal proceedings. In civil proceedings the statutory framework is to be found in the Civil Evidence Act 1995 (CEA 1995); in criminal proceedings it is found in the Criminal Justice Act 2003 (CJA 2003). While there are some differences between the statutory definitions of hearsay in civil and criminal proceedings, the core concepts are similar as they were both based on the same common law rule. This chapter will consider the definition of the rule against hearsay under the CEA 1995 and under the CJA 2003.

The rule against hearsay is not simply an exclusionary rule: there are many exceptions to it in both civil and criminal proceedings. Chapter 12 will consider the effects of the rule in civil proceedings, and Chapter 13 will consider the exceptions in criminal proceedings.

11.2 The common law rule

At common law the rule against hearsay prevented hearsay evidence being adduced at trial unless it could be brought within one of the recognised exceptions. The rule was usually cast in the following terms:

> Any statement other than one made by a witness while giving testimony in the proceedings in question is inadmissible as evidence of the facts stated.

There are therefore three key elements to the common law rule against hearsay:

- statement;
- made out of court (ie other than by a witness while giving evidence in the proceedings); and
- inadmissible as evidence of the facts stated.

Each part of the definition at common law also forms part of the statutory definitions of the rule in the CEA 1995 and CJA 2003. Accordingly, many of the principles derived from decisions made under the common law still apply to the statutory rules under the CEA 1995 and CJA 2003. The statutory definition of hearsay in civil proceedings will itself be considered in further detail at **11.5** and the definition in criminal proceedings at **11.6**.

11.3 Justifications for the rule against hearsay

A question that some commentators (and many students) have asked is whether there is any need for a hearsay rule at all. What is the rationale for the rule? The primary purpose for the rule against hearsay is to ensure that witnesses give evidence as to facts that are within their own knowledge, facts that they have personally perceived, rather than facts they have heard about.

A fuller justification for the rule against hearsay was given by Lord Normand in *Teper v R* [1952] AC 480:

> It is not the best evidence and it is not delivered on oath. The truthfulness and accuracy of the person whose words are spoken to by another witness cannot be tested by cross-examination, and the light which his demeanour would throw on his testimony is lost.

Lord Normand's remarks may be broken down into four separate justifications for the rule:

(a) *It is not the best evidence* The best evidence would be the evidence that could be given by the person who perceived the original event and made the statement that is now being adduced. In *Riat* [2013] 1 Cr App R 2, at [3] *per* Hughes LJ: 'It is necessarily second hand and for that reason very often second best.' For this reason, the hearsay rule has been said to encourage the substitution of weaker evidence for stronger evidence. However, this argument hardly holds water if hearsay is the only evidence available.

(b) *It is not delivered on oath* Taking an oath in the formal setting of the court is very different from telling a friend a story in a relaxed or informal environment. The oath should serve as a strong reminder of the importance of telling the truth and the sanction for failing to do so, although it clearly does not have this effect in every case.

(c) *The truthfulness and accuracy of the person who perceived the original event cannot be tested by cross-examination* The opposing party has no opportunity to cross-examine the maker of the statement in order to probe his veracity, sincerity, powers of perception, means of knowledge, etc. In *Al Khawaja and Tahery v UK* [2012] 52 EHRR 23, the Grand Chamber of the ECHR observed that:

> Experience shows that the reliability of evidence, including evidence which appears cogent and convincing, may look very different when subjected to a searching examination.

Ordinarily, the witness's perception, recollection, insincerity, and narration can be tested and challenged through cross-examination. Therefore, concerns about the reliability of a witness's evidence regarding what they have personally perceived can be addressed, at least in part, at trial. However, where the witness is simply repeating a statement he or she has 'heard said', as the maker of the statement is not present, questions about the maker's perception, recollection, insincerity, and narration cannot be put. As a result, there is no means of effectively testing the reliability of the evidence at trial.

This objection loses force where hearsay takes the form of a previous consistent statement and the speaker is called as a witness: in these circumstances, although neither on oath nor open to observation or cross-examination at the time when the statement was made, the witness can repeat the statement in open court on oath and then be cross-examined upon it.

(d) *The court has no opportunity to observe the demeanour of the person who perceived the original event* The tribunal of fact has no opportunity to properly observe the speaker's demeanour, inflection, tone of voice, etc so as to be able to assess the speaker's truthfulness and accuracy.

Other justifications have also been put forward:

(e) *The jury may attach too much weight to the evidence* It has been argued that juries find it difficult to properly evaluate hearsay evidence. In *Horncastle* [2010] 2 WLR 47, SC, at [21] Lord Philips observed that:

> ... the weight to be given to such evidence was less easy to appraise than that of evidence delivered by a witness face to face with the defendant and subject to testing by cross-examination.

(f) *To admit hearsay is to increase the opportunities for fraud or the deliberate manufacture of evidence* However, statements made at the time of, or shortly after, the events in question are often likely to be much more reliable than statements made months or years later. By the time of trial, the witnesses may have forgotten, be ill, or be dead.

(g) *To admit hearsay is often to admit superfluous material and raise side issues, both of which result in an undue protraction of the trial* However, the rule against hearsay may also operate to exclude highly relevant evidence that cannot be described as 'superfluous'.

The justifications for the rule against hearsay are largely concerned with the reliability of the evidence. The reliability of a statement may be affected by problems arising in connection with the following:

(a) *Faulty perception* This may affect the reliability of evidence in two ways:
   (i) the maker of the statement may have inaccurately perceived the original event; or
   (ii) the witness may have inaccurately perceived what the maker of the statement told him or her, for example, he or she may have misheard.

(b) *Inaccurate recollection* This may affect the reliability of the evidence in two ways:
   (i) the maker of the statement may inaccurately remember the events originally perceived when relating them to the witness; or
   (ii) the witness may inaccurately remember what the maker of the statement told him or her.

(c) *Insincerity* This may affect the reliability of the evidence in two ways:
   (i) the maker of the statement may lie when speaking to the witness. The maker may exaggerate or falsify the facts in his or her statement; or
   (ii) the witness may lie when giving evidence at court. The witness may exaggerate or falsify his or her evidence.

(d) *Ambiguous narration* This may affect the reliability of the evidence in two ways:

(i) the maker of the statement may ambiguously narrate the facts he or she originally perceived when recounting them to the witness. For example, in a case of dangerous driving the witness may say that the car was travelling fast. However, what this means is ambiguous. What is fast to one person may not be to another; or

(ii) the witness may ambiguously narrate the statement when recounting it to the court.

For a fuller examination of arguments for and against the hearsay rule, see, generally, Law Commission Report No 245, *Evidence in Criminal Proceedings: The Hearsay Rule and Related Topics*, Cm 3670, 1997, and the Law Commission Report No 216, *The Hearsay Rule in Civil Proceedings*, Cm 2321, 1993.

11.4 Original evidence

Before turning to the statutory definition of hearsay under the CEA 1995 and CJA 2003, it is worth noting that not all statements made out of court are hearsay statements. Where a witness gives evidence of another person's out of court statement, and where the purpose of repeating the statement in evidence is not to establish the truth of what was asserted in the statement but to establish some other fact, this is *not* hearsay evidence. If the statement is not being tendered to prove that what was said was true but for some other reason, the statement is original evidence. The distinction between hearsay and original evidence is central to the rule against hearsay. However, it is not always an easy distinction to draw. For an example where, it is submitted, the Divisional Court erred, see *West Midlands Probation Board v French* [2009] 1 WLR 1715. For criticism of this decision, see D Ormerod, 'Case Comment' [2009] Crim LR 283.

In *Ratten v R* [1972] AC 378, PC, Lord Wilberforce elucidated the distinction between hearsay and original evidence as follows:

> The mere fact that evidence of a witness includes evidence as to words spoken by another person who is not called, is no objection to its admissibility. Words spoken are facts just as much as any other action by a human being. If the speaking of the words is a relevant fact, a witness may give evidence that they were spoken. A question of hearsay only arises when the words spoken are relied on 'testimonially', i.e., as establishing some fact narrated by the words.

The key is to identify the purpose for which the statement is being adduced. If the purpose is not to prove the truth of the facts stated but some other purpose, it is original evidence.

A statement may be adduced for a variety of reasons other than proving the truth of the facts contained in it. The most commonly occurring types of original evidence are statements adduced to show:

- the state of mind or knowledge or belief of the maker of the statement;
- the state of mind or knowledge or belief of the hearer of the statement;
- that the statement was made;
- that the statement was false; and
- that there is an association between an accused and a document.

We will consider each in turn.

11.4.1 To show the state of mind or knowledge or belief of the maker of the statement

A statement is admissible as original evidence where it is adduced to show the state of mind or knowledge or belief of the maker of the statement. To take an example from a criminal context, in a case of assault where the defence is accident, the fact that the defendant said to the victim immediately prior to the assault, 'You are the most hateful wretch I have ever known! You deserve this!' is evidence of the defendant's malice, which is relevant as tending to disprove the defence of accident. The statement is not being relied upon for the truth of the facts stated (ie it is not relied on to show that the victim was in fact the most hateful wretch the defendant had ever known or that the victim deserved to be met with violence). Rather, the statement is being relied upon because it reveals the state of mind of the maker.

In *Thomas v Connell* (1838) 4 M & W 267, the issue was whether or not the defendant knew that he was insolvent. Proof of a statement in which he said that he was insolvent was held to be admissible as original evidence of his state of mind. It would have been hearsay if it were being adduced to prove the fact of his insolvency. This issue was proved by other evidence.

In *Toussaint-Collins* [2009] EWCA Crim 316, the accused was charged with the murder of G in revenge for the killing of S. A letter written by a third party which protested that no one had avenged S's death and which had been kept by the accused was held to have been properly adduced at trial as original evidence of the accused's state of mind in relation to G.

11.4.2 To show the state of mind or knowledge or belief of the hearer of the statement

A statement is admissible as original evidence where it is adduced to show the state of mind or knowledge or belief of the hearer of the statement. For example, in a case of theft of a necklace where the defence is duress, evidence that a third party had said, 'Unless you steal that necklace I will beat you to a pulp' is evidence of the defendant's state of mind that would tend to show that the defendant may have acted under duress. Similarly, in a case of misrepresentation, evidence from the claimant of the defendant's statement is admissible as original evidence to show that he was misled by the defendant, ie to show what the claimant, on hearing the statement, thought or believed.

In *Subramaniam v Public Prosecutor* [1956] 1 WLR 965, PC, the accused was found in a wounded condition by certain members of the security forces. When he was searched there was found around his waist a leather belt with three pouches containing 20 live rounds of ammunition but no weapon of any description was found upon him or in the immediate vicinity. He was charged with the possession of ammunition contrary to the Emergency Regulations, 1951, of the Federation of Malaya, r 4(1)(b). His defence was that he had been captured by terrorists and that at all material times he was acting under duress. It was held that evidence of threats made to the accused by the terrorists should have been admitted in order to show whether they might reasonably have induced in the accused an apprehension of immediate death if he failed to comply with their wishes, which was of direct relevance to the issue of duress. The threats were not adduced with the purpose of showing them to be true.

11.4.3 To show that the statement was made

A statement is admissible as original evidence where it is adduced to show that the statement was in fact made; this is distinct from any question of the truth of that statement. Certain statements in themselves have legal consequences. For example, in a marriage ceremony the words 'I do' have legal effect. It is by speaking those words that a person enters into a marriage. Such statements have been termed 'verbal acts'. Commonly occurring examples include the following:

- *Statements of offer and acceptance which constitute an alleged contract in a contract case where the formation of the contract is disputed* For example, 'I will sell you this smartphone for £50'. As it is not necessary to establish that an offer to sell the smartphone was genuine, it is not necessary to prove that the maker of the offer to sell the smartphone meant to sell it. Therefore, it does not matter whether the statement 'I will sell you this smartphone for £50' was true or not. All that must be established is that an offer was made (ie that the words were spoken). Therefore, the statement (including the exact words used) will be admissible as original evidence.
- *Statements which constitute an offence* For example, saying 'I am going to kill X' could amount to an offence of threats to kill under the Offences Against the Person Act 1861, s 16. In proving its case the prosecution would have to establish that a threat to kill was made (ie that the words were spoken) but not that the defendant was in fact going to kill X. Therefore, the statement would not be adduced to show that the words spoken were true but simply to show that the threat was made.
- *Statements amounting to acts of ownership* For example, the granting of leases/licences ('I lease you my flat at £500 per month') and the making of gifts ('I give and bequeath my house to my children').

For an example of a case in which evidence of an out of court statement was adduced to show that the statement had been made consider *Woodhouse v Hall* (1980) 72 Cr App R 39, DC. In this case the defendant was charged with 'acting in the management of a brothel'. The prosecution case was that the massage parlour she ran was in fact a brothel. A brothel is a premises at which more than one woman offers herself as a participant in physical acts of indecency for the sexual gratification of men. To prove that the massage parlour was in fact a brothel, police officers were called to give evidence that they had visited the massage parlour in the guise of customers and that, while being massaged by the defendant's employees, these employees had offered them sexual services. The evidence of these offers being made was held not to constitute hearsay evidence. It was the fact that offers of sexual services were made that was relevant, not whether these offers were true.

11.4.4 To show that the statement was false

An out-of-court statement may be admitted as original evidence if tendered not for the truth of its contents, but for its falsity. In such cases the purpose is not to prove the truth of words narrated in the statement but to prove that the statement was made. Alongside further evidence showing that the statement was not true a tribunal of fact can conclude that the statement was, in fact, a lie.

In *Attorney-General v Good* (1825) M'Cle & Yo 286, evidence of a wife's demonstrably untrue statement that her husband was away from home was admissible in order to show the husband's intention to defraud his creditors.

In *Mawaz Khan v R* [1967] 1 AC 454, PC, both defendants were charged with murder. In addition to various items of circumstantial evidence, the prosecution sought to prove statements made by each co-defendant individually in which they alleged that they were, at the time of the murder, at a particular club. The prosecution also called other witnesses who contradicted this alibi evidence. The trial judge then told the jury that the alibi statements could be used in determining whether or not the co-defendants had fabricated an alibi and had therefore cooperated after the murder. This direction to the jury formed the basis of the appeal to the Privy Council that the evidence should not have been left to the jury because it was hearsay. The Board concluded that this was not the case. The purpose of adducing the evidence was not to prove that the matters stated were true (ie to show that the two co-defendants were at the club). Rather, the statements were admissible as original evidence. What was relevant was that the statements were made at all (ie to show that the defendants had said they were at the club). Proof of that fact alongside the witnesses who effectively said that the co-defendants were not present would lead the jury to conclude that the statements were false. From this fact the jury could infer not only that each defendant had lied, but that they had cooperated in doing so.

As to lies generally, see **15.2** and **15.3**.

11.4.5 To show evidence of an association between the accused and a document

A document will not be hearsay evidence where it is relied on to show an association between the accused and a document, as opposed to relying on the truth of any statements contained within the document itself. Inferences may be drawn from this association. In *R v Lydon* (1987) 85 Cr App R 221, CA, the accused was charged with robbery and raised the defence of alibi. The prosecution was permitted to tender a piece of paper found near a gun believed to have been used in the robbery. Someone had written the words 'Sean rules' and 'Sean rules 85' on the paper. Ink found on the gun was of a similar appearance and composition to the ink used on the paper. The Court of Appeal held that the paper was properly admitted at trial as circumstantial evidence, which created an inferential link with the accused, whose first name was Sean. The document was not hearsay evidence; it was not adduced to prove the truth of the words 'Sean rules'.

11.5 Hearsay in civil proceedings

11.5.1 Definition

In civil proceedings the rule against hearsay has been put on a statutory footing by the CEA 1995. The CEA 1995, s 1(2) provides that:

In this Act—

(a) 'hearsay' means a statement made otherwise than by a person while giving oral evidence in the proceedings which is tendered as evidence of the matters stated; and

(b) references to hearsay include hearsay of whatever degree.

Section 13 provides that:

'statement' means any representation of fact or opinion, however made.

The definition contains three of the key elements of the rule at common law:

- statement;
- made otherwise than by a person giving oral evidence in the proceedings; and
- tendered as evidence of the matters stated, ie to prove the truth of the statement.

Hearsay under the CEA 1995 differs from the common law rule in that evidence is not rendered inadmissible in civil proceedings merely on the ground that it is hearsay. The definition in s 1(2)(b) covers multiple hearsay, and by s 13 it encompasses expert and other forms of opinion hearsay evidence. It is unclear whether an implied assertion is a 'statement' for the purposes of the CEA 1995. An implied assertion is an assertion from which a particular fact that is not expressly articulated in the statement can be inferred.

11.5.2 Identifying hearsay in civil proceedings

Although hearsay in civil proceedings is admissible under CEA 1995, it is still important to identify whether evidence is hearsay or original evidence. This is because hearsay evidence is only admissible subject to the conditions and safeguards identified in CEA 1995. These will be considered further in **Chapter 12**. A statement made out of court, adduced to prove something other than the matter stated is original evidence (see **11.4**) and may be admitted as long as it is sufficiently relevant.

In order to identify hearsay in civil proceedings one can employ a four-stage test:

(a) Identify the statement.

(b) Identify whether the statement was made out of court (ie other than by a witness while giving evidence in the proceedings).

(c) Identify the relevance of the statement (ie the purpose for which the statement is being admitted).

(d) Identify whether, in order to achieve that purpose, the statement has to be true or whether the purpose can be achieved by simply showing that the statement was made. If the statement has to be true to achieve its purpose, it is hearsay evidence. If to achieve its relevant purpose, the statement simply has to be made, then the statement is original evidence.

11.6 Hearsay in criminal proceedings

11.6.1 The definition of hearsay in criminal proceedings

In criminal proceedings, the common law rule has been replaced by the statutory framework in the CJA 2003. The definition of hearsay is found in the CJA 2003, s 114(1):

In criminal proceedings a statement not made in oral evidence in the proceedings is admissible as evidence of any matter stated if, but only if—

(a) any provision of this Chapter or any other statutory provision makes it admissible,

(b) any rule of law preserved by section 118 makes it admissible,

(c) all parties to the proceedings agree to it being admissible, or

(d) the court is satisfied that it is in the interests of justice for it to be admissible.

The rule has been drafted in inclusionary (*'admissible ... if ...'*), as opposed to exclusionary (*'inadmissible ... unless ...'*) terms. However, at the committee stage of the passage of the Criminal Justice Bill through Parliament this inclusionary language was rightly described as nothing more than 'mood music' because the rule is still an exclusionary rule to which there are a number of exceptions. Had the provision been drafted in exclusionary terms it would have had precisely the same effect.

The definition therefore contains three of the key elements of the rule at common law:

- statement;
- not made in oral evidence in the proceedings; and
- inadmissible as evidence of any matter stated (unless certain conditions are satisfied).

11.6.2 The definition of a 'statement'

Section 115 of the Act provides:

> (1) *In this Chapter references to a statement or to a matter stated are to be read as follows.*
>
> (2) *A statement is any representation of fact or opinion made by a person by whatever means; and it includes a representation made in a sketch, photofit or other pictorial form.*

A statement for the purposes of hearsay as outlined by s 114(1) of the CJA 2003 is broadly defined under s 115. It covers statements made on oath in previous proceedings (*Berkeley Peerage Case* (1811) 4 Camp 401). The phrase 'by whatever means' encompasses gestures or conduct; for example, in *Chandrasekera v R* [1937] AC 220, PC, a woman whose throat had been cut described her attacker using sign language and nodded when asked whether the appellant was her attacker. Importantly, a statement must be made by a person. Any representation that is generated purely mechanically cannot be hearsay under the CJA 2003; for example, still or moving images generated by CCTV cannot be hearsay evidence (*Dodson* [1984] 1 WLR 971 and *Fowden* [1982] Crim LR 588). It follows that s 115(2) preserves the rule in *R v Wood* (1982) 76 Cr App R 23, CA, which permitted the use of evidence of the printout, reading, or other information produced by a computer or other electronic or mechanical device used to produce information, that is, a tool that does not contribute its own knowledge but merely performs a calculation or other mechanical or electronic function, which could have been done manually. Such a printout, reading, or other information is not a statement made 'by a person' and so is admissible as real evidence.

In *R v Wood* (1982) 76 Cr App R 23, CA, the prosecution sought to prove that certain metal was part of a stolen consignment. To that end the prosecution adduced evidence of an analysis of the chemical composition of the metal. During the analysis the computer was programmed to carry out the relevant calculations and was operated by a chemist. The Court of Appeal held that the computer printout showing the results of these calculations was not hearsay because the computer was being used to perform a sophisticated calculation that could have been done manually. The printout was merely a piece of real evidence, comparable to a piece of litmus paper in a laboratory experiment, the actual proof and relevance of which depended on the testimony of the computer programmer. It was still necessary to prove by non-hearsay evidence the formula that had been programmed into the computer and the data that had been fed into it. Once this had been done, the computer itself was not making any statement for hearsay purposes. In other words, it was the mathematical calculations based on the data that was not hearsay.

The CJA 2003, s 129 provides:

> (1) *Where a representation of any fact—*
>
> (a) *is made otherwise than by a person, but*
>
> (b) *depends for its accuracy on information supplied (directly or indirectly) by a person, the representation is not admissible in criminal proceedings as evidence of the fact unless it is proved that the information was accurate.*
>
> (2) *Subsection (1) does not affect the operation of the presumption that a mechanical device has been properly set or calibrated.*

Section 129 regulates statements made by a machine that performs a calculation on the basis of information supplied by a person. Section 129(1) reflects the requirement in *Wood* that the data entered into a machine has to be proven by non-hearsay evidence. However, it goes further than the requirement in *Wood* in that it makes the accuracy of the information a precondition of admissibility. It would therefore appear to require that the tribunal of law determine the accuracy of the data supplied to such a machine before it can be adduced as evidence in front of the tribunal of fact.

11.6.3 The definition of 'matters stated'

Evidence is hearsay under the CJA 2003, s 114(1) only if it is relied on as 'evidence of the matter stated', ie where it is relied on to establish the truth of that matter.

Section 115 of the Act provides:

> *(1) In this Chapter references to a statement or to a matter stated are to be read as follows.*
>
> . . .
>
> *(3) A matter stated is one to which this Chapter applies if (and only if) the purpose, or one of the purposes, of the person making the statement appears to the court to have been—*
>
> *(a) to cause another person to believe the matter, or*
>
> *(b) to cause another person to act or a machine to operate on the basis that the matter is as stated.*

In other words, even where a statement that is adduced to prove the truth of the facts stated, it will only be hearsay under the CJA 2003 where the purpose, or one of the purposes, of the maker of the statement was:

- to cause another person to believe the facts stated, ie to believe that the facts are true; or
- to cause another person to act or a machine to operate on the basis that the facts are as stated, ie that the facts are true.

Care must always be taken to ascertain the 'matter stated'. For example, where a car is alleged to have been involved in an offence, and an eyewitness to the offence gives an account of the car's registration number to a police officer, it is hearsay evidence for the police officer to give evidence of that registration number at court for the purpose of establishing the truth of the eyewitness's account. The statement (the registration number) was made out of court, it is adduced to prove the truth of the matter stated, and it must have been the witness's intention to cause the police officer to believe that the registration number was as they (the witness) described and/or act on the basis that the account is true, for example by conducting further investigation in to the ownership of that vehicle.

11.6.3.1 Implied assertions and the matter stated

At common law both express and implied assertions were caught by the common law rule against hearsay (*R v Kearley* [1992] 2 AC 228). An implied assertion is an assertion from which a fact that is not expressly asserted in the statement can be inferred.

In *R v Kearley* [1992] 2 AC 228, HL, the police executed a search warrant of Kearley's house. They found drugs there but not in sufficient quantities to raise the inference that he was a dealer. After the search, the police remained at his premises for several hours and intercepted ten telephone calls in which each caller asked to speak to Kearley and asked for drugs. While the police were still on the premises, seven persons arrived at the flat, some with money, also asking for Kearley and asking to be supplied with drugs. Kearley denied a charge of possession with intent to supply. At trial, the prosecution was allowed to call the police officers who had intercepted the calls or received the visitors at the flat to give evidence of the conversations they had had with the callers or visitors. The House of Lords, by a majority of three to two, held that evidence of such a request was not relevant because it could only be evidence of the state of mind of the person making the request, which was not a relevant issue at the trial. The issue at trial was Kearley's state of mind, namely whether he intended to supply drugs, and in so far as evidence of a request was relevant to that issue (as an implied assertion that Kearley was a supplier of drugs), it was inadmissible hearsay in the same way that an express out-of-court assertion to the same effect would be inadmissible hearsay.

The purpose of CJA 2003, s 115(3) was to reverse the decision in *Kearley* and render implied assertions admissible as original evidence. In *R v Singh* [2006] 2 Cr App R 12, CA, it was confirmed that the common law rule against the admissibility of hearsay is abolished by the CJA 2003 and replaced with a new rule against hearsay that does not extend to implied assertions. The Court of Appeal revisited the decision in *Kearley* and stated that what was said by the callers in *Kearley* would now be admissible as direct evidence of the fact that there was a ready market for the supply of drugs from the premises, from which could be inferred an intention by an occupier to supply drugs. The purpose of the makers of the statements was not to cause someone to believe or act on the basis that Kearley was a drugs dealer. However, the rule still gave rise to difficulties. For example, in *R v Leonard* [2009] Crim LR 802, the Court of Appeal held that statements in text messages to the accused impliedly asserting that he was a drug dealer were properly classified as hearsay. It is submitted that the court clearly erred in reaching this conclusion (see D Ormerod, *R v Leonard* (Case Comment) [2009] Crim LR 802 for a critical analysis of the court's reasoning).

Previous case law on the difficult area of implied assertions must now be seen in the light of *R v Twist* [2011] 2 Cr App R 17. In *Twist*, a series of conjoined appeals, the Court of Appeal stated that the CJA 2003 had created a new rule against hearsay which sought to exclude implied assertions. Hughes LJ observed:

> The Act does not use the expression 'assertion'. Instead it speaks of a 'statement' and the 'matter stated' in it. This seems likely to have been because its framers wished to avoid the complex philosophical arguments which beset the common law, as explained in *DPP v Kearley* [1992] 2 AC 28, as to when an utterance contains an implied assertion ...
>
> It is therefore helpful, as it seems to us, that the Act avoids the use of the expression 'assertion' altogether, and with it the difficult concept of the 'implied assertion'.

11.6.3.2 Application of s 115(3) following *Twist*

In *Twist*, Hughes LJ went on to propose that the following approach should be taken to identify hearsay:

> Generally ... it is likely to be helpful to approach the question whether the hearsay rules apply in this way:
>
> (i) identify what relevant fact (matter) it is sought to prove;
> (ii) ask whether there is a statement of that matter in the communication. If no, then no question of hearsay arises (whatever other matters may be contained in the communication);
> (iii) If yes, ask whether it was one of the purposes (not necessarily the only or dominant purpose) of the maker of the communication that the recipient, or any other person, should believe that matter or act upon it as true? If yes, it is hearsay. If no, it is not.

In *Twist*, the Court of Appeal considered four appeals concerning the admissibility of text messages and, taking the above approach, held that none of the messages were hearsay. In the first two appeals, the appellants had been convicted of possession with intent to supply and the text messages under consideration were mostly requests for drugs.

Taking the first step in the approach, the Court of Appeal found that the matter sought to be proved was that the appellants supplied drugs. Taking the second step, there was no statement of that matter in the text messages; the messages were simply requests for drugs. Accordingly, no question arose as to whether the messages were hearsay and they were admissible as relevant evidence.

In the third appeal, the appellants had been convicted of a gunpoint robbery of two girls and the text message under consideration, which had been recovered from one appellant's phone on the morning of the robbery, read, 'Need dat gun today so can sell it and give you lot da tenner back. Does faws still want it?' Taking the first step in the approach, the matter sought to be proved was that the appellants had been in possession of a gun just as the girls had said. Taking the second step in the approach, the court held that there may have been a statement of this in the text message. However, taking the third step, it was not the intention of the sender of the message to cause the appellant to believe that he himself was in possession of a gun; this was assumed by the sender.

In the final appeal, the appellant had been convicted of the rape of his girlfriend. Both he and his girlfriend were 15 years old at the time of the rape. The court held that text messages sent by the appellant to his girlfriend in which he confessed and expressed remorse were not hearsay. Although they obviously contained statements of the matter sought to be proved (that the appellant had committed rape), the appellant's purpose in sending the messages was not to cause his girlfriend to believe that she had been raped, which they both knew had happened: the purpose was to confess and express remorse.

Following the strong approval *Twist* received from the Court of Appeal in *R v Mateza & Mateza* [2011] EWCA Crim 2587, CA, the approach in *Twist* is being followed by the criminal courts. For example, in the case of *Khan* [2013] EWCA Crim 2230, the prosecution sought to rely on an intercepted conversation in which the two parties to the conversation referred to the appellant by his nickname, 'Bana'. The question in issue was whether one of the parties to the conversation knew the appellant. On appeal it was held that the statement 'Bana' was relied on by the prosecution to show that the appellant was well known to the speakers but that, because neither speaker had intended to demonstrate that he knew Bana, no issue of hearsay arose. Similarly, in *Noble* [2017] EWCA Crim 2219, a series of messages sent between the accused and his girlfriend, which included a reference by the girlfriend to the accused's possession of a gun, were not held to be hearsay. The purpose of the statements to the accused about his having a gun was not to cause him to believe that he had a gun or to act on that basis. As observed by the Court of Appeal, '[He] knew if he did or did not have a gun'.

While a 'common understanding' between the parties was a feature of all the communications considered in *Twist*, it is not a necessary feature of all statements saved from the hearsay rule by s 115(3). In *R v Midmore* [2017] EWCA Crim 533, a crime that involved throwing a drain cleaning product over the complainant, a WhatsApp message sent to a third party which comprised a picture of the product and the caption 'this is the one face melter' was held not to be hearsay. Although it was held that the message amounted to a 'statement or representation of fact', it was not intended to make the recipient believe that the sender intended to use the product to melt a face and therefore not hearsay.

11.6.4 Negative hearsay

The decision in *DPP v Leigh* [2010] EWHC 345 makes it clear that 'negative hearsay' contained in records is not caught by the statutory definition of hearsay. The defendant was charged with failing to give information relating to the identity of the driver under the Road Traffic Act 1988, s 172(3). A prosecution witness gave evidence that the police records showed that no reply had been received from the defendant. The Divisional Court held that no statement within the meaning of s 115(2) was being relied upon, nor was the evidence being adduced for the purpose of establishing a 'matter stated' so as to fall within s 115(3). The significance of the records lay not in what they said, but in what they did not say, ie the fact that they said nothing. A person could not be said, by failing to make an entry in the records, to be asserting that no reply had been received. Whether an inference can be drawn in any particular case will depend on the evidence with respect to such matters as the reliability of the record, the care of the checker, etc.

11.6.5 Identifying hearsay in criminal proceedings

In order to identify hearsay in criminal proceedings the following five-stage approach may be helpful. The approach draws on the test in the CJA 2003, s 115 and on the analysis in *R v Twist* [2011] 2 Cr App R 17 (which the courts now follow).

(a) Identify the statement the party wishes to adduce.

(b) Ask if the statement was *not* made in oral evidence in the proceedings.

(c) Ask what matter does the party seeking to admit the statement say the statement proves? (ie what is the matter stated?)

(d) Identify whether there is actually a 'statement' of that matter in the statement. If the answer is 'no', it is not hearsay.

(e) If there is a 'statement' of the matter the party seeks to prove, was one of the purposes of the maker of the statement to cause another person to believe the matter *or* to cause another to act (or a machine to operate) on the basis that the matter is true? If the answer is 'yes', then the statement is hearsay.

11.7 The potential for injustice

As set out above, the rationale for the rule against hearsay is that it excludes potentially unreliable evidence. However, not all hearsay evidence is unreliable and where reliable hearsay evidence is excluded at trial the potential for injustice is created. Consider the following examples:

- In *Sparks v R* [1964] AC 964, PC, the defendant was tried for indecent assault of a 4-year-old girl. Soon after the incident the girl had said to her mother, when questioned as to the description of the assailant: 'It was a coloured boy.' The girl did not give evidence at trial. Sparks was white and at trial sought to lead evidence from the girl's mother that this comment had been made to establish that he could not have been the assailant. The Privy Council held that the evidence was hearsay.
- In *R v Turner* (1975) 61 Cr App R 67, CA, the defendant was charged with robbery. There was evidence that a third party, not called as a witness, had admitted that he had committed the offence. However, the defendant was not permitted to call the evidence of a person who had heard him make this confession as the evidence was inadmissible hearsay.
- In *Jones v Metcalfe* [1967] 1 WLR 1286, DC, the accused was convicted of driving without due care and attention, the police alleging that his lorry collided with a car. A witness called for the prosecution said that he saw the collision and gave the

lorry's number to a police officer. A police officer gave evidence that, as a result of information received, he had interviewed the accused who had admitted that he drove the lorry bearing the registration number in question at the time and place of the incident, but had denied being involved in any collision. The Divisional Court set the conviction aside on the grounds that there was no evidence that the accused's lorry was the one involved in the accident. What the witness had said to the police was inadmissible hearsay and there was simply no admissible evidence of the registration number of the lorry involved in the collision.

It is cases such as these that led to the development of common law and statutory exceptions to the hearsay rule. Because the rule against hearsay is not simply an exclusionary rule, it follows that when a possible issue of hearsay arises the practitioner is required to first determine whether the statement is hearsay and, if it is hearsay, determine whether it is admissible under one, or more, of the exceptions to the rule. In **Chapters 12** and **13** we will consider the circumstances in which hearsay is admissible in civil and criminal proceedings respectively.

12

Hearsay evidence in civil proceedings

12.1 Definition

The definition of hearsay for civil proceedings is found in the Civil Evidence Act 1995, (CEA 1995), s 1(2), which provides that:

In this Act—

(a) 'hearsay' means a statement made otherwise than by a person while giving oral evidence in the proceedings which is tendered as evidence of the matters stated; and

(b) references to hearsay include hearsay of whatever degree.

Further details can be found at **11.5**.

12.2 Admissibility of hearsay in civil proceedings

The admissibility of hearsay in civil proceedings is governed by the CEA 1995. Section 11 of the Act defines civil proceedings as civil proceedings, before any tribunal, in relation to which the strict rules of evidence apply, whether as a matter of law or by agreement of the parties. Accordingly, hearsay provisions under the CEA 1995 have broad application, beyond mainstream civil disputes.

CEA 1995, s 1 provides:

(1) In civil proceedings evidence shall not be excluded on the ground that it is hearsay.

By virtue of s 1(1), in civil proceedings, a hearsay statement will be admissible unless it falls to be excluded under another exclusionary rule. This is so whether the statement is oral or documentary, whether first-hand or multiple (s 1(2)(b)), or whether hearsay is given by an anonymous witness (*Welsh v Stokes* [2007] EWCA Civ 796). Thus the Act prevents the hearsay nature of the evidence being the reason it cannot be admitted. This does not mean, however, that all hearsay is admissible. If the evidence is inadmissible because of some other evidentiary rule, the CEA 1995 will not render such evidence admissible. For example, save for proceedings held in the Court of Protection (Court of Protection Rules 2007, r 95(d) and (e) as amended), these provisions do not allow the proof of out-of-court statements made by a person who would not be competent as a witness (s 5). (See **4.2** and **4.2.4** for the rules of competence in civil proceedings.)

Even though hearsay evidence is now generally admissible, it is still necessary to determine whether the evidence is hearsay or original evidence and whether it would be admissible under some other provision in any event. This is because the admissibility of hearsay remains subject to conditions and safeguards; by contrast, original evidence may be admitted as long as it is sufficiently relevant and it does not fall foul of an exclusionary rule.

12.3 Safeguards

The 1995 Act introduced four safeguards to prevent a party against whom a hearsay statement is adduced from being unfairly prejudiced:

- a requirement to give advance notice;
- the power to call the maker of the statement for cross-examination;
- guidance as to assessing the weight of hearsay evidence; and
- the power to adduce evidence relevant to the credibility of the maker of the statement.

12.3.1 The requirement to give notice

A party proposing to adduce hearsay evidence shall give such notice (if any) as is reasonable and practicable for the purpose of enabling the other parties to deal with any matters arising from its being hearsay (s 2). This requirement must be met unless the parties agree to exclude the notice provisions or the person to whom notice should be given waives that requirement (s 2(3)). However, failure to give such notice will not prevent the evidence from being admitted. The party failing to comply with the notice requirements of s 2 may suffer other sanctions:

(a) under s 2(4)(a), the court may exercise its powers against the defaulting party by adjourning the case and requiring the defaulting party to pay the costs wasted as a result; and

(b) under ss 2(4)(b) and 4(2)(f), the court may attach less weight to the hearsay evidence.

The detailed rules on the notice procedure are contained in CPR, rr 33.2 and 33.3:

Notice of intention to rely on hearsay evidence

33.2 (1) Where a party intends to rely on hearsay evidence at trial and either—

(a) that evidence is to be given by a witness giving oral evidence; or

(b) that evidence is contained in a witness statement of a person who is not being called to give oral evidence;

that party complies with section 2(1)(a) of the Civil Evidence Act 1995 by serving a witness statement on the other parties in accordance with the court's order.

(2) Where paragraph (1)(b) applies, the party intending to rely on the hearsay evidence must, when he serves the witness statement—

(a) inform the other parties that the witness is not being called to give oral evidence; and

(b) give the reason why the witness will not be called.

(3) In all other cases where a party intends to rely on hearsay evidence at trial, that party complies with section 2(1)(a) of the Civil Evidence Act 1995 by serving a notice on the other parties which—

(a) identifies the hearsay evidence;

(b) states that the party serving the notice proposes to rely on the hearsay evidence at trial; and

(c) gives the reason why the witness will not be called.

(4) The party proposing to rely on the hearsay evidence must—

(a) serve the notice no later than the latest date for serving witness statements; and

(b) if the hearsay evidence is to be in a document, supply a copy to any party who requests him to do so.

Circumstances in which notice of intention to rely on hearsay evidence is not required

33.3 *Section 2(1) of the Civil Evidence Act 1995 (duty to give notice of intention to rely on hearsay evidence) does not apply—*

(a) to evidence at hearings other than trials;

(aa) to an affidavit or witness statement which is to be used at trial but which does not contain hearsay evidence;

(b) to a statement which a party to a probate action wishes to put in evidence and which is alleged to have been made by the person whose estate is the subject of the proceedings; or

(c) where the requirement is excluded by a practice direction.

There are, therefore, broadly three types of hearsay statement that require different degrees of notification, as follows:

(a) *Hearsay contained in a witness's statement* The notice is given when the witness statement is served through the normal procedure.

(b) *Hearsay contained in a statement of a person who will not be called as a witness at trial* Notice has to be given by the date for the exchange of witness statements and must state the evidence is to be relied on as hearsay and give the reason why the witness is not being called at the trial.

(c) *Where the hearsay is not contained in a witness statement (for example hearsay in a document that will be produced at trial)* In such circumstances it will not be possible to give notice by service of a witness statement so it is necessary to serve a notice:

  (i) identifying the hearsay evidence;

  (ii) stating that the hearsay will be relied upon; and

  (iii) identifying why the maker of the hearsay statement will not be called to give evidence.

Note that under CPR, Part 27.2, CPR, Part 33 does not apply to civil claims allocated to the small claims track.

12.3.2 The power to call the maker of the statement for cross-examination

Under the CEA 1995, s 3, there is provision for the rules to require the maker of a hearsay statement who is not called as a witness to attend trial to be cross-examined, but only with the leave of the court. This provision reflects the fact that where a party relies on hearsay evidence but does not call the maker of the hearsay statement as a witness, the other parties to the proceedings may want to challenge the statement by cross-examining the statement-maker either on the accuracy of the statement or on the statement-maker's credibility. Although it is the party contesting the evidence who wishes the witness to be called, the rules treat the witness in question as though he or she had been called by the person relying on the evidence. The rules are contained in CPR, r 33.4.

(1) Where a party—

(a) proposes to rely on hearsay evidence; and

(b) does not propose to call the person who made the original statement to give oral evidence,

the court may, on the application of any other party, permit that party to call the maker of the statement to be cross-examined on the contents of the statement.

(2) *An application for permission to cross-examine under this rule must be made not more than 14 days after the day on which a notice of intention to rely on the hearsay evidence was served on the applicant.*

Where the court considers that the maker of the statement should attend court and be cross-examined but the party seeking to rely on the evidence refuses to comply with the order of the court, the court has powers under CPR, r 32.1 to exclude the statement. Consequently, the party disobeying the order will not normally be permitted to rely on the hearsay evidence (*Polanski v Condé Nast Publications Ltd* [2004] 1 WLR 387, CA).

12.3.3 Assessing the weight of hearsay evidence

It is for the court to determine what weight to give to hearsay evidence. This includes giving it little or no weight (*TSB (Scotland) Plc v James Mills (Montrose)* Ltd [1992] SLT 519, a decision under the Civil Evidence (Scotland) Act 1988). The decision as to what weight to give hearsay evidence involves the exercise of judgement (see, eg, *Janan George Harb v Prince Abdul Aziz Bin Fahd Bin Abdul Aziz* [2016] EWCA Civ 556). Section 4 sets out the considerations to which the court may have regard in deciding what, if any, weight ought to be attached to a hearsay statement admissible under the 1995 Act. There is no rule prohibiting the court giving weight to uncorroborated hearsay evidence, simply because it is uncorroborated and cannot be tested. Section 4 provides:

(1) *In estimating the weight (if any) to be given to hearsay evidence in civil proceedings the court shall have regard to any circumstances from which any inference can reasonably be drawn as to the reliability or otherwise of the evidence.*

(2) *Regard may be had, in particular, to the following—*

(a) *whether it would have been reasonable and practicable for the party by whom the evidence was adduced to have produced the maker of the original statement as a witness;*

(b) *whether the original statement was made contemporaneously with the occurrence or existence of the matters stated;*

(c) *whether the evidence involves multiple hearsay;*

(d) *whether any person involved had any motive to conceal or misrepresent matters;*

(e) *whether the original statement was an edited account, or was made in collaboration with another or for a particular purpose;*

(f) *whether the circumstances in which the evidence is adduced as hearsay are such as to suggest an attempt to prevent proper evaluation of its weight.*

Section 4(2)(d) refers to 'any person' with a motive to conceal or misrepresent. In the case of multiple hearsay, therefore, the court should consider whether any person repeating the hearsay statement may have had such a motive and therefore may have misrepresented the facts in question.

An example of where the circumstances in which the evidence is adduced as hearsay are such as to suggest an attempt to prevent proper evaluation of its weight (s 4(2)(f)) would be where the party producing the hearsay evidence fails to give such notice as was reasonable and practicable (s 2(4)(b)).

12.3.4 The power to adduce evidence relevant to the credibility of the maker of the statement

Where the maker of the statement does not attend for cross-examination, the Act makes provision for challenging the credibility of the evidence. Section 5(2) provides:

Where in civil proceedings hearsay evidence is adduced and the maker of the original statement, or of any statement relied upon to prove another statement, is not called as a witness—

(a) evidence which if he had been so called would be admissible for the purpose of attacking or supporting his credibility as a witness is admissible for that purpose in the proceedings; and

(b) evidence tending to prove that, whether before or after he made the statement, he made any other statement inconsistent with it is admissible for the purpose of showing that he had contradicted himself.

Provided that evidence may not be given of any matter of which, if he had been called as a witness and had denied that matter in cross-examination, evidence could not have been adduced by the cross-examining party.

By s 5(2) the hearsay evidence can be challenged by evidence in the same way that a witness attending to give evidence may be challenged. In other words, the Act allows the operation of the normal rules on cross-examination of witnesses. Section 5(2) allows two forms of evidence to be adduced by the challenging party:

(a) evidence undermining the credibility of the witness; and

(b) evidence of statements inconsistent with the hearsay statement.

It applies both to the maker of the original hearsay statement and to any statement relied on to prove another statement. Thus, not only may the credibility of the original maker of the hearsay statement be challenged, but also the credibility of any person, not called as witness, who repeats the hearsay statement. Given that the Act has not changed the rules of evidence except in relation to hearsay evidence, all other restrictions as to what may or may not be adduced in evidence still apply. Note in particular that evidence cannot be adduced if it would offend the rule of finality.

Section 5(2)(a) states that evidence '*for the purpose of attacking or supporting his credibility… is admissible for that purpose*' and s 5(2)(b) states that evidence is '*admissible for the purpose of showing that he had contradicted himself*'. It follows that such evidence as is admitted under s 5 will only go to the issue of credibility rather than to prove the truth of a statement's contents.

For the notice requirements where a person wishes to challenge the credibility of a hearsay statement, see CPR, r 33.5:

(1) Where a party—

(a) proposes to rely on hearsay evidence; but

(b) does not propose to call the person who made the original statement to give oral evidence; and

(c) another party wishes to call evidence to attack the credibility of the person who made the statement,

the party who so wishes must give notice of his intention to the party who proposes to give the hearsay statement in evidence.

(2) A party must give notice under paragraph (1) not more than 14 days after the day on which a hearsay notice relating to the hearsay evidence was served on him.

12.4 Conditions of admissibility

12.4.1 The requirement of competence

Section (5)(1) of the CEA 1995 provides that hearsay evidence shall not be admitted if it consists of, or is proved by means of, a statement made by a person who at the time he or she made the statement was not competent as a witness (as to competence, see **4.2** and **4.2.4**).

12.4.2 The requirement of leave

Under the 1995 Act leave is generally not required before hearsay evidence will be admitted. The one exception to this rule is where the maker of the statement in question has or will be called to give evidence. This exception is set out in s 6(2) of the 1995 Act:

> *(2) A party who has called or intends to call a person as a witness in civil proceedings may not in those proceedings adduce evidence of a previous statement made by that person, except—*
>
> *(a) with the leave of the court, or*
>
> *(b) for the purpose of rebutting a suggestion that his evidence has been fabricated.*
>
> *This shall not be construed as preventing a witness statement (that is, a written statement of oral evidence which a party to the proceedings intends to lead) from being adopted by a witness in giving evidence or treated as his evidence.*
>
> ...
>
> *(4) Nothing in this Act affects any of the rules of law as to the circumstances in which, where a person called as a witness in civil proceedings is cross-examined on a document used by him to refresh his memory, that document may be made evidence in the proceedings.*

The effect of s 6 is that previous consistent statements, with the exception of statements in rebuttal of an allegation of recent fabrication (see **6.5.1.2**) and memory-refreshing documents that have become evidence following cross-examination (see **6.4.9**), are only admissible where the court grants leave.

12.5 Proof of a hearsay statement

Although the 1995 Act renders hearsay statements admissible, it is important not to overlook the fact that they still must be proved. Where the statement is oral hearsay this will be achieved by proving, whether by a witness at trial or through an admissible hearsay document, that the statement was made. However, the statement cannot be proved by a person who is not a competent witness (s 5(1)).

The proof of hearsay statements contained in documents is governed by ss 8–10 of the Act. Section 8 provides:

> *(1) Where a statement contained in a document is admissible as evidence in civil proceedings, it may be proved—*
>
> *(a) by the production of that document, or*
>
> *(b) whether or not that document is still in existence, by the production of a copy of that document or of the material part of it,*
>
> *authenticated in such manner as the court may approve.*
>
> *(2) It is immaterial for this purpose how many removes there are between a copy and the original.*

Under s 13, a document is defined broadly as '*anything in which information of any description is recorded*', for example maps, plans, videotapes, audio tapes, photographs, discs, or graphs. Where the hearsay is contained in a document it is not adequate merely to hand the document to the court (*per* Staughton LJ in *Ventouris v Mountain* (No 2) [1992] 1 WLR 817). At common law, there are rules as to how a document may be proved and the reference in s 8(1)(a) to 'production' must be read accordingly. A witness must attend court to identify the document and to verify its authenticity by oral testimony.

What if the document is available but no person is available to verify it? May hearsay evidence be used to prove the document? This was the problem faced in *Ventouris v Mountain* (No 2) [1992] 1 WLR 817, a case concerning the similar provision under the Civil Evidence Act 1968. There the document in question was a tape recording of a conversation between G and a number of divers who had been hired to blow up a boat for insurance purposes. The defendants, who were the insurers of the boat, wished to adduce this evidence to exempt them from having to make an insurance payment to the plaintiff. G was not available to give evidence. However, he had told an English solicitor what the tape recordings concerned. The Court of Appeal was satisfied that the solicitor would have been able to prove the tapes by repeating what G had told him about the tapes. That this logic would apply to proof of a document by another document is strengthened by s 1(2)(b), which allows hearsay 'of whatever degree' to be admitted. Clearly, a fact stated in a letter by C referred to in a document written by B that was mentioned in a letter written by A would be admissible upon formal proof of A's letter.

Section 8(1)(b) states that a copy of a document (or even a copy of a copy) shall be admissible as evidence even if the original document is in existence. However, the copy must be 'authenticated', ie the court must be satisfied that it is an accurate copy.

Sections 9 and 10 make particular provision for the admissibility of particular documents without having formally to 'prove' those documents. Section 9 concerns any document forming part of the records of a business or of public authorities. A document falling within that section will be admissible if a signed certificate is produced. Section 9(3) allows for the proof of negative hearsay; the absence of an entry in the records of businesses or public authorities may be proved by affidavit. 'Records' is defined in s 9(4) as *'records in whatever form'* and 'business' as *'any activity regularly carried on over a period of time, whether for profit or not, by any body ... or by an individual'*. 'Public authority' includes any government department or public undertaking.

Section 10 provides for the admissibility of the Ogden tables in personal injuries cases but this section is not currently in force.

12.6 Preservation of the common law rules

Section 7 of the 1995 Act preserves some of the common law exceptions to the traditional hearsay rule. These exceptions include:

- works of reference;
- statements contained in a public document or record;
- statements made by deceased persons to prove matters of pedigree;
- statements made by deceased persons to prove the existence of a public or general right; and
- evidence of a person's general reputation.

Section 1 of the CEA 1995 provides that:

...

(3) Nothing in this Act affects the admissibility of evidence admissible apart from this section.

(4) The provisions of sections 2 to 6 (safeguards and supplementary provisions relating to hearsay evidence) do not apply in relation to hearsay evidence admissible apart from this section, notwithstanding that it may also be admissible by virtue of this section.

It follows that where the evidence is admissible under one of these exceptions there is no requirement to comply with the safeguards at s 2 (notice requirements, see **12.3.1**), s **4** (determining the weight of hearsay, see **12.3.3**), and s 5 (adducing evidence relevant to the credibility of the maker of the statement, see **12.3.4**), or with the leave requirements (see **12.4.2**).

12.6.1 Works of reference

Published works dealing with matters of a public nature (such as histories, scientific works, dictionaries, maps, etc) will be admissible as evidence of facts of a public nature stated in them.

12.6.2 Public documents and records

Under this exception the following types of public document will be admissible:

- public documents (such as public registers, and returns made under public authority); and
- records (such as the records of courts, treaties, etc).

This exception was considered by the House of Lords in *Sturla v Freccia* (1880) 5 App Cas 623, in which it was stated that in order to come within this category of exception the document must:

- concern a public matter;
- be made by a person under a duty to inquire into the matter and record the findings of that inquiry; and
- be retained so that the public might refer to it or inspect it.

12.6.3 Statements as to pedigree or the existence of a marriage

A statement made by a person concerning a matter of pedigree (such as legitimacy, dates of birth, etc) or the existence of a marriage will be admissible, after the maker's death, to prove the truth of the facts stated (see, eg, the *Berkley Peerage Case* (1811) 4 Camp 401).

12.6.4 Statements as to the existence of a public or general right

Where the existence of a public right is relevant to an issue, any statement by persons affirming the existence of that public right that was made before the dispute arose shall be admissible, after the maker's death, to prove the existence of that right (see, eg, *Mercer v Denne* [1905] 2 Ch 638). The statement must relate to rights possessed by the general public or by particular classes of persons, not to those possessed by an individual.

12.6.5 Evidence of a person's general reputation

The rule in *R v Rowton* (1865) Le & Ca 520, 169 ER 1497 provides that the character of a person should be proven by evidence of the general reputation of that person in the community where he lived rather than by evidence of specific acts. Proof by this means relies upon statements made by numerous other unidentified people and is therefore proof by hearsay evidence. The rule in *Rowton* does not establish when evidence of character is admissible, simply how it is proven. For the rules concerning the admissibility of evidence of the character of parties and witnesses in civil cases, see **Chapter 8**.

12.7 Hearsay admissible under other statutory provisions

As noted earlier, s 1 of the CEA 1995 provides that:

> (3) *Nothing in this Act affects the admissibility of evidence admissible apart from this section.*
>
> (4) *The provisions of sections 2 to 6 (safeguards and supplementary provisions relating to hearsay evidence) do not apply in relation to hearsay evidence admissible apart from this section, notwithstanding that it may also be admissible by virtue of this section.*

It follows that where hearsay evidence is admissible under another statutory provision, the safeguards and supplementary provisions set out in ss 2–6 do not apply (s 1(4)). The main statutory provisions under which hearsay will be admitted apart from the CEA 1995 are:

- Bankers' Books Evidence Act 1879;
- Children Act 1989; and
- Child Support Act 1991.

12.7.1 Bankers' Books Evidence Act 1879

The Bankers' Books Evidence Act 1879, s 3 provides that:

> ... *a copy of any entry in a bankers' book shall in all legal proceedings be received as prima facie evidence of such an entry, and of the matters, transactions and accounts therein recorded.*

Section 4 adds that proof that the book in question is a bankers' book must be given by a partner or officer of the bank either orally or by a sworn affidavit. Important considerations are what is meant by 'bank' and what is meant by 'bankers' book'. As originally enacted, the definitions restricted the utility of the exception reflecting the early state of development of the banking system in the nineteenth century. The Bankers' Books Evidence Act 1879 as amended currently uses broader definitions. It defines a 'bank' as a deposit taker (as defined at s 9(1A), (1B), and (1A) of the Act) or the National Savings Bank.

'Bankers' books' include ledgers, day books, cash books, account books, and other records used in the ordinary business of the bank, whether these records are in written form or are kept on microfilm, magnetic tape, or any other form of mechanical or electronic data retrieval mechanism (s 9(2)).

12.7.2 Children Act 1989 and Child Support Act 1991

The Children (Admissibility of Hearsay Evidence) Order 1993 (made under the Children Act 1989, s 96) provides that in civil proceedings before the High Court or a county court and in family proceedings and civil proceedings under the Child Support Act 1991 in a magistrates' court, evidence may be given in connection with the upbringing, maintenance, or welfare of a child notwithstanding that the evidence in question would otherwise be inadmissible because of the hearsay rule.

12.7.3 Miscellaneous

Statutory exceptions to the rule against hearsay also include the Marriage Act 1949, s 65(3); the Births and Deaths Registration Act 1953, s 34; and the Solicitors Act 1974, s 18.

13

Hearsay evidence in criminal proceedings

13.1 Definition

As set out in **Chapter 11**, the definition of the hearsay rule in criminal proceedings is to be found in the Criminal Justice Act 2003 (CJA 2003), s 114:

> (1) *In criminal proceedings a statement not made in oral evidence in the proceedings is admissible as evidence of any matter stated if, but only if—*
>
> (a) *any provision of this Chapter or any other statutory provision makes it admissible,*
>
> (b) *any rule of law preserved by section 118 makes it admissible,*
>
> (c) *all parties to the proceedings agree to it being admissible, or*
>
> (d) *the court is satisfied that it is in the interests of justice for it to be admissible.*

However, the definition must be read together with s 115(2), which defines 'statement', and s 115(3), which in defining 'matter stated' requires that the purpose of the person making the statement was:

- to cause another person to believe the matter stated; or
- to cause another person to act or a machine to operate on the basis that the matter is as stated.

As stated earlier in **Chapter 11,** hearsay in criminal proceedings may be identified using an approach which draws on the analysis in the case of *R v Twist* [2011] 2 Cr App R 17 (see **11.6.5**). Where evidence is hearsay, it is inadmissible unless an exception to the rule applies. Accordingly, having identified evidence as hearsay, the next step should be to consider whether it may be brought under one of the four headings for admissibility, for which see **13.2**. It is important to remember that even where hearsay evidence could be admissible under one of these grounds, it is still necessary to consider the application of appropriate safeguards, for which see **13.9**.

'Criminal proceedings' are defined in s 140 as '*criminal proceedings in relation to which the strict rules of evidence apply*'. In *R v Bradley* [2005] 1 Cr App R 24, the Court of Appeal concluded that this meant criminal trials and Newton hearings. Thus, hearsay will be admissible in proceedings for breach of bail (*R (Thomas) v Greenwich Magistrates' Court* [2009] Crim LR 800).

13.2 Admissibility

Section 114 provides that there are four grounds of admissibility for hearsay evidence:

- the statement is admissible under a statutory provision of the 2003 Act (or any other statutory provision);
- the statement is admissible under a preserved common law exception;
- all of the parties in the proceedings agree to its admissibility; or
- it is in the interests of justice for the evidence to be admitted.

13.3 Admissibility under a statutory provision of the Criminal Justice Act 2003

The Act provides for the admissibility of evidence in three main situations:

- the maker of the statement is unavailable as a witness (s 116);
- the statement was made in a business or professional document (s 117); and
- the statement is a specific type of previous statement made by a witness (ss 119 and 120).

The Act also provides for the admissibility of a statement prepared by an expert for the purposes of criminal proceedings (s 127).

It is worth remembering that the CJA 2003, s 114(1)(d) allows the court to admit evidence in the interests of justice if it is not otherwise admissible. Therefore, even where a statement does not meet all the requirements of a statutory exception it may still be admissible under the inclusionary discretion.

13.3.1 Statements where the maker is unavailable as a witness

Section 116 of the CJA 2003 provides:

> *(1) In criminal proceedings a statement not made in oral evidence in the proceedings is admissible as evidence of any matter stated if—*
>
> *(a) oral evidence given in the proceedings by the person who made the statement would be admissible as evidence of that matter,*
>
> *(b) the person who made the statement (the relevant person) is identified to the court's satisfaction, and*
>
> *(c) any of the five conditions mentioned in subsection (2) is satisfied.*
>
> *(2) The conditions are—*
>
> *(a) that the relevant person is dead;*
>
> *(b) that the relevant person is unfit to be a witness because of his bodily or mental condition;*
>
> *(c) that the relevant person is outside the United Kingdom and it is not reasonably practicable to secure his attendance;*
>
> *(d) that the relevant person cannot be found although such steps as it is reasonably practicable to take to find him have been taken;*
>
> *(e) that through fear the relevant person does not give (or does not continue to give) oral evidence in the proceedings, either at all or in connection with the subject matter of the statement, and the court gives leave for the statement to be given in evidence.*

(3) For the purposes of subsection (2)(e) 'fear' is to be widely construed and (for example) includes fear of the death or injury of another person or of financial loss.

(4) Leave may be given under subsection (2)(e) only if the court considers that the statement ought to be admitted in the interests of justice, having regard—

(a) to the statement's contents,

(b) to any risk that its admission or exclusion will result in unfairness to any party to the proceedings (and in particular to how difficult it will be to challenge the statement if the relevant person does not give oral evidence),

(c) in appropriate cases, to the fact that a direction under section 19 of the Youth Justice and Criminal Evidence Act 1999 (c. 23) (special measures for the giving of evidence by fearful witnesses etc) could be made in relation to the relevant person, and

(d) to any other relevant circumstances.

(5) A condition set out in any paragraph of subsection (2) which is in fact satisfied is to be treated as not satisfied if it is shown that the circumstances described in that paragraph are caused—

(a) by the person in support of whose case it is sought to give the statement in evidence, or

(b) by a person acting on his behalf,

in order to prevent the relevant person giving oral evidence in the proceedings (whether at all or in connection with the subject matter of the statement).

Section 116 allows a hearsay statement to be admitted if the person who made the statement:

- could have given admissible oral evidence of it;
- can be identified; and
- is unavailable for one of the specified reasons.

Note that s 116 covers oral statements, statements by gesture, and statements made or contained in a document.

The precursor to s 116 was the Criminal Justice Act 1988, s 23. It is submitted that many of the principles established in the case law relating to s 23 will continue to apply. For that reason, it is appropriate to make reference to cases pre-dating the enactment of the CJA 2003 in the discussion that follows.

13.3.1.1 Oral evidence would have been admissible

Section 116(1)(a) requires that if oral evidence were to be given in the proceedings by the person who made the statement, it would be admissible as evidence of the matter stated. The effect of the CJA 2003, s 116(1)(a) is to prevent the exception from being used to admit otherwise inadmissible evidence. For example, if the person who made the statement was simply expressing an inadmissible opinion (see **Chapter 17**) then it will remain inadmissible even if the other provisions of s 116 could be satisfied.

One of the most significant effects of s 116(1)(a) is that it restricts s 116 to admitting only first-hand hearsay as opposed to multiple hearsay (*R v JP* [1999] Crim LR 401). The phrase 'person who made the statement' has been interpreted to mean the person who communicated the statement to the witness. The person who communicated the statement to the witness may or may not be the person who witnessed the event described in the statement. Consider the following example: W1 witnesses a robbery and describes the appearance of the robber to W2 who then passes the information on to W3. Where W1 makes a statement to W2 who repeats it to W3, and W3 is then called to give evidence of it, W2 will be the 'person who made the statement'. In such circumstances, s 116 will not permit W3 to give evidence of what he heard W2 say because, if W2 were to give evidence of the statement, it would itself be hearsay and thus inadmissible. Of course, s 116(1)(a) would be no bar to W2 giving evidence of what he heard W1 say. In this situation, W1 is the person who made the statement and, as they witnessed the robbery, they could give admissible evidence of what they had seen.

13.3.1.2 Maker of the statement can be identified

The CJA 2003, s 116(1)(b) requires that the court must be satisfied as to the identity of the maker. The question arises as to what amounts to satisfactory identification. In *R v Mayers* [2009] 1 WLR 1915, CA, it was held that s 116(1)(b) requires the witness's name to be known and disclosed to the defence, the rationale for the requirement being to enable the opposing party to challenge the absent witness's credibility under s 124 of the Act (see 13.9.2). While s 114(1)(d) might appear to be an alternative route to admissibility if identity cannot be established, it was held in *R v Mayers* that the interests of justice exception does not allow for the admission of anonymous hearsay (see 13.6). The approach in *Mayers* was confirmed in *R v Horncastle* [2009] 2 Cr App R 15 in which it was held *per curiam* that the CJA 2003 is concerned with identified but absent witnesses and does not permit the admission of the evidence of anonymous witnesses, to whom different considerations apply.

13.3.1.3 Proof of the maker's unavailability

The party seeking to rely upon the statement must prove that the witness is unavailable for one of the five specified reasons set out in s 116(2) to the satisfaction of the judge. If it is the prosecution who seek to rely on the statement, they must meet the criminal standard of proof, namely they must satisfy the judge beyond reasonable doubt (*R v Acton Justices, ex p McMullen* (1990) 92 Cr App R 98; *R (Meredith) v Harwich Justices* [2006] EWHC 3336 (Admin)); the defence need only satisfy the judge on the balance of probability (*R v Mattey* [1995] 2 Cr App R 409).

For the purposes of s 116(2), it is the circumstances of the maker of the statement at the time of trial that are material rather than the circumstances at the time when the statement was made.

None of the conditions for admissibility will be satisfied if it is proven to the court that the maker's unavailability was brought about by the person seeking to admit the statement (s 116(5)(a)) or by a person acting on that person's behalf (s 116(5)(b)).

We will consider each of the reasons for unavailability in turn.

13.3.1.4 Death

An example of how this might arise in practice would be where the complainant, who is elderly, makes a statement to the police regarding the offence but dies before the matter reaches trial.

13.3.1.5 Unfitness to be a witness owing to bodily or mental condition

The exception applies where the maker of the statement is 'unfit to be a witness' and not simply unfit to attend court. The provision is not therefore focused on the witness's ability to attend court but once there, their fitness to give evidence. Under the equivalent provision of the Criminal Justice Act 1988, s 23 (the predecessor to the CJA 2003, s 116) it was held that the exception would apply where, owing to their physical or mental condition, the witness could not give meaningful testimony (*R v Setz-Dempsey* [1994] Crim LR 123, CA). The terms of s 116 are broad enough to include the accused. Although the circumstances are likely to be rare and exceptional, where a defendant is genuinely unfit to give oral evidence at trial, s 116 may permit the defendant to put his account before the jury by way of hearsay (*Hamburger* [2017] EWCA Crim 273).

In deciding whether a person is unfit to be a witness, the judge may give consideration to whether special measures could be used to assist the witness to give evidence (see *R v Ferdinand* [2014] EWCA Crim 1243). Where such special measures could be used so as to enable a witness to give evidence who would not otherwise be able to do so, the witness will not be deemed 'unfit' (see **4.11** for special measures directions).

13.3.1.6 Outside the United Kingdom and securing attendance not reasonably practicable

Evidence that the witness is in fact outside the United Kingdom must be established by admissible evidence; a declaration to that effect in the witness statement itself will not suffice (*R v Case* [1991] Crim LR 192). However, it is not enough to simply prove that the witness is outside the UK; it is also necessary to demonstrate that securing their attendance is not reasonably practicable. What is reasonable will depend on the circumstances but, to ensure a fair trial, a prosecutor seeking to rely on s 116 should be in a position to provide compelling and detailed reasons for a witness's absence: see *Price v UK* [2016] ECHR 753. In *R v Castillo* [1996] 1 Cr App R 438, the Court of Appeal held that the mere fact that it is possible for the witness to attend does not mean that the exception does not apply. Instead, regard should be had to the following three factors:

- the importance of the evidence the witness could give;
- the expense and inconvenience in securing attendance; and
- the validity of the reasons put forward for not attending.

For example, in *Gyima* [2007] EWCA Crim 429, it was held that the refusal of the parents of a child witness to cooperate with the prosecution's efforts to secure his attendance and the cost of alternative measures were proper for the court to consider under s 116(2)(c).

The expression 'reasonably practicable' must be judged on the basis of the steps taken, or not taken, by the party seeking to secure the attendance of the witness: *C & K* [2006] 1 WLR 2994. In this case, it was also noted that evidence should be provided as to whether a witness's account could have been given via a video link, or some other method that would enable the defendant to challenge that witness's account. The same point was made by Hughes LJ in *Riat* [2013] 1 Cr App R 2; absence abroad will satisfy s 116(2)(c) '*only if it is not reasonably practicable to bring the witness to court, either in person or by video link*'.

Where a party has satisfied the court that it is not reasonably practicable to secure the attendance of the witness, the court must go on to consider whether to exercise its powers under s 126 of the 2003 Act and s 78 of the 1984 Act (see **13.9.4**).

13.3.1.7 Maker cannot be found despite reasonably practicable steps having been taken

As with s 116(2)(c) above, evidence of the reasonable steps taken to secure the attendance of the witness at trial will be required to satisfy this criteria, and what is reasonable will depend on the particular circumstances. The courts have emphasised the importance of keeping track of witnesses before trial. In *Riat* [2013] 1 Cr App R 2, Hughes LJ said '*[i]f the witness is lost, all reasonably practicable steps must have been taken to get him to court: this will include not only looking for him if he disappears but also keeping in touch with him to avoid him disappearing*'. In *R v Adams* [2008] 1 Cr App R 35, it was held that simply leaving a message on a mobile telephone the last working day before trial in circumstances in which no contact had been had with the witness in the four months since the trial date had been set was not taking such steps as are reasonably practicable. In *R v Murphy* [2014] EWCA Crim 1457, it was held that the judge was entitled to conclude that the prosecution had taken reasonable steps in contacting the witness on the last working day before trial and then seeking a witness summons which was served on the witness before he refused to attend court and disappeared without leaving an address. It was held that the question of whether the prosecution have taken reasonable steps is a question of fact for the judge to determine and that, in this case, while the prosecution should have acted more promptly, the prosecution's subsequent actions in seeking to secure the witness's attendance were sufficient.

13.3.1.8 Maker in fear

Section 116(2)(e) may be relied upon to prove a statement where the witness fails to attend to give evidence, attends but refuses to give evidence, stops giving evidence, or gives evidence but avoids reference to particular matters; however, proof of a causal link between the fear and the failure or refusal to give evidence is required.

Section 116(3) of the CJA 2003 provides that fear should be widely construed and specifically mentions fear of death or injury to persons other than the maker of the statement and the fear of financial loss. The test has been held to be subjective (*R v Doherty* (2007) 171 JP 79, CA) and so fear can even be based on misunderstanding (*R v Martin* [1996] Crim LR 589, CA). In *R v Horncastle* [2009] 2 Cr App R 15, it was noted that fear need not be attributable to the accused. It may include fear to which a police officer has contributed, for example, by advising witnesses as to the potential risk of harm presented by the defendant.

The question of whether the witness is in fear should be considered at the time when the witness is due to give evidence rather than days or weeks beforehand, although there might be some practical necessity to resolve the matter at the beginning of the trial (*R v H* [2001] Crim LR 815, CA). The fear must be established by admissible evidence (*Neill v North Antrim Magistrates Court* [1992] 1 WLR 1221, HL). It was thought that courts would be ill-advised to seek to test the basis of fear by calling witnesses before them, not least because this would undermine the very purpose of s 116 (*R v Davies* [2007] 2 All ER 1070); instead fear could be proved by witness statement (*R v Rutherford* [1998] Crim LR 490, CA; *R v Davies*) or by other persons (*R v Acton Justices, ex p McMullen* (1991) 92 Cr App R 98). However, in *Shabir* [2012] EWCA Crim 2564 the Court of Appeal endorsed the view that every effort must be made to get the witness to court so that the judge may test the evidence of fear rigorously, explore all possibilities of the witness attending to give oral evidence, and be satisfied that every effort has been made to get the witness to court (see also *R v Riat* [2013] 1 Cr App R 2). In the majority of cases, close scrutiny of the witness's fear should be conducted in court, although there may be some cases where this would be inappropriate (*Harvey* [2014] EWCA Crim 54).

Unlike the other grounds for the application of the CJA 2003, s 116(2) evidence can only be admitted under s 116(2)(e) if the judge grants leave. Section 116(4) requires the court, in determining leave, to consider any 'relevant circumstances' but specifically requires consideration of the contents of the statement, the effect of any special measures directions that could be made, and the risk of unfairness to any party in the proceedings in either admitting or excluding the evidence.

13.3.2 Statements in business documents

Section 117 of the CJA 2003 provides:

> (1) *In criminal proceedings a statement contained in a document is admissible as evidence of any matter stated if—*
>
> (a) *oral evidence given in the proceedings would be admissible as evidence of that matter,*

> (b) *the requirements of subsection (2) are satisfied, and*
>
> (c) *the requirements of subsection (5) are satisfied, in a case where subsection (4) requires them to be.*
>
> (2) *The requirements of this subsection are satisfied if—*
>
> (a) *the document or the part containing the statement was created or received by a person in the course of a trade, business, profession or other occupation, or as the holder of a paid or unpaid office,*
>
> (b) *the person who supplied the information contained in the statement (the relevant person) had or may reasonably be supposed to have had personal knowledge of the matters dealt with, and*
>
> (c) *each person (if any) through whom the information was supplied from the relevant person to the person mentioned in paragraph (a) received the information in the course of a trade, business, profession or other occupation, or as the holder of a paid or unpaid office.*
>
> (3) *The persons mentioned in paragraphs (a) and (b) of subsection (2) may be the same person.*
>
> (4) *The additional requirements of subsection (5) must be satisfied if the statement—*
>
> (a) *was prepared for the purposes of pending or contemplated criminal proceedings, or for a criminal investigation, but*
>
> (b) *was not obtained pursuant to a request under section 7 of the Crime (International Co-operation) Act 2003 (c. 32) or an order under paragraph 6 of Schedule 13 to the Criminal Justice Act 1988 (c. 33) (which relate to overseas evidence).*
>
> (5) *The requirements of this subsection are satisfied if—*
>
> (a) *any of the five conditions mentioned in section 116(2) is satisfied (absence of relevant person etc), or*
>
> (b) *the relevant person cannot reasonably be expected to have any recollection of the matters dealt with in the statement (having regard to the length of time since he supplied the information and all other circumstances).*
>
> (6) *A statement is not admissible under this section if the court makes a direction to that effect under subsection (7).*
>
> (7) *The court may make a direction under this subsection if satisfied that the statement's reliability as evidence for the purpose for which it is tendered is doubtful in view of—*
>
> (a) *its contents,*
>
> (b) *the source of the information contained in it,*
>
> (c) *the way in which or the circumstances in which the information was supplied or received, or*
>
> (d) *the way in which or the circumstances in which the document concerned was created or received.*

The rationale behind s 117 is that business records are ordinarily compiled by disinterested persons, ie persons not influenced by personal advantage, and are likely to be accurate. Accordingly, s 117 allows business documents to be admissible at trial because they are likely to be reliable.

As with s 116 of the CJA 2003, s 117(1)(a) does not allow the admission of evidence in a document where that evidence would be inadmissible under other rules of evidence. However, unlike s 116 there is no requirement that the maker of the statement be able to give admissible oral evidence of the facts stated in the statement. It follows that multiple hearsay may be admitted under s 117.

Unlike s 116, s 117 is only concerned with the admissibility of statements contained in documents (s 117(1)). Oral statements or gestures are not admissible under s 117 unless they have been recorded in a document. Document is defined by s 134(1) as anything in which information of any description is recorded.

The precursor to s 117 was the Criminal Justice Act 1988, s 24. It is submitted that many of the principles established in the case law relating to s 24 will continue to apply. For that reason, cases pre-dating the enactment of the CJA 2003 will be referred to in the discussion that follows.

13.3.2.1 Documents to which CJA 2003, s 117 applies

Section 117 regulates the admissibility of two types of document:

- ordinary business documents; and
- documents prepared for pending or contemplated criminal proceedings or during criminal investigations.

To be admissible under the CJA 2003, s 117, the following criteria must be met:

(a) The document must have been created or received in the course of a trade, business, profession, etc (s 117(2)(a)). Note, therefore, that a letter written by someone in a non-professional capacity but received by someone in a professional/business capacity is covered by the section.

(b) The supplier of the information in the document must be shown to have personal knowledge of the facts related (s 117(2)(b)). Section 117(2)(b) also allows the court to infer such personal knowledge from the nature of the document (see *R v Foxley* [1995] 2 Cr App R 523; *Vehicle and Operator Services Agency v Jenkins Transport Ltd* [2003] EWHC 2879 (Admin)).

(c) Where the document contains information that has been passed from person to person, each person receiving the information must have done so in the course of a trade, business, profession, etc (s 117(2)(c)).

Consider the following example. Alf is charged with theft of computer parts from Stock Room D of the building where he works as a packer. The prosecution alleges that the goods went missing on the evening of 3 March. The computer parts were found in Alf's house and the serial numbers for each part were identified. The following are items of evidence:

1. A timesheet recording that Alf worked in Stock Room D on 3 March from 3 pm to 11 pm. The person who filled out the timesheet, Anil, can attend court but cannot remember any details. The system for filling out the sheet is that each stock room has a foreman who informs Anil who was in that room on each day, when they started and when they left.
2. A checklist that records the serial numbers of all parts consigned to each warehouse. On the list the serial numbers for the computer parts found at Alf's house appear in the column headed 'Stock Room D'. A witness can prove that the usual process for recording the information is either for the person compiling the list to look at the parts himself or for him to have a colleague call the numbers out to him. However, there is no evidence as to who compiled the list.

Neither statement can be admitted under s 116. The hearsay statement contained in the timesheet is that Alf was present in Stock Room D from 3 pm to 11 pm. The statement was originally made orally by the foreman who passed the information to Anil who then made the written record. Not only is the timesheet multiple hearsay, and thus inadmissible by virtue of s 116(1)(a), but Anil, who made the statement that is recorded in the document, is available to attend court and give evidence.

The hearsay statement contained in the checklist is the serial numbers of the computer parts later recovered from Alf's house. If the information was passed to the person who wrote the checklist, then the statement is clearly multiple hearsay. However, even if there was no intermediary, the statement will not be admissible under s 116(1)(b) because the maker of the statement cannot be identified.

However, both statements would be admissible under s 117. Oral evidence would be admissible of the facts stated in statements (s 117(1)(a)). There can be no doubt that the documents were created by a person during the course of a business (s 117(2)(a)). Furthermore, the supplier of the information (ie the foreman and the compiler or his colleague) can reasonably be supposed to have had personal knowledge of the matters dealt with (s 117(2)(b)). Where applicable, each person through whom the information passed, received the information in the course of their employer's business (s 117(2)(c)). Unlike s 116, there is no need to prove the unavailability of the maker of the statement.

Maher v DPP (2006) 170 JP 441 usefully illustrates the effect of s 117(2)(c). The defendant was involved in a collision with the complainant's vehicle but drove away without stopping. However, the collision was witnessed by a passer-by who made a note of the registration number of the defendant's vehicle, which she left under the windscreen wiper of the complainant's vehicle. The complainant returned to find her car damaged and the note giving the registration number of the defendant's vehicle. The complainant telephoned the police and passed the registration number on to them. The number was recorded in an incident log. By the time of the trial the note had been lost. The magistrates' court admitted evidence of the log under the CJA 2003, s 117. The Divisional Court held that the evidence of the log was not admissible under s 117(2)(c) because the complainant had not received the information in the course of a trade, business, etc. However, the Divisional Court concluded that the evidence was admissible under s 121(1)(c) as multiple hearsay on the grounds that the value of the evidence, taking into account its apparent reliability, was so high that the interests of justice required its admissibility.

13.3.2.2 Documents prepared for criminal investigations or proceedings

To prevent s 117 from undermining s 116 by admitting witness statements in circumstances where the s 116(2) reasons for unavailability cannot be satisfied, s 117(4) and (5) additionally require that a document prepared for the purposes of pending or contemplated criminal proceedings or for the purpose of a criminal investigation may only be admitted under s 117 where the supplier of the information either:

(a) is unavailable for one of the five conditions mentioned in section 116(2); or

(b) cannot reasonably be expected to have any recollection of the matters dealt with in the statement (having regard to the length of time since he supplied the information and all other circumstances).

13.3.3 Previous inconsistent statements

The admissibility of previous inconsistent statements to prove a matter stated is governed by s 119(1), which is considered at **7.7**.

13.3.4 Previous consistent statements

The admissibility of previous consistent statements to prove a matter stated is considered at **6.5**.

13.4 Admissibility under preserved common law exceptions

Section 118(1) of the CJA 2003 preserves the following common law exceptions to the rule against hearsay:

- public information;
- evidence of reputation;

- *res gestae*;
- confessions;
- admissions by agents;
- common enterprise; and
- expert evidence.

Otherwise all of the common law rules concerning the admissibility of hearsay evidence in criminal proceedings are abolished by the CJA 2003, s 118(2).

13.4.1 Public information

Section 118(1) provides the following description of the preserved common law rules regarding certain public documents:

> *(1) Any rule of law under which in criminal proceedings—*
>
> *(a) published works dealing with matters of a public nature (such as histories, scientific works, dictionaries and maps) are admissible as evidence of facts of a public nature stated in them,*
>
> *(b) public documents (such as public registers, and returns made under public authority with respect to matters of public interest) are admissible as evidence of facts stated in them,*
>
> *(c) records (such as the records of certain courts, treaties, Crown grants, pardons and commissions) are admissible as evidence of facts stated in them, or*
>
> *(d) evidence relating to a person's age or date or place of birth may be given by a person without personal knowledge of the matter.*

The rule presumes that entries in documents made by public officers can be relied upon (*Irish Society v Bishop of Derry* (1846) 12 Cl & F 641). For further details on the operation of this exception, see **12.6.2**. Although preserved under s 118, various statutes allowing for the admissibility of certain documents, and, in particular, s 117 of the CJA 2003, have greatly diminished the importance of this rule.

13.4.2 Reputation

Section 118(1), paras 2 and 3 preserve the following rules:

Reputation as to character

> *(2) Any rule of law under which in criminal proceedings evidence of a person's reputation is admissible for the purpose of proving his good or bad character.*

Note

The rule is preserved only so far as it allows the court to treat such evidence as proving the matter concerned.

Reputation or family tradition

> *(3) Any rule of law under which in criminal proceedings evidence of reputation or family tradition is admissible for the purpose of proving or disproving—*
>
> *(a) pedigree or the existence of a marriage,*
>
> *(b) the existence of any public or general right, or*
>
> *(c) the identity of any person or thing.*

Note

The rule is preserved only so far as it allows the court to treat such evidence as proving or disproving the matter concerned.

For further details on the operation of this exception, see **12.6.5**. Proof of the character of a person by reputation is only permitted where the proof of the character in question is admissible evidence: see, generally, **Chapters 8**, **9**, and **10**. In *R v Phillips* [2010] EWCA Crim 378, the defendant was identified as being at the scene of the offence by a witness, but the witness had only learned of the defendant's surname from others after the offence. It was held that the attribution of the surname by the witness to the defendant fell within the common law exception of reputation to prove identity preserved under s 118(3)(c).

13.4.3 *Res gestae*

Section 118(1) states the rule that is preserved under the heading '*res gestae*' as follows:

...

> *(4) Any rule of law under which in criminal proceedings a statement is admissible as evidence of any matter stated if—*
>
> *(a) the statement was made by a person so emotionally overpowered by an event that the possibility of concoction or distortion can be disregarded,*
>
> *(b) the statement accompanied an act which can be properly evaluated as evidence only if considered in conjunction with the statement, or*
>
> *(c) the statement relates to a physical sensation or a mental state (such as intention or emotion).*

Paragraph 4 is not intended to define the *res gestae* rule, merely to identify it. The definition of *res gestae* is a matter for the common law.

Statements forming part of the *res gestae* fall into a number of different categories. The phrase '*res gestae*' is used by the law to identify the event in question. The various *res gestae* exceptions loosely conform to a principle that the statement must be made at or about the same time as the matter to which it relates. In other words, there is some requirement of contemporaneity. Quite what the statement relates to for each exception varies, as shall be seen in the following sections. The logic of these exceptions is that statements made at the time of the event or matter are less likely to be made up or distorted than statements made at a later point.

13.4.3.1 Statements contemporaneous to an emotionally overpowering event

This category of *res gestae* statement is one that is made by someone as an event is taking place and where the event is dominating or overwhelming the mind of the person making the statement.

The test for admissibility for this type of *res gestae* statement is set out in *R v Andrews* [1987] AC 281, where a man was attacked and mortally wounded by two others. The prosecution called police officers to give evidence that the victim told them that Andrews was one of the attackers. Clearly this was a hearsay statement adduced to prove that fact. The House of Lords held that nonetheless the statement was admissible under the *res gestae* exception. In doing so Lord Ackner defined the test of admissibility (at [300]) as follows:

> 1. The primary question which the judge must ask himself or herself is—can the possibility of concoction or distortion be disregarded?
> 2. To answer that question the judge must first consider the circumstances in which the particular statement was made, in order to satisfy himself or herself that the event was so unusual or startling or dramatic as to dominate the thoughts of the maker so that his utterance was an instinctive reaction to that event, thus giving no real opportunity for reasoned reflection. In such a situation the judge would be entitled to conclude that the involvement or the pressure of the event would exclude the possibility of concoction or distortion, providing that the statement was made in conditions of approximate but not exact contemporaneity.

Therefore:

(a) The primary test is whether concoction or distortion can be disregarded.

(b) This test is passed if the judge concludes (ie it is proved to him) that:

(i) there was an 'unusual or *startling* or dramatic' *event*;

(ii) that event therefore *dominated the thoughts* of the maker of the statement;

(iii) as a result of that domination of the thoughts, the statement was an 'instinctive reaction' to the event. In other words, the statement was *spontaneous*;

(iv) the statement was *approximately contemporaneous*.

Lord Ackner made the following additional points:

(a) On the issue of spontaneity, Lord Ackner said:

(i) the statement must be '*so closely associated with the event ... that it can fairly be said that the mind of the declarant was still dominated by the event*';

(ii) the judge must be satisfied that the '*event, which provided the trigger mechanism was still operative*';

(iii) that the statement is a response to a question is only a factor to consider in deciding whether the statement was sufficiently spontaneous.

(b) The judge should consider any factors other than the passage of time that might, in the circumstances of each case, support any argument that the statement was concocted or distorted. In *R v Andrews*, for example, it was alleged that the victim had a malicious motive to fabricate evidence against Andrews. In such cases the judge must be satisfied that there was no possibility of any concoction or distortion having regard to the allegations of malice.

(c) Generally, any risk that the person hearing and repeating the statement has made an error goes to the weight not the admissibility of the statement. However, where a special feature is alleged to have caused the mistake, such as drunkenness (as was the case in *R v Andrews*) or short sightedness, the judge must '*consider whether he can exclude the possibility of error*'. If not, it would seem the judge may have to exclude the statement.

Whether or not a particular statement comes within this exception will have to be established by evidence. In *Teper v R* [1952] AC 480, PC, the statement was shouted to a passing motorist by an unknown person. It was held that as it was not known who had made the statement, it was *unlikely* that the statement would be admissible under this exception. This is because it is unlikely that the prosecution would be able to prove that the maker's mind was dominated by the event in the absence of knowing who the maker is. However, there may be circumstances in which there is evidence to suggest that the statement was made by an unknown person whose mind was dominated.

The statement must be approximately contemporaneous. This will be a question of fact in each case. In *Tobi v Nichols* [1988] RTR 343, DC, a statement made 20 minutes after a collision was determined not to be sufficiently contemporaneous. However, it was also considered that the event, a road traffic accident, was not sufficiently mind-dominating. It is submitted that there is a correlation between the nature of the event and how long after it a statement may be roughly contemporaneous. The more traumatic the event, the stronger the argument that it is still dominating the mind of the maker at a later point. In *R v Carnall* [1995] Crim LR 944, for example, a statement made an hour after a murderous assault was held to have been rightly admitted. As the statement must be a reaction to or part of the event, statements made before the event in question cannot be part of this category of *res gestae* exception (*R v Newport* [1998] Crim LR 581). Consider also *Ibrahim v CPS* [2016] EWHC 1750 (Admin) and *Morgan v DPP* [2016] EWHC 3414 (Admin), in which the victims of domestic violence in each case were assaulted some 90 minutes and 60 minutes respectively before seeking assistance from the emergency services; evidence of their statements in seeking assistance was admitted under the *res gestae* rule.

There are no particular requirements that the person who made the statement is dead or unavailable at the time of trial (*R v Nye* (1977) 66 Cr App R 252, CA). Even statements made by the accused can be part of the *res gestae* and therefore admitted by either party. In *R v Glover* [1991] Crim LR 48, CA, the accused said: 'I am David Glover ... we will not think twice about shooting you and your kids.' As the trial issue was identity, the prosecution was allowed to call this statement as part of the *res gestae*. However, in *R v Andrews*, Lord Ackner observed that it would be wrong to use this *res gestae* exception to avoid calling the witness in question so as to deprive other parties of an opportunity to cross-examine the maker of the statement. In *Attorney-General's Reference (No 1 of 2003)* [2003] 2 Cr App R 453, the Court of Appeal ruled that there was no requirement that a witness was unavailable before a statement made by that witness would be admissible under the doctrine of *res gestae*. However, where the prosecution sought to rely on a *res gestae* statement made by a person who could be called as a witness but whom the prosecution did not propose to call, the trial judge had a discretion under s 78 of PACE 1984 to exclude the *res gestae* statements. In deciding whether to do so the court would have regard to the circumstances in which the statement was made and how easy it would have been to call the witness.

In *Barnaby* [2015] EWHC 232 (Admin), hearsay statements in the form of agitated statements made by the complainant during a 999 call in which she claimed that her boyfriend, the accused, had tried to strangle her were admitted as part of the *res gestae*. The complainant remained afraid of the accused and, although present at court during the trial, neither party called her to give evidence. The Court of Appeal noted that the court has a cardinal responsibility to ensure that a defendant receives a fair trial but did not find that admitting the hearsay evidence was unfair even though the complainant was available as a witness. In doing so the court observed that the prosecution's decision not to call the complainant was a sensible decision in recognition of the potentially dangerous position in which the complainant had been placed as a prosecution witness.

A similar approach was adopted in *Ibrahim v CPS* [2016] EWHC 1750 (Admin) and *Morgan v DPP* [2016] EWHC 3414 (Admin). Both cases involved domestic violence in which statements made by the victim were admitted under the *res gestae* exception. These cases recognise that where a victim of domestic violence is in fear, the prosecution should have regard for a witness's well-being. However, where a witness does not give oral evidence through fear, *res gestae* should not be used as a means to circumvent the requirements under s 116(2)(e) (unavailable witness in fear) and the importance of a witness giving live evidence at court whenever possible. In *Wills v CPS* [2017] EWHC 3779 (Admin), the magistrates' decision to immediately consider the application of the *res gestae* rule when a complainant unexpectedly failed to attend as a witness was held to have been inappropriate without first determining the reason for the witness's non-attendance; the reasons for the failure to attend were relevant to determining the exercise of the court's discretion to exclude evidence under PACE 1984, s 78.

So as to prevent the *res gestae* rule creating decisions at odds with the provisions under s 116(2)(e) (absent witnesses in fear) and under s 114(1)(d) (in the interests of justice), the Court of Appeal in *S* [2017] EWCA Crim 1908 noted that the criteria for applying the interests of justice exception under s 114(1)(d) (see 13.6) are likely to assist the court in determining the exercise of its discretion in cases involving *res gestae* statements.

13.4.3.2 Contemporaneous statements accompanying an act

There are three requirements:

(a) the statement must be approximately contemporaneous to the act. In *Howe v Malkin* (1878) 40 LT 196, it was said that such a statement was admissible because it was mixed up with the event in question;

(b) the statement must be made by the person performing the act (*Peacock v Harris* (1836) 5 Ad & El 449); and

(c) the act should itself be relevant to the issues in the case (in *R v McCay* [1990] 1 WLR 645, CA, the statement 'It's number 8' was made at the same time as a person was identified in an identification parade).

13.4.3.3 Contemporaneous statements relating to the maker's physical or mental state

A statement made by a person in which he refers to his current physical state will be admissible to prove that physical state.

The statement can prove the physical state but not its cause (*R v Gloster* (1888) 16 Cox CC 471). Therefore, in *R v Thomson* [1912] 3 KB 19, CCR, statements by a woman that she had recently operated upon herself were not admissible to prove the cause of a miscarriage.

The statements do not have to be made at the exact time that the feelings are being experienced: whether a statement is contemporary to the feeling is a question of degree. In *Aveson v Lord Kinnaird* (1805) 6 East 188, statements made by a woman as to symptoms she said she had been suffering for some time were admitted to prove that not only was she suffering those symptoms when she made the statement but also that she had suffered them some days earlier.

So far as the maker's state of mind is concerned, statements revealing that a person was of a particular frame of mind may be original evidence in cases from which a state of mind is inferred, ie because A said a particular thing we can infer a particular state of mind or particular emotional state (eg *Thomas v Connell* (1838) 4 M & W 267, as confirmed by the approach of the courts in *R v Blastland* [1986] AC 41, HL and *R v Kearley* [1992] AC 228, HL). Clearly, however, where a person expressly states that he is of a particular state of mind (such as 'I hate that man' or 'I believe he is the one who stole my watch') there can be little doubt that the statement is hearsay evidence.

However, such a statement will be admissible as an exception to the rule against hearsay evidence if it is sufficiently contemporaneous. Statements of one's state of mind at an earlier time are not admissible (*R v Moghal* (1977) 65 Cr App R 56, CA).

A particular difficulty arises from this rule where a statement of a contemporaneous fact is used to prove what happened at a later date. The usual case is one in which the statement reveals the intention of the maker and the issue is whether the maker later acted on that intention. Consider the following cases:

(a) *R v Buckley* (1838) 13 Cox CC 293. A statement made by a police officer that he intended to keep a watch on the accused was admitted to prove that he had later been keeping a watch on the accused when he was murdered.

(b) *R v Moghal* (1977) 65 Cr App R 56, CA. A statement made by S that she intended to kill R was held to be admissible to prove that she and not the accused had killed R even though the statement had been made six months before.

(c) *R v Callender* [1998] Crim LR 337, CA. Statements made by a person two weeks before he was arrested on explosives charges that he intended to carry false explosive devices for publicity purposes were held not to be admissible.

The case law in this area appears confused. It is submitted that the best view to take of cases about current intentions is that such statements of intention are admissible under this exception but only if relevant. If the statements are not sufficiently relevant, they should not be admitted. This was the view taken in *R v Blastland* in which the statement in *R v Moghal* was criticised as insufficiently relevant. For a further criticism of *R v Callender*, see ***Blackstone's Criminal Practice***.

13.4.4 Confessions and admissions

Section 118(1), para 5 provides for the continued operation of the admissibility of confessions and mixed statements as an exception to the rule against hearsay. Confession evidence is dealt with in detail in **Chapter 14**. Mixed statements are considered at **6.5.2.5.3**.

A confession is only admissible against the maker under the common law exception. However, s 114(1)(d) is potentially available for all types of hearsay including confessions by third parties (see *R v McLean* [2008] 1 Cr App R 11, CA; *R v Y* [2008] 1 Cr App R 34).

Section 118(1), para 6 provides for the continued operation at common law of the rule whereby admissions made by an agent (*R v Turner* (1975) 61 Cr App R 67, CA) or a person appointed by the defendant to answer questions on the defendant's behalf (*Williams v Innes* (1808) Camp 364) will be admissible in evidence against the defendant. The agency must be proven by evidence independently of the agent's assertions (*R v Evans* [1981] Crim LR 699, CA).

In *R v Turner* (1975) 61 Cr App R 67, CA, the Court of Appeal identified three principles which operated in respect of admissions made by agents:

(a) an authorised agent may make an admission on behalf of his principal;

(b) a party seeking to rely on an admission must prove the agent was so authorised; and

(c) a court is entitled to assume that what is said in court by a barrister on his client's behalf is said with his client's authority.

The third principle extends to admissions made by a barrister orally or in writing, and admissions made both at trial and at pre-trial proceedings. As regards pre-trial proceedings, *R (Firth) v Epping Magistrates' Court* [2011] 1 Cr App R 32, DC, illustrates how the third principle may apply. The accused was charged with assault and made her first appearance in the magistrates' court represented by counsel. On a case progression form, required to be completed to assist in the management of a criminal case under the Criminal Procedure Rules, her counsel entered information about the issues in the case in a box headed, 'Trial Issues ...'. The information entered by counsel was, 'assault on def by complainant. Only contact made was in self-defence'. At a committal hearing the accused argued that the prosecution witness statements did not establish a prima facie case. To support its argument in reply that there *was* a prima facie case, the prosecution sought to adduce the case progression form as evidence of an admission by the defendant of a physical encounter with the complainant. The Divisional Court held that the magistrates' court had been correct to admit the evidence under s 118(1), para 6 and the third principle in *Turner*. According to the court, there was no reason why s 118(1), para 6 could not apply to admissions entered by legal representatives on court management forms in pre-trial proceedings.

However, *Firth* must be seen in the light of *R v Newell* [2012] EWCA Crim 650, a case in which the Court of Appeal considered the admissibility, for use by the prosecution, of information recorded in a case progression form by the accused's counsel. It was held that although in principle such information could be admissible under s 118(1), para 6, ordinarily it would fall to be excluded under PACE 1984, s 78. The court observed that case progression forms should be seen primarily as a means to give information for the purposes of effective case management under the Criminal Procedure Rules. Accordingly, where the case was being conducted in accordance with the letter and spirit of the rules, information in a case progression form should not, within the discretion of the court under s 78, be admitted in evidence by the prosecution as a statement to use against the defendant. Only in rare cases would such information be so admitted. It is submitted that the principle in *Newell* does not apply to a co-defendant who seeks to admit information in the defendant's case progression form, since the discretion to exclude under s 78 applies only to evidence the prosecution seeks to admit.

13.4.5 Common enterprise

Paragraph 7 of s 118(1) preserves:

> *(7) Any rule of law under which in criminal proceedings a statement made by a party to a common enterprise is admissible against another party to the enterprise as evidence of any matter stated.*

Where, in the course of committing a crime, A makes a statement that proves that B was also committing the same crime, the common law permits the statement to be admitted as proof of the fact that B committed the crime. This rule should be contrasted with the rule that generally a confession is only admissible against the person who makes it and not another person.

Before a statement will be admissible under this exception, however, it must be established that:

- there was a common criminal purpose or enterprise; and
- the statement was made to pursue or further that purpose.

13.4.5.1 Common purpose

A common purpose is wider than a conspiracy. In *R v Jones* [1997] 2 Cr App R 119, CA, for example, the doctrine was applied to the offence of evading the prohibition on the importation of drugs (drug smuggling) even though there was no charge of conspiracy on the indictment. However, there does have to be some common element of commission of the offence. In *R v Gray* [1995] 2 Cr App R 100, there had been an allegation of a 'network' between various co-accused as to insider dealing but each accused was charged with separate offences. The Court of Appeal concluded that, in the absence of some allegation that the offences had been committed jointly, the rule did not apply. Usually such an allegation would arise from the way in which the accused persons were charged. Therefore the rule will generally only apply where the parties are jointly charged, whether as principals or as secondary parties. The court did leave open the possibility that future cases may involve a common purpose even if the various parties were charged with separate offences but did not explain how that might be the case.

The existence of the common purpose must be proved by evidence independent to the statement to be admitted under the exception (*R v Blake* (1844) 6 QB 126). In other words, what is said in the statement cannot prove that there was a common purpose and the jury should be directed that it cannot rely on the statement itself to prove the existence of such a common purpose (*R v Williams* [2002] EWCA Crim 2208). However, the court can conditionally admit the evidence of the statement subject to proof at some later stage of the common purpose (*R v Governor of Pentonville Prison, ex p Osman* [1990] 1 WLR 277, DC). If the existence of a common purpose cannot subsequently be proven by independent evidence, the statement will have to be excluded from the case against any co-accused (*R v Donat* (1985) 82 Cr App R 173, CA) and, in jury trials, a direction will have to be given directing the jury to ignore the evidence or it may have to be discharged.

13.4.5.2 Furtherance of the common purpose

A statement made after the criminal purpose has been achieved or one that simply explains what another member has done without advancing it in any way, will not be 'in furtherance' of the common purpose and therefore is not admissible (*R v Walters* (1979) 69 Cr App R 115, CA; *R v Steward* [1963] Crim LR 697, CCA).

What is capable of being a statement in furtherance of a common purpose will depend on the facts of the case. In *R v Devonport* [1996] 1 Cr App R 221, CA, the statement concerned the intended division of proceeds from a drug deal. This was treated as in furtherance of the common purpose. However, in *R v Blake* (1844) 6 QB 126, a cheque proving that B had received his share of the proceeds from a conspiracy was held not to be in furtherance of the common purpose. In the former case the statement assisted or encouraged the commission of the offence whereas in the latter case it was simply a consequence of it.

Where the evidence that is alleged to prove the common purpose is a document, it will be necessary to prove (a) it was either made in a particular (and relevant) way or to have been found in an incriminating way, and (b) that it suggests the involvement of the defendants in the common purpose (*R v Jenkins* [2003] Crim LR 107, CA). Merely producing the document without proving it in this way will not render it admissible as evidence of the common purpose.

The courts have interpreted what furthers the purpose quite loosely. In *R v Ilyas* [1996] Crim LR 810, CA, the diary of A was admitted to prove that B, C, and D had received stolen cars, Latham J appearing to extend the definition to documents 'created *in the course of*, or furtherance, of the conspiracy'. Were this case to be decided again today it is unlikely that the diary entries would come within the statutory definition of hearsay by virtue of the CJA 2003, s 115(3) (see *R v N* [2006] EWCA Crim 3309).

13.4.6 Expert evidence

Section 118(1), para 8 preserves:

> *(8) Any rule of law under which in criminal proceedings an expert witness may draw on the body of expertise relevant to his field.*

Expert evidence is considered in detail in **Chapter 17**. There it will be seen that experts are, understandably, entitled to rely upon hearsay in the sense that they can rely on the observations and writings of other experts in their field of expertise.

However, the rule that the data upon which the expert's opinion is based have to be proven by admissible evidence has been relaxed by the CJA 2003, s 127, which provides that an expert can base his opinion on information contained in a statement prepared for criminal purposes if the fact that the expert will do so is notified to the other parties. The other parties have the opportunity to object to such a use of the statement. Where such a statement is used, s 127(3) provides that the statement becomes evidence of its contents.

13.5 Admissibility by agreement

By virtue of s 114(1)(c), where all of the parties agree, hearsay evidence may be admitted at trial. There is no definition of 'agreement' under the CJA 2003 but it appears that agreement may be express or implied (*Shah* [2012] EWCA Crim 212). A failure to object to hearsay being admitted is not necessarily an indication of agreement (*Williams v Vehicle Operator Services Agency* [2008] EWHC 849 (Admin) and *Bhagchandka* [2016] EWCA Crim 700).

13.6 Admissibility in the interests of justice

Section 114(1)(d) creates a broad inclusionary discretion that permits a judge to admit hearsay evidence whenever it is in the interests of justice to do so. The Court of Appeal has stressed that s 114(1)(d) must not be viewed as a 'safety valve' (*Sak v Crown Prosecution Service* (2008) 172 JP 89, DC). There is nothing in the provision that suggests it is a limited inclusionary discretion to be used only in exceptional circumstances. While s 114(1)(d) must not be viewed as a mere safety valve, it must nevertheless be cautiously applied, since otherwise the conditions laid down by Parliament in the other exceptions would be circumvented. There is a particular tension between s 116 and s 114(1)(d). Where evidence is not admissible under s 116, the Court of Appeal has stated that s 114(1)(d) cannot and should not be applied so as to render s 116 nugatory and the Court of Appeal has been slow to admit statements of unavailable witnesses under s 114(1)(d) where the reason for absence does not come within s 116(2) (see *R v O'Hare* [2006] EWCA Crim 2512; *R v Y* [2008] 1 WLR 1683, CA; *R v Marsh* [2008] All ER (D) 338 (Jul), CA; *R v Sadiq* [2009] EWCA Crim 712; *R v Z* [2009] 1 Cr App R 500, CA; and *R v CT* (2011) 175 JP 462).

However, case law provides numerous examples of hearsay statements that have been admitted under s 114(1)(d). For example, in *R v Lynch* [2008] 1 Cr App R 24, the witness, at an identification parade, identified the defendant and stated that 'when another boy had knocked V over, D was swearing at him'. The statement was not admissible under any other provision, but the Court of Appeal held that it was admissible in the interests of justice under s 114(1)(d). In *R v L* [2008] 2 Cr App R 18, CA, the accused's wife made a statement to the police concerning an allegation of the rape of her daughter by the defendant. She no longer wished to give evidence against the defendant by the time of trial and, by virtue of s 80 of PACE 1984, she could not be compelled to do so (see **4.2.2.3**). The trial judge admitted her statement as evidence under s 114(1)(d). In *R v Sadiq* [2009] EWCA Crim 712, a crucial witness for the prosecution sustained very significant injuries during the offence, as a result of which he was only able to communicate by pointing to letters on an alphabet board. At the first trial, the witness gave evidence painstakingly through an intermediary. The witness was unwilling to participate in a subsequent retrial but the court admitted the transcript of his evidence from the first trial under s 114(1)(d). In contrast, note that it has been held that where the CJA 203, s 131 permits hearsay evidence to be admitted in a retrial (a) by agreement, (b) under s 116, or (c) under s 114(1)(d), s 114(1)(d) should be the provision least capable of covering a situation in which a witness refused to give evidence on a retrial; a judge will have to consider with care the circumstances of refusal, just as he will where a witness is unavailable through fear under s 116, before the evidence could be admitted under s 114(1)(d) (*R v R* [2013] EWCA Crim 708). In *R v Steen* [2008] 2 Cr App R 380, CA, the accused refused to agree the circumstances of a conviction admissible under the bad character provisions of the 2003 Act, but the prosecution successfully applied to adduce a summary of his police interviews and the evidence he gave at the trial for that offence.

While the test is the same for both prosecution and defence, it appears that the test may be more strictly applied where the prosecution seek to rely upon s 114(1)(d) (*R v Y*

[2008] 1 WLR 1683, CA). Considerable care will need to be taken in any case in which a hearsay statement would provide the prosecution with a case, when otherwise it would have none. Similarly, the Court of Appeal has observed that the test to be applied to a defendant's application, where the defendant is being tried for a serious criminal charge, will often be less exacting than the test which would apply to a prosecution application, although it does not follow that the interests of justice are synonymous with the interests of the defendant (*R v Marsh* [2008] All ER (D) 338 (Jul), CA).

Section 114(1)(d) does not extend to anonymous hearsay evidence. The written note of a witness who wished to remain anonymous which identified the registration number of a getaway car was held to be inadmissible (*R v Ford* [2010] EWCA Crim 2250).

Section 114(2) provides a list of criteria to which the judge should have regard when exercising his discretion under s 114(1)(d). It provides:

> *(2) In deciding whether a statement not made in oral evidence should be admitted under subsection (1)(d), the court must have regard to the following factors (and to any others it considers relevant)—*
>
> *(a) how much probative value the statement has (assuming it to be true) in relation to a matter in issue in the proceedings, or how valuable it is for the understanding of other evidence in the case;*
>
> *(b) what other evidence has been, or can be, given on the matter or evidence mentioned in paragraph (a);*
>
> *(c) how important the matter or evidence mentioned in paragraph (a) is in the context of the case as a whole;*
>
> *(d) the circumstances in which the statement was made;*
>
> *(e) how reliable the maker of the statement appears to be;*
>
> *(f) how reliable the evidence of the making of the statement appears to be;*
>
> *(g) whether oral evidence of the matter stated can be given and, if not, why it cannot;*
>
> *(h) the amount of difficulty involved in challenging the statement;*
>
> *(i) the extent to which that difficulty would be likely to prejudice the party facing it.*

In *R v T* [2006] 2 Cr App R 14, CA, it was stated that a judge, in determining whether to admit evidence in the interests of justice under s 114(1)(d), is not required to reach a conclusion in relation to all nine factors. It is a matter for the judge, having regard to any factors identified in the course of argument and to any factors he considers relevant, to determine the interests of justice test. The Court of Appeal will be slow to interfere with a proper exercise of judgement and will only do so if incorrect application of principles was involved or if it was outside the bounds of legitimate decision (*Finch* [2007] 1 WLR 1645 and *Musone* [2007] 1 WLR 2467).

Some of the factors under the CJA 2003, s 114 concern the probative value of the hearsay evidence. Under s 114(2)(a) the court must consider how much probative value the statement has (assuming it to be true) in relation to a matter in issue in the proceedings, or how valuable it is for the understanding of other evidence in the case. This means that the question for the court is how much impact it would have on the case if accepted by the jury, not whether the jury is likely to accept it as true. Evidence that would undermine the defence and point powerfully to a conviction has been held to make the other factors even more significant, and in particular s 114(2)(g) (*R v Z* [2009] 1 Cr App R 500, CA).

Under paras (e) and (f) the court must consider any evidence of the reliability of both the maker of the statement and the circumstances of the making of the statement. The judge is required to make an assessment of reliability; it is not permissible to reason that the jury may assess reliability (*Musone* [2007] 1 WLR 2467). At the very least, the judge must be satisfied that the evidence is properly capable of being considered reliable by a jury (*R v Sliogeris* [2015] EWCA Crim 22).

Other factors concern the importance of the evidence to the trial. For example, s 114(2)(b) requires consideration of the availability of alternative evidence and s 114(2)(c) requires consideration of the importance of the evidence or the matter in issue in the proceedings in the context of the case as a whole.

Given that hearsay evidence is not intended to substitute oral evidence, the court is required to consider the availability of oral evidence (s 114(2)(g)). In *R v Z* [2009] 1 Cr App R 500, the Court of Appeal held that it will be rare that potentially prejudicial evidence will be admitted where a witness is available, although reluctant, and the reluctance is not due to fear. See also *R v Jones* [2015] EWCA Crim 1317. The difficulties of challenging the evidence fall to be considered under s 114(2)(h).

The final criterion concerns the extent to which the evidence could cause prejudice to the party facing it (s 114(2)(i)).

It has been held that the factors listed in s 114(2)(a)–(i) may be regarded as useful *aides memoire* when assessing admissibility of hearsay evidence under any other hearsay provision, or its exclusion under PACE 1984, s 78 (*R v Riat* [2013] 1 Cr App R 2, CA).

13.7 Multiple hearsay

Section 121 of the CJA 2003 provides:

> *(1) A hearsay statement is not admissible to prove the fact that an earlier hearsay statement was made unless—*
>
> *(a) either of the statements is admissible under section 117, 119 or 120,*
>
> *(b) all parties to the proceedings so agree, or*
>
> *(c) the court is satisfied that the value of the evidence in question, taking into account how reliable the statements appear to be, is so high that the interests of justice require the later statement to be admissible for that purpose.*
>
> *(2) In this section 'hearsay statement' means a statement, not made in oral evidence, that is relied on as evidence of a matter stated in it.*

Multiple hearsay (eg 'he told me that she said ...') tends to be less reliable than first-hand hearsay. It is for this reason that s 121 allows for limited use of multiple hearsay only where the conditions under s 121(1)(a)–(c) apply.

Section 121(1)(a) needs to be read very carefully. It does not create an exception to the rule against hearsay, but imposes an additional requirement on a party seeking to adduce a hearsay statement to prove the fact that an earlier hearsay statement was made. In such a situation, each limb of the multiple hearsay statement must be admissible through one of the established hearsay exceptions, but one of the limbs must be admissible under s 117, 119, or 120. So, for example, X witnesses an assault and describes the assailant to Y who immediately passes that information on to Z. However, X dies before the trial and Y is available to give evidence but can no longer recall what X told him. In these circumstances, under s 120(4) and (6), Z could give evidence of the fact that Y had told him that X had made a statement describing the assailant and X's statement too would be admissible under s 116(2)(a). In *R v Xhabri* [2006] 1 Cr App R 26, a police officer gave evidence that an individual had told him that the complainant was being held against her will. The complainant gave evidence that she had told a security guard, who fitted the description of the person who spoke to the police officer, that she was being held against her will. The Court of Appeal concluded that the complainant's evidence was admissible under s 120(4) and (7) and so the requirement in s 121(1)(a) had been satisfied.

Although similar, the interests of justice test in s 121(1)(c) is stricter than that in s 114(1)(d). It requires the value of the evidence to be *so high* that the interests of justice require its admission. In *R v Xhabri*, the court considered it likely that the evidence could also have been admitted under s 121(1)(c) given that its evidential value was so great. Note also that where a party wishes to rely on a hearsay statement to prove an earlier hearsay statement, then although the earlier statement might have been admissible under s 114(1)(d) and s 114(2), the test in s 121(1)(c) remains an additional test which must be met before the later statement can be admitted (*R v Walker* [2007] EWCA Crim 1968).

13.8 Article 6 of the ECHR

13.8.1 Hearsay and Article 6(3)(d)

Article 6(1) and (3)(d) of the ECHR provide:

> 1. *In the determination … of any criminal charge against him, everyone is entitled to a fair and public hearing*
>
> …
>
> 3. *Everyone charged with a criminal offence has the following minimum rights:*
>
> …
>
> *(d) to examine or have examined witnesses against him and to obtain the attendance and examination of witnesses on his behalf under the same conditions as witnesses against him.*

The issue of whether a defendant can receive a fair trial if he is deprived of the opportunity to cross-examine a witness has been considered by the European Court of Human Rights (ECtHR) on a number of occasions. The leading authority on the relationship between Article 6 and the hearsay provisions under the CJA 2003 is *Al-Khawaja and Tahery v UK* (2012) 54 EHRR 23. In this case, the Grand Chamber of the European Court of Human Rights reviewed UK national and Strasbourg jurisprudence relating to the admissibility of hearsay evidence and set out the following principles (see *Al-Khawaja and Tahery v UK* (2012) 54 EHRR 23, [118]–[124]).

1. The Court noted that the guarantees in para 3(d) of Article 6 are specific aspects of the right to a fair hearing which must be taken into account in any assessment of the fairness of proceedings. The Court's primary concern under Article 6(1) is to evaluate the overall fairness of the criminal proceedings as a whole, having regard to the rights of the defence but also to the interests of the public and the victims that crime is properly prosecuted.
2. The admissibility of evidence is a matter for regulation by national law and the national courts and that the Court's only concern is to examine whether the proceedings have been conducted fairly.
3. Article 6(3)(d) enshrines the principle that, before an accused can be convicted, all evidence against him must normally be produced in his presence at a public hearing with a view to adversarial argument. Exceptions to this principle are possible but must not infringe the rights of the defence.
4. There are two requirements which follow from the above general principles. First, there must be a good reason for the non-attendance of a witness. Second, when

a conviction is based solely or to a decisive degree on depositions that have been made by a person whom the accused has had no opportunity to examine or to have examined the rights of the defence may be restricted to an extent that is incompatible with the guarantees provided by Article 6 (the so-called 'sole or decisive rule').

5. The requirement that there be a good reason for admitting the evidence of an absent witness is a preliminary question which must be examined before any consideration is given as to whether that evidence was sole or decisive. Even where the evidence of an absent witness has not been sole or decisive, the Court will still find a violation of Article 6(1) and (3)(d) when no good reason has been shown for the failure to have the witness examined. This is because as a general rule witnesses should give evidence during the trial and that all reasonable efforts will be made to secure their attendance. Thus, when witnesses do not attend to give live evidence, there is a duty to enquire whether that absence is justified.
6. Where a witness has died, in order for his or her evidence to be taken into account, it will be necessary to adduce his or her witness statement. Absence owing to fear calls for closer examination. A distinction must be drawn between fear which is attributable to threats or other actions of the defendant or those acting on his or her behalf and fear which is attributable to a more general fear of what will happen if the witness gives evidence at trial. When a witness's fear is attributable to the defendant or those acting on his behalf, it is appropriate to allow the evidence of that witness to be introduced at trial without the need for the witness to give live evidence or be examined by the defendant or his representatives even if such evidence was the sole or decisive evidence against the defendant. To allow the defendant to benefit from the fear he has engendered in witnesses would be incompatible with the rights of victims and witnesses. Consequently, a defendant who has acted in this manner must be taken to have waived his rights to question such witnesses under Article 6(3)(d).
7. There is no requirement that a witness's fear be attributable directly to threats made by the defendant in order for that witness to be excused from giving evidence at trial. Fear of death or injury of another person or of financial loss are all relevant considerations in determining whether a witness should not be required to give oral evidence. This does not mean that any subjective fear of the witness will suffice. The trial court must determine whether or not there are objective grounds for that fear and whether those objective grounds are supported by evidence.
8. Given the extent to which the absence of a witness adversely affects the rights of the defence, allowing the admission of a witness statement in lieu of live evidence at trial must be a measure of last resort. Before a witness can be excused from testifying on grounds of fear, the trial court must be satisfied that all available alternatives, such as witness anonymity and other special measures, would be inappropriate or impracticable.

The principles in *Al-Khawaja and Tahery v UK* were re-examined by the Grand Chamber in *Schatschaschwili v Germany* (2016) 63 EHRR 14. The Grand Chamber decided that a good reason for a witness's absence was no longer a precondition for hearsay evidence to be admitted. The lack of a good reason for a witness's non-attendance will not be conclusive of the fairness of a trial; instead it is a very important factor in assessing the overall fairness of a trial and may tip the balance towards finding a breach of Article 6. Careful scrutiny of a witness's reasons for non-attendance is required and the court must make all reasonable efforts to secure a witness's attendance at trial.

13.8.2 Sole or decisive hearsay

What approach should be taken where hearsay evidence is the sole or decisive evidence against the defendant? Before the matter was resolved by the Grand Chamber in *Al-Khawaja and Tahery*, this was a difficult question. In *Luca v Italy* (2003) 36 EHRR 807, it was held that where a conviction is based solely or to a decisive degree on statements that have been made by a person whom the accused has had no opportunity to question, the rights of the defence are restricted to an extent that is incompatible with the guarantees provided by Article 6. Similarly, in an earlier decision by the ECtHR in the case of *Al-Khawaja and Tahery v UK* (2009) 49 EHRR 1 the Strasbourg court held that it was doubtful if any counterbalancing factors could be sufficient to justify the admission of hearsay evidence that would be the sole or decisive evidence on which a conviction is based.

However, in *R v Horncastle* [2009] 2 Cr App R 15, the Court of Appeal declined to follow the decisions of the ECtHR. It held that *Luca* had failed to properly distinguish between the different approaches taken to absent and anonymous witnesses in the Strasbourg case law. The case law showed that the Article 6(3)(d) right is not absolute and could be restricted, provided that the trial is still fair. The court stated that Part 11, Chapter 2 of the CJA 2003 contains a crafted code intended to ensure that evidence is admitted only when it is fair that it should be, that allows for the defence to test the credibility and reliability of evidence, and contains an overriding safeguard in the power of the judge to stop a trial where the evidence is unconvincing. Provided the provisions of the CJA 2003 are observed, there is no breach of Article 6 and in particular Article 6(3)(d), even if the conviction is based solely or to a decisive degree on hearsay evidence admitted under the Act. In *R v Horncastle* [2010] 2 WLR 47, the Supreme Court agreed with the Court of Appeal's view that the CJA 2003 is intended to admit hearsay evidence only when it is fair that it should be and also provides additional safeguards in ss 124–126 that are designed to further the same end. Their Lordships noted that Strasbourg case law accepts that derogation from the specific Article 6 rights is permissible as long as the proceedings as a whole are fair. The Supreme Court concluded that the CJA 2003 creates a scheme that only admits hearsay evidence that is reliable and consistent with the need to ensure a fair trial and contains sufficient counterbalancing measures.

Following the Supreme Court's decision in *Horncastle*, the Grand Chamber of the Strasbourg court was invited by the UK Government to consider the decision in *Al-Khawaja and Tahery v UK* (2009) 49 EHRR 1. In *Al-Khawaja and Tahery v UK* (2012) 54 EHRR 23, the Grand Chamber of the European Court of Human Rights held, by 15 votes to 2, that a conviction based on sole or decisive hearsay did not automatically breach Article 6(3)(d). The Grand Chamber noted that in Strasbourg jurisprudence, the Strasbourg court had always interpreted Article 6(3) by reference to the overall fairness of proceedings and had taken into account factors such as statutory safeguards and how they were applied, procedural safeguards to counterbalance difficulties experienced by the defence and how proceedings were conducted by the trial judge. This meant that the sole or decisive rule was not inflexible, even though previous *dicta* of the Strasbourg court might have suggested otherwise. Nonetheless, the Grand Chamber emphasised that even though the rule was not inflexible, the reasons for the rule remained valid and the dangers associated with sole or decisive hearsay were acute. Consequently, where the prosecution sought to admit sole or decisive hearsay evidence, strong counterbalancing measures would be required. The Grand Chamber accepted that the safeguards contained in the CJA 2003 Act, supported by those contained in s 78 of PACE 1984 and the common law, are in principle strong safeguards designed to ensure fairness.

As a result of the Grand Chamber's decision in *Al-Khawaja and Tahery*, the Supreme Court's decision in *Horncastle* is not incompatible with the Strasbourg jurisprudence on the question of whether convictions may be based solely or decisively on hearsay evidence.

In revisiting the principles set out in *Al-Khawaja and Tahery* in the case of *Schatschaschwili v Germany* (2016) 63 EHRR 14, the Grand Chamber held that where hearsay evidence is significant, but where the court could not be clear that it is sole or decisive, the sufficiency of counter-balancing measures should still be examined. The requirement to consider whether counter-balancing measures are sufficient is not limited to cases involving sole or decisive hearsay. The more important the evidence, for the trial to be fair, the more weight the counter-balancing measures must carry.

The principles set out in *Schatschaschwili v Germany* were applied in *Seton v UK* [2016] ECHR 318 and *Price v UK* [2016] ECHR 753. In *Seton v UK* the ECtHR found that the non-attendance of a reluctant witness whose evidence was adduced under s 114(1)(d) did not breach Article 6 and was not conclusive of the fairness of the trial despite the fact that the court was not persuaded that all reasonable efforts had been made to secure the witness's attendance. The Court also held that the witness's evidence was not sole or decisive and that there were sufficient safeguards to ensure a fair trial given the relative the importance of the absent witness. In *Price*, the ECtHR held that hearsay statements adduced under s 116(2)(e) (unavailable witness in fear) were not decisive given the other evidence in the case but that, following *Schatschaschwili v Germany*, consideration of the sufficiency of counter-balancing measures was required.

13.8.3 Approach to be taken to Strasbourg decisions

In respect of what approach should be taken by the Crown Courts when managing evidence of hearsay in everyday criminal trials, five 'central propositions' were stated by the Court of Appeal in *R v Riat* [2013] 1 Cr App R 2:

(a) The law is and must be accepted to be as stated in the CJA 2003.

(b) Where, on close analysis, there is any difference between the Supreme Court's decision in *R v Horncastle* and the decision of the Grand Chamber in *Al-Khawaja and Tahery*, the obligation is to follow the former.

(c) There are differences in the way principle is stated, but these differences may well be more of form than substance; specifically, the importance of hearsay evidence in the context of the case is a vital consideration when assessing admissibility and treatment, but there is no over-arching rule in Strasbourg or English law that because of this, sole or decisive hearsay is automatically inadmissible.

(d) On the basis of (b) and (c) above, a Crown Court judge need not ordinarily be concerned with close analysis of the two strands of jurisprudence and generally need only look to the CJA 2003 and the decision in *R v Horncastle*.

(e) Neither under the CJA 2003 nor *R v Horncastle* can hearsay simply be treated as if it were first-hand evidence and automatically admissible.

Guidance of a more general nature is provided in *R (Hicks) v Commissioner of Police of the Metropolis* [2014] EWCA Civ 3. In *R (Hicks)*, the Court of Appeal (Civil Division) distilled the following 'clear principles' from domestic case law concerning what approach should be taken by domestic courts to Strasbourg decisions that interpret the scope of provisions of the ECHR:

(a) National courts have a duty to uphold Convention rights which have been enacted domestically.

(b) The meaning of the Convention must be interpreted ultimately by the Strasbourg court.

(c) Where the Grand Chamber gives an interpretation of a provision of the Convention, the UK courts are bound to follow it as authoritative, unless it is apparent that the Grand Chamber has overlooked or misunderstood an important feature of UK law or practice which, if properly explained, would lead to the Grand Chamber reviewing its interpretation by reference to domestic law or practice.

(d) The principle stated at (c) above also applies to a clear and consistent line of decisions of the Strasbourg court, other than decisions of the Grand Chamber.

(e) The European Convention sets out 'high level' human rights, which have to be given effect and implemented in detail by domestic law.

(f) In respect of ambiguities in Strasbourg law about the scope and application of a provision of the Convention, a 'real judicial choice' will have to be made at national court level.

13.9 Safeguards

Hearsay evidence is potentially unreliable and its admission deprives the party against whom it is adduced of the opportunity to test the evidence through the cross-examination of the maker of the statement. The CJA 2003 only allows hearsay evidence to be admitted where it is from an unavailable witness, from a witness who is present for cross-examination, or where the hearsay is otherwise apparently reliable. The Act also provides a series of safeguards that aim to ensure that the admission of hearsay evidence will be fair. Where hearsay evidence may be admissible under the CJA 2003, regard must be had to these safeguards; they act as statutory countermeasures to prevent unfairness. As was noted earlier, the Court of Appeal in *R v Horncastle* [2009] 2 Cr App R 15 and the Supreme Court in *R v Horncastle* [2010] 2 WLR 47 carefully considered the adequacy of the safeguards in the CJA 2003 and concluded that they are sufficient to ensure that the admission of hearsay will not jeopardise the fairness of the trial. In respect of sole or decisive hearsay, see **13.8.2**.

13.9.1 Capability

Hearsay evidence should not be used to sidestep the rules on the competence of witnesses (see **4.2**). Therefore, the CJA 2003, s 123 creates rules that regulate how the court should proceed when the issue of competence is raised. CJA 2003, s123 provides:

(1) Nothing in section 116, 119 or 120 makes a statement admissible as evidence if it was made by a person who did not have the required capability at the time when he made the statement.

(2) Nothing in section 117 makes a statement admissible as evidence if any person who, in order for the requirements of section 117(2) to be satisfied, must at any time have supplied or received the information concerned or created or received the document or part concerned—

(a) did not have the required capability at that time, or

(b) cannot be identified but cannot reasonably be assumed to have had the required capability at that time.

(3) For the purposes of this section a person has the required capability if he is capable of—

(a) understanding questions put to him about the matters stated, and

(b) giving answers to such questions which can be understood.

(4) Where by reason of this section there is an issue as to whether a person had the required capability when he made a statement—

(a) proceedings held for the determination of the issue must take place in the absence of the jury (if there is one);

(b) in determining the issue the court may receive expert evidence and evidence from any person to whom the statement in question was made;

(c) the burden of proof on the issue lies on the party seeking to adduce the statement, and the standard of proof is the balance of probabilities.

The maker of a statement adduced under s 116, 119, or 120 must have been 'capable' of giving evidence when the statement was made for the statement to be admissible. Capability is defined in s 123(3) in similar terms to the competence test under the YJCEA 1999, s 53(3), namely that the witness must be able to understand questions put to him and able to give understandable answers to them.

Section 123(2) of the CJA 2003 applies the same test of competence to all persons involved in the transfer of information under the CJA 2003, s 117, that is to say, the supplier of the information and any person who received the information, or created any document containing the information or received any document with the information in it. The relevant time for each person is the point at which they supplied, created, or received the information or document. As tracing all persons in a chain of communication would be potentially impossible, s 123 requires the court to consider whether any identifiable person was not capable (s 123(2)(a)) and whether any unidentifiable person 'cannot reasonably be assumed to have the required capability at that time'. It seems likely on the language of para (b) that the courts will be willing to presume that a person was capable unless there is evidence that prevents that being reasonably assumed.

Section 123(4) of the CJA 2003 makes provision for the proof of the capability of the person in question. The issue should be tried in the absence of the jury (s 123(4)(a)) and the burden of proof is upon the party seeking to prove capability on the balance of probabilities irrespective of whether it is the prosecution or defence seeking to adduce the hearsay statement. Clearly, the court cannot (in contrast to practice under the YJCEA 1999, s 53) make its own inquiries as to the competence of the maker, at the time of the making of a statement, given the statement was made some time in the past. The court will be reliant on such direct and circumstantial evidence of the maker's mental state at that time as it can obtain.

This section does not apply in relation to statements admitted as exceptions to the rule against hearsay preserved under the CJA 2003, s 118 or under any other statutory exception including s 114(1)(d), although it is submitted that it will rarely be in the interests of justice to admit hearsay evidence of a witness who lacks competence.

13.9.2 Attacking the credibility of the maker of the statement

One of the main problems with hearsay evidence is that it is not possible to test the reliability of the statement, or the credibility of the person who made the statement, by cross-examination. Section 124 of the CJA 2003 makes provision for challenges to the credibility of hearsay statements:

(1) This section applies if in criminal proceedings—

(a) a statement not made in oral evidence in the proceedings is admitted as evidence of a matter stated, and

(b) the maker of the statement does not give oral evidence in connection with the subject matter of the statement.

(2) In such a case—

(a) any evidence which (if he had given such evidence) would have been admissible as relevant to his credibility as a witness is so admissible in the proceedings;

(b) evidence may with the court's leave be given of any matter which (if he had given such evidence) could have been put to him in cross-examination as relevant to his credibility as a witness but of which evidence could not have been adduced by the cross-examining party;

(c) evidence tending to prove that he made (at whatever time) any other statement inconsistent with the statement admitted as evidence is admissible for the purpose of showing that he contradicted himself.

(3) If as a result of evidence admitted under this section an allegation is made against the maker of a statement, the court may permit a party to lead additional evidence of such description as the court may specify for the purposes of denying or answering the allegation.

(4) In the case of a statement in a document which is admitted as evidence under section 117 each person who, in order for the statement to be admissible, must have supplied or received the information concerned or created or received the document or part concerned is to be treated as the maker of the statement for the purposes of subsections (1) to (3) above.

And the CJA 2003, s 119(2) provides:

(2) If in criminal proceedings evidence of an inconsistent statement by any person is given under section 124(2)(c), the statement is admissible as evidence of any matter stated in it of which oral evidence by that person would be admissible.

Section 124 of the CJA 2003 applies to any hearsay evidence admitted in criminal proceedings. It therefore also applies where the evidence is admitted under one of the exceptions to the rule against hearsay preserved in s 118 as much as it applies to other statements admissible under other sections of the CJA 2003. However, s 124 does not apply where the maker of the statement gives evidence. It, therefore, does not apply where the hearsay statement is admitted under s 119 or 120. Nor will it apply to hearsay statements admitted under s 118 where the maker is called as a witness (such as where the defendant made a *res gestae* statement and gives evidence at trial as happened, for example, in *R v Glover*, CA, referred to at **13.4.3.1**). In so far as the statement is admitted under s 117, evidence relevant to the credibility of any of the persons involved in the transfer of the information is potentially admissible under this section (s 124(4)).

Section 124(2) makes provision for the challenge of the person in three ways. Section 124(2)(a) and (c) reflects what could have been done had that person given evidence, while s 124(2)(b) goes further:

(a) Section 124(2)(a) allows evidence that would have been admissible as relevant to his or her credibility as a witness to be adduced (eg any proof of the witness's bad character which would have been admissible under the CJA 2003, s 100 had the witness been present at trial (*Harvey* [2014] EWCA Crim 54) or proof of other facts permitted by the rule against finality).

(b) Section 124(2)(b) allows evidence to be given of a matter that could have been put in cross-examination as relevant to his credibility even though, had the maker actually been a witness at trial, such evidence could not have been adduced. Remember that the rules concerning cross-examination allow questions to be asked affecting the credit of a party, but the rule of finality provides that only some of those matters can be proved in evidence if the witness denies the facts alleged during cross-examination. Because the maker of the statement is not present to give evidence, the questions cannot be put to him. Therefore, s 124(2)(b) allows the evidence to be put before the tribunal of fact. However, to maintain the distinction between those things admissible as exceptions to the rule against finality and those matters that are not, evidence of matters that do not fit within any of those exceptions are only admissible with the leave of the court. For the rule of finality, see **7.10**.

(c) Section 124(2)(c) allows proof of previous inconsistent statements. As the maker of the statement is not present to give evidence, the procedure for establishing inconsistency under the Criminal Procedure Act 1865, ss 3, 4, and 5 cannot be adopted. Therefore, a statement inconsistent with the hearsay statement admitted is admissible as of right. By virtue of s 119(2), a statement admitted under s 124(2)(c) is admissible as evidence of any matter stated of which oral evidence by the maker would be admissible.

In respect of the existence of evidence which might affect the credibility of an absent witness for the prosecution, it is expected that very full inquiries will be made (more than a simple check for convictions on the Police National Computer) and all relevant material disclosed to the defence. Where the absent witness is a witness for the defence, it is expected that the defendant will disclose sufficient information to permit proper checks to be made. Further, throughout the trial, both counsel and judge must keep under review the issue of disclosure of material which might affect the credibility of the absent witness (see *R v Riat* [2013] 1 Cr App R 2). Section 124(3) of the CJA 2003 allows any party to counter the attacks on the credibility of the maker of the statement under s 124(2) by proof of further evidence.

13.9.3 Stopping a case

The CJA 2003, s 125 provides the court with the power to stop a case where the evidence admitted poses the danger of an unsafe conviction.

Section 125 provides:

(1) If on a defendant's trial before a judge and jury for an offence the court is satisfied at any time after the close of the case for the prosecution that—

(a) the case against the defendant is based wholly or partly on a statement not made in oral evidence in the proceedings, and

(b) the evidence provided by the statement is so unconvincing that, considering its importance to the case against the defendant, his conviction of the offence would be unsafe,

the court must either direct the jury to acquit the defendant of the offence or, if it considers that there ought to be retrial, discharge the jury.

(2) Where—

(a) a jury is directed under subsection (1) to acquit a defendant of an offence, and

(b) the circumstances are such that, apart from this subsection, the defendant could if acquitted of that offence be found guilty of another offence,

the defendant may not be found guilty of that other offence if the court is satisfied as mentioned in subsection (1) in respect of it.

...

(4) This section does not prejudice any other power a court may have to direct a jury to acquit a person of an offence or to discharge a jury.

This section allows the court to stop the prosecution case where it is based 'wholly or partly' on hearsay evidence (s 125(1)(a)) and the evidence is so unconvincing that a conviction would be unsafe. The court must consider both the probative value of the evidence and the importance that it has in determining trial issues. If the court considers the evidence to have minimal probative value but its importance to the trial issues is such that it poses the risk of an unsafe conviction, then the court must either direct the jury to acquit the defendant, or must discharge the jury and order a retrial.

Where the defendant is acquitted, by virtue of this section, of an offence to which a lesser verdict could be returned, that lesser verdict must not be returned if it also depends on the unconvincing hearsay evidence that has been withdrawn (s 125(2)). Therefore, if the hearsay evidence that is unconvincing relates to the identity of a defendant alleged to have intentionally caused grievous bodily harm on the victim contrary to the Offences Against the Person Act 1861, s 18, the withdrawal of the evidence would not permit a conviction for an offence contrary to the Offences Against the Person Act 1861, s 20. However, if the evidence related only to the intention to cause such an injury to the victim, the acquittal for the s 18 offence would not necessarily preclude the jury from continuing to consider the s 20 offence.

13.9.4 Exclusion of evidence

13.9.4.1 General discretions to exclude evidence

Section 126(1) of the CJA 2003 creates a general discretion to exclude hearsay evidence and s 126(2) preserves the operation of the exclusionary discretions that apply to criminal law generally in relation to such evidence.

Section 126(1) states:

> *(1) In criminal proceedings the court may refuse to admit a statement as evidence of a matter stated if—*
>
> *(a) the statement was made otherwise than in oral evidence in the proceedings, and*
>
> *(b) the court is satisfied that the case for excluding the statement, taking account of the danger that to admit it would result in undue waste of time, substantially outweighs the case for admitting it, taking account of the value of the evidence.*

The exclusion applies to any hearsay evidence that would otherwise be admitted in criminal proceedings. Therefore, it could restrict the admissibility of hearsay evidence admitted under a common law exception preserved under s 118 as much as under any exception under the CJA 2003. The section also applies to restrict hearsay evidence irrespective of which party is seeking to adduce it.

In *Drinkwater* [2016] 1 Cr App R 471, the Court of Appeal upheld a decision to exclude an internally inconsistent, confusing, and contradictory confession given by a third party who had since died, which had been tendered by the defence. The Court found that the evidence was of no value in determining the guilt or innocence of the defendant. The Court held that there was no difference in the test for the exclusion of evidence under s 126 where that evidence was tendered by the defence as opposed to the prosecution. The Court also indicated a 'strong preliminary view' that s 126 creates a general discretion for the exclusion of evidence that 'lacks significant probative value' and that it is not limited to cases in which the admission of the hearsay evidence would generate an undue waste of time.

Section 126(2) of the CJA 2003 expressly retains the exclusionary discretions that apply to the criminal law in general. Section 126(2) provides:

> *(2) Nothing in this Chapter prejudices—*
>
> *(a) any power of a court to exclude evidence under section 78 of the Police and Criminal Evidence Act 1984 (c. 60) (exclusion of unfair evidence), or*
>
> *(b) any other power of a court to exclude evidence at its discretion (whether by preventing questions from being put or otherwise).*

In *R v Cole and Keet* [2008] 1 Cr App R 5, the Court of Appeal observed that the operation of the s 78 discretion was unlikely to provide a different result from the interests of justice test in s 114(1)(d). In that case, and in many cases since, the courts have considered the interests of justice criteria in s 114(2) when exercising discretion under s 78. Indeed, in *R v Riat* [2013] 1 Cr App R 2, the factors listed in s 114(2) were, as stated earlier, commended as useful *aides memoire* when considering the admissibility of hearsay under any provision or its exclusion under s 78.

13.9.4.2 Business documents, etc

Section 117(6) of the CJA 2003 states that the court can direct that any document otherwise admissible under s 117 should be excluded where the statement is unreliable having regard to the contents of the documents, the source of the information, how the information was supplied or received, or how the document was created or received (s 117(7)).

13.9.5 Rules of court

Section 132 of the CJA 2003 provides for the making of rules of court to regulate the process of proof of hearsay evidence, in particular about procedure to be followed and conditions for admissibility of such evidence (s 132(2)) and the provision of notices (s 132(3)). Section 132(4) provides for the making of a rule that a failure of a party to challenge the admissibility of evidence under the notice procedure can amount to agreement as to the admissibility of that evidence.

The effect of failure to comply with the notice provisions is dealt with by the CJA 2003, s 132(5)–(7):

> *(5) If a party proposing to tender evidence fails to comply with a prescribed requirement applicable to it—*
>
> *(a) the evidence is not admissible except with the court's leave;*
>
> *(b) where leave is given the court or jury may draw such inferences from the failure as appear proper;*
>
> *(c) the failure may be taken into account by the court in considering the exercise of its powers with respect to costs.*
>
> *(6) In considering whether or how to exercise any of its powers under subsection (5) the court shall have regard to whether there is any justification for the failure to comply with the requirement.*
>
> *(7) A person shall not be convicted of an offence solely on an inference drawn under subsection (5)(b).*

The rules of court are to be found in Crim PR, r 20. Under r 20.2, written notice must be served on the court officer and all other parties where a party wishes to tender hearsay evidence under s 114(1)(d) (interests of justice), s 116 (unavailable witness), s 117(1)(c) (business document prepared for the purposes of criminal proceedings), or s 121 (multiple hearsay). Other forms of hearsay do not require notice. If the party proposing to tender hearsay evidence fails to comply with the prescribed procedure, the evidence is not admissible except with the leave of the court. Where leave is granted, the court or jury may draw adverse inferences from the failure to comply with the prescribed requirements (s 132(5)), but a conviction may not be based solely on such an inference (s 132(7)). The court has a wide power to dispense with notice requirements or to allow notice to be given in a different form, including orally. Similarly, a party entitled to receive notice may waive that entitlement.

Where a defendant seeks to rely on hearsay evidence but fails to comply with the notice requirement, the court should not grant leave where this might cause incurable unfairness to the prosecution or to a co-accused, but leave may be granted if any unfairness can be cured, for example by an adjournment, and where the interests of justice would otherwise require that evidence to be admitted (*R v Musone* [2007] 1 WLR 2467).

13.9.6 Judicial direction on hearsay

Where hearsay evidence is admitted at trial, the jury must receive a direction on the dangers of relying on hearsay evidence and should be invited to scrutinise the evidence with particular care. Indeed, the requirement for judicial direction on hearsay was noted to be one of the 'principle safeguards designed to protect a defendant against unfair prejudice as a result of the admission of hearsay evidence' in *Horncastle* [2010] 2 WLR 47, SC. The direction should assist the jury in properly assessing the reliability and probative value of the hearsay evidence.

Where hearsay is adduced at trial, the judge should discuss the terms of the direction with counsel and deliver a direction tailored to the circumstances of the case. The ***Crown Court Compendium*** gives guidance on appropriate directions for all forms of hearsay evidence. In particular, the jury should be warned about the inability to test the maker of the statement by cross-examination, the fact that the statement was not made on oath, and that there has been no opportunity to assess the maker's demeanour at the time they made the statement. It is also desirable for the jury to be told to consider the hearsay evidence in the context of all of the evidence, and for the judge to draw attention to its strengths and weaknesses (*Grant v The State* [2006] UKPC 2 and *Shabir* [2012] EWCA Crim 2564). Failure to give an adequate or an appropriate direction may render the trial unfair but will not necessarily do so.

13.10 Other statutory exceptions to the rule against hearsay in criminal cases

With the exception of confessions (for which see **Chapter 14**) other statutory exceptions to the rule against hearsay in criminal cases all relate to documentary evidence. Other statutes have created exceptions to the rule against hearsay, including:

(a) the Bankers' Books Evidence Act 1879, ss 3 and 4, which provide for the use of bankers' books to evidence banking transactions (see **12.7.1**);

(b) the Criminal Justice Act 1967, s 9, which provides that the written statement of a witness shall be admissible 'as evidence to the like extent as oral evidence' of the maker. This will only happen, however, if no other party has objected to the use of the statement instead of calling the witness (see **4.4.1.1**);

(c) the Theft Act 1968, s 27(4), which provides for the proof of facts by statutory declarations relating to goods in transmission.

This list is not comprehensive. See ***Blackstone's Criminal Practice*** for a more extensive consideration of documentary evidence in criminal cases.

14 Confessions and illegally or improperly obtained evidence

14.1 Confessions

14.1.1 Admissibility

The admissibility of a confession is governed by PACE 1984.

14.1.2 The definition of 'confession'

Section 82(1) of PACE 1984 provides that:

'confession' includes any statement wholly or partly adverse to the person who made it, whether made to a person in authority or not and whether made in words or otherwise.

This is a very wide definition. However, the statement must have been adverse when made (*R v Sat-Bhambra* (1988) 88 Cr App R 55). Statements that were favourable when made but later proved to be adverse, for example, statements which put forward a false alibi, are not confessions (*R v Park* (1995) 99 Cr App R 270) *R v Hasan* [2005] UKHL 22).

Where a confession is admissible, it is the whole of the statement that is admissible. This means that a statement which is partly exculpatory and partly adverse (ie mixed) cannot be divided and is taken as one confession (*R v Garrod* [1997] Crim LR 445). See 6.5.2.5.3 for more detail on mixed statements.

14.2 Confessions adduced by the prosecution

14.2.1 PACE 1984, s 76(1)

Section 76(1) of PACE 1984 provides that:

In any proceedings a confession made by an accused person may be given in evidence against him in so far as it is relevant to any matter in issue in the proceedings and is not excluded by the court in pursuance of this section.

Generally, a confession may only be evidence of facts that are known by the person who makes it. In *R v Hulbert* (1979) 69 Cr App R 243, the defendant was charged with handling stolen goods and confessed that the person from whom she bought the goods told her that they were stolen. Although her confession was evidence that she believed that the goods were stolen, it was not evidence that they were in fact stolen.

14.2.2 Confession of a defendant incriminating a co-defendant

When the prosecution adduces a confession made by a defendant that also incriminates a co-defendant it is evidence against the defendant as the maker of the confession but is generally not evidence against the co-defendant. Where the defendant makes a confession which contains adverse statements about the co-defendant, the whole confession is admissible even though parts of it incriminate the co-defendant (*R v Pearce* (1979) 69 Cr App R 365). The co-defendant is only protected by a direction by the judge to state that the confession by one defendant is not evidence against a co-defendant (see Crown Court Compendium 2017, Part 1, 14–15). The question of whether a confession by a defendant should be edited to protect a co-defendant who might be incriminated by it was raised in *R v Silcot* [1987] Crim LR 765. In this case, it was suggested that the trial judge had a common law discretion to order editing in such cases. An order for editing would effectively have involved excluding an item of defence evidence where the prejudicial effect of admitting those parts which a co-defendant called to have edited out, outweighed the probative value of admitting them. However, the Privy Council case of *Lobban v R* [1995] 1 WLR 877 determined that the discretion to exclude applies only to prosecution evidence and, on this basis, it can be said that a judge would not have the power to order editing of a confession which incriminates a co-defendant where it effectively involved the exclusion of defence evidence (see also *R v Mitchell* [2005] EWCA Crim 3447). The proposition that confessions are only admissible against the maker is subject to certain exceptions, principally those outlined below.

14.2.2.1 Confessions in the presence of the co-defendant

Where the confession is made in the presence of the co-defendant and he or she acknowledges the incriminating parts so as to make them, in effect, his or her own, then the confession will be admissible against both parties.

14.2.2.2 Defendant's guilt used to establish a co-defendant's guilt

In a joint trial of two (or more) defendants for a joint offence where the case against defendant A is based solely on a confession made out of court, the jury is entitled to consider first the case in respect of defendant A and then to use their findings of A's guilt and the role A played as a fact to be used evidentially in respect of co-defendant B (*R v Hayter* [2005] 1 WLR 605). However, the jury must be sure of the truthfulness of defendant A's confession and must be directed that when deciding the case against defendant B, they must disregard entirely everything said by defendant A in the confession which might otherwise be thought to incriminate the defendant. The case of *Hayter* concerned a murder trial in which the jury, having concluded that the first defendant (the victim's wife) was guilty of murder for having arranged for the contract-killing of her husband, and (by virtue of his out-of-court confession to his girlfriend) that the third defendant was the killer, were entitled to use those conclusions as part of the building blocks in the case against the second defendant (the middleman who had engaged the killer and passed the money to him). The circumstances in which the jury can rely on the confession of the co-defendant as evidence against the defendant are strictly confined (*Persad v State of Trinidad and Tobago* [2008] 1 Cr App R 1).

14.2.3 Restrictions on the admissibility of confessions adduced by the prosecution

A confession on which the prosecution proposes to rely may be excluded under the following provisions:

(a) PACE 1984, s 76(2);
(b) PACE 1984, s 78;
(c) CJA 2003, s 126; and
(d) the common law exclusionary discretion.

We will consider each in turn.

14.2.3.1 PACE 1984, s 76(2)

Section 76(2) of PACE 1984 provides that if the defence represent to the court that the confession was obtained either:

(a) by oppression; or
(b) as a result of something said or done to the defendant which was likely to render any resulting confession unreliable,

then the confession must be excluded unless the prosecution proves that the confession was not so obtained. The standard of proof is beyond reasonable doubt.

The wording of s 76 is as follows:

> *(2) If, in any proceedings where the prosecution proposes to give evidence of a confession made by an accused person, it is represented to the court that the confession was or may have been obtained—*
>
> *(a) by oppression of the person who made it; or*
>
> *(b) in consequence of anything said or done which was likely, in the circumstances existing at the time, to render unreliable any confession which might be made by him in consequence thereof,*
>
> *the court shall not allow the confession to be given in evidence against him except in so far as the prosecution proves to the court beyond reasonable doubt that the confession (notwithstanding that it may be true) was not obtained as aforesaid.*
>
> *(3) In any proceedings where the prosecution proposes to give in evidence a confession made by an accused person, the court may of its own motion require the prosecution as a condition of allowing it to do so, to prove that the confession was not obtained as mentioned in subsection (2).*

Section 67(11) of PACE 1984 provides that the court *shall* take account of the PACE codes in determining any question (where relevant) arising in any proceedings, which means that breaches of the Codes of Practice issued under PACE will add weight to an application to exclude evidence under s 76. A recent but unsuccessful attempt to rely upon alleged breaches of the PACE Codes in excluding a confession can be found in *R v Rashid* [2017] EWCA Crim 2.

14.2.3.1.1 Oppression (s 76(2)(a))

Oppression is defined in s 76(8) of PACE 1984 as '*torture, inhuman or degrading treatment, and the use or threat of violence (whether or not amounting to torture)*'.

In *R v Fulling* [1987] QB 426, Lord Lane held that 'oppression' was to be given its ordinary dictionary meaning. The ***Oxford English Dictionary*** in its third definition of the word runs as follows: '*exercise of authority or power in a burdensome, harsh, or wrongful manner; unjust or cruel treatment of subjects, inferiors, etc., or the imposition of unreasonable or unjust burdens.*'

There is no reference to Article 3 of the ECHR in s 76, nor are the words 'the use or threat of violence' further defined in PACE 1984. 'Torture' is a criminal offence under s 134 of the Criminal Justice Act 1988 and 'violence' or 'force' is broadly defined in s 8 of the Public Order Act 1986 (where it includes violent conduct to property and person).

In *R v Paris* (1992) 97 Cr App R 99, CA, the fact that the defendant had a solicitor present did not deprive the interview of its oppressive character. The police had continued to shout at the suspect even though he had denied the charge over 300 times.

In *R v Parker* [1995] Crim LR 223, CA, and *Re Proulx* [2001] 1 All ER 57, it was held that a breach of the PACE Codes of Practice would not automatically lead to a confession being excluded. It was important to look at the context in which the term oppression was used to judge whether or not the confession had been obtained by oppression.

In considering the question of whether or not 'oppression' has occurred, the character and attributes of the accused may be relevant. In *R v Miller* [1986] 1 WLR 1191, it was said *per* Watkins LJ that it might be oppressive to put questions to an accused who is known to be mentally ill so as to 'skilfully and deliberately' induce a delusionary state in him. In *R v Seelig* [1992] 1 WLR 128, Henry J took account of the fact that the accused was an 'experienced merchant banker' and was 'intelligent and sophisticated' when he assessed whether he had been questioned in an oppressive way.

14.2.3.1.2 *Unreliability (s 76(2)(b))*

Bad faith is not required to render a confession inadmissible under s 76(2)(b). Moreover, the court is not concerned with the reliability of the confession per se, but the reliability of any confession which might be made by the defendant in consequence of the thing said or done.

The case of *R v Barry* (1992) 95 Cr App R 384 gives guidance on how to approach the question of the reliability of confessions during a police interview:

1. Identify the thing 'said or done' (the judge must take into account everything 'said or done' by the police).
2. Ask whether or not the thing 'said or done' was likely in the circumstances to render unreliable any confession made in consequence.
3. Ask whether the prosecution have proved beyond reasonable doubt that the confession was not obtained in consequence of the thing 'said or done'.

Steps 1 and 2 are objective, and the third step is a question of fact (see Code C, PACE 1984).

The words 'said or done' do not include anything said or done by the person making the confession. In *R v Goldenberg* (1989) 88 Cr App R 285, CA, a heroin addict was interviewed at a time when he may have been withdrawing from the effects of heroin. It was held that since the section states 'in consequence of', it was intended that there should be a causal link between what was 'said and done' and the making of the confession. It followed that the words 'said or done' were limited to something external to the person making the confession.

Breaches of PACE Code C can amount to 'things done'. Examples include a failure to caution a suspect (*R v Doolan* [1988] Crim LR 747, CA), or improper denial of access to a solicitor (*R v McGovern* (1991) 92 Cr App R 228, CA). The test is whether the breach is significant and substantial: see *R v Delaney* (1989) 88 Cr App R 338, CA, where a confession made at the end of an interview which had not been recorded in accordance with Code C was ruled inadmissible. It is also noteworthy that things said or done in a police interview which are likely to render a confession unreliable may be said or done by persons other than the police officers conducting the interview. In *R v M* [2000] 8 Arch News 2, M's solicitor, by intervening during his client's interview in an attempt to secure a confession, rendered the resultant confession unreliable.

14.2.3.1.3 *Procedure for a PACE 1984, s 76 application*

The *voir dire* procedure is used when determining admissibility under PACE 1984, s 76. *R v Sat-Bhambra* (1988) 88 Cr App R 55, CA, established that where an objection was made to the admissibility of a confession under s 76, the time to make the objection was before the confession was given in evidence. At common law, where a confession was admitted, and it subsequently emerged during the trial that the admissibility of the confession was questionable, the judge was precluded from applying s 76. However, the judge could direct the jury in several ways:

- to disregard the statement;
- to direct its attention to the matters that might affect the weight attached to the confession; or
- if the matter could not be solved by a suitable direction, he could discharge the jury.

The judge's power to take such action derives from the common law principle to take such steps that are necessary to prevent injustice, which is preserved by PACE 1984, s 82(3) (see **14.2.3.4**).

While a *voir dire* is generally inappropriate in summary proceedings, as the magistrates are the tribunal of both fact and law, s 76(2) places a statutory obligation on the magistrates to hold one (*Liverpool Juvenile Court, ex p R* [1988] QB 1). Where the defendant's pre-trial statements are excluded under s 78, the correct approach is for the magistrates to seek the views of the parties and then consider whether the substantive hearing should be dealt with by a differently constituted bench (*DPP v Lawrence* [2008] 1 Cr App R 147). It is submitted that the same approach should be taken in relation to s 76.

14.2.3.2 PACE 1984, s 78

Section 78 of PACE 1984 creates a discretion to exclude evidence. Section 78 provides that:

> (1) *In any proceedings the court may refuse to allow evidence on which the prosecution proposes to rely to be given if it appears to the court that, having regard to all the circumstances, including the circumstances in which the evidence was obtained, the admission of the evidence would have such an adverse effect on the fairness of the proceedings that the court ought not to admit it.*
>
> (2) *Nothing in this section shall prejudice any rule of law requiring a court to exclude evidence.*

14.2.3.2.1 *Confessions, s 78, and PACE 1984 Codes of Practice*

The discretion to exclude a confession is likely to be exercised when deliberate impropriety or bad faith is present, resulting in unfairness. However, the simple fact that there has been a breach of a PACE code does not necessarily lead to a confession being excluded, nor is it necessary to show bad faith. The key question is whether it would be unfair to admit the confession because of the breach. Arguably, the Human Rights Act 1998 means that the courts should be more 'rights-orientated' in their application of s 78, so, for example, where a confession has been obtained after an unjustified refusal of access to a solicitor (in breach of an individual's rights under PACE, s 58, Code C, para 6.1), it should be excluded.

What are a person's rights under PACE in relation to access to a solicitor, which may act as a fundamental safeguard against self-incrimination (see *Ibrahim v UK* [2016] ECHR 750)? A person who is arrested and held in custody at a police station has a right, at his or her request, to consult with a solicitor at any time, privately (PACE 1984, s 58). Article 6(3) of the ECHR requires that consultation must take place out of the hearing of a third party (in particular a police officer) (*Brennan v UK* (2002) 34 EHRR 507). In the magistrates' court it is not a statutory right but it is a common law right to have access to a solicitor as soon as is reasonably practicable.

The right is a right to advice and not a right to have a legal adviser present during interview; however, Code C, para 6.8 states that if the detainee has been permitted to consult a solicitor he is entitled on request to have a solicitor present at his interview (subject to some exceptions listed in Code C, para 6.6).

The police may delay access to a solicitor on the grounds that to wait could prejudice the investigation (*R (Thompson) v Chief Constable of the Northumberland Constabulary* [2001] 1 WLR 1342). In *Samuel* [1988] QB 615, the Court of Appeal held that if the police seek to deny access to a solicitor they must show more than a substantial risk of their fears being realised. If delay is authorised, the reasons must be given and noted in the custody record. Specific grounds for delaying access to a solicitor by those suspected of committing indictable offences are set out in Code C, para 6.6 and Annex B. They include an officer of the rank of at least superintendent having reasonable grounds to believe that access might lead to interference with evidence, interference or harm to other people, alerting other suspects not as yet arrested, hindering the recovery of property obtained as a result of the commission of an indictable offence, and unreasonable delay to the process of investigation.

14.2.3.2.2 Procedure for a PACE 1984, s 78 application

A *voir dire* is necessary in the Crown Court to determine whether a confession should be excluded under s 78.

There is no *voir dire* in summary proceedings for applications under s 78, as the magistrates are the tribunal of both fact and law. In fact, there is no general rule as to when issues of admissibility should be decided as each case is different. However, where magistrates exclude evidence of a defendant's pre-trial statements, the correct approach is for the magistrates to seek the views of the parties and then consider whether the substantive hearing should be dealt with by a differently constituted bench (*DPP v Lawrence* [2008] 1 Cr App R 147).

14.2.3.3 Criminal Justice Act 2003, s 126

Section 126 of the CJA 2003 provides:

> *(1) In criminal proceedings the court may refuse to admit a statement as evidence of a matter stated if—*
>
> *(a) the statement was made otherwise than in oral evidence in the proceedings, and*
>
> *(b) the court is satisfied that the case for excluding the statement, taking account of the danger that to admit it would result in undue waste of time, substantially outweighs the case for admitting it, taking account of the value of the evidence.*

This exclusionary discretion applies to hearsay evidence. As a confession is a type of hearsay evidence, it follows that the court also has the power to exclude it under this provision. However, as previously stated, s 126 seems designed to exclude hearsay evidence that has little probative value or is superfluous. Since confessions are normally highly probative and the issues arising over their admissibility are to do with oppression, unreliability, and unfairness, s 126 is unlikely to be relied upon. See further **13.9.4.1**.

14.2.3.4 Common law discretion

Section 82(3) of PACE 1984 preserves the common law discretion to exclude evidence pre-PACE 1984 and provides that:

Nothing in part of this Act shall prejudice any power of a court to exclude evidence (whether by preventing questions being put or otherwise) at its discretion.

In practice the common law discretion is seldom used as it has been largely superseded by s 78 of PACE 1984.

14.2.4 Effects of excluding a confession

What effect will the exclusion of a confession have on the admissibility of evidence discovered as a result of that confession? The answer differs according to the power under which it has been excluded.

14.2.4.1 PACE 1984, s 76

Section 76(4)–(6) of PACE 1984 provides that:

(4) *The fact that a confession is wholly or partly excluded in pursuance of this section shall not affect the admissibility in evidence—*

(a) *of any facts discovered as a result of the confession; or*

(b) *where the confession is relevant as showing that the accused speaks, writes or expresses himself in a particular way, of so much of the confession as is necessary to show that he does so.*

(5) *Evidence that a fact to which this subsection applies was discovered as a result of a statement made by an accused person shall not be admissible unless evidence of how it was discovered is given by him or on his behalf.*

(6) *Subsection (5) applies—*

(a) *to any fact discovered as a result of a confession which is wholly excluded in pursuance of the section; and*

(b) *to any fact discovered as a result of a confession which is partly so excluded, if the fact is discovered as a result of the excluded part of the confession.*

The effect of s 76(4)–(6) is that, where a confession is excluded under s 76(2), any facts which have been discovered as a result of the confession are admissible. However, the prosecution cannot prove that those facts were discovered as a result of an excluded confession.

14.2.4.2 PACE 1984, s 78, Criminal Justice Act 2003, s 126, and the common law discretion

If a confession is excluded under PACE 1984, s 78, the CJA 2003, s 126 or the common law discretion, then s 76(4)–(6) cannot be invoked. However, the ordinary principles of relevance will apply should the prosecution wish to admit facts arising from the confession. Furthermore, where a confession has been excluded under one of these principles, any evidence that has been obtained as a result is itself liable to exclusion under s 78 or the common law discretion.

14.2.5 'Mentally handicapped persons'

At common law, where the prosecution case relies wholly on a confession by a person suffering a mental handicap to a significant degree and the confession is unconvincing to the extent that a jury properly directed could not properly convict on it, then the judge should withdraw the case from the jury (see *R v MacKenzie* [1993] 1 WLR 453, CA, which adapted the principles of *R v Galbraith* [1981] 1 WLR 1039 to cases involving confessions by mentally handicapped persons).

The provisions of PACE 1984 also bite where confessions have been made by persons who have a mental handicap. The confession of a mentally handicapped person may be excluded under s 76(2)(b) where the person's mental handicap renders the confession unreliable. Therefore, where a person with a mental handicap makes confessions in police interviews when no solicitor or appropriate independent person was present, the confession would almost certainly be excluded (see *R v Moss* (1990) 91 Cr App R 371). Such a confession might also be excluded under PACE 1984, s 78, where to admit the confession would have such an adverse effect on the fairness of the proceedings that it ought not to be admitted (see **14.2.3.2**).

Additionally, PACE 1984, s *77* specifically imposes an obligation on the judge to warn the jury about a confession made by a mentally handicapped person in certain circumstances. It states that where the case against the accused depends wholly or substantially on a confession by an accused who is mentally handicapped and which was not made in the presence of an independent person, '*the court shall warn the jury that there is a special need for caution before convicting the accused in reliance on the confession*'. If the judge fails to give this warning, it is likely that the conviction will be quashed (*R v Lamont* [1989] Crim LR 813, CA; see **5.5**).

The relevant provisions of the PACE Code of Practice that govern the treatment of persons with a mental handicap are to be found in Code C and Annex E. Breaches of these provisions may provide a sound basis upon which to argue that a confession by a mentally handicapped person should be excluded.

14.3 Confessions adduced by a co-defendant

14.3.1 Admissibility

In *R v Myers* [1998] AC 124, HL, it was held that where the accused has made a confession, and the confession is relevant to the defence of a co-accused, then the co-accused will be allowed to adduce evidence of that confession unless the way in which it was obtained would have rendered it inadmissible for the prosecution by virtue of PACE 1984, s 76(2). However, where a confession is inadmissible for the prosecution under PACE 1984, s 78, it could still be admissible for the co-accused.

The admissibility of a confession on behalf of a co-defendant is now governed by s 76A(1) which provides:

> (1) *In any proceedings a confession made by an accused person may be given in evidence for another person charged in the same proceedings (a co-accused) in so far as it is relevant to any matter in issue in the proceedings and is not excluded by the court in pursuance of this section.*

R v Nazir [2009] EWCA Crim 213 provides a straightforward example of how a confession by a co-accused is admissible under s 76A. M and N were convicted of the murder of S in a so-called 'honour killing'. M, who was unrelated to S, made statements to the police in which he sought to take all the blame. N's defence was that, while he was present when M killed S, he had no involvement. It was held that the trial judge was wrong to direct the jury that they could not consider M's statements to the police in relation to N's defence as the statements were admissible under s 76A.

Section 76A has no application, however, where a co-accused has pleaded guilty. In *R v Finch* [2007] 1 Cr App R 439, the Court of Appeal held that it has been well-established law for many years that a defendant who has pleaded guilty and who is not on trial before the jury is not a 'person charged with an offence' in the proceedings for the purpose of his status as a witness and accordingly s 76A did not apply to any confession he has made. Additionally, the provision will not apply unless the co-accused's statement is actually a confession for the purposes of PACE 1984, s 82(1) and, where the statement is not a confession, its admissibility will be determined by the CJA 2003, s 114 (see *R v Y* [2008] 1 WLR 1683).

14.3.2 Exclusion

Where a co-defendant proposes to rely upon the defendant's confession, the court has no power to exclude it under PACE 1984, s 78 or at common law, as these powers only apply to prosecution evidence. However, the court is given a power to exclude a co-defendant's evidence under:

(a) PACE 1984, s 76A(2); and

(b) CJA 2003, s 126.

14.3.2.1 PACE 1984, s 76(A)(2)

Section 76A of PACE 1984 provides:

> *(2) If, in any proceedings where a co-accused proposes to give in evidence a confession made by an accused person, it is represented to the court that the confession was or may have been obtained—*
>
> *(a) by oppression of the person who made it; or*
>
> *(b) in consequence of anything said or done which was likely, in the circumstances existing at the time, to render unreliable any confession which might be made by him in consequence thereof, the court shall not allow the confession to be given in evidence for the co-accused except in so far as it is proved to the court on the balance of probabilities that the confession (notwithstanding that it may be true) was not so obtained.*

It can be seen that this provision follows very closely the provision in s 76(2) (see **14.2.3.1**). The key difference is that because the co-defendant bears the burden of disproving that the confession was obtained by oppression or in consequence of something said or done likely to render any confession made by the defendant unreliable, the standard of proof is the balance of probabilities.

14.3.2.2 Criminal Justice Act 2003, s 126

As previously stated at **14.2.3.3**, s 126 of the CJA 2003 creates a discretion to exclude hearsay evidence. The discretion is not limited to prosecution evidence and so, in theory, it could be relied upon by the co-defendant to exclude evidence of his or her confession on which the defendant proposes to rely. However, it is submitted that, in practice, where the confession is relevant to the issues between the defendant and the co-defendant, it is unlikely that the case for excluding the confession would substantially outweigh the case for admitting it.

14.3.2.3 Effects of excluding a confession

Section 76A(4)–(6) of PACE 1984 allows for evidence that has been discovered as the result of a confession to be admitted notwithstanding that the confession has itself been excluded under s 76A(2):

> *(4) The fact that a confession is wholly or partly excluded in pursuance of this section shall not affect the admissibility in evidence—*
>
> *(a) of any facts discovered as a result of the confession; or*
>
> *(b) where the confession is relevant as showing that the accused speaks, writes or expresses himself in a particular way, of so much of the confession as is necessary to show that he does so.*

(5) *Evidence that a fact to which this subsection applies was discovered as a result of a statement made by an accused person shall not be admissible unless evidence of how it was discovered is given by him or on his behalf.*

(6) *Subsection (5) above applies—*

(a) *to any fact discovered as a result of a confession which is wholly excluded in pursuance of this section; and*

(b) *to any fact discovered as a result of a confession which is partly so excluded, if the fact is discovered as a result of the excluded part of the confession.*

This power does not apply to confessions which have been admitted under the CJA 2003, s 126. Where that is the case, then any evidence discovered as the result of a confession will be admissible as long as it is relevant and is not otherwise liable to exclusion under another principle of evidence.

14.4 Illegally or improperly obtained evidence other than confessions

It is well established that a judge retains at common law a discretion to exclude evidence that may be admissible where the prejudicial effect of the evidence outweighs its probative value. This principle is applied on a case-by-case basis.

Where the evidence has been obtained unlawfully or improperly, the evidence may be excluded under s 78. In *R v Sang* [1980] AC 402, the House of Lords held that at *common law* the court did not have a discretion to exclude this type of evidence unless its probative value was outweighed by its prejudicial effect or the evidence amounted to a confession (eg where a defendant was induced into providing a specimen, which was then used to show that he was unfit to drive: see *R v Payne* [1963] 1 WLR 637).

However, a defendant is not *entitled* to have unlawfully obtained evidence excluded simply because it has been so obtained (see *R v P* [2002] 1 AC 146). An application to exclude unlawful or improperly obtained evidence under s 78 will turn on its facts. Generally, an application under s 78 should succeed where the unlawful or improper means used to obtain the evidence affect its quality, or where there has been bad faith or a breach of one of the defendant's fundamental rights.

In *R v Khan (Sultan)* [1997] AC 558, the House of Lords upheld the Court of Appeal's decision that evidence obtained by a bugging device, attached by the police to a private house without the knowledge of the owner, was admissible. Lord Nolan (at [582]) stated that the significance of any breach of any relevant law or Convention will normally be determined by its effect on the fairness of the proceedings, rather than its irregularity or unlawfulness. This case was considered further in the European Court in *Khan v UK* [2000] Crim LR 684, where it was asserted that there had been a breach of Article 8, respect for private life, and therefore a breach of Article 6(1), fair trial. The court decided that there was no breach of Article 6, despite finding that the United Kingdom had violated Article 8. Since this decision, the Regulation of Investigatory Powers Act 2000 (RIPA) has been enacted governing how the police conduct covert surveillance.

R v Khan [2013] EWCA Crim 2230 was a case which involved covert surveillance which exceeded permission granted under RIPA to conduct the surveillance. In *Khan*, permission had been granted under RIPA to make surveillance recordings for the purposes of obtaining evidence to prove or disprove the defendant's involvement in a crime, but the recording in question (of incriminating statements) was made, albeit in good faith, after the defendant had been charged. It was held that although the recording had been made in excess of authority and there had been a breach of the defendant's right to privacy under Article 8, the judge had been correct in refusing to exclude the evidence under s 78: the touchstone of the law is fairness in the criminal trial process and it was not unfair to admit evidence of the recording.

In *R v Smurthwaite; R v Gill* (1994) 98 Cr App R 437, CA, it was held that entrapment itself did not result in the exclusion of evidence. However, the court gave guidance on the factors that might render evidence obtained by entrapment inadmissible. Key among them was the question of whether the police had enticed a person into committing a crime which that person might otherwise not have committed. *R v Loosely; Attorney General's Reference (No 3 of 2000)* [2002] 1 Cr App R 29 reviewed the issue of entrapment and Lord Hoffmann stated that the more appropriate remedy in cases of entrapment would be staying the prosecution as an abuse of process rather than excluding the evidence. For further comment on abuse of process, see *R v Latif; R v Shahzad* [1996] 2 Cr App R 92, HL.

14.4.1 Illegally or improperly obtained evidence in civil proceedings

In civil proceedings judges have the power under CPR, r 32.1(2) to exclude evidence that would otherwise be admissible. The power must be exercised in accordance with the overriding objective in Part 1 of the CPR, to deal with cases justly. The discretion was explained by Lord Hoffmann in *A v Home Secretary (No 2)* [2006] 2 AC 221 in the following way: 'There is a discretion in all cases to exclude evidence if its admission would dishonour the administration of justice or compromise the integrity of the judicial process.' This means that evidence may be excluded in civil proceedings on grounds that it has been obtained illegally or improperly. However, the manner in which the evidence was obtained is just one factor to be considered by the civil courts when deciding whether to exclude under CPR, r 32.1(2). In *Jones v Warwick University* [2003] 1 WLR 954, the Court of Appeal (Civil Division) stated that any unlawfulness in how evidence was obtained had to be balanced against the importance of the court reaching the correct decision on the basis of all the available evidence. So, in civil cases, as in criminal cases, the fact that evidence has been obtained by illegal or improper means is not necessarily a bar to its admissibility. Further, the fact that such evidence should have been excluded in criminal proceedings does not mean that it must be excluded in related civil proceedings. In *Olden v Serious Organised Crime Agency* [2010] EWCA Civ 143, it was held that material discovered by the police following an unlawful arrest and subsequent searches, even though inadmissible in the accused's criminal trial, was admissible in related confiscation proceedings.

15

Lies and silence

15.1 Introduction

In the last chapter we considered how the courts will use confessions obtained (usually but not exclusively) by police officers investigating a criminal offence. Clearly not all persons who are questioned will confess their guilt. Others may seek to lie to deflect the police from investigating them further. So, to what extent can the court use the fact either that someone remained silent or that they lied?

Consider the following scenario. Ollie is alleged to have stolen a car. When arrested by the police he is in possession of a car radio (that, it later turns out, is the same as the car radio that has been taken from the stolen car). Ollie refuses to say anything about the radio when asked to do so by the police. Ollie is taken to the police station. He is interviewed and says that he does not know anything about the car in question and that when it went missing he was at work. The police tell him (correctly) that they found his wallet in the back of the car. He asks to see his solicitor and, having taken the solicitor's advice, he refuses to answer any other questions.

What if anything does Ollie's conduct prove? How might the following situations change the way in which a tribunal of fact might treat Ollie?

(a) At trial, Ollie alleged that he lied about his whereabouts because he was visiting his girlfriend, of whom his parents do not approve, and he didn't want them to know. He found the radio on the road.

(b) In addition to (a) above, his solicitor advised him not to answer any questions because the police officer interviewing him had a reputation for planting evidence.

(c) Instead of (a) and (b) above, Ollie alleges at trial that he did not answer questions because his solicitor advised him that he had a right to remain silent and that it was for the police to obtain all the evidence to prove the case against him without his help.

(d) Instead of (a)–(c) above, Ollie gives no evidence at trial in his own defence but his barrister has cross-examined the police witnesses to suggest that the wallet was planted in the car by racist police officers (Ollie is black and has been in trouble with the police before).

The detail of the answers to these questions will be considered later. However, for the time being, it is worth considering the issues that the questions have raised.

(a) What is the evidential value of a lie? Does it show that the liar is guilty of the offence about which he has lied? Should it be adduced in evidence in a criminal trial?

(b) What is the evidential value of refusing to answer questions or allegations at the time of arrest and later questioning?

(c) What is the effect of raising a defence for the first time at trial? Does it show that the accused was trying to hide his defence from the prosecution until he put it before the jury? If so, does that mean that he is more likely to be guilty?

(d) What if the refusal to explain or answer questions is due to legal advice?

(e) What is proved by the fact that an accused person does not testify in his own defence? Does this show that he is conscious of his own guilt?

(f) Does it make a difference if a person does not testify but uses his lawyer to advance the defence through cross-examination?

Before looking at these areas in depth, it should be noted that what this chapter looks at is the evidential value of lies or silence on the part of a party. It is not about the evidential value of the thing that the party lied or was silent about. Consider the example just given. Ollie was found with a car radio like the one from the car and his wallet was found in the car. These are items of circumstantial evidence unaffected by the law covered in this chapter. They are admissible at Ollie's trial, in so far as they are relevant. What this chapter considers, among other things, is the evidential value of *failures to explain those other items of admissible evidence*. Do not confuse the two (it is very easy to do so).

As is common with the rules of evidence, we shall see that there is a very different approach between the civil and the criminal courts. We shall consider the civil rules first.

15.2 Civil cases

The common law governs the position in civil cases in respect of both lies and silence. The courts have treated silence or a lie like any other item of evidence: it is admissible if it is relevant to a fact in issue and the weight to be attached to it is a matter for the tribunal of fact and will depend on the facts and issues in each case. Examples include the following cases:

- In *Bessela v Stern* (1877) LR 2 CPD 265, the plaintiff confronted the defendant over a promise to marry her. He made no reply. The defendant's silence was treated as admissible evidence to prove that there had been such a promise because he would have denied that fact if it had not been true.
- In *Wiedmann v Walpole* [1891] 2 QB 534, the defendant did not reply to an accusatory letter written by the plaintiff. The court held that the letter was not admissible as evidence to prove that the accusations were true. The failure to reply to the letter simply did not go far enough in proving that the accusation was true. There was a number of reasons why a person might not reply to such a letter.
- In *Francisco v Diedrick*, The Times, 3 April 1998, where a plaintiff had made out a prima facie case, the defendant's failure to testify was circumstantial evidence that supported the plaintiff's case.

15.3 Lies in criminal cases

The evidential value of lies, as opposed to silence, in the face of accusation or questioning, is governed by the common law. Evidence of lies is generally admissible. The statements alleged to be lies will be admissible as original, as opposed to hearsay, evidence (see **11.4.4**). The rules set out below apply to lies told either outside of court or in the witness box.

15.3.1 Directing the jury on lies

Where the defendant is alleged to have lied, the judge will ensure that the jury is given careful guidance as to how it should deal with the alleged lie as evidence. The leading case is *R v Lucas* [1981] QB 720, where Lord Lane CJ said (at [724]) that the jury must be directed that, to be capable of being evidence against the accused, the alleged lie must be:

- said deliberately;
- concerned with a material issue in the case;
- motivated by a realisation of guilt and fear of the truth; and
- shown to be untrue.

All four matters must be identified to the jury in summing up and the jury must be told that before it uses the alleged lie as evidence of the accused's guilt, it must be satisfied beyond reasonable doubt that the statement is a lie (*R v Burge* [1996] 1 Cr App R 163).

On the issue of the motive for the lie, Lord Lane said in *R v Lucas*:

> The jury should in appropriate cases be reminded that people sometimes lie [not from a sense of guilt but], for example, in an attempt to bolster up a just cause, or out of shame or out of a wish to conceal disgraceful behaviour from their family.

Clearly, a statement made by the defendant that is alleged to be untrue will potentially be a lie within the meaning of *Lucas*. However, what if the statement is made by another person in the presence of the defendant? It seems that whether it is capable of being used against the defendant as the basis of a lie will depend on the particular facts of each case. In *R v Collins* [2004] 2 Cr App R 11, C and B were arrested together on suspicion of having recently kidnapped H. When B was asked where he had been he told the police officers (in C's presence) that both he and C had been at a particular public house. However, in interview and at trial C maintained that he had been with H but that he had not kidnapped him. At trial the judge gave a *Lucas* direction against C. The Court of Appeal quashed C's conviction. The court concluded that where a question was asked and an untrue answer was given in the presence of a defendant, the jury could conclude that his reaction to that question and answer could amount to his adoption of that answer, if the jury were satisfied that: (a) the question called for some response from the defendant; and (b) by his reaction the defendant had adopted the answer made. In the circumstances of that case the jury had not been properly directed to adopt that approach and, in any event, there was not sufficient evidence adduced at trial for the jury to reach such a conclusion from the question and answer posed.

15.3.2 When a *Lucas* direction is required

The four-part direction just set out is not always necessary. A *Lucas* direction is only required where lies are of direct relevance to the offence charged, for example, false alibi (*R v Smith* [1995] Crim LR 305). In *R v Burge* [1996] 1 Cr App R 163, the Court of Appeal identified four situations in which such a direction would be necessary:

(a) where the accused raised an alibi;

(b) where the judge has directed the jury to look for supporting evidence for particular witnesses and has made reference to potential lies as a possible source of such support (on the need for the judge to issue such a direction, see **Chapter 5**);

(c) where the prosecution has sought to rely on an alleged lie as evidence of the accused's guilt; and

(d) where the prosecution has not explicitly sought to rely on the alleged lie but there is a real danger that the jury will do so.

Situation (d) identified in *R v Burge* clearly places an obligation on the trial judge to consider the likely effect of any untrue statements made during or before trial and take what steps are thought necessary. In *R v Nash* [2004] EWCA Crim 164, the defendant was charged with criminal damage, it being alleged that he had fired pellets from an airgun at car windows. The only evidence against the defendant was that: (a) he was seen near the scene of the crime acting suspiciously; (b) he denied owning an air rifle; and (c) an air rifle was found at his flat. Despite it seeming clear that the denial in (b) could be a lie, no *Lucas* direction was given. The Court of Appeal concluded that, in such circumstances, a direction should have been given as there was a real danger that the jury might use the defendant's lie as evidence of guilt even though the prosecution did not so rely upon it.

The list identified in *R v Burge* is not exhaustive. The Court of Appeal has noted that the identification of certain categories in *Burge* does not reduce the general principle that a *Lucas* direction is required where there is a danger that the jury may regard the fact that the defendant has told lies as probative of his guilt; see *R v Jefford* [2003] EWCA Crim 1987. In *Jefford*, the need for the direction arose as a result of the significance that the judge attached to potential lies and inconsistencies, even though the prosecution had placed no particular reliance upon those lies.

Although it should generally be clear in each case whether such a situation arises, this may not always be so. The court in *R v Burge* stated that the judge and counsel should consider the need for a *Lucas* direction before the judge starts summing up to the jury; this ought to minimise the possibility of a complaint afterwards. Further, the Court of Appeal would generally be unwilling to overturn a conviction due to the lack of a *Lucas* direction if defence counsel did not identify the need for one at trial. This is because the lawyers and the trial judge are in a better position than the Court of Appeal to evaluate the issues and to determine whether a *Lucas* direction should have been given in any particular case. If the lawyers did not identify the need for a direction at trial, the Court of Appeal is unlikely to conclude that the absence of a direction renders a conviction unsafe (*R v McGuinness* [1999] Crim LR 318).

On some occasions where the jury rejects the accused's account (ie concludes he is lying) it will have no choice but to convict. In such circumstances, there is no need for the judge to direct the jury in respect of the lie (*R v Patrick* [1999] 6 Arch News 4). Clearly, when the effect of rejecting the defence case is the conviction of the accused, there is little purpose to be served by also considering whether the lie is evidence that the accused was guilty of the offence.

See also the ***Crown Court Compendium Part 1*** 2017, section 16-2 at <https://www.judiciary.gov.uk/wp-content/uploads/2016/06/crown-court-compendium-pt1-jury-and-trial-management-and-summing-up-nov2017-v3.pdf>.

15.4 Silence in criminal cases

Parliament has created a number of rules that allow the failure of the accused to answer allegations to be adduced as evidence to show the accused's guilt.

It is not difficult to understand why a lie might prove that a person is guilty of an offence. A lie suggests that the person lying is trying to cover up for his or her guilty behaviour. But what about a refusal to answer questions or to explain matters? Clearly, it is *possible* to infer from such silence that the suspect does not have an explanation that will stand up to any scrutiny. However, there are numerous reasons why a person might refuse to answer questions or innocently explain incriminating evidence; being guilty is only one of them. Therefore, as we shall see, the courts have sought to ensure that juries are carefully directed only to use silence as evidence if any innocent explanations have been rejected.

Furthermore, using the silence of the accused as evidence of his or her guilt offends some fundamental principles of the criminal justice process. Clearly, such evidence runs contrary to the right to silence and the privilege against self-incrimination. These principles are enshrined in Article 6 of the ECHR. For this reason, the statutory provisions set out in this section have been the subject of frequent scrutiny to determine whether they comply with the right to a fair trial.

Instead of a single rule relating to inferences from silence, Parliament has provided different rules for inferences to be drawn in respect of silence at different stages in the criminal process. In an approximate chronological sequence, these are:

- silence upon being questioned (see **15.4.1**);
- silence when confronted about certain types of incriminating evidence (see **15.4.2**);
- refusal to give 'body samples' to the police (see **15.4.3**);
- failure to disclose the defence case (see **15.4.4**);
- failure to testify (see **15.4.5**); and
- failure to call evidence (see **15.4.6**).

Of these, the most significant are usually seen as silence on being questioned and a failure to testify at trial. All of the various stages will be dealt with in turn.

15.4.1 Silence upon being questioned

15.4.1.1 Failure to disclose a fact

Adverse inferences may be drawn in certain circumstances if the accused has not explained his defence at an early opportunity. Before considering when this might happen, it is worth making sure that you understand the powers of the police to question suspects (see Chapter 2 of the ***Criminal Litigation and Sentencing*** manual). One thing we must be clear on, though, is this: it is not silence as such that gives rise to any inference being drawn against the accused but the *non-disclosure* of a fact that triggers the possibility of an adverse inference. An accused may say many things upon being questioned; he or she may disclose many significant facts and make important admissions, so that he or she could not be said to be silent during questioning. If, however, he or she says nothing about a particular fact that he or she relies on in his or her defence at trial, the omission to disclose that fact can count against him or her.

15.4.1.2 The Criminal Justice and Public Order Act 1994, s 34

Section 34 of the Criminal Justice and Public Order Act 1994 states:

> *(1) Where, in any proceedings against a person for an offence, evidence is given that the accused—*
>
> *(a) at any time before he was charged with the offence, on being questioned under caution by a constable trying to discover whether or by whom the offence had been committed, failed to mention any fact relied on in his defence in those proceedings; or*
>
> *(b) on being charged with the offence or officially informed that he might be prosecuted for it, failed to mention any such fact,*
>
> ...

> (2) *Where this subsection applies—*
>
> ...
>
> (c) *the court, in determining whether there is a case to answer; and*
>
> (d) *the court or jury, in determining whether the accused is guilty of the offence charged, may draw such inferences from the failure as appear proper.*

Section 34 places a suspect under an obligation to explain his or her potential defence under specified circumstances. These circumstances will be discussed in more detail. The duty is not absolute. There is no automatic sanction for failing to explain a defence: the failure to mention a fact simply gives the fact-finders an option to treat that failure as something that can strengthen the prosecution case.

15.4.1.3 No inference will be drawn if the fact relied on is true

It has been said that no inference should be drawn under s 34 if the fact in question has been shown to be true; see *R v Wisdom* (CA, 10 December 1989), approved in *R v Webber* [2004] 1 All ER 770. However, this rarely occurs in the course of a trial prior to the verdict being reached.

15.4.1.4 When is the accused required to disclose the facts of his defence?

The court can draw inferences from the accused's failure to explain his or her defence in two situations:

- Upon being questioned, but only if:
  - he or she has been cautioned; and
  - he or she has not yet been charged with the offence.
- Upon being charged with the offence, at which point he or she will be cautioned again.

The wording of the caution differs slightly depending upon whether it is being administered at upon questioning or upon charge. The wording of the caution to be given upon being questioned under PACE Code C, para 10.5 is:

> You do not have to say anything. But it may harm your defence if you do not mention *when questioned* something which you later rely on in court. Anything you do say may be given in evidence.

The wording of the caution to be given upon being charged under PACE Code C, para 16.2 is:

> You do not have to say anything. But it may harm your defence if you do not mention *now* something which you later rely on in court. Anything you do say may be given in evidence.

Not all questions asked by a police officer are governed by s 34(1)(a). In such situations (for detail, see Annex C to Code C of the PACE Codes of Practice), to the extent that a prosecutor seeks to rely on the defendant's failure to provide answers to questions, the common law rules apply (see later).

It is likely that failure to mention facts in response to being charged would occur most often in situations where the police did not feel that there was a need to question the accused because they already have sufficient evidence to charge him or her. However, s 34(1)(b) will also apply if no inferences can be drawn from the interview because it has been excluded under s 78 (see **Chapter 14**). In those circumstances, inferences can be drawn from the failure to mention a defence on charge even though the accused was questioned fully prior to charge (*R v Dervish* [2002] 2 Cr App R 105).

Note that s 34 also applies to situations in which the prosecution will be commenced other than by charging the accused (see Chapter 2 of the ***Criminal Litigation and Sentencing*** manual). In such circumstances the obligation to explain facts arises upon the accused being told that he or she will be prosecuted.

15.4.1.5 The fact that is not mentioned must later be relied upon as part of a defence

This is a very important feature of s 34. Inferences cannot be drawn simply because the accused did not answer questions during interview (or upon caution). They may only be drawn if the accused:

- relies on a fact in his or her defence; and
- he or she did not mention that fact when questioned under caution or charged.

In other words, it is the last-minute use of a defence (or facts supporting a defence) that leads to the inference rather than the simple exercise of the right to silence. But in what circumstances has a person relied upon a fact in his or her defence? Where the accused gives evidence, it is relatively simple to spot such reliance. But what if either the accused does not give evidence or the question as to s 34 inferences arises before the accused has had an opportunity to do so (eg during a submission of no case to answer)?

Think again about the case concerning Ollie at **15.1**. Have a look at situations (a) and (d) identified there. In which of the two situations does Ollie rely on a fact in his defence?

In situation (a), it is clear that Ollie has relied upon an alibi defence (he was visiting his girlfriend) and also that he found the radio on the road. In addition to any adverse inferences that might result from having lied, he could be subject to adverse inferences under s 34.

Situation (d) has presented more difficulty for the courts. To what extent does a defendant rely on a fact if he does not give evidence or call any witnesses? Does cross-examination of the police witnesses that the wallet was 'planted' amount to reliance upon a fact? In *R v Webber* [2004] 1 All ER 770, the House of Lords considered the meaning of 'fact' within s 34 at some length. Lord Bingham said (at [33]) that the word 'fact' in s 34:

> should be given a broad and not a narrow or pedantic meaning. The word covers any alleged fact which is in issue and is put forward as part of the defence case: if the defendant advances at trial any pure fact or exculpatory explanation or account which, if it were true, he could reasonably have been expected to advance earlier, s 34 is potentially applicable.

For this reason, the House concluded that a party relies on a fact within the meaning of s 34 not only when the defendant gives evidence of that fact but also when the defendant's advocate '*puts a specific and positive case to prosecution witnesses, as opposed to asking questions intended to probe or test the prosecution case*' and that was the position whether or not the witness in question accepted the allegation put to him or her by defence counsel.

It is therefore necessary to distinguish between cross-examination that tests the prosecution evidence (such as suggesting that an identification witness was mistaken) and cross-examination that suggests a positive defence (putting to the same witness that the accused was at another place at the time of the offence). The former will not amount to reliance on a fact under s 34 but the latter probably will.

The use of the phrase 'facts relied on in defence' may appear to give the prosecution and the court an opportunity to invoke s 34 whenever there is a small detail raised by the defendant at trial that he did not mention during a previous interview. However, in *R v Brizzalari* [2004] EWCA Crim 310, the Court of Appeal recognised that it was a matter for the trial judge to determine whether facts mentioned by the defendant were sufficiently important to fall within s 34.

15.4.1.6 The failure to mention the fact must be unreasonable

Section 34 states that a fact that is not mentioned must be '*a fact which in the circumstances existing at the time the accused could reasonably have been expected to mention*'.

In many cases, the defendant will have a reason (for having failed to answer questions) which should be presented to the jury and which the jury must consider. In *R v Cowan* [1996] 1 Cr App R 1, a case concerning s 35 of the 1994 Act, which also allows adverse inferences to be drawn unless there are good reasons for the defendant's silence, it was noted that there would have to be evidence before the jury of the reasons for silence. It was not possible for counsel simply to give those reasons in the absence of an evidential foundation.

In *R v Nickolson* [1999] Crim LR 61, the Court of Appeal held that a suspect could not be expected to give an innocent explanation of potentially incriminating evidence that was not presented to him at interview.

In *R v Turner* [2004] 1 All ER 1025, the Court of Appeal stated that, where possible, the prosecution should challenge the defendant about any unmentioned fact in cross-examination and give the defendant an opportunity to provide an explanation.

Section 34 will not apply if the accused mentioned the fact in a prepared statement even if he then refuses to answer further questions during interview (*R v Ali* [2001] EWCA Crim 863; *R v Knight* [2003] EWCA Crim 1977).

Have another look at the scenarios concerning Ollie at **15.1**. Now consider situations (a)–(c). In which of those situations should the jury be allowed to draw an adverse inference from Ollie's failure to explain his defence at the police station?

In relation to situation (a), the reason Ollie did not give the real explanation was fear of his parents. It will be a matter for the jury as to whether it accepts this as a genuine reason. If not, it may decide that he did not give his explanation because he was guilty. Note the similarity of approach adopted in relation to the lie he told: the jury will have to decide whether his reason for lying or not mentioning a fact was a consciousness of guilt. It should also be noted that no explanation appears to have been given for the failure to explain the presence of the radio. As he has not put forward any reason for failing to mention how he came by the incriminating radio, the jury would simply have to decide whether his failure to mention the finding of the radio was evidence that he might be guilty of the offence. In other words, where the defendant attempts to give an explanation for his failure to mention facts at trial, the jury will have to undertake a more complicated analysis before drawing adverse inferences against him.

In situations (b) and (c), Ollie's failure to put forward defences at the police station *are* explained at trial. However, the jury is not bound to accept the reasons he gives.

15.4.1.6.1 Legal advice

Situations (b) and (c) in our scenario involve a solicitor's legal advice. The mere fact that a defendant remains silent because of legal advice to that effect does not determine whether or not inferences should be drawn. In *R v Condron* [1997] 1 Cr App R 185, two suspects being investigated for drug offences had been interviewed under caution but both remained silent. At trial the two accused put forward innocent explanations of all the prosecution evidence, which explanations could have been given at the police station. They also testified that their solicitor had advised them not to answer questions because he felt that they were suffering from heroin withdrawal. The police (acting on the advice of the police doctor) had decided the suspects were fit to be interviewed. The jury was directed that it could draw an inference from the failure of the accused to explain their defences at the police station. The Court of Appeal affirmed their convictions. Legal advice could not determine whether or not s 34 applied. Instead, the jury should have regard to the reasons given by the accused (including legal advice) and consider whether it is the legal advice or the consciousness of guilt that is the reason for the failure to mention the fact. The matter was taken to the European Court of Human Rights (*Condron and Condron v UK* [2000] Crim LR 679) where it was decided that it was necessary that the jury be directed that it should only draw an adverse inference if it concluded (beyond reasonable doubt) that the *only* reason for failing to mention the fact was that the suspect had no answer to the questions (or none that would stand up to cross-examination) (see *R v Daly* [2002] 2 Cr App R 201 and *R v Petkar* [2004] 1 Cr App R 270).

In *R v Argent* [1997] Crim LR 346, the Court of Appeal stated that the jury should take into consideration the circumstances in which advice was given and the personality of the accused in deciding the real reason for remaining silent. It was also said that the reasons for the legal advice should not determine whether or not adverse inferences should be drawn. The jury should not be concerned with the correctness of the advice but with its impact upon the accused's conduct at the police station. Therefore, it is not the fact (or the accuracy) of the legal advice that determines whether or not it amounts to a good reason for remaining silent. Rather, the jury will have to consider whether the advice was the cause of the silence or whether it was some other matter and should only infer guilt where it concludes that the other reason was the guilty mind of the accused. As it was put by the Court of Appeal in *R v Beckles* [2005] 1 Cr App R 23, the jury should be told to consider whether the defendant had 'genuinely and reasonably relied' on the legal advice given to him. In our scenario, there is no real difference between situations (b) and (c) except in so far as the jury is likely to accept one or the other as more or less likely to have influenced Ollie's decision. The fact that the advice in situation (c) is clearly wrong (in that it overlooks s 34) is simply a matter for the jury to take into account.

As legal advice can be (but is not necessarily) a good reason for failing to mention a fact it will occasionally be necessary to prove what legal advice was given. The accused could testify as to what his legal adviser told him (this would not be hearsay evidence because it is admitted to prove the fact not the truth of the advice: see **Chapter 11**). However, it may be necessary to call the legal adviser to testify as to what advice he gave to assist in deciding whether the decision to remain silent was really based on the legal advice given (*R v Roble* [1997] Crim LR 449). In *R v Bowden* [1999] 4 All ER 43, it was said that where the accused or his solicitor had given evidence as to not just the fact of advice having been given to keep silent but also the reasons for that advice, the accused '*voluntarily withdrew the veil of privilege and having done so could not resist questioning directed to the nature of that advice and the factual premises on which it was based*' (*per* Lord Bingham CJ at [47]). While it is not generally permissible for one party to enquire into the legal advice that another has received (see legal professional privilege in **Chapter 19**), it is possible for this rule to be waived and following *R v Bowden,* the giving of evidence as to the legal advice received constitutes such waiver. The witness (whether the solicitor or his or her client) could be cross-examined about that advice.

This point was elaborated in *R v Loizou* [2006] EWCA Crim 1719, where the Court of Appeal drew a distinction between two situations:

(a) where an allegation of recent fabrication had been made against the accused that effectively left her with no alternative but to disclose what was said—this would not result in a waiver of privilege; and

(b) where no such allegation had been made (as here because examination-in-chief was taking place) and in effect the accused went beyond the task of simply telling the court that her refusal to answer questions had been based upon the legal advice given. Where she voluntarily disclosed the reasons for the legal advice she had received (here stating that her solicitor had advised her that what was being alleged 'did not amount to a criminal charge')—this would amount to a waiver and expose the accused to cross-examination so that the court could understand the context. This would help the court to answer 'the s 34 question', namely whether it was the advice rather than the absence of a satisfactory explanation that had caused the accused to stay silent.

15.4.1.7 The nature of the questioning

Section 34 only applies if the questioning relates to whether or by whom the offence has been committed. A failure to explain other matters cannot be used to support an inference under s 34 (although it may do so at common law: see **15.4.1.12**).

15.4.1.8 Who must conduct the questioning

While s 34(1) refers to a constable, the section also applies to *'persons (other than constables) charged with the duty of investigating offences or charging offenders'* (s 34(4) and see *R v Ali* [2001] EWCA Crim 863). Where questioning is conducted by someone who does not have a duty of investigating offences, the rules at common law apply.

15.4.1.9 Access to legal advice

When questioning takes place in an 'authorised place of detention' (which includes but is not limited to a police station: see s 38(2A)) then inferences cannot be drawn if the suspect was not given an opportunity to consult a solicitor (s 34(2A) and see *Murray v United Kingdom* (1996) 22 EHRR 29). If the accused declines the right to consult a solicitor, it would appear that inferences could be drawn (as the opportunity has been given) although the matter has not been determined by case law. However, if the police exercise the power to delay access to legal advice under s 58 of PACE 1984 (see **Chapter 14**) then inferences could not be drawn from the failure to mention a fact.

15.4.1.10 The effect of the failure to mention the fact

Where the jury decides that there has been a failure to mention a fact in the circumstances just set out it may draw 'such inferences as appear proper' (s 34(2)). However, in *R v Petkar* [2004] 1 Cr App R 270, the Court of Appeal accepted that the trial judge should give guidance as to what inferences might be drawn in each case.

15.4.1.11 Direction to the jury

Where the prosecution has not sought to rely on s 34, the judge should not invite the jury to draw an adverse inference from the alleged failure of the accused to mention a defence without first discussing the matter with counsel (*R v Khan* [1999] 2 Arch News 2). Where s 34 is relied upon, there will be a need for some form of judicial direction (*R v Webber* [2004] 1 All ER 770, ostensibly rejecting the approach in *R v Mountford* [1999] Crim LR 575).

The suggested content of a judicial direction relating to s 34 and an example of such directions can be found in Chapter 17-1 of the ***Crown Court Compendium Part 1*** 2017, available at: <https://www.judiciary.gov.uk/wp-content/uploads/2016/06/crown-court-compendium-pt1-jury-and-trial-management-and-summing-up-nov2017-v3.pdf>.

In essence the jury should be directed that:

(a) a suspect is not bound to answer police questions;

(b) an inference from silence cannot prove guilt on its own;

(c) the prosecution must have established a case to answer before any inference may be drawn;

(d) it is for the jury to decide whether the defendant could reasonably be expected to have mentioned the defence. If it thinks the defence should have been mentioned then the jury may, but not must, draw inferences against the accused; and

(e) it can draw an inference *only* if satisfied that the defendant was silent because he or she had no answer or none that would stand up to investigation (see *R v Daly* [2002] 2 Cr App R 14).

The judge should identify the facts it is alleged the accused has relied upon that give rise to this inference (*R v Chenia* [2003] 2 Cr App R 83). Simple reference to a general failure to answer questions at interview creates the risk that the jury will convict on the silence at interview alone rather than on the failure to mention a fact later relied on in defence (*R v Turner* [2004] 1 All ER 1025).

The judge in summing up should not only identify any reasons given by the defendant for failing to mention a fact, but should do so as part of the direction on s 34 rather than when summing up on the defence case (*R v Petkar* [2004] 1 Cr App R 270).

The Court of Appeal has indicated that it will look in a practical way at the content and effect of the judge's direction to the jury on s 34 (see *Boyle* [2006] EWCA Crim 2101). In *Boyle*, the court accepted that the s 34 direction had been defective but it did not accept that it had been unfair. In fact, in the court's opinion, the direction had been more advantageous to B than a full direction would have been, since it had minimised the risk of any adverse inference being drawn. The court also noted that the terms of the s 34 direction had been agreed between counsel for B and for his co-accused and that no submission had been made on the direction at trial and concluded that B's conviction was safe. A pragmatic approach to the direction may be required. For example, where a defendant gave one explanation on being questioned, and a second explanation at trial, then technically of course this could trigger an s 34 direction. The Court of Appeal has taken the view that it would be simpler to direct the jury that one of the explanations (at least) was dishonest and to draw its own conclusions from that; a full s 34 direction would be inappropriate. See *R v Maguire* [2008] EWCA Crim 1028.

Where there are multiple accused in a trial and each requires s 34 direction, it will usually be desirable for the judge to give a separate s 34 direction in respect of each of them: *R v Miah* [2009] EWCA Crim 2368.

15.4.1.12 The position at common law

Section 34 will not apply if:

- the person questioning is not a police officer or authorised investigator;
- the questioning or accusation does not take place under caution;
- the questioning takes place after the accused has been charged;
- the accused does not rely on a fact in his or her defence;
- the questioning did not concern whether or by whom an offence had been committed; or
- the failure to mention the fact now relied upon was not unreasonable.

As noted earlier, if s 34 does not apply, the common law rules on inferences from silence may apply (*R v McGarry* [1999] 1 WLR 1500). However, the common law rules will be of limited application because:

(a) a person could only be subject to adverse inferences arising from his or her failure to answer questions or accusations if:
   (i) the accused had not been cautioned; and
   (ii) the questioner/accuser and the accused were on equal terms (*Parkes v R* [1976] 1 WLR 1251);

(b) where the person questioning or making accusations is a police officer or equivalent, they will not be on equal terms (*Hall v R* [1971] 1 WLR 298), although an *obiter dictum* in *R v Chandler* [1976] 1 WLR 585 suggested that a person might be on equal terms with police officer if he or she was accompanied by a solicitor. Furthermore, in *R v Horne* [1990] Crim LR 188, CA, an unprompted accusation was made by a victim of an attack in the presence of the defendant and police officers. The Court of Appeal ruled that the defendant's failure to respond to that accusation had been rightly admitted.

The main situation in which the common law rule will apply is where the person making the accusations or asking the questions is another member of the public (as was the case in *Parkes v R*).

15.4.1.13 'Counterweight' directions

If the accused does not advance a new defence or new facts in support of a defence at trial, s 34 will not apply. As the accused was questioned under caution, the common law rules concerning inferences do not apply either.

However, s 34(3) allows the prosecution to prove the silence under questioning (a 'no-comment' interview) before or after the accused relies on a fact. This is a pragmatic rule which allows the accused's interview to be proved as an ordinary part of the prosecution case, rather than requiring the prosecution to reopen its case when the accused later raises a new fact or defence and therefore triggers s 34. It is very rare in practice for an interview (other than those excluded under s 76 or 78 of PACE 1984) not to be proved during the prosecution case.

Where the prosecution has proved the interview but the accused does not then advance any new defence or facts, the tribunal of fact will have heard or read the interview and may draw an adverse inference of its own accord. In such situations not only should the judge not issue a s 34 direction, he should also issue a further direction (a 'counterweight direction') that the jury should not hold the accused's silence against him (*R v McGarry* [1999] 1 WLR 1500). However, the judge should have regard to whether on the particular facts there is any real risk that the jury would draw an adverse inference in the absence of any comment by the judge on the matter (*R v La Rose* [2003] EWCA Crim 1471). Where, for example, a direction is to be made under s 35 (see **15.4.5**) the jury would have been sufficiently warned about the right to remain silent, so any further direction would simply be confusing.

15.4.1.14 Where the prosecution seek merely to challenge credibility

A direction under s 34 is unnecessary if the prosecution do not seek an inference under s 34, but merely wish to rely upon earlier inconsistent accounts to undermine a defendant's credibility. A 'common-sense' issue as to credit is very different to the sort of inference that is sought under s 34 (*R v Harris* [2015] EWCA Crim 1293).

15.4.1.15 Interaction between s 34 and the *Lucas* direction

As was noted at **15.4.1.2**, it is the failure to mention a fact later relied upon that triggers s 34, not silence per se. A defendant may tell the police officer facts that the prosecution say are lies *and* rely at trial on different facts. Take, for example, the case of *Rana* [2007] EWCA

Crim 2261 where, after a pub brawl, R was questioned by police and denied any involvement. Later, on being shown CCTV footage, R accepted that he had been there and took part in the brawl but only in defence of his friend. On the question of whether the trial judge should have given both a s 34 direction and a *Lucas* direction, the Court of Appeal said that it was quite common for there to be an overlap between the two situations—lies and failure to disclose—and the best way to address this was not to give both directions to the jury but rather to use a modified version of one direction. Here, the trial judge had given a modified s 34 direction in which he had explicitly told the jury that the earlier failure—by lying—to disclose the true nature of the defence case was only capable of supporting the prosecution's case if the jury were satisfied that there was no innocent reason for the non-disclosure, such as the shame asserted by R here. That was an acceptable way to deal with the overlap.

15.4.2 Silence upon confrontation about particular types of incriminating evidence

There are two inferences of a similar nature. Both arise when a person is confronted about particular types of incriminating evidence. Unlike inferences under s 34, they do not arise because the accused later relies upon a defence that he or she has not mentioned at an earlier point but simply because he or she does not offer an explanation when invited to do so. In other words, it is the simple exercise of the right to silence in incriminating circumstances that gives rise to the inferences here.

15.4.2.1 Failure to account for objects, substances, or marks

Section 36 of the Criminal Justice and Public Order Act 1994 provides:

> *(1) Where—*
>
> *(a) a person is arrested by a constable, and there is—*
>
> *(i) on his person; or*
>
> *(ii) in or on his clothing or footwear; or*
>
> *(iii) otherwise in his possession; or*
>
> *(iv) in any place in which he is at the time of his arrest, any object, substance or mark, or there is any mark on any such object; and*
>
> *(b) that or another constable ... reasonably believes that the presence of the object, substance or mark may be attributable to the participation of the person arrested in the commission of an offence specified by the constable; and*
>
> *(c) the constable informs the person arrested that he so believes, and requests him to account for the presence of the object, substance or mark; and*
>
> *(d) the person fails or refuses to do so,*
>
> *then if, in any proceedings against the person for the offence ... evidence of those matters is given, subsection (2) below applies.*
>
> *(2) Where this subsection applies—*
>
> *...*
>
> *(c) the court, in determining whether there is a case to answer; and*
>
> *(d) the court or jury, in determining whether the accused is guilty of the offence charged, may draw such inferences from the failure or refusal as appear proper.*
>
> *(3) Subsections (1) and (2) above apply to the condition of clothing or footwear as they apply to a substance or mark thereon.*

In addition to the above points, the following should be noted:

(a) Section 36 allows the court to draw adverse inferences from the failure to explain the object, substance, or mark only if the accused has been arrested and the effect of the failure to explain the incriminating object, etc has been explained to the accused. Note, however, that the object, substance, or mark itself is evidence in its own right and there are no particular rules or conditions for its admissibility (other than the usual rules of evidence).

(b) The inference can only be drawn if the suspect has been told of the reasons for suspicion and of the effect of failing to comply with this section (s 36(4)). The officer does not have to identify the precise offence. In *R v Compton* [2002] EWCA Crim 2835, CA, it was considered sufficient that the police officer had said that he was investigating 'drug trafficking'.

(c) Code C sets out the text of the special warnings that should be given to the accused under s 36 at para 10.11.

(d) Section 36 applies to questions raised by customs and excise officers as well as police officers (s 36(5)). However, in contrast to s 34, other officers with a duty of investigating offences are not specifically mentioned. It would therefore appear that only confrontations or questions about objects, substances, or marks by police or customs officers will lead to adverse inferences.

(e) Where the accused was in a place of authorised detention, inferences are only possible if the accused was offered access to a solicitor. This is likely to be a common feature of s 36 inferences as the section only arises upon arrest, at which stage the police should generally take a suspect to a police station before questioning him or her.

15.4.2.2 Failure to account for presence at the scene of a crime

Section 37 of the 1994 Act provides:

> *(1) Where—*
>
> *(a) a person arrested by a constable was found by him at a place at or about the time the offence for which he was arrested is alleged to have been committed; and*
>
> *(b) that or another constable investigating the offence reasonably believes that the presence of the person at the place at that time may be attributable to his participation in the commission of the offence; and*
>
> *(c) the constable informs the person that he so believes, and requests him to account for that presence; and*
>
> *(d) the person fails or refuses to do so,*
>
> *then if, in any proceedings against the person for the offence, evidence of those matters is given, subsection (2) below applies.*
>
> *(2) Where this subsection applies—*
>
> . . .
>
> *(c) the court, in determining whether there is a case to answer; and*
>
> *(d) the court or jury, in determining whether the accused is guilty of the offence charged, may draw such inferences from the failure or refusal as appear proper.*

The points noted in relation to s 36 apply equally to s 37.

15.4.3 Refusal to give body samples

Body samples are used to prove issues by scientific evidence, usually by DNA profiles. During the investigation of a crime, samples or substances such as blood or semen might be taken, for example from the scene of the crime or from a victim. To prove that the accused committed the offence, the DNA profile of the sample and a profile from a sample taken from the accused must be matched.

The taking of bodily samples is governed by ss 62 and 63 of PACE 1984. This is covered in more detail in **Chapter 16**. However, at this point it is worth noting that bodily samples are defined in two classes, as follows:

(a) *Non-intimate samples* Such samples can be taken without the consent of the owner in certain circumstances (s 63). If the conditions for taking such a sample without consent do not apply and the owner declines to consent without good reason, the court may draw inferences of guilt from that refusal at common law (*R v Smith* (1985) 81 Cr App R 286).

(b) *Intimate samples* Such samples cannot be taken without the consent of the owner in any circumstances. However, if the owner refuses to consent to the taking of such samples without good cause, the court may draw such inferences from that refusal as appear proper. These inferences can be used in determining the issue of guilt and in determining whether there is a case to answer.

15.4.4 Failure to disclose the defence case

The inferences that we have already considered all relate to pre-trial investigation. Those that follow all relate to the trial process itself.

The Criminal Procedure and Investigations Act 1996, s 5 places the accused under an obligation to disclose his defence by way of a defence statement. See the ***Criminal Litigation and Sentencing*** manual for the detailed rules of procedure. In outline, a defence statement should set out in general terms the nature of the accused's defence and matters with which he or she takes issue with the prosecution case and the basis of any such dispute (s 6A). The logic of this procedure is that the accused is then committed to the defence to be run at trial. Where the accused intends to rely on an alibi defence (ie that he or she was at some other specific place at the time of the offence) there are additional obligations. Section 11 of the 1996 Act makes provision for any failure on the part of the accused to comply with his or her obligations under s 5. The court may draw inferences when deciding the guilt of the accused *but not when deciding whether there is a case to answer* if the accused:

- does not give a defence statement;
- gives the defence statement late;
- runs a defence at trial that is inconsistent with that in his or her defence statement; or
- seeks to establish an alibi without having complied with the additional notice requirements for alibi defences.

The Court of Appeal has said that the mandatory nature of s 5 and the consequences of failure under s 11 do not breach an accused's human rights under Article 6 of the ECHR: *Essa* [2009] EWCA Crim 43. In summary proceedings, the giving of a defence statement is voluntary (s 6) but, if one is given, it must comply with the requirements in s 5 as to the form and content of the statement. However, under s 11 inferences can be drawn if the accused:

- gives the defence statement late;
- runs a defence at trial which is inconsistent with that in his or her defence statement; or
- seeks to establish an alibi without having complied with the additional notice requirements for alibi defences.

The accused cannot be convicted solely on the basis of an inference under s 11 (s 11(10)). The court should take care to ensure that the jury is properly directed as to the nature of any discrepancy and the reasons that the accused may give for it (*R v Wheeler* (2000) 164 JP 565). There may be particular difficulties where the accused states that the defence statement was not drafted under his or her instructions (in other words that a solicitor drafted it) and that therefore its contents do not reflect his or her intended defence. It is not possible to force the accused to sign the statement (*R (Sullivan) v Crown Court at Maidstone* [2002] 1 WLR 2747, CA). However, under the Criminal Procedure and Investigations Act 1996, s 6E(1), where an accused's solicitor purports to give a defence statement on behalf of the accused, there is a rebuttable presumption that it was given with the accused's authority.

See also chapter 17-4 of the ***Crown Court Compendium Part 1*** 2017.

15.4.5 Failure to testify

The traditional right of an accused not to testify has been modified by s 35 of the Criminal Justice and Public Order Act 1994, which provides:

> *(1) At the trial of any person for an offence, subsection … (3) below applies unless—*
>
> *(a) the accused's guilt is not in issue; or*
>
> *(b) it appears to the court that the physical or mental condition of the accused makes it undesirable for him to give evidence;*
>
> …
>
> *(3) Where this subsection applies, the court or jury, in determining whether the accused is guilty of the offence charged, may draw such inferences as appear proper from the failure of the accused to give evidence or his refusal, without good cause, to answer any question.*

Such inferences can only be drawn if the accused has either been warned by the court of the effect of the failure to give evidence (s 35(2)) or has stated that he or she will give evidence and then fails to do so (s 35(1)). The text of any warnings to the accused is set out in Chapter 17-5 of the ***Crown Court Compendium Part 1*** 2017, at para 21, pp 17–23 and in Criminal Practice Direction VI, Part 26P. The section applies to a person who refuses to answer questions in evidence unless the refusal is justified (under s 35(5)):

- on the grounds of legal privilege (see **Chapter 19**);
- because another statute excludes the evidence that would be contained in the answer; or
- because the court rules that the question need not be answered.

Note that inferences can only be drawn when determining whether the accused is guilty. Inferences cannot be used to determine whether there is a case to answer, not least of all because the accused has not had the opportunity to give evidence by that point in proceedings (*Murray v DPP* [1994] 1 WLR 1, HL).

Section 35 allows the judge to direct the jury (or requires the magistrates) to take into account the failure of the accused to testify if the conditions in s 35(1) are satisfied and the warnings have been issued under s 35(2). Further, the prosecution is entitled to comment on the failure of the accused to testify.

15.4.5.1 The accused's guilt is not in issue

There are situations in which the accused could give evidence in his or her 'defence' even though his or her guilt is not in issue. The most obvious example is a 'Newton' hearing at which the issue is not whether the accused committed a particular crime but how serious his or her commission of the offence was so that an appropriate sentence can be passed (see the ***Criminal Litigation and Sentencing*** manual).

15.4.5.2 'Physical or mental condition'

There must be evidence that the physical or mental condition of the accused is such that an inference should not be drawn (*R v A* [1997] Crim LR 883).

If a court rejects medical evidence from the defence that is offered to show that the defendant's physical/mental condition makes it undesirable for him or her to testify in court, the jury or magistrates ought nevertheless to consider that medical evidence when assessing the reliability of any evidence from the defendant; see *R v Tabbakh* [2009] EWCA Crim 464. This would be put in the balance alongside a s 35 direction: see *R v Anwoir* [2009] 1 WLR 980.

15.4.5.3 The direction to the jury

In *R v Cowan* [1996] 1 Cr App R 1, CA, Lord Taylor stated that a direction to the jury should contain the following elements:

(a) The accused has a right not to give evidence but he has been warned that a failure to do so may lead to the jury drawing inferences.

(b) A failure to give evidence cannot on its own prove guilt but it can assist in deciding whether the accused is guilty.

(c) If a reason for not testifying has been advanced the jury should consider it and:

  (i) if it accepts the reason advanced, it cannot draw any inference against the accused;

  (ii) if it rejects the reason advanced, it may draw an inference but is not obliged to do so.

(d) If the jury concludes that the only sensible explanation for his decision not to give evidence is that he has no answer to the case against him, or none that could have stood up to cross-examination, then it would be open to it to hold against him his failure to give evidence. It is for the jury to decide whether it is fair to do so.

See also chapter 17-5 of the ***Crown Court Compendium Part 1*** 2017.

The House of Lords observed in *R v Becouarn* [2006] 1 Cr App R 2 that it appears to have stood the test of time but that '*trial judges have full discretion to adapt even a tried and tested direction if they consider that to do so gives the best guidance to a jury and fairest representation of the issues*'.

It is important that the jury is told clearly that it should consider the evidence against the accused before turning to consider the effect of his or her failure to testify. In particular, it should be told that it must find there is a prima facie case against the accused before it can draw any inferences from the accused's silence. Although this has been described as an 'absolute requirement' (*R v Birchall* [1999] Crim LR 311, CA), subsequent cases have clarified that it does not need to be spelled out to the jury in such terms, so long as the effect of the judge's summing up is to clearly direct the jury to consider the evidence *against* the accused first, to ask itself 'whether there is something in this', before considering the silence of the accused (see *R v Bromfield* [2002] EWCA Crim 195 and *R v Whitehead* [2006] EWCA Crim 1486).

Note that the jury can be invited to infer the fact of guilt from the failure to testify if a prima facie case has been made out. Lord Mustill described the matter in this way in *Murray v DPP* (a case concerning Northern Ireland legislation with provisions which were materially the same):

> If ... the defendant does not go on oath ... the fact finder may suspect that the defendant does not tell his story because he has no story to tell or none which will stand up to scrutiny; and this suspicion may be sufficient to convert a possible prosecution case into one which is actually proved.

Lord Mustill also said that whether such inferences should be drawn depended upon whether the accused should be able to give his or her own account of the particular matter in question. Developing this point, the Court of Appeal concluded in *R v McManus* [2001] EWCA Crim 2455 that a direction under s 35 was inappropriate where there was no factual dispute in the case. The only issue in that case was whether a particular property could in law constitute a 'disorderly house', the facts that supported such a conclusion being agreed between the defence and prosecution. The accused's testimony could not have assisted on this matter so a s 35 inference was inappropriate.

15.4.5.4 Causing or allowing a child or vulnerable adult to die or suffer serious physical harm

Ordinarily, a s 35 adverse inference may be drawn only if the jury are satisfied that the prosecution has established that the defendant has a case to answer (*R v Cowan* [1996] 1 Cr App R 1). However, the position is different in relation to murder or manslaughter charges when they are coupled with a charge under s 5 of the Domestic Violence, Crime and Victims Act 2004 (DVCVA 2004). Under s 5 of the DVCVA 2004, it is an offence to cause or to allow the death of a child or a vulnerable adult as a result of an unlawful act. The child or vulnerable adult must have lived in the same household as the defendant and the defendant must have been either the person to have caused the harm or a person who ought to have been aware of the risks and yet failed to take steps to protect the child or vulnerable adult. Such a defendant may also be charged with murder or manslaughter. Sections 6 and 6A of the DVCVA 2004 provide that where an adverse inference from silence could be drawn under s 35 as to a defendant's guilt in relation to the s 5 offence, an 'enhanced inference' may be drawn that the defendant is guilty of murder or manslaughter even if there would otherwise be no case to answer in relation to the murder or manslaughter charge. Whilst this circumvents the ordinary *Cowan* principle, there is good public policy justification for it, namely to break the 'wall of silence' that otherwise may 'hamper a proper investigation into a death' (*R v Quinn* [2017] EWCA Crim 1071 at [73]).

15.4.6 Failure to call evidence

At common law it is permissible for the judge to comment on the failure of the accused to call a particular witness. The principle is that the judge should exercise care before doing so and the comments made to the jury should not generally invite the court to equate the failure to call the witness with the accused's account being untrue (*R v Weller* [1994] Crim LR 856). It is especially important that no comment should be made about the failure to call a witness if there may be a valid reason for not calling the witness (*R v Couzens* [1992] Crim LR 822, CA).

PACE 1984, s 80A provides that the failure to call a spouse should not be commented upon by the *prosecution* (the spouse of an accused person not being compellable on his or her behalf under s 80 of that Act: see **Chapter 4**). However, there is no prohibition on the *judge* commenting on the failure to call a spouse. In *R v Naudeer* [1984] 3 All ER 1036, though, the Court of Appeal took the view that great care should be exercised by the judge before any such comment was made.

15.4.7 Summary on inferences from silence in criminal cases

There are two broad categories of inference, as follows:

(a) *Silence before a criminal prosecution is commenced* This category includes:

(i) silence under questioning (Criminal Justice and Public Order Act 1994, s 34);
(ii) failure to explain objects, substances, or marks on the suspect's person (Criminal Justice and Public Order Act 1994, s 36);
(iii) failure of the accused to testify in his or her own defence (Criminal Justice and Public Order Act 1994, s 35); and
(iv) failure to provide bodily samples (PACE 1984, s 62).

(b) *Silence after a criminal prosecution has been commenced* This category includes:

(i) failure to produce a defence statement (Criminal Procedure and Investigations Act 1996, s 11);
(ii) failure of the accused to testify in his own defence (Criminal Justice and Public Order Act 1994, s 35); and
(iii) failure to call witnesses (common law).

There are many differences between the various sections but the essential difference between the two categories is that silence before commencement of a prosecution case can be used to raise a case for the accused to answer while silence after commencement cannot.

All of the inferences in criminal cases, however, have certain common features, whether as a result of statute or common law. While expressed differently in different situations, the common features are that:

(a) before an inference can be drawn it must be established that the motive for the failure must be a realisation of guilt rather than some other reason (and the jury should be told that it must rule out any other reason);
(b) the tribunal of fact is never obliged to draw an inference in any of the cases noted: the facts simply establish that an inference may (rather than must) be drawn; and
(c) the inference can never prove guilt on its own.

16 Identification evidence

16.1 Introduction

We have already looked at situations where the fact-finders may need to be alerted to the possible danger of relying on a particular source of evidence—see **Chapter 5**. Usually, this happens on a case-by-case, witness-by-witness basis. But there is one whole category of evidence where it is thought that the risk of unreliability is much greater than normal, or at least greater than the inexperienced fact-finder would expect. This is identification evidence. Courts have tried to minimise the danger by requiring a warning to be given by the judge to the jury where a case turns on such disputed evidence. We shall look first at the rationale behind the concerns (**16.2**) and then at the methods now used to deal with them (**16.3–16.8**). Finally, we will look at how evidence is produced to prove identification in court and the procedures that must be followed (**16.9**).

16.2 Identification evidence and miscarriages of justice

Intuitively, most people consider that identification evidence is very reliable and accurate. Indeed, identification witnesses themselves often think so and come into the witness box convinced that they have identified the criminal correctly. That there are dangers in over-reliance on such evidence has been plain since at least the early twentieth century and the case of Adolf Beck. Beck was twice convicted wrongly (in 1896 and 1904) of offences of fraud. In the 1870s, when Beck claimed to have been in South America, a 'John Smith' was convicted in England of several frauds. Each offence alleged that Smith had become intimate with a woman, persuaded her to put valuable jewellery into his possession, and then disappeared. In 1895, several more women were called as witnesses at a new trial. The offences seemed identical. Each woman identified the accused, this time Adolf Beck. The prosecution even called two police officers to testify that Adolf Beck and John Smith were the same man. Beck was convicted and sentenced to seven years' imprisonment. After his release, the offences started again. In 1904, Beck was again convicted on the word of several women, each of whom claimed to have been intimate with him. While Beck was held in custody, awaiting sentence, John Smith was caught committing another offence. Smith's appearance matched the descriptions given by the women, which included the fact that their seducer was circumcised. Prison records from the 1870s indicated that 'John Smith' was circumcised. Beck was not circumcised. Beck was released and pardoned, and received a substantial sum in compensation. Following this case, the Court of Criminal Appeal was set up and the first set of general instructions on the conduct of identification parades was issued.

However, miscarriages of justice continued to occur in cases based upon identification evidence. As Lord Devlin has pointed out (*The Judge*, 1981):

In 1912 a man on a charge of murder was identified by no less than 17 witnesses, but fortunately was able to establish an irrefutable alibi. In 1928 Oscar Slater, after he had spent 19 years in prison ... had his conviction for murder quashed; he had been identified by 14 witnesses. Nevertheless, cases continued to be left to the jury as if they raised only a simple issue between the identifier and the accused as to which was telling the truth ... In 1974 two shattering cases of mistaken identity came to light within four weeks of each other.

16.3 The special need for caution—*Turnbull* warnings

In May 1974, Lord Devlin was invited to chair a committee to investigate the law and procedure on identification and his committee's report (*Report to the Secretary of State for the Home Department of the Departmental Committee on Evidence of Identification in Criminal Cases*) was published in April 1976. It made several recommendations for changes to the gathering of identification evidence and its treatment in the courtroom, all of which were intended to be effected by statute. However, as Lord Devlin has observed:

The Court of Appeal decided to forestall legislation by giving in July 1976 ... a comprehensive judgment laying down a new approach.

That judgment was given in *R v Turnbull* [1977] QB 224 by Lord Widgery CJ. The 'new approach' is as follows (see pp 228–230 of the report).

(a) First, whenever the case against an accused depends wholly or substantially on the correctness of one or more identifications of the accused which the defence alleges to be mistaken, the judge should warn the jury of the special need for caution before convicting the accused in reliance on the correctness of the identification or identifications. In addition he should instruct them as to the reason for the need for such a warning and should make some reference to the possibility that a mistaken witness can be a convincing one and that a number of such witnesses can all be mistaken. Provided this is done in clear terms the judge need not use any particular form of words.

(b) Second, the judge should direct the jury to examine closely the circumstances in which the identification by each witness came to be made. How long did the witness have the accused under observation? At what distance? In what light? Was the observation impeded in any way, as for example by passing traffic or a press of people? Had the witness ever seen the accused before? How often? If only occasionally, had he any special reason for remembering the accused? How long elapsed between the original observation and the subsequent identification to the police?

(c) Was there any material discrepancy between the description of the accused given to the police by the witness when first seen by them and his actual appearance?

(d) If in any case, whether it is being dealt with summarily or on indictment, the prosecution have reason to believe that there is such a material discrepancy they should supply the accused or his legal advisers with particulars of the description the police were first given. In all cases if the accused asks to be given particulars of such descriptions, the prosecution should supply them. Finally, he should remind the jury of any specific weakness which had appeared in the identification evidence.

(e) Recognition may be more reliable than identification of a stranger; but even when the witness is purporting to recognise someone whom he knows, the jury should be reminded that mistakes in recognition of close relatives and friends are sometimes made.

(f) When the quality (of the identifying evidence) is good, as for example when the identification is made after a long period of observation, or in satisfactory conditions by a relative, a neighbour, a close friend, a workmate and the like, the jury can safely be left to assess the value of the identifying evidence even though there is no other evidence to support it: provided always, however, that an adequate warning has been given about the special need for caution.

(g) When, in the judgment of the trial judge, the quality of the identifying evidence is poor, as for example when it depends solely on a fleeting glance or on a longer observation made in difficult conditions, the situation is very different. The judge should then withdraw the case from the jury and direct an acquittal unless there is other evidence which goes to support the correctness of the identification. This may be corroboration in the sense lawyers use that word; but it need not be so if its effect is to make the jury sure that there has been no mistaken identification.

(h) The trial judge should identify to the jury the evidence which he adjudges is capable of supporting the evidence of identification. If there is any evidence or circumstances which the jury might think was supporting when it did not have this quality, the judge should say so.

(i) Care should be taken by the judge when directing the jury about the support for an identification which may be derived from the fact that they have rejected an alibi. False alibis may be put forward for many reasons: it is only when the jury is satisfied that the sole reason for the fabrication was to deceive them and there is no other explanation for its being put forward can fabrication provide any support for identification evidence. The jury should be reminded that proving the accused has told lies about where he was at the material time does not by itself prove that he was where the identifying witness says he was.

Note that identification evidence given by police officers has no special status. Typically, officers receive training in observation and they might be thought to possess greater ability to identify people than is possessed by ordinary members of the public. However, in *Reid v R* (1990) 90 Cr App R 121, the Privy Council stated that:

> experience has undoubtedly shown that police identification can be just as unreliable and is not therefore to be excepted from the now well established need for the appropriate warnings.

This remains the position, even where the police witness claims to have recognised the accused at the scene of crime, having known him previously (see *R v Bowden* [1993] Crim LR 379).

16.4 Form of a *Turnbull* warning

When a trial judge directs a jury about identification evidence in the summing up, there is no set form of words which is needed for the *Turnbull* warning. In *Mills v R* [1995] 1 WLR 511, the Privy Council stated that *Turnbull* was not a statute and did not require the incantation of a formula. A judge has:

> a broad discretion to express himself in his own way when he directs a jury on identification. All that is required ... is that he should comply with the sense and spirit of the guidance in ... *Turnbull*.

Notwithstanding the discretion that a judge clearly has, there is an example direction in the ***Crown Court Compendium Part 1*** 2017, chapter 15-1 at p 15-3):

> You must be cautious when considering this evidence because experience has shown that any witness who has identified a person can be mistaken even when the witness is honest and sure that he is right. Such a witness may seem convincing but may be wrong. This is true even though a witness knows a person well and says that he has recognised that person. The witness could still be mistaken. You can only rely on the identification evidence if you are sure that it is accurate.
>
> You need to consider carefully all the circumstances in which D was identified. So you must ask yourselves:
>
> - For how long could W see the person he says was D and, in particular, for how long could he see the person's face?

- How clear was W's view of the person, considering the distance between them, the light, any objects or people getting in the way and any distractions?
- Had W ever seen D before the incident? If so, how often and in what circumstances? If only once or occasionally, had W any special reason for remembering D?
- How long was it between the time of the incident and the time when W identified D to the police?
- Is there any significant difference between the description W gave of the person and D's appearance?

You should also think about whether there is any evidence which, if you accept it, might support the identification. In particular you should consider {specify}. However the evidence of {specify} cannot support the identification because {explain}.

You will also have to look to see if there are any weaknesses in any of the identification evidence, or if there is any evidence which, if you accept it, might undermine the identification evidence. In particular, you should consider {specify}.

While it is the duty of the judge to identify for the jury potential weaknesses in identification evidence, the extent of the duty depends entirely on the state of the evidence in an individual case. If the judge does identify points which the defence rely on as weaknesses, he should also normally remind the jury of all the evidence affecting such points. He is not required in effect to make a second speech for the defendant (*Stoutt v The Queen* [2014] UKPC 14).

16.5 Poor-quality identification evidence—submissions of no case

You have seen, in **16.3**, points (g)–(i), how the Court of Appeal in *R v Turnbull* [1977] QB 224 recognised that identification evidence may sometimes be of poor quality. The suggestion was that cases based on such weak evidence should be stopped on a submission of no case to answer unless there was some evidence that might support the accuracy of the identification.

At the conclusion of the prosecution evidence in a trial, the defence may make a submission of no case to answer. Generally, such submissions are governed by the principles set out in *R v Galbraith* [1981] 1 WLR 1039, but in cases where evidence of identification is disputed, the submission will be based upon *R v Turnbull*, as follows:

(a) Where there is no identification evidence at all, the judge's decision is simple. The submission succeeds.

(b) Where there is identification evidence but it is of poor quality and is unsupported by other evidence, again the judge should withdraw the case from the jury. First, the judge should assume the identification evidence to be honest (ie he does not need to form a view about the credibility of the prosecution witness). Then if the judge considers that the identification evidence has a base that is so slender that it is unreliable and thus not sufficient to found a conviction, he should uphold the submission and order the defendant's acquittal on the charge (see, eg, *Daley v R* [1993] 4 All ER 86).

(c) Where there is identification evidence of poor quality but which is potentially supported by other evidence, the judge will allow the case to go to the jury. The judge should tell the jury what other evidence is capable of supporting the accuracy of the identification (see **16.6**). According to *R v Akaidere* [1990] Crim LR 808, a judge should not tell a jury that the identification evidence is of poor quality and the case would have been withdrawn if there was no supporting evidence. The reason for this ban is that, while it is for the judge to decide if there is evidence *capable* of supporting the identification, it is a question of fact for the jury to decide whether it does support it. The jury might be inappropriately influenced in its decision if it knew of the judge's view.

We shall now consider how identification evidence may be supported.

16.6 Support for poor-quality identification evidence

One possible form of support was specifically considered in *R v Turnbull* [1977] QB 224—the fact that the defendant had put forward a false alibi (see point (i), **16.3**). If a defendant's alibi is rejected as a lie, this fact can offer support but a careful direction is required (*R v Keane* (1977) 65 Cr App R 247; ***Crown Court Compendium Part 1*** 2017, chapter 15-1, p 15-3 para 13 and p 15-5 sample direction). It does not follow that, because an alibi has been rejected by the jury as false, the defendant was wherever the identification witness says he was. The jury should consider if there is a reason why the defendant might have offered a false alibi, consistent with his innocence. An example might be where he was with a girlfriend and did not want his wife to find out about it, so offered a different, false, alibi. You will see the parallel with the general treatment of lies by the accused (*R v Lucas* [1981] QB 720; see **15.3.1**).

Evidence of a defendant's previous 'bad character' may be used to support weak identification where the nature of the previous bad character has similarities to the allegations in the present case (see, eg, *R v Richardson* [2014] EWCA Crim 1785; *R v LN* [2014] EWCA Crim 506; *R v Randall* [2006] EWCA Crim 1413).

In the absence of other sources of evidence to support a poor-quality identification (eg D's fingerprints on the murder weapon), the judge should consider whether several identification witnesses may support each other. If they have each been hampered in their observation (eg passengers on a night bus passing an incident on the street), the judge may have to withdraw the case from the jury and direct an acquittal. A series of poor-quality identifications as the sole or decisive evidence generally is not capable of safely supporting a conviction (*R v Younas* [2012] EWCA Crim 2022). However, if they have observed in satisfactory conditions (eg several spectators at a sunny daytime football match observe an assault by a fellow spectator), then their evidence may be presented to the jury as capable of supporting each other's identification evidence. In that situation, the judge should also direct the jury that several honest witnesses can all be mistaken (see *R v Weeder* (1980) 71 Cr App R 228 and *R v Breslin* (1985) 80 Cr App R 226).

In some situations, several identification witnesses may offer mutual support even though they have each witnessed a different incident, where it is alleged that each incident involved the same offender.

16.7 Situations in which a *Turnbull* warning may be unnecessary

The concern that lay behind the decision in *R v Turnbull* [1977] QB 224 was that an identification witness may be mistaken but persuasive because he appears to be sincere and convincing. In fact, he is sincere and has probably convinced himself that his identification is accurate. But he may still be wrong. The *Turnbull* warning is intended to alert the jury to the danger of being misled. But what if *mistaken* identification is not an issue at the trial? This may arise in three ways:

(a) There may be no possibility of mistake. If so, there is no need for a *Turnbull* warning. One example is when the only person who could be the offender is the defendant. In *R v Slater* [1995] 1 Cr App R 584, an offence took place in a nightclub and the accused accepted that he had been there. The accused was two metres tall and the Court of Appeal noted that there was no evidence to suggest that anyone remotely similar in height to the accused was present in the nightclub where the offence took place; no *Turnbull* warning was needed. Conversely, in *R v Thornton* [1995] 1 Cr App R 578, an offence occurred at a wedding reception. The accused accepted that he was at the reception. There were a number of people present who were dressed similarly to the accused (black leather jacket, black trousers) and several people were allegedly involved in the offence. The Court of Appeal thought that a mistaken identification was clearly possible; a *Turnbull* warning should have been given.

(b) Where the defence alleges that the identification witness is lying, mistake is simply not a live issue for the jury to consider. The issue now is simply the veracity of the witness. Does the jury believe the identification witness or not? In *R v Courtnell* [1990] Crim LR 115, the Court of Appeal accepted that point but noted that if there was evidence that might support the contention of mistaken identification, the judge should direct the jury accordingly, even though the defence had not raised that issue at the trial. In *R v Courtnell*, there was no such evidence and the judge had not erred in omitting a *Turnbull* direction. Similarly, in *R v Cape* [1996] 1 Cr App R 191, the defendants were alleged to have been involved in a fight in a pub. The pub landlord, who knew the men, testified that they were so involved. The defendants admitted being in the pub at the time but denied involvement; they suggested the landlord was lying and motivated by a grudge. The issue for the jury was simply whether they accepted the evidence of the landlord as truthful; that did not call for a *Turnbull* warning.

In *Beckford v R* (1993) 97 Cr App R 409, the Privy Council reiterated the need to consider carefully all of the issues before the jury. Beckford and two co-accused were tried for murder. The sole witness to the crime identified all three men as being present. At trial, the accused all ran alibi defences and alleged that the witness was lying because either: (i) he was a compulsive and inveterate liar; or (ii) he was susceptible to mental aberrations (having previously been a patient in a mental hospital). The Privy Council considered that there were two questions for the jury to address:

(i) Is the witness honest? This was at the heart of the defence case. If the jury found he was not honest, it would disregard his evidence. If the jury found him to be an honest witness, it would need to consider (and be directed on) a second question.

(ii) Could the witness be mistaken? If this were a possibility, on the evidence, it would require a *Turnbull* direction from the judge. The direction should then be given even if the defence did not rely on the possibility of mistake. In a more recent case, in which the defendant ran a defence that the identification witness who claimed to have recognised him was lying, the Court of

Appeal held that a limited *Turnbull* direction could have been given by the judge (even if the witness was honest, he might be mistaken), but that the failure to do so was not a misdirection such as to make the conviction unsafe. (See *R v Giga* [2007] Crim LR 571, considering the decision of the Privy Council in *Capron v R* [2006] UKPC 39 and concluding that a full *Turnbull* direction would have been misleading.)

(c) Where the evidence does not identify a person. Where an eyewitness gives evidence only of *description* (eg clothing or general characteristics), this is not identification evidence. In *R v Gayle* [1999] 2 Cr App R 130, the Court of Appeal noted that the danger of an honest witness being mistaken about distinctive clothing, or the general description of a person he has seen (eg short or tall, black or white, direction of movement) is minimal. What the jury needs to concentrate upon is the honesty of the witness.

Where the prosecution tries to prove that a defendant was present at a particular place by calling witnesses who will say that they saw *a man* driving a car, and they can identify *the car*, then a full *Turnbull* warning is not needed. The prosecution will need to produce other evidence to prove that the defendant was driving the car at the material time. This was the view taken by the Court of Appeal in *R v Browning* (1991) 94 Cr App R 109. The explanation for the distinction between identification of a person and of a car was said to be that, whereas people may change their appearance frequently (eg facial expression or bodily posture), cars do not change their shape, colour, or size (unless of course they are altered deliberately). Nevertheless, a jury should still be directed about any difficulties regarding observation of the car (eg if the witness was a driver who got a fleeting glance at the car while being overtaken).

16.8 Appeals and identification evidence

A failure to observe the *Turnbull* guidelines will often lead to a successful appeal (see *R v Hunjan* (1979) 68 Cr App R 99). Indeed, the Privy Council said in *Reid v R* (1990) 90 Cr App R 121 that it had:

> no hesitation in concluding that a significant failure to follow the identification guidelines as laid down in *Turnbull* ... will cause a conviction to be quashed because it will have resulted in a substantial miscarriage of justice ... If convictions are to be allowed upon uncorroborated [unsupported] identification evidence there must be strict insistence upon a judge giving a clear warning of the danger of a mistaken identification which the jury must consider before arriving at their verdict. It is only in the most exceptional circumstances that a conviction based on uncorroborated identification evidence will be sustained in the absence of such a warning.

An example of such 'exceptional circumstances' may be found in *Freemantle v R* [1994] 3 All ER 225. Here, the Privy Council said that if the identification evidence was of exceptionally good quality, this would be an exceptional circumstance. Among the factors that the Privy Council thought showed the exceptionally good quality of the identification evidence, was a dialogue between the accused, Freemantle, and one of the eyewitnesses, Campbell. Campbell shouted to the man he saw, 'Freemantle me see you'; the man's reply was regarded as an implied acknowledgement of the accuracy of that identification. (See also *Scott v R* [1989] AC 1242.)

16.9 Establishing a link between the accused and the crime

16.9.1 Ways to make a link

Suppose that a defendant (or suspect) denies being the offender? There are several ways to produce evidence which can show that he or she is the offender. For example:

- visual identification by an eyewitness;
- aural (voice) identification by an ear witness;
- prints left at the crime scene—these could be prints made by fingers, palm, foot, or even ear;
- fibres left at the crime scene;
- DNA left at the crime scene;
- handwriting left at the crime scene; or
- fingerprints, etc or property from the crime scene that have been found to match ones found on the defendant or on his or her clothing, among his or her possessions, or in his or her house.

We now need to consider what must be done in order to turn any of these pieces of information into admissible evidence which could be used in a trial. In all of these situations, there will be a witness as to the facts. This person must make a witness statement to say 'I heard something', 'I saw someone', 'I found this letter', 'I picked up this cigarette butt', and so on. A comparison must then be made between that information and the defendant (or suspect).

Comparison by an eye or ear witness is usually done by letting the witness see or hear the suspect in controlled conditions (eg an identification parade). In order to insulate the witness from attack in cross-examination at trial, the witness should give a description of the person he or she saw or heard before comparing his or her recollection with the suspect's appearance or voice (see Code D, para 3.1).

Finders will need to send their discoveries elsewhere for testing. They should protect their discoveries by sealing them in plastic bags, to avoid possible contamination. Such bags must be labelled so that the expert making the comparison can show the connection between what he or she is testing and what was found. Defence counsel may object at trial either that a discovery has been contaminated by coming into contact with other material, or that there is no evidence to link the sample tested in a laboratory by an expert witness to what was found at the crime scene.

In the case of prints, fibres, DNA, or handwriting, comparison must be made with a specimen obtained from the suspect. DNA and fingerprints may already be available to the police, following the suspect's conviction on an earlier occasion. Otherwise, a specimen must be obtained now. We will consider how that happens in **16.9.6**. Once we have the specimen, we need an expert to make the comparison. If there is a sufficient match, we will have our evidence of identity. The expert witness must provide an expert report, to be disclosed to the defence and used at trial. The probative value of that evidence will vary from case to case. A fingerprint or DNA match may be very probative but some fibres or types of glass, for example, may be in very common use and so have a low probative value. If they were rare, for example pieces of hand-blown medieval glass from a church window, the match would have a higher probative value. Even with a good match and uncommon material, we have only circumstantial evidence to link the suspect to the crime scene. This means that the match may be explained away at trial by the defence, or somehow shown to be less probative. For example, in the trial of several youths for the murder of Damilola Taylor at the Old Bailey in 2002, the prosecution alleged that the fatal injury to the victim was caused by a shard from a glass bottle. Fragments of the bottle were recovered at the crime scene. One of the accused youths possessed a pair of trainers on which was found a tiny piece of glass. Scientific tests showed it to match the type of glass that had been found at the crime scene. Thus, the police had evidence to make a link between the youth and the crime scene. At trial, the defence explained this apparently damaging match by showing that the youth had visited the crime scene a day or two after the death of Damilola Taylor. This was confirmed by police officers who were present at the time. The piece of glass could have got onto his trainer then, quite innocently. There are other ways to challenge expert evidence (on identification and other matters), which we will consider in **Chapter 17**.

16.9.2 Admissibility and exclusion of evidence

Quite apart from the risks that attach to identification evidence in general (to which the *Turnbull* direction relates), questions arise as to the ways in which identification evidence should be: (a) gathered; and (b) presented in court. Some forms of identification evidence, for example, dock identifications, are thought to carry such a risk of prejudice to the accused that the courts have frequently excluded such evidence. Exclusion is at the court's discretion either at common law or under PACE 1984, s 78 (see **14.2.3.2**). Generally, an application under s 78 should succeed where the identification evidence is unreliable, where there has been bad faith or where the evidence has been obtained in breach of one of the defendant's fundamental rights. A code of practice (Code D) has been laid down by virtue of s 66 of the 1984 Act to ensure that identification evidence is gathered in 'controlled circumstances' in an attempt to maximise its quality.

Many Court of Appeal decisions illustrate that non-compliance with Code D may be an important factor in deciding whether to exclude the evidence pursuant to s 78 of the 1984 Act (see, eg, *R v Leckie* [1983] Crim LR 543; *R v Gall* (1990) 90 Cr App R 64; *R v Conway* [1990] Crim LR 402).

However, breaches of Code D do not automatically lead to the exclusion of the identification evidence (see *R v Quinn* [1990] Crim LR 581; *R v Penny* [1992] Crim LR 184; *R v Palmer* [2002] EWCA Crim 2645; *R v Alan Jones, Tina Jones* [2005] EWCA Crim 3526; *R (Marsh) v DPP* [2007] Crim LR 162). For example, in *R v Forbes* [2001] AC 473, the House of Lords held that two street identifications by an eyewitness had been rightly allowed in as evidence at a trial, notwithstanding non-compliance with Code D.

Whether there is a breach of Code D or not, s 78 of the 1984 Act would need to be considered. For example, evidence of a street identification, in the absence of an identification parade, *might* be excluded. In the final analysis, the fairness of allowing the other identification evidence to be called will depend on a variety of factors which are usually taken into consideration under s 78.

Where the judge decides that there has been a breach of Code D the direction to the jury should make specific reference to the breaches. The judge should explain to the jury that compliance with Code D is a positive obligation rather than a question of desirability (*R v Gojra* [2010] EWCA Crim 1939). The significance of any breaches of the Code and the prejudice or possible prejudice which these might cause to the defence should also be explained (*R v Forbes* [2001] 1 AC 473; *R v Preddie* [2011] EWCA Crim 312). A sample direction for cases involving a breach of Code D can be found in the ***Crown Court Compendium Part 1*** 2017, chapter 15-1 p 15-5).

16.9.3 Cases in which the link between the accused and the crime is based upon an eyewitness

This topic is dealt with generally in Code of Practice D, issued under PACE 1984. Code D and the Annexes A–D are particularly important. The current Code D came into effect on 23 February 2017. In considering the use to be made of an eyewitness, we must start by distinguishing between two situations:

(a) where an eyewitness identifies the accused as the offender in court, while giving evidence at the trial (see **16.9.3.1**); or

(b) where an eyewitness identifies the accused as the offender before the trial begins (see **16.9.3.2**).

16.9.3.1 In-court eyewitness identification (usually called 'dock identification')

Dock identification should not generally be allowed (*R v Howick* [1970] Crim LR 403). The reason for this ban is the lack of probative value of a dock identification. It is easy for a witness to 'identify' the alleged criminal when he is standing rather obviously in the dock and the exercise adds little or nothing to a previous act of identification. In the absence of a previous identification by that witness, to allow a dock identification would flout the basic principles that govern the production of identification evidence (through an identification parade, for example). In *R v Tido* [2011] 2 Cr App R 336, it was held by the Privy Council that although there is no rule of law which renders dock identifications inadmissible per se or admissible only in exceptional circumstances, the trial judge must always be alert to whether permitting a dock identification would endanger a fair trial for the accused.

A dock identification may be permissible when a defendant refuses to attend a parade (*R v John* [1973] Crim LR 113, CA and *R v Tido* [2011] 2 Cr App R 36) or renders a parade impracticable, for example, by changing his appearance (*R v Mutch* [1973] 1 All ER 178, CA). It may also be admissible where the witness claims to recognise the defendant as someone he already knows well (*R v Tido* [2011] 2 Cr App R 36), but a formal identification procedure will be required where the witness has seen the suspect only once or on only a few occasions (see para 3.12(ii) of Code D and *R v France* [2012] UKPC 28).

Where a dock identification has occurred then, according to *R v Tido* [2011] 2 Cr App R 36, the jury must be directed carefully in the following way:

(a) They must be directed on the danger of relying on it.

(b) They must be warned of the disadvantages to the defendant of having been denied a formal identification procedure, specifically about the possibility of an inconclusive result which could have been used by the defence to challenge the dock identification.

(c) They must be warned about the obvious danger that even a well-meaning person might automatically assume the defendant in the dock was the person who committed the crime, simply by virtue of the fact that the defendant is in the dock.

There is no logic in making a distinction between a dock identification in a Crown Court and in a magistrates' court. However, in road traffic offences it is usually necessary to prove that the defendant was the driver of the car at the time of the offence. Generally, there is no dispute that the accused was the driver, but a failure to call any evidence on that issue is likely to result in an acquittal. In summary trials for road traffic offences, the custom has evolved where a witness (usually a police officer) is asked, 'Do you see the driver in court?'. Because of the sheer number of such offences that are tried by magistrates, if there had to be an identification parade in every case where the accused did not expressly admit that he was the driver, '*the whole process of justice in a magistrates' court would be severely impaired*' (*Barnes v Chief Constable of Durham* [1997] 2 Cr App R 505). Thus, it seems that in this type of case the onus is on the accused to raise the issue of disputed identification before the trial starts and seek an identification procedure.

16.9.3.2 Out-of-court eyewitness identification

The obvious way to avoid the prejudice of a dock identification is to refer to an out-of-court identification made in less prejudicial circumstances. Code D lays down a regime for ensuring this (so far as is possible). All forms of out-of-court identification would seem to be admissible as prior consistent statements under the CJA 2003, s 120(4) and (5) (see **6.5.2.2**).

16.9.3.2.1 Where a suspect's identity is not known

A suspect becomes 'known' to the police when there are reasonable grounds to suspect a particular person of involvement in an offence (Code D, para 3.1A). In cases when the suspect's identity is not known, where practicable a record should be made of any description of the suspect as first given by an eyewitness (Code D, para 3.1, 3.2(a)). Two types of identification procedure may then be appropriate. An eyewitness may be taken to a particular neighbourhood or place to see whether they can identify the person they saw on a previous occasion. Care must be taken not to direct the witness's attention to any individual unless, taking into account all the circumstances, this cannot be avoided (Code D, para 3.2). Further or alternatively, the eyewitness may be shown photographs of potential suspects, in accordance with Code D, Annex E.

16.9.3.2.2 Where a suspect's identity is known and the suspect is available

Where a suspect's identity is known, the suspect may either be 'available' or 'unavailable'. An 'available' suspect is one who is immediately available, or will be available within a reasonably short time, in order that they can be invited to take part in at least one of the eyewitness identification procedures (para 3.1A).

If the suspect does not dispute identification by a witness, no identification procedure is necessary unless the officer in charge of the investigation considers it would be useful (paras 3.12 and 3.13). If identification is disputed, and there is a witness who expresses an ability to identify the suspect, or where there is a reasonable chance of the witness being able to do so, an identification procedure shall be held unless it is not practicable or it would serve no useful purpose in proving or disproving whether the suspect was involved in committing the offence (para 3.12).

Examples of when a procedure would serve no useful purpose are where the suspect admits being at the scene of the crime and gives an account of what took place and the witness did not see anything which contradicts the suspect's version, or when it is not disputed that the suspect is already known to the witness who claims to have recognised the suspect as the person he saw committing the crime (para 3.12(ii)). *R v Abbott* [2006] EWCA Crim 151, CA provides another example of when a procedure would serve no useful purpose. In *Abbott*, two witnesses to a robbery described the height and build of the robbers, their clothing, which included balaclavas and ski masks, and their eyes, which were either 'light-coloured' or 'blue'. Defendant A had deep-brown eyes. The Court of Appeal held that there had been no need to hold an identification procedure (nor give a *Turnbull* warning) as this was not an eyewitness identification case, considering the witnesses had not in fact purported to identify the suspect. Although A disputed involvement, an identification procedure would have served no useful purpose; his involvement was shown purely through circumstantial evidence such as fingerprints. *R v Robinson* [2005] EWCA Crim

3307 is a curious example of a situation where an identification procedure *did* serve a useful purpose. R denied involvement in a robbery and sought to challenge that he had been correctly identified in almost every conceivable way. One of the three other alleged robbers became a Crown witness and picked out R in an identification parade. That was probative evidence because the fellow robber had only known R by sight and by his nickname of 'Rambo'; the Crown needed to establish that 'Rambo' and R were one and the same.

If an identification procedure is to be used, when the identity of the suspect is known to the police and he is available, three forms of identification procedure may be used. In a *video identification procedure*, the witness is shown images of a suspect, together with images of at least eight other people who resemble the suspect. Ordinarily, the images must be moving images (para 3.5 and Annex A). An *identification parade* puts the suspect into a line-up of at least eight other people who resemble the suspect as far as possible (see Annex B). *Group identification* is less formal—the suspect is put into an informal group of people, perhaps walking through a shopping centre or in a queue at a bus station (see Annex C).

The conditions in which a video identification procedure or an identification parade take place can be controlled far more satisfactorily than the conditions in which a group identification takes place. Therefore, the starting point for the officer in charge of the case will be to consult with the identification officer as to the suitability and practicability of holding either a video identification or an identification parade. (An identification officer is the officer responsible for the arrangement and conduct of identification procedures, usually an inspector: para 3.11.) A video identification will normally be offered to the suspect unless it is not practicable or an identification parade or a group identification would be practicable and more suitable (paras 3.14 and 3.16). The suspect may refuse the offered procedure and may then make representations as to why a different procedure should be used. The identification officer shall then offer an alternative procedure if one is suitable and practicable.

16.9.3.2.3 *Where a suspect's identity is known and the suspect is not available*

A suspect will be 'unavailable' if not immediately available to participate in a procedure and will not become available within a reasonably short time. Failure or refusal to participate by the suspect may be treated as not being available (see Code D, paras 3.4 and 3.21). Arrangements may be made for covert video identification or covert group identification (para 3.21). As a last resort, if none of the other procedures are practicable, a *confrontation* may be arranged. *Confrontation* involves a direct confrontation between witness and suspect. This will usually take place in a police station and the witness will be asked, 'Is this the person?'. If the witness identifies the person but is unable to confirm the identification (eg the witness says, 'yes I think it is the person, but am not sure'), the witness will be asked how sure he or she is (see Annex D).

In *R v Nolan (Mercedes)* [2005] EWCA Crim 3661, M refused to participate in a video parade and the officer then compiled a series of still photos which did not require M's active involvement. M changed her mind about participating in the video procedure although it is unclear whether this happened (and the police officer was told) before or after her photo was picked out by the witness. The Court of Appeal held that the officer had acted properly in the circumstances of the case. The court did observe, however, that:

> ... the inspector running the [identification] procedure should consider carefully any timely and clearly communicated change of mind on the part of a suspect, resulting in an agreement by him or her to cooperate. If it is still reasonably possible to organise a fair video/moving image identification procedure without materially endangering the willingness of the witnesses to cooperate or otherwise prejudicing the identification procedure, the inspector should consider whether

fairness dictates that he should revert to a video/moving image identification. Whether or not he should accede to a request/change-of-mind of this kind will always depend on the circumstances of the case.

16.9.3.2.4 *Identification after the conclusion of an identification procedure.*

If an eyewitness makes an identification after an identification parade has ended, the suspect and his solicitor should be informed. The police should also consider whether to give the witness a second opportunity at a parade (Code D, Annex B, para 20). Where two witnesses are put into the same room after taking part in a parade, and only one has identified the suspect but later the second makes a statement doing so, neither witness's evidence has to be excluded. See *R v Willoughby* [1999] 2 Cr App R 82, where the Court of Appeal held that merely 'firming up' a tentative identification at a parade does not come within the ambit of what is now Annex B, para 20. As to the witness who had not previously identified the suspect, the court observed that even if para 20 is breached, so long as the breach is relatively minor and innocent (eg no coaching has occurred), the trial judge may decide not to exclude that evidence under s 78 of the 1984 Act. See, by way of contrast, *R v Ciantar* [2005] EWCA Crim 3559, where an eyewitness who attended a video identification some six weeks after a fatal stabbing did not pick out anyone at the time but immediately afterwards told the investigating officer that she had been nervous and scared during the procedure and that the man whose image was numbered five '*had a look about him that frightened* [her] *and reminded* [her] *of the guy at* [the restaurant]'. C's image was number five. She had not picked him out as she thought that she needed to be 100 per cent sure before doing so. The witness's evidence was allowed in the trial following a *voir dire*. The Court of Appeal held that the trial judge had been correct not to put it to the jury as a positive identification but rather as a 'qualified' identification whose weight was less than that of a positive identification. (For further guidance on 'qualified' identifications, see *R v George* [2003] Crim LR 282.)

16.9.4 Recognition by showing films, photographs, and other images

A defendant may be recognised in a controlled environment, for example, a police station or in court. Alternatively, a defendant may be recognised in an uncontrolled environment, such as on social media. Each of these situations will be dealt with in turn.

16.9.4.1 Controlled recognition through films, photographs, and other images

16.9.4.1.1 *The jury*

The jury can look at a CCTV film or a still photograph and form its own view as to whether the person shown is the accused sitting in the dock (see *Kajala v Noble* (1982) 75 Cr App R 149, DC and *R v Dodson and Williams* [1984] 1 WLR 971). According to *R v Blenkinsop* [1995] 1 Cr App R 7, a full *Turnbull* warning would not be appropriate in such cases. However, it may be preferable to call a witness who knows the accused and recognises the accused on the film (in which case a *Turnbull* hearing would generally be appropriate).

In *R v McNamara* [1996] Crim LR 750, the Court of Appeal held that where a jury requested a view of the accused to compare with a man on a video, no inference could properly be drawn if the accused chose to absent himself from the dock.

16.9.4.1.2 *Police officers and others who know the accused*

R v Fowden [1982] Crim LR 588, *R v Grimer* [1982] Crim LR 674, *Taylor v Chief Constable of Cheshire* [1987] 1 All ER 225, and *R v Caldwell* (1994) 99 Cr App R 73 are authorities which considered the situation where witnesses (usually police officers) who know the accused are called upon to identify him as the person caught on film, or appearing in a photograph. The propositions that emerge from these cases are as follows:

(a) Where there are several witnesses, they should not be allowed to view the film, etc together but should be asked to view the film individually and state whether they recognise the person on the film (see also Code D, Annex A).

(b) At trial, attempts should be made not to reveal to the jury that the witness knows the accused through previous encounters in the course of investigations into other criminal offences.

(c) A *Turnbull* warning should be given to the jury.

All of these cases were considered and approved by the Court of Appeal in *Attorney-General's Reference (No 2 of 2002)* [2003] 1 Cr App R 21.

In *R v Smith* [2009] 1 Cr App R 36 (approved by *Chaney* [2009] 1 Cr App R 512), the Court of Appeal noted that in cases where the suspect is identified by a police officer from a CCTV recording there is a danger that the officer may assert that he recognised someone without any objective means of testing the accuracy of the recognition. The Court of Appeal, while unclear as to whether Code D applied at that time, thought that the safeguards which the Code is designed to put in place are as important in such cases as they are for other identifying witnesses. Therefore, there should always be a record set out of police officers' initial reactions to the recording, including matters such as:

- how many times the officer viewed the video before identifying the suspect;
- the words that officer used by way of recognition;
- the failure of the officer to pick anybody else out;
- any words of doubt expressed by the officer; and
- what it is about the image that triggered the alleged recognition.

Following *Smith*, and possibly due to the increasing prevalence and use of recording media in the identification of suspects, changes were made to Code D so that it now applies to recognition of suspects from films, photographs, and other visual images. The procedure to be followed is set out in Code D, paras 3.34–3.37. Films, photographs, or images should be shown on an individual basis to avoid the possibility of collusion and reduce the risk of mistaken recognition. The procedure should as far as possible follow the principles for video identification contained in Annex A if the suspect is known or, if the suspect is not known, the principles for identification by photographs in Annex E (para 3.35). Very importantly, a careful and detailed record *must* be made of the circumstances and conditions under which the person is given an opportunity to recognise the individual (para 3.36) and the record must be made by the person who views the images or sees the individual and makes the recognition (para 3.37). Matters which the record must include are listed below in para 3.36, (a)–(k).

3.36 …

(a) Whether the person knew or was given information concerning the name or identity of any suspect.

(b) What the person has been told before the viewing about the offence, the person(s) depicted in the images or the offender and by whom.

(c) How and by whom the witness was asked to view the image or look at the individual.

(d) Whether the viewing was alone or with others and if with others, the reason for it.

(e) The arrangements under which the person viewed the film or saw the individual and by whom those arrangements were made.

(f) Whether the viewing of any images was arranged as part of a mass circulation to police and the public or for selected persons.

(g) The date, time and place images were viewed or further viewed or the individual was seen.

(h) The times between which the images were viewed or the individual was seen.

(i) How the viewing of images or sighting of the individual was controlled and by whom.

(j) Whether the person was familiar with the location shown in any images or the place where they saw the individual and if so, why.

(k) Whether or not on this occasion, the person claims to recognise any image shown, or any individual seen, as being someone known to them, and if they do:

(i) the reason

(ii) the words of recognition

(iii) any expressions of doubt

(iv) what features of the image or the individual triggered the recognition.

In *R v Lariba* [2015] EWCA Crim 478, the Court of Appeal (endorsing *R v Forbes* [2001] AC 473) held that, when an investigator may make an identification from CCTV in informal circumstances, there remains an obligation to hold a formal identification procedure under Code D unless it would be impracticable or serve no useful purpose (eg if the witness already knows the suspect well and saw him commit the crime). The formal procedure provides the witness with the opportunity in controlled conditions to entertain second thoughts.

Where a crime has been seen by an eyewitness as well as being recorded on a surveillance video, the witness may be allowed to view the video and to amend his witness statement in the light of what he sees on it (see *R v Roberts* [1998] Crim LR 682).

Where a security tape exists, and it shows an offence being committed, but does not show the accused who is now on trial, that tape is material evidence which must be disclosed to the defence (see *Sangster v R* [2002] UKPC 58).

16.9.4.2 Uncontrolled recognition through films, photographs, and other images

16.9.4.2.1 Images circulated by the police

If police circulate images as part of an appeal to identify or trace a suspect, whether on social media or otherwise, a copy of the relevant material released to the media must be kept. Any person who viewed the material will have done so outside of an environment that is controlled and supervised by the authorities. Therefore, any person who comes forward following such an appeal should be asked to give details of the circumstances and conditions in which the viewing was made (Code D, Part 3(C)).

The weight of a positive identification by an eyewitness might be affected if that eyewitness had seen images circulated by the police prior to the identification procedure. Therefore, any eyewitness should also be asked, after any identification procedure, whether they have seen any film, photograph, or image relating to the offence or any description of the suspect which has been broadcast or published, and their reply recorded. If they have, they should be asked to give details of the circumstances.

16.9.4.2.2 Images not circulated by the police

Code D does not apply directly where images were not circulated by the police. However, the principles inherent in Code D, Part 3(C) apply by extension, in that as much detail as possible about the circumstances of the identification should be recorded. A record should be kept of the images that were viewed and a statement should be taken from the witness so that the jury are able to make a proper assessment of its reliability (see *R v Alexander* [2013] 1 Cr App R 26). Concerning the reliability of so-called 'identification by Facebook', it is submitted that important factors are likely to be whether the witness had the name of the suspect before looking for him on the internet, whether the witness read information about the suspect, for example in 'personal profiles', and whether the witness was prompted in any way by other persons.

16.9.4.3 Expert evidence

In *R v Stockwell* (1993) 97 Cr App R 260, the Court of Appeal accepted that the opinion evidence of a facial-mapping expert is admissible, particularly in cases where there is a possibility that the person caught on the film was disguised. However, one must take care that the opinion evidence of a facial-mapping expert stays within acceptable bounds. It is acceptable to call such an expert at trial to demonstrate to a jury particular characteristics or a combination thereof, with the aid of specialist enhancement techniques if appropriate. It had been stated that it was not acceptable for such an expert to offer an estimate of probabilities or to state the degree of support provided by particular facial characteristics. These were said to be subjective opinions and thus inadmissible until such time as a '*national database or agreed formula or some other such objective measure is established*' (see *R v Gray* [2003] EWCA Crim 1001). However, in *Atkins* [2009] EWCA Crim 1876, the Court of Appeal distinguished *Gray* and said that facial mapping was a legitimate field for expert evidence and should be admissible. It would still be wrong for an expert to offer an opinion in such a way as to present it as scientific fact. That it was the expert's subjective opinion was something to be considered by the jury and explored in cross-examination. In *Atkins*, the expert had erred by ascribing numerical values to his opinions—0 = 'Lends no support' up to 5 = 'Lends powerful support'—this may wrongly have suggested that a measurable scale was involved. For a helpful collection of the authorities on the use and usefulness of facial mapping, see 'Identification from CCTV: The Risk of Injustice' [2007] Crim LR 591.

In *R v Clarke* [1995] 2 Cr App R 425, the Court of Appeal held that evidence of facial mapping by way of video superimposition (of police photographs of the accused upon photographs of the offender taken by a security camera) was admissible as a species of real evidence to which no special rules applied.

In *R v Clare* [1995] 2 Cr App R 333, the Court of Appeal accepted that a police officer, who had viewed a security video of a crowd disturbance at a football match over 40 times (having the facility to stop the video and examine it in slow motion), had thereby become an expert on that video so as to justify calling him to give evidence interpreting the video and the role and identification of the person caught on the video. In *R v Thomas* (1999) LTL 22/11/99, the Court of Appeal held that there is no obligation on the prosecution to put the accused on an identification parade before people on whom neither the police nor the Crown ever intend to rely as identification witnesses. Before T was put on trial for four bank robberies, a police officer studied CCTV videos and single-frame shots of the robberies 'repeatedly'. The Court of Appeal said that the officer had '*acquired special knowledge that the* [trial] *court did not possess*'; in effect, he had become an 'expert' and there was no purpose in seeing if he could pick out T on a parade.

16.9.5 Cases in which the link between the accused and the crime is made by recognition of voice

An alleged recording of an accused's voice should be heard by the jury but expert evidence on it should also be presented (see *R v Bentum* (1989) 153 JP 538; *R v Robb* (1991) 93 Cr App R 161).

In *R v Deenik* [1992] Crim LR 578, a witness testified to recognising the accused's voice (as that of the person who had committed the offence) on overhearing the accused being interviewed. It was held that it was not necessary to exclude the evidence merely because the accused was unaware that the witness was listening to the interview. The

Court of Appeal has said that where a witness identifies a suspect by hearing his voice, Code D has no application and there is no obligation to hold a voice identification parade. However, reference to Code D shows that a witness attending an identification parade may ask to hear any member speak (see Code D, Annex B, para 18).

A tape of the perpetrator's voice may be played to the jury, if the accused has given evidence, so it may form its own judgement of the opinions of the experts (*R v Bentum* (1989) 153 JP 538).

In *R v Flynn* [2008] 2 Cr App R 20, the Court of Appeal made some observations about voice identification evidence and issued some guidance on best practice where police officers give evidence of voice identification based at least in part on recordings. First, the Court of Appeal observed:

- voice identification is more difficult than visual identification;
- voice identification is more likely to be reliable when done by an expert, using appropriate equipment, rather than by a 'lay listener' (such as a police officer);
- a lay listener's ability to identify a voice is subject to variables, about which not enough is yet known. However, a confidently made identification may be wrong just as with a visual identification; and
- an expert can show his technique and explain how his work supports his conclusions; conversely, the lay listener's method of analysis is 'fundamentally opaque' and consequently hard to explain and harder to challenge.

Where the prosecution relies on the evidence of police officers who have listened to recordings of a suspect's voice, best practice is as follows:

- Where police officers set out to obtain voice identification evidence, the process ought to be recorded properly. Officers need to log the time they have individually spent in contact with the suspect in order to show their familiarity with the suspect.
- When a police officer prepares a transcript of a recording, that police officer should log the date of this action and the time taken to do it.
- If that officer also makes notes on the transcript showing his thoughts as to the identity of the speaker(s), he should record this fact.
- When a police officer makes an attempt at voice identification, he should not be given a transcript but, if one is supplied, the transcript should not be one previously annotated by an earlier listener to show who he thought was speaking.
- It is highly desirable that a voice recognition exercise, if it is to be carried out by a police officer at all, should be performed by an officer who is independent of the investigation.

The judge should direct the jury using a suitably adapted form of *Turnbull* warning. Research suggests that identification by voice is less reliable than visual identification, so the warning should be in stronger terms. (See further *R v Hersey* [1998] Crim LR 281; *R v Gummerson* [1999] Crim LR 680; *R v Roberts* [2000] Crim LR 183; *R v Chenia* [2002] EWCA Crim 2345.) The ***Crown Court Compendium Part 1*** 2017, chapter 15-7 provides guidance on how a judge should direct a jury in respect of evidence of identification by voice. Judges are advised that an explicit modified *Turnbull* direction is required and that the direction should draw the jury's attention to any failure to hold a voice comparison exercise (a voice identification procedure). Judicial comment should also be made where expert evidence is adduced which is based solely on auditory phonetic analysis rather than quantitative acoustic analysis, since auditory phonetic analysis is unable to distinguish between vocal mechanisms of voices. *Karsten v Wood Green Crown Court* [2014] EWHC

2900 (Admin) provides an example of how a Bench directed itself in relation to voice identification evidence in an appeal to the Crown Court from the magistrates' court.

16.9.6 Cases in which the link between the accused and the crime is made by fingerprints or DNA profiles

The problem here is primarily how fingerprints or body samples can *properly* be obtained from the accused. The governing statutory provisions in this regard are to be found in PACE 1984, ss 61–65 (as amended) and supplemented by Code D, Part 4 (fingerprints) and Part 6 (body samples).

16.9.6.1 Fingerprints and ear impressions

PACE 1984, s 61 sets out when fingerprints may be taken. The judge's discretion to admit fingerprint evidence depends upon all the circumstances. Although *R v Buckley* (1999) 163 JP 561 suggested that fingerprints with less than eight matching characteristics were highly unlikely to be admitted, the ***Crown Court Compendium Part 1*** 2017, chapter 15-6 notes that 'the police fingerprint bureau in England and Wales have since adopted a non-numerical standard. The latest guidelines emphasise the role of subjective evaluation in the comparison of prints.' The judge should therefore consider the other facts outlined in Buckley, namely whether there were any dissimilar characteristics between the print and that taken from the accused, and the size, quality, and clarity of the print relied upon.

Expert evidence may also be given of comparisons of ear prints (*R v Dallagher* [2003] 1 Cr App R 11). However, care needs to be taken—such evidence may be reliable when it shows a correspondence of minutiae and precise details, but when it shows an imprecise match only of the 'gross features' of the ear, factors such as flexibility, movement, or pressure may make the evidence unreliable. See *R v Kempster* [2008] 2 Cr App R 19.

16.9.6.2 Body samples (DNA profiles)

The governing provisions are PACE 1984, ss 62 and 63. Section 62 deals with intimate samples and s 63 deals with non-intimate samples.

'*Intimate sample*' means:

(a) a sample of blood, semen, or any other tissue fluid, urine, or pubic hair;

(b) a dental impression; or

(c) a swab taken from any part of the genitals (including pubic hair) or from a person's body orifice other than the mouth.

('*Intimate search*' means a search that consists of the physical examination of a person's body orifices other than the mouth).

'*Non-intimate sample*' means:

(a) a sample of hair other than pubic hair;

(b) a sample taken from a nail or from under a nail;

(c) a swab taken from any part of a person's body other than a part from which a swab taken would be an intimate sample;

(d) saliva; or

(e) a skin impression, which means any record of the skin pattern and other physical characteristics or features of the whole or any part of the foot or of any other part of the body.

Section 64 of the 1984 Act makes provision for the destruction of samples where suspects are eventually cleared of any offence (see Code D, Annex F). Regarding the effect of breaches of these statutory rules, see *R v Nathaniel* [1995] 2 Cr App R 565, in which it was held that the trial judge should have applied PACE 1984, s 78, to exclude evidence obtained from a blood sample that should have been destroyed. Lord Taylor CJ said:

> To allow that blood sample to be used in evidence ... when the sample had been retained in breach of statutory duty and in breach of undertakings to the accused must ... have had an adverse effect on the fairness of the proceedings.

Subsequently, the House of Lords has drawn a distinction between trying to use a DNA profile as evidence in a trial when it should have been destroyed (as was the position in *R v Nathaniel*), and using such a profile as part of a criminal investigation. The position is governed by different parts of ss 64–64(3B)(a) and (b), respectively. In *R v B (Attorney-General's Reference (No 3 of 1999))* [2001] 1 Cr App R 475, the House of Lords considered the use of a DNA profile from a man (B) acquitted of burglary. The profile had been placed on the national DNA database but, contrary to s 64(3B)(b), was not removed following his acquittal. Subsequently, the profile provided a match with DNA obtained from a rape victim. B was arrested and one of his hairs was removed, legally but without his consent. The hair provided another DNA match. At trial, the prosecution did not rely on the first DNA profile. B was convicted and appealed. The House of Lords held that the 1984 Act did not stipulate a consequence for a breach of s 64(3B)(b) and that the subsection did not legislate that evidence obtained as a result of the prohibited investigation was inadmissible. Section 64(3B)(b) had to be read in conjunction with s 78 of the 1984 Act. Section 64(3B)(b) prohibited the use of a sample liable to destruction for the purposes of any investigation of other offences. It would not prohibit the use of any evidence resulting from such investigation in any subsequent criminal proceedings. The House also considered Article 8 of the ECHR and concluded that its interpretation of s 64(3B)(b) did not contravene the Convention. This should now be read in the light of the decision of the Grand Chamber of the European Court of Human Rights in *S and Marper v United Kingdom* [2009] Crim LR 355, which found that the wrongful retention of DNA samples, taken from defendants who had either been acquitted or against whom proceedings had been discontinued, constituted a breach of Article 8, the right to respect for one's private life. The Crime and Security Act 2010 sets out the statutory framework to govern the destruction of fingerprints and DNA samples, in response to the *Marper* judgment.

16.9.6.2.1 Adducing evidence of DNA profiles

In *R v Reed* [2009] EWCA Crim 2698, Thomas LJ held that compliance with Part 33 (now Part 19) of the Crim PR, dealing with expert evidence, is of paramount importance. Part 19 provides a 'very important safeguard' as to the admissibility of DNA evidence. In particular, r 19.4(f) and (g) require 'each expert to identify where there is a range of opinion on the matters dealt with in his report. In such a case, the expert must summarise the scope of opinion and give reasons for his own opinion. If the expert cannot give his opinion without qualification, he must state the qualification. Compliance with this obligation will identify for the other party an area where there is a range of opinion; it is particularly important that this rule is followed in the expert report obtained by the Crown.' Part 19 also 'enables clear identification of what is in issue before the trial begins. Under r 19.6(2) the court has power to direct experts to discuss expert issues in the proceedings and prepare a statement for the court of the matters on which they agree and disagree giving their reasons. If an expert does not comply with this, that party may not call the expert to give evidence without the permission of the court [(r 19.6(4))]'. Accordingly, in cases involving DNA evidence, Thomas LJ concluded that:

- It is particularly important to ensure that the obligation under Rules 19.4(f) and (g) is followed and also that, where propositions are to be advanced as part of an evaluative opinion, that each proposition is spelt out with precision in the expert report.

- Expert reports must, after each has been served, be carefully analysed by the parties. Where a disagreement is identified, this must be brought to the attention of the court.
- If the reports are available before the PTPH, this should be done at the PTPH; but if the reports have not been served by all parties at the time of the PTPH (as may often be the case), it is the duty of the Crown and the defence to ensure that the necessary steps are taken to bring the matter back before the judge where a disagreement is identified.
- It will then in the ordinary case be necessary for the judge to exercise his powers under Rule 19.6 and make an order for the provision of a statement.
- We would anticipate, even in such a case, that ... much of the science relating to DNA will be common ground. The experts should be able to set out in the statement under Rule 19.6 in clear terms for use at the trial the basic science that is agreed, in so far as it is not contained in one of the reports. The experts must then identify with precision what is in dispute—for example, the match probability, the interpretation of the electrophoretograms or the evaluative opinion that is to be given.
- If the order as to the provision of the statement under Rule 19.6 is not observed and in the absence of a good reason, then the trial judge should consider carefully whether to exercise the power to refuse permission to the party whose expert is in default to call that expert to give evidence. In many cases, the judge may well exercise that power. A failure to find time for a meeting because of commitments to other matters, a common problem with many experts as was evident in this appeal, is not to be treated as a good reason.

16.9.6.2.2 *DNA evidence and a case to answer*

There is no evidential or legal principle which prevents a case solely dependent on the presence of the defendant's DNA profile on an article left at the scene of a crime being considered by a jury (*R v Tsekiri* [2017] EWCA Crim 40).

Where it is clear that DNA had been directly deposited in the course of the commission of a crime by the offender, a very high DNA match with the defendant would be sufficient without more to give rise to a case for the defendant to answer (see *R v FNC* [2016] 1 Cr App R 13). However, where there are moveable articles left at the scene of the crime, the position will depend upon the facts. Relevant factors will include the following matters (*R v Tsekiri*):

- Is there any evidence of some other explanation for the presence of the defendant's DNA on the item other than involvement in the crime?
- Was the article apparently associated with the offence itself? For example, did the defendant leave DNA on a door handle of a car that was used by the offender in the course of committing the offence? In which case there can be no doubt that the offender did touch the article in question. The position could be different if the article was not necessarily so connected with the offence, eg if a DNA profile were to be found on a cigarette stub discarded at the scene of a street robbery.
- How readily movable was the article in question? A DNA profile on a small article of clothing or something such as a cigarette end at the scene of a crime might be of less probative force than the same profile on a vehicle.
- Is there evidence of some geographical association between the offence and the offender?
- In the case of a mixed profile is the DNA profile which matches the defendant the major contributor to the overall DNA profile?
- Is it more or less likely that the DNA profile attributable to the defendant was deposited by primary or secondary transfer?

16.9.6.2.3 *Directing the jury on DNA evidence*

A comprehensive jury direction on DNA evidence can be found at chapter 15-8 of the ***Crown Court Compendium Part 1*** 2017.

17

Opinion evidence

17.1 General rule

You may recall an occasion when someone (a parent or teacher perhaps) said to you, 'When I want your opinion, I'll ask for it!'. In the courtrooms of England and Wales, the approach is effectively the same. In civil and criminal cases, the opinions of witnesses are not generally admissible.

Opinions, and conclusions, are for the court to reach, based upon the information placed before it. If a conclusion on a point of law is required, the court will base its conclusion upon the legal arguments put before it by the advocates. Any factual conclusion will be based upon the evidence in the trial (or other form of hearing). Any witness should normally be confined to stating the facts.

When reaching conclusions of fact, the court should make its decisions for itself. So, a rule evolved that a witness should not be asked questions, or offer answers, which require the witness to venture an opinion on a fact in issue. To do so could appear to exert improper influence over the court. This is sometimes known as the 'ultimate issue' rule.

There is also a risk that the court might be unaware of the factual basis (or lack of it) on which the witness's opinion is founded. What the court really needs are the original facts, upon which the witness's opinion is based.

Finally, in situations where the court is quite capable of forming an opinion on the fact in issue, it would be a waste of time to allow a witness to state his or her opinion on that fact.

Any description of the rule against opinion evidence, even if it is supported with examples, fails to give a true impression of the impact of the rule upon the questioning of witnesses. An objection to a particular question is often made on the basis that the witness is being invited to state opinion. Sometimes the question itself is really nothing more than comment on the witness's evidence.

The general rule excluding opinion evidence is subject to two important exceptions. These arise in cases where the court lacks the witness's competence to form an opinion on a particular issue. That may arise through: (a) lack of the necessary direct knowledge; or (b) lack of the necessary expertise.

17.2 Witnesses of fact who offer their opinion

Statements of opinion by an eyewitness (E) to the facts in issue are often really a convenient way of stating several facts. Thus, an assertion by E that the defendant was drunk is a convenient way of stating the various facts that E saw (or heard or smelled), which led him to form that opinion. Such a statement will generally be admissible as long as a proper appraisal of the facts does not call for any special expertise.

In civil cases this exception has been put into statutory form: the Civil Evidence Act 1972, s 3(2):

> *It is hereby declared that where a person is called as a witness in any civil proceedings, a statement of opinion by him on any relevant matter on which he is not qualified to give expert evidence, if made as a way of conveying relevant facts personally perceived by him, is admissible evidence of what he perceived.*

If a degree of precision is required, then a witness's best guess or estimate by itself will probably not do. In a case concerning a road accident it will often be necessary to consider the speed at which the vehicles involved were travelling and E may be allowed to state his opinion on this issue. However, if the charge is driving over the speed limit or driving with an amount of alcohol in the blood that exceeds the maximum prescribed by law, precision is needed. See, for example, the Road Traffic Regulation Act 1984, s 89 (see **5.2.2**), which states that it is insufficient to use the opinion of just one witness to prove a speeding case.

17.3 Expert opinion evidence

17.3.1 General principle

There are many situations in which an issue that a court is required to determine is so far removed from the court's experience that it needs the opinions of experts to help it to determine the issue in question. When such need arises, the opinion of an expert *is* admissible. This was recognised as long ago as *Folkes v Chadd* (1782) 3 Doug KB 157. The converse is also true: if an issue calls for expert evidence, the evidence of a non-expert should not be admitted (see *R v Inch* (1989) 91 Cr App R 51). Where a litigant wishes to instruct an expert with a view to providing a report, the court may place limits on this (see CPR, r 35.7, and the use of a single joint expert, for example); it may even require the litigant to seek the court's permission before instructing an expert at all (see, generally, **17.3.8.1** below and CPR, r 35.4).

It is not possible to list all the matters in respect of which expert evidence may be required; some matters (eg medical and scientific) obviously call for the opinions of experts. However, the line between matters that do call for expert evidence and matters that do not is often extremely fine (especially in relation to psychiatric evidence) and the courts consider the question most carefully. In *R v Turner* [1975] QB 834, CA, at p 841, Lawton LJ put the point very effectively in this way:

> The fact that an expert witness has impressive scientific qualifications does not by that fact alone make his opinion on matters of human nature and behaviour *within the limits of normality* any more helpful than that of the jurors themselves; but there is a danger that they may think it does. [Author's emphasis]

In a similar vein, note the views of the Australian Northern Territory Supreme Court on the absence of need for expert help in assessing the credibility and likelihood of fabrication for a normal 9-year-old boy (see case commentary on *R v Joyce* [2005] NTSC 21, [2006] Crim LR 276).

Evidence 'of the practices, mores and associations of gangs', including evidence of gang territories, conflicts, and associations, as well as gang signs and tattoos, may be the subject of expert evidence (*Myers v The Queen* [2015] UKPC 40).

So, expert evidence will usually be excluded if it merely offers an opinion on normal human behaviour. But this sometimes begs the question, 'What is normality?'. In a development from the position in *R v Turner*, expert evidence may now be called not merely where the accused is alleged to be suffering from a recognised mental illness, but also if it could show that the accused is suffering from a personality disorder that would tend to affect the reliability of the confession or other evidence (see, eg, *R v Pinfold* [2004] 2 Cr App R 5).

There are particular difficulties in criminal cases when there *is* evidence of *abnormality* but the central issue in the case turns on the application of an objective test. By definition the 'reasonable man' cannot be assumed to be abnormal. In so far as an expert's evidence would *only* be relevant if such an assumption could be made then it would appear to be inadmissible. You should refer to practitioner works to review the (sometimes contradictory) case law on this subject. It has affected such issues as duress, recklessness, and provocation.

It should be noted that evidence of fact must not be confused with expert evidence, even where it is given by a witness whose qualifications would entitle that witness to give expert evidence (*Kirkman v Euro Exide Corporation* [2007] CP Rep 19).

Expert evidence is probably encountered most frequently in civil cases (and there are many rules of civil procedure which relate to expert evidence—see Sime, ***A Practical Approach to Civil Procedure*** or the ***White Book***). We saw earlier that witnesses of fact can express their opinion on an issue, even though it may be an 'ultimate issue' for the court to decide. The same is true for an expert witness. In civil cases, this is established by the Civil Evidence Act 1972, s 3(1) and (3):

> (1) *Subject to any rules of court made in pursuance of this Act, where a person is called as a witness in any civil proceedings, his opinion on any relevant matter on which he is qualified to give expert evidence shall be admissible in evidence.*
>
> ...
>
> (3) *In this section 'relevant matter' includes an issue in the proceedings in question.*

Sometimes, an expert may seem to trespass into ultimate issues in criminal cases: for example, in *R v Stockwell* (1993) 97 Cr App R 260, which featured an early use of facial-mapping evidence. There is no statutory equivalent of the Civil Evidence Act 1972 to permit experts in criminal cases to offer their opinions on ultimate issues but it seems to be a matter of the form that questions take now, rather than their substance, 'since counsel can bring the witness so close to opining on the ultimate issue that the inference as to his view is obvious' (*R v Stockwell, per* Lord Taylor CJ).

17.3.2 Who is an 'expert'?

Where a matter calls for expert evidence, only a suitably qualified expert can give it. Indeed, the starting point in examining-in-chief an expert witness is to establish his expertise. But this does not necessarily mean that there must be formal qualifications. Examples are *R v Silverlock* [1894] 2 QB 766—a solicitor who had for many years studied handwriting as a hobby (handwriting expert)—and *Ajami v Comptroller of Customs* [1954] 1 WLR 1405—a banker with 24 years' experience of Nigerian banking law (foreign law expert). (Matters of *foreign* law are generally treated as calling for expert evidence.) However, it will not be easy to satisfy a judge that a witness is an expert in a field if he lacks formal qualifications. See, for example, *R v Stockwell* (1993) 97 Cr App R 260, where the 'expert' in facial mapping had '*no scientific qualifications, no specific training, no professional body and no database*'. In *R v Atkins* [2009] EWCA Crim 1876, CA, it was held that 'self-certification' as an expert is insufficient to establish that the evidence tendered has come from an expert source. The Court of Appeal observed that judges should be rigorous in ensuring that evidence advanced as 'expert evidence' is based upon specialised knowledge, experience, and study. Police officers may qualify as experts if they have made a sufficient study, whether by formal training or through practical experience, to assemble what can properly be regarded as a balanced body of specialised knowledge which would not be available to the tribunal of fact. In *Myers v The Queen* [2015] UKPC 40, the police officer in question was held to have been rightly treated as an expert on gangs. He was a member of a small police unit charged with targeting gangs in Bermuda. He regularly patrolled the streets where gangs congregated. He saw and frequently spoke to their members, most of whom he knew by name. He had studied their territories, and the markings which they put on walls within them, and their structures. He had undergone specialist training in gang monitoring and study from the FBI, both locally and in the USA and he was in communication with that institution's head and field offices in Washington, DC.

It has sometimes been said that an expert witness would be disqualified from giving evidence in a trial if he had an interest in the proceedings (see, eg, *Liverpool Roman Catholic Archdiocesan Trustees Inc v Goldberg (No 3)* [2001] 1 WLR 2337, disapproved in *R (Factortame Ltd) v Secretary of State for Transport, Local Government and the Regions (No 8)* [2003] QB 381). Such a situation might arise where the expert is an employee of one of the litigants, or is related to one. It ought to be clear that the expert owes an overriding duty to the court, not to himself or to a litigant (see, eg, CPR, r 35.3, and Crim PR, r 19.2). In *Myers v The Queen* [2015] UKPC 40 it was held that it is particularly important that a police expert should fully understand that once he is tendered as an expert he is not simply a part of the prosecution team, but has a separate duty to the court to give independent evidence, whichever side it may favour. In particular, a police expert needs to be especially conscious of the duty to state fully any material which weighs against any proposition which he is advancing, as well as all the evidence on which he has based that proposition. When considering an application by the Crown to adduce the evidence of a police expert, it is incumbent upon the judge to satisfy himself that these duties are recognised, and discharged.

Currently, the position is that a litigant who wishes to call an expert as a witness should disclose to the other litigant(s) and the court any interest that the expert has, or may seem to have. There is also an obligation on the expert to disclose any potential conflict of interest; this may be done by attaching the expert's curriculum vitae to the report (see *Toth v Jarman* [2006] 4 All ER 1276). That interest will not automatically disqualify the expert, although disqualification may be required on the facts of the particular case. It has been said that it is '*the nature and extent of the interest or connection which matters, not the mere fact of the interest or connection*' (see Nelson J in *Armchair Passenger Transport Ltd v Helical Bar plc* [2003] EWHC 367). Apparent bias is not enough to disqualify an expert from being called as a witness.

The key questions are:

- Does the person have relevant expertise?
- Is he aware of the overriding duty as an expert to the court, and willing and able to fulfil it?

If allowed to testify, the interest or connection may still be relevant to the weight of the evidence given by the expert. In conclusion, '*it is always desirable that an expert should have no actual or apparent interest in the outcome of the proceedings in which he gives evidence*', according to Lord Phillips MR in *R (Factortame Ltd) v Secretary of State for Transport, Local Government and the Regions (No 8)* [2003] QB 381. The same basic principles apply in criminal trials—see *Stubbs* [2006] EWCA Crim 2312. S was tried for his part in a conspiracy to defraud a bank via its online banking system. A bank employee, R, was called by the Crown to give expert evidence about the system's operation. On the appeal against conviction, the Court of Appeal held that the fact that R was an employee of the bank went only to the weight of his evidence, not its admissibility. It was a matter for the jury to decide whether R displayed any bias or lack of objectivity.

We must also note the litigation involving Sir Roy Meadow (see *Meadow v General Medical Council* [2007] 2 WLR 286, on appeal from the Administrative Court in [2006] 1 WLR 1452). Sir Roy Meadow had given evidence as an expert for the prosecution in several 'battered baby' or sudden infant death trials. Following successful appeals by several women, such as Sally Clark and Angela Cannings (see **17.3.4**), the General Medical Council—the professional body responsible for Sir Roy Meadow—found him guilty of serious professional misconduct and struck him off its register of medical practitioners. He sought judicial review of the decisions. At first instance, it was held that expert witnesses ought to have limited immunity from suit arising out of their evidence given in a court, as a matter of public policy (to have no immunity was thought likely to dissuade many experts from testifying). The Court of Appeal took the view that it would be wrong to grant immunity from suit by limiting the powers of a professional 'fitness to practice panel'; in general, the threat of such proceedings was in the public interest (see, eg, the speech of Sir Anthony Clarke MR at paras 30–34). Whatever the nature of the proceedings, it was critical that the lawyers representing the party calling the expert should ensure that his evidence was confined to matters within his expertise and was limited to relevant and admissible issues in the hearing. However, on the facts of the present case, a finding of serious professional misconduct was not justified.

17.3.3 Status of expert evidence

Expert evidence should be treated like the evidence of any other witness. It is a misdirection to tell a jury that they must accept it. See, for example, the speech of Lord Diplock in *R v Lanfear* [1968] 2 QB 77. However, in *R v Anderson* [1972] 1 QB 304, it was held that it would equally be a misdirection to tell a jury that they could disregard expert evidence that had been given by only one witness and which, if accepted, dictated one answer. See also, to the same effect, *R v Bailey* (1978) 66 Cr App R 31.

In civil cases, it has been said by Lord Rodger of Earlsferry in *Fairchild v Glenhaven Funeral Services Ltd* [2003] 1 AC 32, HL, that:

> even though it is always for the judge rather than for the expert witness to determine matters of fact, the judge must do so on the basis of the evidence, including the expert evidence. The mere application [by a judge] of 'common sense' cannot conjure up a proper basis for inferring that an injury must have been caused in one way rather than another when the only relevant evidence is undisputed scientific evidence which says that either way is equally possible.

Similarly, where two or more experts have been called as witnesses, Lord Phillips of Worth Matravers MR in *English v Emery Reimbold and Strick Ltd* [2002] 3 All ER 385 said that:

> 'a coherent reasoned opinion expressed by a suitably qualified expert should be the subject of a coherent reasoned rebuttal'. This does not mean that the judgment should contain a passage which suggests that the judge has applied the same, or even a superior, degree of expertise to that displayed by the witness. He should simply provide an explanation as to why he has accepted the evidence of one expert and rejected that of another. It may be that the evidence of one or the other accorded more satisfactorily with facts found by the judge. It may be that the explanation of one was more inherently credible than that of the other. It may simply be that one was better qualified, or manifestly more objective, than the other. Whatever the explanation may be, it should be apparent from the judgment.

However, the Divisional Court has said that it is trite law that a court is not obliged to accept the evidence of a witness, even the unchallenged evidence of an expert (see *Hackney London Borough Council v Rottenberg*, The Times, 9 February 2007). This was a case about an allegedly noisy neighbour; the Divisional Court said that whether this amounted to a noise nuisance was a matter of subjective judgment for the trial judge to decide, notwithstanding evidence from environmental and pollution control officers of the local authority to the effect that the conduct amounted to a statutory nuisance.

17.3.4 Reliability of expert evidence

It may be difficult for a jury in a criminal trial to evaluate the reliability of expert evidence. Prior to amendment of the Crim PR and Criminal Practice Direction in 2014, the approach regularly adopted by the courts was to put its faith in a jury to reach the correct conclusion on a specialist matter by favouring admissibility of expert opinion evidence and relying upon in-trial cross-examination and judicial direction to flush out unreliable evidence (see, eg, *Atkins* [2009] EWCA Crim 1876). The difficulty in assessing the reliability of expert evidence is well illustrated by the case of Angela Cannings (*R v Cannings* [2004] 1 WLR 2607), in which a mother was convicted of the murders of two of her children on the basis of expert evidence as to sudden infant deaths. Quashing her convictions, the Court of Appeal observed that:

> Not so long ago, experts were suggesting that new born babies should lie on their tummies. That was advice based on the best-informed analysis. Nowadays, the advice and exhortation is that babies should sleep on their backs ... This advice is equally drawn from the best possible known sources. It is obvious that these two views cannot both simultaneously be right ... [R]esearch in Australia [suggests] that the advice that babies should sleep on their backs had not achieved the improvement in the rate of cot deaths attributed to modern practice ... Our point is to highlight the fact that even now contrasting views on what might be thought to have been settled once and for all are current.

As the Court of Appeal noted in *R v Holdsworth* [2008] EWCA Crim 971:

> Particular caution is needed where the scientific knowledge of the process or processes involved is or may be incomplete. As knowledge increases, today's orthodoxy may become tomorrow's outdated learning.

In 2011, the Law Commission published a report, 'Expert Evidence in Criminal Proceedings in England and Wales'. The report contained a draft Criminal Evidence (Experts) Bill which provided for a reliability-based admissibility test by which evidence would only be admissible if it was judged to be sufficiently reliable to go before a jury, thereby creating a clear threshold that would have to be passed before a jury would be required to consider the expert evidence. Rather than legislate, amendments were made to the Crim PR and the Criminal Practice Directions. The rules on expert evidence are now found in Part 19 of the Crim PR. Rule 19.4(h) requires that the expert report must include such information as the court may need to decide whether the expert's opinion is sufficiently reliable to be admissible as evidence. Criminal Practice Directions V, paras 19A.4–19A.6 provide:

> *19A.4 In its judgment in R v Dlugosz and Others [2013] EWCA Crim 2, the Court of Appeal observed (at paragraph 11): 'It is essential to recall the principle which is applicable, namely in determining the issue of admissibility, the court must be satisfied that there is a sufficiently reliable scientific basis for the evidence to be admitted. If there is then the court leaves the opposing views to be tested before the jury.' Nothing at common law precludes assessment by the court of the reliability of an expert opinion by reference to substantially similar factors to those the Law Commission recommended as conditions of admissibility, and courts are encouraged actively to enquire into such factors.*

19A.5 Therefore factors which the court may take into account in determining the reliability of expert opinion, and especially of expert scientific opinion, include:

(a) the extent and quality of the data on which the expert's opinion is based, and the validity of the methods by which they were obtained;

(b) if the expert's opinion relies on an inference from any findings, whether the opinion properly explains how safe or unsafe the inference is (whether by reference to statistical significance or in other appropriate terms);

(c) if the expert's opinion relies on the results of the use of any method (for instance, a test, measurement or survey), whether the opinion takes proper account of matters, such as the degree of precision or margin of uncertainty, affecting the accuracy or reliability of those results;

(d) the extent to which any material upon which the expert's opinion is based has been reviewed by others with relevant expertise (for instance, in peer-reviewed publications), and the views of those others on that material;

(e) the extent to which the expert's opinion is based on material falling outside the expert's own field of expertise;

(f) the completeness of the information which was available to the expert, and whether the expert took account of all relevant information in arriving at the opinion (including information as to the context of any facts to which the opinion relates);

(g) if there is a range of expert opinion on the matter in question, where in the range the expert's own opinion lies and whether the expert's preference has been properly explained; and

(h) whether the expert's methods followed established practice in the field and, if they did not, whether the reason for the divergence has been properly explained.

19A.6 In addition, in considering reliability, and especially the reliability of expert scientific opinion, the court should be astute to identify potential flaws in such opinion which detract from its reliability, such as:

(a) being based on a hypothesis which has not been subjected to sufficient scrutiny (including, where appropriate, experimental or other testing), or which has failed to stand up to scrutiny;

(b) being based on an unjustifiable assumption;

(c) being based on flawed data;

(d) relying on an examination, technique, method or process which was not properly carried out or applied, or was not appropriate for use in the particular case; or

(e) relying on an inference or conclusion which has not been properly reached.

As to reliability, disagreement between prosecution and defence experts will not lead to their expert evidence being excluded where both experts agree that each other's opinion is valid and tenable. *R v Hookway* [2011] EWCA Crim 1989 concerned disagreement between the prosecution and defence expert on whether the accused's DNA components were present in two mixed DNA profiles at a sufficiently high level to enable statistical interpretation. The prosecution expert said that they were, but the defence expert disagreed. Both experts were able to find support for their respective views from the scientific community and both agreed that each other's opinion was valid and tenable. The Court of Appeal held that the disagreement did not mean that the expert evidence was unreliable and ought to be excluded. Such evidence could properly go to the jury for their consideration, and it would be for them to make an assessment of what weight to attach to each opinion. In doing so, they could have regard for their conclusions about other non-expert evidence in the case.

17.3.5 Upon what can an expert base an opinion?

An expert's opinion will be based upon much more than the facts of the particular case he is considering. It will be based on the expert's experience and any information that he has obtained from extraneous sources such as textbooks, articles, and journals. Such information (often referred to as secondary facts) is not treated as hearsay but simply as part of the basis for the expert opinion. Obviously, the facts of the particular case on which the opinion is given (the primary facts) should be proved by admissible evidence (whether or not by the expert).

For example, an expert valuer of antiques may be called to give opinion evidence of the value of certain Chinese vases. The opinion may be based on his own knowledge of previous sale prices of similar vases; it may also be based on secondary facts—reports of sales at foreign auction rooms or books published for the antiques trade specialist. However, if the valuation is based on the 'primary fact' that these vases date from the era of the Ming dynasty in China and are in excellent condition, these primary facts must themselves be proved by admissible evidence. This might be done either by this witness testifying about what he observed when looking at the vases (maker's marks, absence of cracks, chips, etc) or by calling other witnesses who have examined the vases. Thus, our expert may need dual expertise—first, on current saleroom prices for excellent-quality Ming vases; second, how to identify an 'excellent-quality Ming vase' (see, generally, *English Exporters (London) Ltd v Eldonwall Ltd* [1973] Ch 415 and *H v Schering Chemicals Ltd* [1983] 1 WLR 143; cf *R v Bradshaw* (1986) Cr App R 79, in which 'as a concession to the defence' a psychiatrist was allowed to base his opinion as to the accused's mental state upon statements made out of court by the accused—ie hearsay).

In *R v Jackson* [1996] 2 Cr App R 420, the Court of Appeal held that although, strictly speaking, an expert witness should not give an opinion based on scientific tests which had been made by assistants (in the expert's absence), maximum use should be made of written statements and formal admissions in proving such tests where it is not disputed that the tests were properly carried out.

A good example of the difference between primary and secondary facts is *R v Abadom* (1983) 76 Cr App R 48. Defendant A was charged with robbery. An expert gave opinion evidence that glass found on A's shoes came from a window that had been broken during the robbery. Samples of glass taken from the shoes and the window had the same refractive index. The expert stated that, according to statistics produced by the Home Office Research Establishment, the chances of the glass being from two distinct sources were minimal. A was convicted and appealed on the grounds that the statistics were hearsay. The Court of Appeal held that the statistics were secondary facts supporting the expert's opinion. So long as the primary facts (ie that the samples compared were: (a) glass taken from A's shoes and (b) glass from the robbery scene and they shared the same refractive index) were proved by admissible evidence, the expert could (indeed should) state why he arrived at his opinion on those facts.

Secondary facts cannot be introduced as evidence in the absence of an expert's opinion. For example, on a drink-driving charge a defendant who is not a medical expert cannot refer to a medical journal to support his defence. See *Dawson v Lunn* [1986] RTR 234. Note that the CJA 2003, s 127 allows proof of the primary facts through hearsay evidence in criminal cases.

17.3.6 Advance notice of expert evidence

17.3.6.1 Civil proceedings

The Civil Evidence Act 1972, s 2(3), made provision for rules of court to be made in relation to advance notice of expert evidence in civil cases. By CPR, r 35.13, a party who fails to disclose an expert's report may not use the report at the trial or call the expert to give evidence orally unless the court gives permission.

A party should be sure that he wishes to use the expert's report as evidence in his case *before* disclosing it to the other side. CPR, r 35.11, provides that *any* party to whom such a report is disclosed can put it in evidence. In general, an expert's advice that is sought by a party for the purposes of pending or contemplated litigation would be protected from disclosure (at any stage of the proceedings) by legal professional privilege (see **Chapter 19**) but r 35.11 makes it clear that the privilege is lost once the report has been disclosed under the advance notice procedure.

Even where a party relies on legal professional privilege in respect of an expert's opinion, it should be remembered that there is no property in a witness. A party who chooses not to use an expert's evidence can claim privilege in respect of the expert's opinion given to that party but he cannot muzzle the expert. Other parties to that litigation are entitled to instruct the expert and seek his opinion (subject to the procedural restrictions; see *Harmony Shipping Co SA v Saudi Europe Line Ltd* [1979] 1 WLR 1380, CA).

The amount of expert evidence that can be used in civil cases is affected by CPR, r 35.7(1), which provides:

Where two or more parties wish to submit expert evidence on a particular issue, the court may direct that the evidence on that issue is to be given by one expert only.

Unless the parties agree on the expert under this rule, the court may select an expert from a list submitted by the parties, or direct how the expert should be selected. Once selected, each instructing party may give instructions to the expert, sending a copy to the other instructing parties.

It has been held that under CPR, Part 35, the meaning of 'expert' is restricted to an expert who is instructed to give or prepare evidence for the purpose of court proceedings. Accordingly, CPR, Part 35 will not apply to a report which already exists and has been prepared by a third party for purposes other than to give or prepare evidence for court proceedings (see *Rogers v Hoyle* [2013] EWHC 1409 (QB)).

17.3.6.2 Criminal proceedings

The prosecution is obliged to disclose its expert evidence to the defence. The defence is also obliged to disclose such evidence. The procedure for disclosing expert evidence is set out in Crim PR, r 19.3:

19.3.—(1) A party who wants another party to admit as fact a summary of an expert's conclusions must serve that summary—

(a) on the court officer and on each party from whom that admission is sought;

(b) as soon as practicable after the defendant whom it affects pleads not guilty.

(2) A party on whom such a summary is served must—

(a) serve a response stating—

(i) which, if any, of the expert's conclusions are admitted as fact, and

(ii) where a conclusion is not admitted, what are the disputed issues concerning that conclusion; and

(b) serve the response—

(i) on the court officer and on the party who served the summary,

(ii) as soon as practicable, and in any event not more than 14 days after service of the summary.

(3) A party who wants to introduce expert evidence otherwise than as admitted fact must—

(a) serve a report by the expert which complies with rule 19.4 (Content of expert's report) on—

(i) the court officer, and

> (ii) *each other party;*
>
> (b) *serve the report as soon as practicable, and in any event with any application in support of which that party relies on that evidence;*
>
> (c) *serve with the report notice of anything of which the party serving it is aware which might reasonably be thought capable of detracting substantially from the credibility of that expert;*
>
> (d) *if another party so requires, give that party a copy of, or a reasonable opportunity to inspect—*
>
> (i) *a record of any examination, measurement, test or experiment on which the expert's findings and opinion are based, or that were carried out in the course of reaching those findings and opinion, and*
>
> (ii) *anything on which any such examination, measurement, test or experiment was carried out.*
>
> (4) *Unless the parties otherwise agree or the court directs, a party may not—*
>
> (a) *introduce expert evidence if that party has not complied with paragraph (3);*
>
> (b) *introduce in evidence an expert report if the expert does not give evidence in person.*

17.3.7 Opinion evidence and the hearsay rule

17.3.7.1 In civil proceedings

In civil proceedings, hearsay statements are rendered admissible by the Civil Evidence Act 1995, subject to ss 5 and 6(2) of the Act. 'Statement' is defined in s 13 of the Act for the purpose of civil proceedings as '*any representation of fact* or opinion *however made*' (author's emphasis). Accordingly, the fact that opinion evidence is presented as hearsay will not generally affect its admissibility in civil cases. This will apply to both expert opinion evidence (typically in the form of an expert report) and also to statements of opinion by witnesses of fact (where covered by the Civil Evidence Act 1972, s 3(2)).

17.3.7.2 In criminal proceedings

By the Criminal Justice Act 1988, s 30:

> (1) *An expert report shall be admissible as evidence in criminal proceedings, whether or not the person making it attends to give oral evidence in those proceedings.*
>
> (2) *If it is proposed that the person making the report shall not give oral evidence, the report shall only be admissible with the leave of the court.*
>
> (3) *For the purpose of determining whether to give leave the court shall have regard—*
>
> (a) *to the contents of the report;*
>
> (b) *to the reasons why it is proposed that the person making the report shall not give oral evidence;*
>
> (c) *to any risk, having regard in particular to whether it is likely to be possible to controvert statements in the report if the person making it does not attend to give oral evidence in the proceedings, that its admission or exclusion will result in unfairness to the accused or, if there is more than one, to any of them; and*
>
> (d) *to any other circumstances that appear to the court to be relevant.*
>
> (4) *An expert report, when admitted, shall be evidence of any fact or opinion of which the person making it could have given oral evidence.*
>
> (5) *In this section 'expert report' means a written report by a person dealing wholly or mainly with matters on which he is (or would if living be) qualified to give expert evidence.*

This section applies to statements of fact *and* opinion in the expert report. The effect is clear. It creates a hearsay exception specifically directed at expert reports. When the expert attends as a witness the report is admissible without leave. However, where the expert is not available as a witness the court's leave to use the report is required.

There is no specific provision applicable to criminal cases to allow out-of-court statements, which are essentially shorthand for facts perceived (cf the Criminal Evidence Act 1972, s 3(2)). However, CJA 2003, ss 114 and 115 allow out-of-court statements to be used in evidence, whether they are statements of fact or opinion.

17.3.8 Guidance for experts

17.3.8.1 Civil litigation

There is a Protocol on the appointment of experts in civil cases (see <http://www.judiciary.gov.uk> for the full content). It should be read in conjunction with CPR, Part 35 on the disclosure and use of expert evidence and PD 35 (PD 35.1).

Consistently with the overriding objective, the Protocol encourages early disclosure of information about expert issues involved in a prospective claim; also, that expert issues should be agreed where possible and as much as possible, prior to commencing litigation. This is in the hope of avoiding or at least minimising litigation. The Protocol applies to all experts who are governed by CPR, Part 35—this covers any expert who is instructed to give or prepare evidence for the purpose of civil proceedings in court (CPR, r 35.2). It follows that if an expert is instructed to provide an opinion to a client but the client does not intend to adduce the report in evidence at court, the Protocol and CPR, Part 35 do not apply to that expert. In particular, there would be no obligation to disclose the expert's report to other litigants, indeed it would usually be protected by legal professional privilege (see further **Chapter 19**).

Regardless of which party has instructed an expert, the expert owes a primary duty to help the court and enable it to comply with the overriding objective. This takes precedence over any duty to the client (CPR, r 35.3). In preparing a report, the expert must be independent—the Protocol suggests that a good test for this is whether the expert would offer the same opinion on an issue if instructed by the opposing party. In order to secure their independence, payment to an expert must not be dependent on their opinion, nor on whether the party instructing them succeeds at court; thus, an expert cannot be instructed on a conditional or contingency fee basis. There is no 'property' in an expert witness—once a report has been disclosed in litigation, it may be used in evidence at trial by any party (CPR, r 35.11).

A party does not need permission from a court to instruct an expert (eg simply to provide advice) but such permission will be needed if the party proposes to call the expert to give evidence, or rely on their report at court (CPR, r 35.4). In making its decision, a court will consider both the issues in the case and the proposed expert. The court looks at the relevance of the proposed expert's opinion to the issues that are disputed in the case and whether that evidence is 'reasonably required to resolve the proceedings' (CPR, r 35.1). The court will also consider whether the proposed expert actually has the necessary expertise and to the appropriate level. Finally, the court will consider whether appointing a single joint expert will do the job, or whether each party needs its own expert (bear in mind the 'independence' factor identified above).

17.3.8.1.1 Content of the expert report

The expert report should be addressed to the court and must contain certain statements: see PD 35. These include an acknowledgement that they are bound by an overriding duty to the court and must comply with CPR, Part 35 and the Protocol; additionally, there must be a 'statement of truth'. In small claims and cases in the fast-track, the written report will usually stand as the expert's evidence and there will be no oral evidence from the expert unless it is necessary in the interests of justice (CPR, r 35.5(2)). Standard form reports can be accessed via professional bodies such as the Expert Witness Institute. The report must set out relevant qualifications of the expert as well as all of the instructions given to them by the party retaining them. The report may contain both material facts ('primary facts') and literature or other material within the field ('secondary facts') on which their opinion is based. Where the content of the report falls outside their direct knowledge—for example, an analytical test was conducted by an assistant—that must be stated clearly. The methodologies used in any scientific tests must be described clearly.

The approach adopted by the CPR follows the guidance was given in the *Ikarian Reefer* case [1993] 2 Lloyd's Reports 68 as to expert evidence:

- expert evidence given to a court should be, and be seen to be, the independent product of the expert, uninfluenced as to form or content by the exigencies of litigation;
- the expert witness should offer independent assistance to the court by stating his objective unbiased opinion on matters within his expertise, and should never become in effect an advocate for a litigant;
- the expert should make it clear if a particular question or issue falls outside his expertise;
- the facts or assumptions upon which the expert's opinion is based must be stated. Material facts that detract from his opinion should be included;
- if the expert feels that he has been supplied with insufficient data properly to research a matter, then his opinion will be provisional and should be identified as such; and
- following exchange of reports, an expert may change his mind on a material matter. If so, the other party or parties (and the court where appropriate) should be told without delay.

17.3.8.1.2 *Changes to an expert report*

Parties who have instructed an expert, and who propose to either rely on a report or call the expert to give evidence at court, should pass on to them any relevant reports from other experts instructed in the proceedings, for consideration and possible comment. Experts may also meet or exchange questions and answers. Meetings may be by agreement or directed by the court (CPR, r 35.12) but will usually be disproportionate costs-wise in small claims and fast-track cases. If, as a result of these steps, the expert changes their opinion, it will be necessary to reduce that into writing. This will often take the form of a simple addendum to their report, signed and dated by the expert but, in a case of a significant change of opinion, the report will need to be amended. In *Stallwood v David* [2007] 1 All ER 206, the county court judge who was handling the pre-trial matters ruled against the claimant being allowed to call a second orthopaedic expert, following a change of mind by his initial expert. On appeal, the High Court said that such applications would rarely be successful. The applicant would need to show a good argument that the first expert had changed his mind (or modified his opinion) for reasons that could not properly support the revised position. Such reasons might include moving outside his field of expertise or otherwise showing himself to be incompetent.

Following disclosure of an expert report, written questions may be put to the expert (CPR, r 35.6). There is usually a limit of 28 days in which to do this. Answers will become part of the report and are covered by the statement of truth in the original report. Failure to answer may result in the court making an order that the party who instructed the expert cannot rely on the expert's evidence, or that the costs of the expert may not be recovered from the other party.

17.3.8.1.3 *Single joint experts*

This is possibly the hardest situation to grasp, given the typically adversarial nature of litigation. The essential point is that a court will look at the broader picture, rather than simply the wishes of the parties in having a 'champion' to advance their case. It is a matter of discretion for a judge whether to use a single joint expert (SJE)—'the court may direct that evidence on [an] issue is to be given by a single joint expert' (CPR, r 35.7). A judge will certainly consider the importance to the parties of the issue on which expert evidence is sought. However, the judge will also look at whether using an SJE is likely to assist with a speedier and more cost-effective resolution to the case than instructing separate experts. Another consideration is keeping the cost proportionate—so the judge will consider the complexity of the issue and the value of the dispute (see PD 35.7). Also, the field may be well settled with little scope for disagreement or it may be that a range of opinions could be offered. The main message is that the CPR (as the Protocol states) 'encourage the use of joint experts ... [and] wherever possible a joint report should be obtained'. They are 'the norm' in small claims and fast-track cases: see CPR, r 35.4(3A).

Once appointed, an SJE may receive instructions from any relevant party to the litigation and each party becomes liable, jointly and severally, for the expert's fees (unless the court directs otherwise). All instructions given to an SJE must be disclosed to the other parties. Once the SJE has reported, written questions can be asked by any relevant party, pursuant to CPR, r 35.6.

17.3.8.2 Criminal litigation

Guidance on expert evidence in criminal proceedings, with the aim of bringing it into line with civil cases, was given by the Court of Appeal in two cases in 2006 (*R v Harris* [2006] 1 Cr App R 5 and *R v Bowman* [2006] EWCA Crim 417). In November 2006, a new Part 33 was added to the Crim PR 2005, setting out a new scheme for adducing expert evidence in criminal trials. That scheme is now found in Part 19 of the Crim PR 2015. The rules explain the duty of the expert to the court—helping the court to achieve the overriding objective by giving his objective and unbiased opinion on matters within his expertise. Rule 19.2 states explicitly that this overrides any duty that the expert owes to the party calling him or paying for his services. In effect, the rules mirror those already well established in the CPR and are very similar to the guidance set out in *Harris* and *Bowman*.

Where both prosecution and defence wish to use expert evidence, the court can direct that their experts should discuss the relevant issues and prepare a statement for the court, identifying the issues on which they agree/disagree and giving reasons (r 19.6). Non-compliance with such direction by a party may result in the court ruling their expert's evidence inadmissible. The most controversial provision is probably r 19.7. This allows the court to direct that, in a case involving multiple defendants, if more than one defendant wishes to call expert evidence on the same issue at trial, they must use an SJE. Each of the defendants may then issue separate instructions to the SJE; those instructions must be disclosed to the other defendants (r 19.8). The court may also give directions about any examination, measurement, test, or experiment which the expert wishes to carry out (r 19.8(3)(b)).

Reference should also be made to the CPS guide for experts that it instructs, available at the CPS website: <https://www.cps.gov.uk/legal-guidance/disclosure-experts-evidence-case-management-and-unused-material-may-2010-guidance>.

This guide makes it clear that where an expert is instructed for the prosecution, the expert is obliged to record, retain, and reveal all the material generated, either in a witness statement or an expert report or, where appropriate, in an index of unused material. The guide follows previous guidance published when the Attorney-General made a statement to the House of Lords in February 2007 about Professor David Southall, an expert paediatrician who had been called as a prosecution witness in various trials but who found himself the subject of proceedings by the General Medical Council. The allegation there was that he had acted '*in a way which was not in the best interests of children and which amounted to keeping secret medical records on them*'. This was understood to affect possibly as many as 4,400 'special files' over a period of some ten years, although the number of cases affected by material non-disclosure (if any) was not clear.

17.3.9 Experts in cases involving children in the family courts

Expert evidence in the family courts is governed by s 13 of the Children and Families Act 2014, which provides that 'a person may not without the permission of the court instruct a person to provide expert evidence for use in children proceedings'. Evidence obtained without such permission will be inadmissible unless the court rules otherwise. The court may only give permission for expert evidence if the court is of the opinion that the expert evidence is necessary to assist the court to resolve the proceedings justly. When considering whether the expert evidence is necessary, the court is to have regard in particular to:

(a) any impact which giving permission would be likely to have on the welfare of the children concerned;

(b) the issues to which the expert evidence would relate;

(c) the questions which the court would require the expert to answer;

(d) what other expert evidence is available (whether obtained before or after the start of proceedings);

(e) whether evidence could be given by another person on the matters on which the expert would give evidence;

(f) the impact which giving permission would be likely to have on the timetable for, and duration and conduct of, the proceedings;

(g) the cost of the expert evidence; and

(h) any matters prescribed by Family Procedure Rules.

Part 25 of the Family Procedure Rules set out requirements in relation to expert witnesses. In order to improve the quality of expert evidence and to minimise delays in proceedings, the Appendix to PD 25B reflects the standards for expert witnesses drawn up by the Family Justice Council. It requires (amongst other things) that the expert has relevant expertise, has been active in the area of work or practice and is familiar with the breadth of current practice or opinion, has received appropriate training, and (if relevant) that the expert is regulated by and accredited to an appropriate registered body.

18

Judgments as evidence of the facts on which they are based

18.1 Introduction

That a judgment in a case that has already been decided can be relevant to a subsequent trial is unlikely to come as a surprise. The earlier case may have established a legal precedent or principle relevant to the issues in the later case or two cases may involve the same parties and issues so reference to the earlier judgment may prevent unnecessary repetition of litigation. A third possibility is that the facts that were proved in the earlier case may be relevant to the facts in a subsequent trial. It is this third option, the use of judgments as evidence of the facts on which they are based, that is the subject of this chapter.

18.2 The rule in *Hollington v F Hewthorn and Co Ltd*

Following the decision in *Hollington v F Hewthorn and Co Ltd* [1943] KB 587, the common law rule is that judgments are inadmissible at subsequent trials as evidence of the facts on which they are based. The case involved a road traffic accident in which the plaintiff's son was killed. The plaintiff brought an action in negligence against the driver of the vehicle and his employer. The driver had previously been convicted of careless driving in respect of the same incident and the plaintiff wished to admit the driver's conviction as evidence of negligence. The Court of Appeal held that the plaintiff was not entitled to do so on the basis that the court had no knowledge of the evidence heard at the criminal trial and the opinion of the criminal court was irrelevant. The use of the word 'irrelevant' in the case of *Hollington v F Hewthorn and Co Ltd* was explained in *Rogers v Hoyle* [2013] EWHC 1409 (QB) not to mean evidence lacking logical probative value, but rather that the opinion of another court is not a matter to which a court required to decide an issue should have regard; it is the duty of the court to form its own opinion on the basis of the evidence put before it.

Although a civil decision, the principle in *Hollington v F Hewthorn and Co Ltd* has been applied not only in the civil courts but also in the criminal courts. For example in *R v Spinks* [1982] 1 All ER 587, F's conviction for wounding with intent to cause grievous bodily harm (in which F was found to have stabbed someone) was held to be inadmissible at Spinks' trial for concealing F's knife with intent to impede the apprehension or prosecution of a person who had committed an arrestable offence, namely F. See also *Hassan* [1970] QB 423 in which a woman's previous convictions for prostitution were inadmissible as evidence against a man charged with living off her immoral earnings.

The result of the common law rule was that civil and criminal trials were often extended; issues that had already been proved in one court had to be proved again in subsequent trials. The inconvenience and the risks of inconsistent outcomes relating to this rule are obvious; the principle attracted much criticism. Since the implementation of the Civil Evidence Act 1968 (CEA 1968), the rule in *Hollington v F Hewthorn* and Co Ltd has been overruled in so far as the CEA 1968 governs the proof of criminal convictions and findings of paternity and adultery in civil proceedings. Similarly, the introduction of s 74 of PACE 1984 overruled the common law principle in so far as it allows for the admissibility of convictions in criminal proceedings. While the common law rule appears to remain valid in respect of other findings, the combined effect of the CEA 1968 and PACE 1984 has been to significantly reduce the impact of the principle in *Hollington v F Hewthorn and Co Ltd*.

18.3 The use of a previous judgment as evidence of the facts in a civil case

18.3.1 Use of a criminal conviction as evidence of the facts upon which it was based in a subsequent civil case

The CEA 1968, s 11 provides as follows:

> (1) *In any civil proceedings the fact that a person has been convicted of an offence by or before any court in the United Kingdom or by a court-martial there or elsewhere shall (subject to subsection (3) below) be admissible in evidence for the purpose of proving, where to do so is relevant to any issue in those proceedings, that he committed that offence, whether he was so convicted upon a plea of guilty or otherwise and whether or not he is a party to the civil proceedings; but no conviction other than a subsisting one shall be admissible in evidence by virtue of this section.*
>
> (2) *In any civil proceedings in which by virtue of this section a person is proved to have been convicted of an offence by or before any court in the United Kingdom or by a court-martial there or elsewhere—*
>
> (a) *he shall be taken to have committed that offence unless the contrary is proved; and*
>
> (b) *without prejudice to the reception of any other admissible evidence for the purpose of identifying the facts on which the conviction was based, the contents of any document which is admissible as evidence of the conviction, and the contents of the information, complaint, indictment or charge-sheet on which the person in question was convicted, shall be admissible in evidence for that purpose.*
>
> (3) *Nothing in this section shall prejudice the operation of section 13 of this Act or any other enactment whereby a conviction or a finding of fact in any criminal proceedings is for the purposes of any other proceedings made conclusive evidence of any fact.*
>
> (4) *Where in any civil proceedings the contents of any document are admissible in evidence by virtue of subsection (2) above, a copy of that document, or of the material part thereof, purporting to be certified or otherwise authenticated by or on behalf of the court or authority having custody of that document shall be admissible in evidence and shall be taken to be a true copy of that document or part unless the contrary is shown.*

This section reverses the rule in *Hollington v F Hewthorn and Co Ltd* in respect of criminal convictions that a party seeks to prove in a subsequent civil trial. Indeed, if the case of *Hollington v F Hewthorn and Co Ltd* were to be determined under s 11 of the CEA 1968, the conviction for careless driving would now be admissible evidence in the civil trial for negligence. It should be noted that under the CEA 1968, s 11, to be admissible the conviction must be a subsisting one, meaning that the conviction has not been quashed on appeal or a guilty plea has not been withdrawn. Further, the conviction must have been made by a UK court or court-martial; s 11 has no application to foreign convictions.

Where a conviction is proved through use of s 11, the CEA 1968, s 11(2) establishes a rebuttable presumption that the person so convicted did commit that offence. Should a party to proceedings deny that the convicted person committed the offence, that party bears the burden of proving that, on the balance of probabilities, the convicted person is not guilty of the offence. It is not enough merely to prove that the conviction was unsafe or that there was some technical defect in the conviction, for example a wrongful admission of evidence or a misdirection to the jury, or that the prosecution was an abuse of process (see *Raja v van Hoogstraten* [2005] EWHC 1642 (Ch)). This effectively reverses the legal burden of proof in respect of the commission of the offence.

18.3.1.1 Rebutting the presumption

There has been a divergence of opinion as to what weight should be attached to a conviction when a challenge is raised to it and a determination of whether a party has successfully rebutted the presumption under s 11(2) must be made. The matter was considered in *Taylor v Taylor* [1970] 1 WLR 1148 when Davies LJ considered (at [1152]) that:

> ... it is obvious that, when a man has been convicted by twelve of his fellow countrymen and countrywomen at a criminal trial, the verdict of the jury is a matter which is entitled to very great weight when the convicted person is seeking, in the words of the statute, to prove the contrary.

The same dispute divided the Court of Appeal in *Stupple v Royal Insurance Co Ltd* [1971] 1 QB 50. In that case, Lord Denning MR expressed similar views to Davies LJ, stating that the conviction was a weighty piece of evidence to overcome in seeking to prove that the offence was not committed. By contrast, Buckley LJ considered that proof of the conviction would simply give rise to the rebuttable presumption under s 11(2) without in itself carrying any evidential weight. While both Lord Denning MR and Buckley LJ's approaches have been followed in subsequent cases, the approach taken by Lord Denning MR is generally considered to best reflect the wording of the statute. Further support for the contention that a conviction carries weight can be found in the case of *Hunter v Chief Constable of the West Midlands Police* [1982] AC 529, in which Lord Diplock stated that a party seeking to challenge the presumption would face an 'uphill task', and more recently in the case of *CXX v DXX* [2012] EWHC 1535 (QB). The practical consequence is that it is likely to be very difficult for a party to successfully challenge the presumption that a convicted person committed the offence of which they stand convicted.

There has been further debate as to whether fresh evidence is required in order for a party to be permitted to challenge a criminal conviction at a subsequent civil trial. In *Brinks Ltd v Abu Saleh (No 1)* [1995] 4 All ER 65, per Jacob J, it was said that a convicted defendant must adduce fresh evidence that 'entirely changes the aspect of the case' in order to be permitted to contest a civil action based on the same facts. By contrast, when the matter was considered in *J v Oyston* [1999] 1 WLR 694, Smedley J held that it was entirely legitimate for Oyston to try and show that he had not committed rape and indecent assault even though he had no additional evidence beyond that which had already been considered at his trial or on appeal. The conflicting authorities were considered in *CXX v DXX* [2012] EWHC 1535 (QB) and the view in *J v Oyston* [1999] 1 WLR 694 was followed; it was held that a defendant to civil proceedings may assert in good faith that he did not commit an offence for which he has been convicted without giving rise to an abuse of process. While it may be difficult for a party to successfully rebut the presumption under s 11, especially without fresh evidence, it must be a matter for that party to decide whether or not to attempt it.

It seems that the position is different however where a claimant initiates civil proceedings with a view to re-litigating a matter that has already been determined against him or her by a criminal court (ie a convicted defendant seeks to challenge the correctness of the conviction by initiating a civil claim against the prosecuting authority). In these circumstances, the claim is likely to be struck out as an abuse of process under CPR, r 3.4(2)(b) (see *Hunter v Chief Constable of the West Midlands Police* [1982] AC 529).

18.3.1.2 Practical considerations

Where a claimant seeks to rely on evidence under s 11, CPR Practice Direction 16, para 8.1 requires that a statement to that effect be included in his or her particulars of claim, together with details of the type of conviction, its date, the court or court-martial that made it, and the issue to which it relates. Section 11(2)(b) provides for the admissibility of certain documents for the purpose of identifying the facts on which the conviction is based, while s 11(4) allows a certified copy of the conviction, indictment, etc to be used to prove the facts on which the conviction was based.

18.3.2 Findings of adultery and paternity

Section 12 of the CEA 1968 enables previous findings of adultery in matri-monial proceedings and findings of paternity to be admissible in subsequent civil proceed-ings for the purpose of proving those facts. Section 12 reflects s 11 in that it creates a rebuttable presumption in relation to those findings. The party seeking to disprove the findings of adultery or paternity must do so on the balance of probabilities (*Sutton v Sutton* [1970] 1 WLR 183). 'Matrimonial proceedings' are defined to include, *inter alia*, any matrimonial cause in the High Court or family courts in England or Wales, or in the High Court in Northern Ireland.

The CEA 1968, s 12 (as amended by the Family Law Reform Act 1987) provides that:

> *(1) In any civil proceedings—*
>
> *(a) the fact that a person has been found guilty of adultery in any matrimonial proceedings; and*
>
> *(b) the fact that a person has been found to be the father of a child in relevant proceedings before any court in England and Wales or Northern Ireland or has been adjudged to be the father of a child in affiliation proceedings before any court in the United Kingdom;*
>
> *shall (subject to subsection (3) below) be admissible in evidence for the purpose of proving, where to do so is relevant to any issue in those civil proceedings, that he committed the adultery to which the finding relates or, as the case may be, is (or was) the father of that child, whether or not he offered any defence to the allegation of adultery or paternity and whether or not he is a party to the civil proceedings; but no finding or adjudication other than a subsisting one shall be admissible in evidence by virtue of this section.*
>
> *(2) In any civil proceedings in which by virtue of this section a person is proved to have been found guilty of adultery as mentioned in subsection (1)(a) above or to have been found or adjudged to be the father of a child as mentioned in subsection (1)(b) above—*
>
> *(a) he shall be taken to have committed the adultery to which the finding relates or, as the case may be, to be (or have been) the father of that child, unless the contrary is proved; and*
>
> *(b) without prejudice to the reception of any other admissible evidence for the purpose of identifying the facts on which the finding or adjudication was based, the contents of any document which was before the court, or which contains any pronouncement of the court, in the other proceedings in question shall be admissible in evidence for that purpose.*

18.3.3 Use of convictions in defamation cases

Following the recommendation of the Fifteenth Report of the Law Reform Committee (1967) (Cmnd 3391), s 13 of the CEA 1968 creates a conclusive presumption in defamation cases that, once a person is proved to have been convicted of an offence, he did commit that offence. This section prevents a convicted criminal from abusing defamation proceedings to attempt to reopen a conviction. It was the view of the Law Reform Committee that no one should be at risk of incurring civil liability through stating that a person had committed an offence for which he or she stood convicted; the legislation aims to protect writers and publishers who rely on a conviction for the truth of what they write or publish. Although s 13 does not give publishers liberty to make general attacks on convicts' characters (see *Levene v Roxhan* [1970] 1 WLR 1322), the effect of s 13 is that an action in defamation will be struck out if it is based on the defendant's assertion that the claimant committed an offence for which the claimant has been convicted.

The CEA 1968, s 13 (as amended by the Defamation Act 1996 and the Armed Forces Act 2006) states:

> (1) *In an action for libel or slander in which the question whether the plaintiff did or did not commit a criminal offence is relevant to an issue arising in the action, proof that, at the time when that issue falls to be determined, he stands convicted of that offence shall be conclusive evidence that he committed that offence; and his conviction thereof shall be admissible in evidence accordingly.*
>
> (2) *In any such action as aforesaid in which by virtue of this section the plaintiff is proved to have been convicted of an offence the contents of any document which is admissible as evidence of the conviction, and the contents of the information, complaint, indictment or charge-sheet on which he was convicted, shall, without prejudice to the reception of any other admissible evidence for the purpose of identifying the facts on which the conviction was based, be admissible in evidence for the purpose of identifying those facts.*
>
> (2A) *In the case of an action for libel or slander in which there is more than one plaintiff:*
>
> (a) *the references in subsections (1) and (2) above to the plaintiff shall be construed as references to any of the plaintiffs, and*
>
> (b) *proof that any of the plaintiffs stands convicted of an offence shall be conclusive evidence that he committed that offence so far as that fact is relevant to any issue arising in relation to his cause of action or that of any other plaintiff.*
>
> (3) *For the purposes of this section a person shall be taken to stand convicted of an offence if but only if there subsists against him a conviction of that offence by or before a court in the United Kingdom or (in the case of a service offence) a conviction (anywhere) of that service offence.*

18.3.4 Use of a criminal acquittal as evidence of the facts upon which it was based in a subsequent civil case

An acquittal is not covered by any exception in the CEA 1968, so it appears that the rule in *Hollington v F Hewthorn and Co Ltd* still applies: the acquittal is inadmissible evidence if used to show that the criminal defendant is innocent of an offence. This may be justified by reference to the different standards of proof that apply in criminal and civil trials.

18.4 Use of a previous judgment as evidence of the facts in criminal cases

18.4.1 Use of a criminal conviction as evidence of the facts upon which it was based in a subsequent criminal case

Under the common law rule, judgments were inadmissible in criminal trials as evidence of the facts on which they were based. For example, if A were charged with handling stolen goods, B's conviction for theft of those goods would be inadmissible at A's trial to prove that the goods were stolen (*R v Turner* (1832) 1 Mood CC 347).

The Eleventh Report of the Criminal Law Revision Committee (Cmnd 4991) recommended that a provision corresponding to the CEA 1968, s 11 be introduced to allow for the admissibility of previous convictions of persons other than the accused. Section 74 of PACE 1984 gave effect to this recommendation, but went further to also allow for the fact of an accused's previous convictions to be presented at trial. Where the fact of the conviction is admissible under PACE 1984, s 74, a rebuttable presumption arises that the relevant person did commit that offence.

PACE 1984, ss 74 and 75 (as amended by the CJA 2003 and Coroners and Justice Act 2009), provide that:

> 74(1) *In any proceedings the fact that a person other than the accused has been convicted of an offence by or before any court in the United Kingdom or any other member state or by a Service court outside the United Kingdom shall be admissible in evidence for the purpose of proving that that person committed that offence, where evidence of his having done so is admissible, whether or not any other evidence of his having committed that offence is given.*
>
> (2) *In any proceedings in which by virtue of this section a person other than the accused is proved to have been convicted of an offence by or before any court in the United Kingdom or any other member state or by a Service court outside the United Kingdom, he shall be taken to have committed that offence unless the contrary is proved.*
>
> (3) *In any proceedings where evidence is admissible of the fact that the accused has committed an offence, if the accused is proved to have been convicted of the offence—*
>
> (a) *by or before any court in the United Kingdom or any other member State; or*
>
> (b) *by a Service court outside the United Kingdom,*
>
> *he shall be taken to have committed that offence unless the contrary is proved.*
>
> 75(1) *Where evidence that a person has been convicted of an offence is admissible by virtue of section 74 above, then without prejudice to the reception of any other admissible evidence for the purpose of identifying the facts on which the conviction was based—*
>
> (a) *the contents of any document which is admissible as evidence of the conviction; and*
>
> (b) *the contents of—*
>
> (i) *the information, complaint, indictment or charge-sheet on which the person in question was convicted, or*
>
> (ii) *in the case of a conviction of an offence by a court in a member State (other than the United Kingdom), any document produced in relation to the proceedings for that offence which fulfils a purpose similar to any document or documents specified in sub-paragraph (i),*
>
> *shall be admissible in evidence for that purpose.*

Like s 11 of the CEA 1968, s 74 is limited to subsisting convictions, meaning that a plea of guilty has not been withdrawn nor has the conviction been quashed on appeal (s 75(4)). Unlike s 11 of the CEA 1968, s 74 applies not only to convictions made by courts in the United Kingdom but also to convictions made in other EU member states. Section 74 also applies to convictions before a 'Service court'; this is a court-martial or any Standing Civilian Court. Foreign convictions made by non-EU states are not covered by s 74 but may now be admissible under the bad character provisions of the CJA 2003, and, if admissible, may be proved under the Evidence Act 1851, s 7. As s 99(1) of the CJA 2003 abolished all 'common law rules governing the admissibility of criminal convictions', the rule in *Hollington v F Hewthorn and Co Ltd* will no longer apply to criminal convictions in criminal courts, including foreign convictions.

Where a conviction is admissible in criminal proceedings, PACE 1984, s 73 provides a method of proving that conviction. This is achieved by producing a certificate of conviction (or acquittal as appropriate) and proving the identity of the person named on that certificate as the person whose conviction (or acquittal) is to be proved. Where the prosecution wishes to rely on a conviction and the accused disputes that he or she is the party named on the certificate, the prosecution must prove that the accused is the person named on the certificate beyond reasonable doubt (see *Pattison v DPP* [2006] 2 All ER 317 for further guidance).

18.4.2 Convictions of persons other than the accused

Under s 74(1) the fact that a person other than the accused has been convicted of an offence is admissible to prove that that person committed that offence. There is no statutory guidance as to when a conviction will be admissible under s 74(1). It follows that PACE 1984, s 74 does not affect the law governing the admissibility of a past misconduct and the normal rules of admissibility apply (for which see the CJA 2003 in **Chapters 9** and **10**). The concept of relevance is of key importance to the rules of admissibility. The original wording of s 74(1) expressly referred to the fact of a conviction being admissible where it was '*relevant to any issue in the proceedings*', in contrast to the current wording which allows for the fact of a conviction to be adduced '*where evidence of his having done so is admissible*'. The difference between the original and current wording is essentially cosmetic; to be admissible the conviction must be relevant to an issue in proceedings, hence cases decided under the original wording of s 74(1) still have application under the current, amended wording.

The conviction of a person other than the accused may be relevant in establishing an essential element of the offence with which the accused is charged. For example, if A transfers goods to B and they are jointly charged with handling stolen goods, A's guilty plea to the offence may now be admissible at B's trial to prove that the goods were stolen. See *R v Pigram* [1995] Crim LR 808, CA. However, in *R v Robertson; R v Golder* [1987] 3 All ER 231, CA, it was held that the commission of an offence may be relevant to less fundamental evidential issues in proceedings. It was also held that s 74(1) could apply to convictions in which the accused on trial participated. In *Robertson*, the defendant was charged with conspiracy to commit burglary. The co-accused entered guilty pleas to some 16 burglaries committed during the period of the conspiracy, but entered a not guilty plea to conspiracy. It was held that the 16 burglary convictions were admissible because it could be inferred from these offences that there had been a conspiracy between Robinson and the co-accused. In *Golder*, the defendant was charged with robbery committed at garage 1 and entered a not guilty plea. Two co-accused entered guilty pleas to that robbery and also to another robbery which took place at garage 2. The prosecution relied on a confession statement made by Golder in which he made reference to both robberies; Golder denied making the confession and suggested that it had been fabricated by the police. It was held that the guilty pleas of the co-accused were admissible as proof that there had been a robbery at garage 1 and as relevant evidence suggesting Golder's guilt because the content of the confession was in accordance with the known facts of the robbery committed by the two co-accused at garage 2. The broad interpretation of relevance to an issue in proceedings as established by *R v Robertson; R v Golder* was applied in the case of *R v Castle* [1989] Crim LR 567, and has been followed in subsequent cases.

Where the fact of a conviction is admissible under s 74(1) of the Act, s 74(2) creates a rebuttable presumption that the person so convicted did commit that offence. Should a party seek to rebut the presumption and disprove the commission of the offence, the legal burden is borne by that party. Where the accused bears the legal burden, he or she discharges it on the balance of probabilities; the standard of proof borne by the prosecution remains beyond reasonable doubt.

18.4.2.1 The discretion to exclude

It should be noted that, where the prosecution seek to rely on the convictions of a person other than the accused under s 74 of PACE 1984, the court may exclude the evidence under s 78 of that Act. In *Robertson* it was stressed that s 74 should be used sparingly and it was noted that there will be occasions where, although the evidence may be technically admissible, it would be wiser not to adduce it. It was also observed that the judge should be careful to explain to the jury the effect of the evidence and its limitations where evidence is admitted under s 74.

There is particular need for care when determining whether to exclude evidence under s 78 in cases involving joint offences like conspiracy and affray. This is clearly illustrated by the case of *O'Connor* (1987) 85 Cr App R 298, in which B and C were jointly charged with conspiracy (with each other and no other parties) to obtain property by deception. B's guilty plea was admitted at C's trial. The Court of Appeal held that B's conviction should have been excluded under PACE 1984, s 78 on the basis that the jury might have inferred from B's conviction for conspiring with C, that C must have conspired with B. In *Curry* [1988] Crim LR 527, it was held that s 74 should be used sparingly in such cases, especially where the fact of a conviction, expressly or by inference, suggests the complicity of the accused.

Whether a conviction that is admissible under s 74 should be excluded under s 78 will ultimately depend on the particular facts of the case. Where a conviction is admissible under s 74, an appeal against the judge's decision not to exclude it under s 78 will only be allowed if the decision was made on a false basis or it was a decision that no judge could reasonably have made. (See *Abdullah* [2010] EWCA Crim 3078, following *Smith* [2007] EWCA Crim 2105.)

18.4.3 Convictions of the accused

Under PACE 1984, s 74(3) an accused's conviction is admissible as evidence of the commission of that offence and the accused shall be taken to have committed that offence unless the contrary is proved. Should the accused seek to rebut this presumption, he or she bears the legal burden of disproving that he or she committed that offence on the balance of probabilities.

Like s 74(1) and (2), s 74(3) does not define the circumstances in which the accused's convictions may be admissible but assists in proving the fact of the conviction where such evidence is admissible. There are four situations when s 74(3) applies. The first arises when the accused denies committing a previous offence on which the prosecution seek to rely as proof of an element of the offence with which the accused is charged. The second arises where the prosecution seek to adduce relevant evidence of the accused's misconduct, or the accused's disposition towards misconduct, that 'has to do with' the alleged facts of the offence charged under the CJA 2003, s 98(a). The third arises where the accused's commission of an offence, other than that with which he or she is charged, is admissible under s 101 of the CJA 2003 as evidence of bad character. The fourth occurs where the conviction has been proved as part of the prosecution case pursuant to statutory provisions such as s 101 of the CJA 2003, s 27(3)(a) of the Theft Act 1968, or s 1(2) of the Official Secrets Act 1911, and the accused disputes the commission of the offence in question.

Where an accused seeks to rebut the presumption under PACE 1984, s 74(3), the principles set out in C [2011] 1 WLR 1942 allow for both sides to adduce evidence without turning the trial into a retrial of the offence in question. Following C, the Court of Appeal in *Lunkulu* [2015] EWCA Crim 1350 noted that, if an accused fails to call any evidence to dispute his guilt in respect of a previous offence of which he was convicted, then the court must presume that he is guilty of that previous offence. It is essential that the accused's defence case statement raises all elements of the case which the accused will advance in order to rebut the presumption so that the prosecution can prepare any necessary admissions of fact and collate their evidence.

Where the prosecution seek to rely on evidence of an accused's previous conviction, such evidence may be excluded under PACE 1984, s 78.

18.4.4 Use of a criminal acquittal as evidence of the facts upon which it was based in a subsequent criminal case

Where an accused or a person other than the accused has been acquitted of an offence, unless there is some exceptional feature, the fact of the acquittal is generally irrelevant and therefore inadmissible at a subsequent trial (see *Hui Chi-ming v R* [1991] 3 All ER 897, PC). The rationale is that the decision of the jury is an irrelevant opinion because it is not possible to say why the jury acquitted. An exception to this rule may arise where a witness's credibility is directly in issue at trial and where it can clearly be inferred from the verdict at a previous trial that the jury rejected that witness's evidence because they did not believe him or her (see *D* [2007] EWCA Crim 684). Even where an acquittal is admissible, it does not conclusively evidence innocence nor does an acquittal mean that all relevant issues were resolved in the accused's favour, rather it records that the prosecution failed to prove all elements of the offence to the criminal standard and make the jury sure of the accused's guilt (see *R v Terry* [2005] QB 996, *Coleman* [2004] EWCA Crim 3252, and *Preko* [2015] EWCA Crim 42).

Where evidence of an acquittal is admissible, PACE 1984, s 73 provides the method for proof of that acquittal, for which see **18.4.1** above.

18.4.5 Use of a civil judgment as evidence of the facts upon which it was based in a subsequent criminal case

Owing to the lower standard of proof in civil trials, any finding of fact would be insufficiently probative to be admissible as evidence in a criminal trial. A civil judgment against an accused would have no material value in establishing the accused's criminal liability in any criminal trial.

19

Privilege and public policy

19.1 Introduction

This chapter concerns the exclusion of relevant evidence on grounds of privilege or public policy. Privilege operates to exclude relevant evidence because the value of admitting it is outweighed by more important principles, namely the rights of parties to be advised confidentially by their legal advisers, to enter into negotiations without being bound by what is said in the negotiation process, and to be free from being compelled to answer questions where to do so would be self-incriminating. Public policy operates to exclude relevant evidence because the value in admitting it is outweighed by the harm that would be caused to the national or public interest.

Privilege and public policy issues are most likely to arise during the pre-trial disclosure process in civil cases (see Sime, ***A Practical Approach to Civil Procedure*** or the ***White Book***) and criminal cases (see the ***Criminal Litigation and Sentencing*** manual), although such issues may also arise during the course of trials.

19.2 Privilege

In broad terms privilege allows a party to prevent evidence from being put before the court on specific grounds. The types of privilege are:

- the privilege against self-incrimination;
- legal professional privilege; and
- 'without prejudice' correspondence.

19.2.1 Privilege against self-incrimination

The privilege against self-incrimination has influenced the development of the rules of evidence and procedure in a number of areas, notably, the exercise of the right to silence (**Chapter 15**) and the compellability of witnesses (**Chapter 4**).

The privilege against self-incrimination has a more general application than legal professional privilege and the privilege that attaches to 'without prejudice' correspondence. Under the privilege, no person is obliged to reveal a fact if doing so renders it reasonably likely that proceedings will be commenced that expose him to the risk of any criminal charge or sanction (*Blunt v Park Lane Hotel Ltd* [1942] 2 KB 253). Explaining this test in

R v Boyes (1861) 1 B & S 311, Cockburn J said that the risk of prosecution and punishment must be '*real and appreciable with reference to the ordinary operation of the law in the ordinary course of things; not a danger of an imaginary and unsubstantial character*'. The privilege does not apply where the risk posed is a civil liability (Witnesses Act 1806) or criminal liability under foreign law (*King of Two Sicilies v Willcox* (1851) 1 Sim NS 301; Civil Evidence Act 1968, s 14) but can extend to penalties under EC law (*Rio Tinto Zinc Corporation v Westinghouse Electric Company* [1978] AC 547).

The privilege against self-incrimination is also enshrined in Article 6 of the ECHR. In *Saunders v United Kingdom* (1996) 23 EHRR 313, it was observed that:

> The right to silence and the right not to incriminate oneself, are generally recognised international standards which lie at the heart of the notion of a fair procedure under article 6 ... the right not to incriminate oneself, in particular, presupposes that the prosecution in the criminal case seek to prove their case against the accused without resort to evidence obtained through methods of coercion or oppression in defiance of the will of the accused. In this sense the right is closely linked to the presumption of innocence contained in article 6(2).

The privilege extends not only to the evidence that the person might give but to documents, items, or information that the person is requested to provide during proceedings.

19.2.1.1 'Real and appreciable danger'

The evidence must *create* the risk of incrimination. If there is already strong evidence against the witness on the matter to which the privilege is said to relate, the privilege will not apply (*Khan v Khan* [1982] 2 All ER 60). Furthermore, if the risk can be avoided, the privilege will not apply. So, in *AT & T Istel v Tully* [1993] AC 45, HL, an offer by the CPS not to prosecute the defendant in respect of any frauds revealed was held to be sufficient protection for the defendant to prevent the privilege from applying. In *Beghal v DPP* [2015] UKSC 49, the Supreme Court held that where answers had been obtained under compulsion (using powers under the Terrorism Act 2000 which made it a criminal offence not to cooperate), it would breach Article 6 of the ECHR which guarantees the right to a fair trial if those answers were used in criminal proceedings. Because such evidence would be excluded from any criminal trial (using the court's power under PACE 1984, s 78) there would be no real and appreciable risk of self-incrimination. This was reiterated in *R (on the application of DPP) v Leicester Magistrates' Court* [2015] EWHC 1295 (Admin), where additionally there was an express assurance from the Crown that the witness would not be prosecuted.

Where the sanction or punishment that is faced is trivial, the court may also conclude that there is no real and appreciable danger (*Rank Film Distributors Ltd v Video Information Centre* [1982] AC 380).

19.2.1.2 To whom does the privilege apply?

In criminal cases the privilege only applies to the person asserting it. In other words, A could not exercise the privilege on the grounds that his answer would incriminate B (this is implicit from *R v Pitt* [1983] QB 25, where a witness was treated as compellable to give evidence against her spouse: this would not have been the case if she could have asserted a privilege against incriminating her spouse). In civil cases the privilege extends to spouses (Civil Evidence Act 1968, s 14(1)(b)).

Companies can also be covered by the privilege (*Triplex Safety Glass Co Ltd v Lancegaye Safety Glass* [1939] 2 KB 395). However, in such circumstances, the privilege excuses an employee of the company from giving testimony (or disclosing evidence) which would incriminate the company; it does not excuse him from incriminating an employee of the company (*Rio Tinto Zinc v Westinghouse Electric*) other than himself.

19.2.1.3 Privileged evidence that is revealed

If a witness answers questions without claiming the privilege, the evidence can be used against the witness in subsequent proceedings (*R v Coote* (1873) LR 4 PC 599). However, if the witness does claim privilege and is wrongly refused (and therefore forced to answer), the evidence must be excluded in the subsequent proceedings (*R v Garbett* (1847) 1 Den CC 236).

19.2.1.4 Statutory exceptions

19.2.1.4.1 Express statutory exceptions

The privilege is subject to numerous statutory exceptions. First of all, the privilege does not protect the accused in criminal proceedings from answering questions in respect of those proceedings (Criminal Evidence Act 1898, s 1(2)).

Evidence that reveals criminal conduct may be admitted in specific types of proceedings, examples of which are set out here. However, in each type of proceedings, there are restrictions on the extent to which the information revealed can be used in subsequent criminal proceedings.

(a) Under the Theft Act 1968, s 31(1), in proceedings concerning the recovery or administration of property, the execution of any trust or an account for property or dealings with property, a person has no privilege against answering questions simply because doing so would reveal that he may have committed an offence. However, any statement or testimony made is not admissible in a subsequent prosecution under the Theft Act 1968. This protection also extends to the spouse of the witness. If the evidence poses a real risk of both a Theft Act and a non-Theft Act prosecution the court will apply the privilege against self-incrimination (*Renworth Ltd v Stephansen* [1996] 3 All ER 244) with the effect that the person is not obliged to answer the question.

(b) A similar provision is contained in the Criminal Damage Act 1971, s 9 in connection with offences under that Act.

(c) A similar provision is contained in the Fraud Act 2006, s 13 in connection with offences under that Act or any 'related offence'. 'Related offence' is defined by the 2006 Act as conspiracy to defraud and any other offence involving any form of fraudulent conduct or purpose (s 13(4)).

(d) Under the Children Act 1989, s 98, in proceedings concerning the care, supervision, or protection of children, a person cannot refuse to answer questions on the grounds that that person or his spouse would be incriminated. Again, however, such evidence will not be admissible in subsequent proceedings other than perjury proceedings (s 98(2)). It has been suggested that this protection extends to oral or written statements made before trial (*Oxfordshire County Council v P* [1995] 2 All ER 225; *Cleveland County Council v F* [1995] 2 All ER 236). However, in *Re G (A Minor)* [1996] 2 All ER 65, the Court of Appeal stated that the protection under s 98(2) should be restricted to evidence in the proceedings and not pre-trial statements. However, the court recognised that the criminal courts were not bound by that view. In *A Chief Constable v A County Council* [2003] 1 FLR 579, the court took the view that statements made by parents to expert witnesses appointed by the court would be covered by s 98(2) privilege and therefore would not be admissible in subsequent criminal proceedings.

(e) Under the Criminal Justice Act 1987, s 2, the Director of the Serious Fraud Office has broad powers to investigate persons in respect of offences of serious or complex fraud (ie those under Part 1 of that Act). Persons investigated can be required to answer questions or provide documentation. Such evidence can only be used at a later trial if the person is being prosecuted for the offence of providing false information under s 2 or subsequently makes a statement inconsistent with it (ie as a previous inconsistent statement—see **7.7**).

(f) Under the Insolvency Act 1986, various statements which a person must make could be incriminating. Section 433(1) of the Act provides that such statements may be used in evidence against the person who made them in subsequent proceedings. Section 433(2), however, provides that in subsequent criminal proceedings such statements may only be admitted (or questions asked about them) if the person who made the statement has already admitted evidence relating to that statement. This restriction does not apply in relation to perjury and related proceedings or criminal proceedings under the Insolvency Act itself.

(g) Similar restrictions to those under the Insolvency Act apply in relation to investigations under the Companies Act 1985, ss 434 and 447 and various other statutes in Sch 3 to the Youth Justice and Criminal Evidence Act 1999.

(h) Under the Terrorism Act 2000, Sch 7 permits an officer to take steps to determine whether a person either is, or has been, concerned in the commission, preparation, or instigation of acts of terrorism. This includes powers to stop and detain a person in order to question them or to search them, powers to require a person to produce document or electronic storage device, and a power to copy and retain that document or electronic data. Failure to comply is a criminal offence, punishable by a fine and a maximum of three months' imprisonment. In *Beghal v DPP* [2015] UKSC 49, the Supreme Court held that it would breach a person's right to a fair trial to use evidence obtained using the Sch 7 power in criminal proceedings and that therefore such evidence would be excluded from a criminal trial using the court's powers under PACE 1984, s 78.

19.2.1.4.2 Implied statutory exceptions

Other statutes, especially those creating investigatory powers, may impliedly abrogate the privilege against self-incrimination on the ground that the power created by the statute would otherwise be largely ineffective. The question of whether a statute which confers a power to ask questions or obtain documents or information excludes the privilege against self-incrimination in one or other of its forms is therefore one of construction. However, in the process of construction, the court must balance the public interest in obtaining the information, the extent to which the right to silence would be affected by the power and the strength of the grounds for preserving it (*R v Hertfordshire CC, ex p Green Environmental Industries Ltd* [2000] 2 AC 412, HL).

Where the privilege is abrogated impliedly it will be without restriction as to the use to which the material may be put. There is a potential breach of Article 6(1) of the ECHR, but this is not always so. In *Brown v Stott* [2001] 2 WLR 817, the Privy Council recognised that Article 6 rights are subject to a limited qualification. Where there was a clear public interest in revoking the privilege, the statutory provision would not necessarily be held to be incompatible with Article 6. In *Office of Fair Trading v X* [2003] 2 All ER (Comm) 183, the High Court upheld powers to search premises and to question persons present about items found during the search where the statutory framework for such searches included guarantees of a suspect's rights. *R v K* [2009] EWCA Crim 1640 concerned the abrogation of the privilege in relation to evidence given in ancillary relief proceedings under the Matrimonial Causes Act 1973 and the operation of Article 6 to limit the use of that evidence in subsequent criminal proceedings. In *K*, it was held that evidence given by parties about their financial circumstances in accordance with obligations under the Family Proceedings Rules 1991 during ancillary relief proceedings under the Matrimonial Causes Act 1973 could not be used in subsequent criminal proceedings for cheating the public revenue. The court held that the Family Proceedings Rules, by stating that a party would be liable to prosecution for perjury if deliberately untruthful, had intended to abrogate the privilege against self-incrimination in ancillary relief proceedings for the obvious purpose of ensuring that the legislation was effective. However, to then use the evidence in criminal proceedings for cheating the public revenue would violate Article 6. Although there was a strong public interest in protecting the public revenue, the court held using evidence disclosed in the face of a threat of imprisonment was a disproportionate means of protecting that interest.

19.2.1.5 Material that is independent of the will of the suspect

The right not to incriminate oneself does not extend to the use in criminal proceedings of material which may be obtained from the accused through compulsory powers but which has an existence independent of the will of the suspect, such as, *inter alia*, documents acquired pursuant to a warrant, breath, blood, and urine samples, and bodily tissue for the purpose of DNA testing (*Saunders v United Kingdom*, referred to earlier). This principle is well established in domestic law (see, eg, *Attorney-General's Reference (No 7 of 2001)* [2001] 2 Cr App R 19 and *R v Hundal and Dhaliwal* [2004] 2 Cr App R 19) and is summarised by Aikens J in *R v Kearns* [2003] 1 Cr App R 7 as follows:

> There is a distinction between the compulsory production of documents or other material which have an existence independent of the will of the suspect or accused person and statements that he has had to make under compulsion. In the former case there is no infringement of the right to silence and the right not to incriminate oneself. In the latter case there could be, depending on the circumstances.

Where the defendant is in possession of a key to access encrypted material on a computer, the key exists independently of his will but his knowledge of the key may attract the privilege against self-incrimination. It follows that when a lawful request is made to disclose it (under s 49 of the Regulation of Investigatory Powers Act 2000) he cannot refuse, although how the prosecution came to access the material could be excluded at trial under PACE 1984, s 78 (*R v S* [2009] 1 All ER 716).

This principle has also been applied in civil proceedings (see *C plc v P (Secretary of State for the Home Office)* [2007] 3 All ER 1034).

19.2.2 Legal professional privilege

Both civil and criminal litigation depends upon parties having access to effective legal advice. This in turn depends upon a party and his lawyer being able to communicate freely and without fear that the content of the discussion will be used by the other side. Furthermore, legal professional privilege is a function of Article 6 of the ECHR (*S v Switzerland* (1991) 14 EHRR 670; *Foxley v United Kingdom* (2001) 31 EHRR 25).

There are two classes of legal professional privilege, which broadly are:

(a) communications between a lawyer and his client (also known as 'lawyer–client privilege' or 'legal advice privilege'); and

(b) communications between the lawyer or client, on the one hand, and third parties, on the other, where such communication relates to pending or contemplated litigation (*Waugh v British Railways Board* [1980] AC 521; also known as 'litigation privilege').

Under both classes the privilege applies to communication with solicitors, barristers, foreign lawyers, and in-house legal advisers (*Re Duncan* [1968] P 306; *Alfred Compton Amusement Machines Ltd v Customs & Excise Commissioners* [1974] AC 405).

19.2.2.1 Lawyer–client privilege

Communications between a lawyer and his client for the purposes of obtaining or giving legal advice are privileged whether or not litigation is contemplated (*Greenough v Gaskell* (1833) 1 My & K 98).

The rationale for the privilege is that if the advice given by lawyers is to be sound, their clients must make them aware of all the relevant circumstances of the problem. Clients will be reluctant to do so, however, unless they can be sure that what they say about any potentially damaging or embarrassing circumstances will not be revealed later (*per* Lord Carswell in *Three Rivers District Council v Bank of England (No 6)* [2005] 1 AC 610).

'Lawyer' for these purposes includes solicitors, barristers, foreign lawyers, and salaried in-house lawyers (*Re Duncan* [1968] P 306; *Alfred Crompton Amusement Machines Ltd v Customs & Excise Commissioners* [1974] AC 405). However, a 'lawyer' does not include professionals other than lawyers even though they may have specialist knowledge of the law and advise on it, for example, accountants with expertise in tax law. In *R (Prudential plc) v Special Commissioners of Income Tax* [2011] 2 WLR 50, CA, it was held that legal professional privilege applied only to members of the legal professions of England and Wales and by extension, foreign legal professionals. It did not cover a person who was not a lawyer, even though that person might be a member of another profession and gave legal advice which he or she was competent to give.

Not all communications between a lawyer and his client are privileged: they must be made in the context of a lawyer–client relationship and for the purposes of legal advice. In *Greenhough v Gaskell* (1833) 1 My & K 98, it was held that communications made before the lawyer–client relationship existed or after it ceased would not be privileged. However, the rule was broadened slightly by *Minter v Priest* [1930] AC 558 where it was held that communications passing between a solicitor and a prospective client with a view to the client retaining the solicitor on professional business were privileged from disclosure, even if the solicitor did not accept the retainer.

What constitutes 'legal advice' was considered in *Balabel v Air India* [1988] Ch 317. The plaintiffs claimed specific performance of an agreement for an underlease, and sought discovery of three categories of documents, namely communications between the defendant and its solicitors other than those seeking or giving legal advice; drafts, working papers, attendance notes, and memoranda of the defendant's solicitors relating to the proposed underlease; and internal communications of the defendant other than those seeking legal advice from the defendant's legal advisers. Upholding the defendant's claim to privilege in the Court of Appeal, Taylor LJ said:

> The test is whether the communication or other document was made confidentially for the purposes of legal advice. Those purposes have to be construed broadly. Privilege obviously attaches to a document conveying legal advice from solicitor to client and to a specific request from this client for such legal advice. But it does not follow that all other communications between them lack privilege. In most solicitor and client relationships, especially where a transaction involves protracted dealings, advice may be required or appropriate on matters great or small at various stages. There will be a continuum of communication and meetings between the solicitor and client. The negotiations for a lease such as occurred in the present case are only one example. Where information is passed by the solicitor or client to the other as part of the continuum aimed at keeping both informed so that advice may be sought and given as required, privilege will attach. A letter from the client containing information may end with such words as 'please advise me what I should

> do'. But, even if it does not, there will usually be implied in the relationship an overall expectation that the solicitor will at each stage, whether asked specifically or not, tender appropriate advice. Moreover, legal advice is not confined to telling the client the law; it must include advice as to what should prudently and sensibly be done in the relevant legal context.

Balabel v Air India was confirmed by the House of Lords in *Three Rivers District Council v Bank of England (No 6)* [2005] 1 AC 610, which concerned the application of legal advice privilege to lawyer–client communications on the presentation of evidence at an inquiry into the collapse of BCCI. In his judgment, Lord Scott drew attention to Taylor LJ's reference to 'the relevant legal context'. He stated that if a solicitor becomes the client's 'man of business', responsible for advising the client on all matters of business, including investment policy, finance policy, and other business matters, the advice may lack a relevant legal context, in which case the communications will not be privileged.

Guidance on the scope of the privilege was also provided in *Hellenic Mutual War Risks Association v Harrison (The Sagheera)* [1997] 1 Lloyd's Rep 160. In this case, Rix J held that the practical emphasis when dealing with this first head of legal professional privilege must be on the purpose of the retainer. If the dominant purpose of the retainer is the obtaining and giving of legal advice, then, although it is in theory possible that individual documents may fall outside that purpose, in practice it is unlikely. If, however, the dominant purpose of the retainer is some business purpose, then the documents will not be privileged. Although, even in that context, if legal advice is requested or given, the relevant documents will probably still attract privilege. For an interesting application of this principle, see *Nederlandse Reassuriante Groep Holding NV v Bacon & Woodrow* [1995] 1 All ER 976, in which it was held that communications between solicitor and client giving advice on the commercial wisdom of entering into a transaction (in respect of which legal advice was also sought) would be privileged.

A 'letter of engagement' from a solicitor to a client will attract legal advice privilege where the letter specifies matters upon which the solicitor will give advice (*Behague v Revenue and Customs Commissioners* [2013] UKFTT 596 (TC)).

Communications intended to be passed on to a third party will not be privileged (*Conlon v Conlon's Ltd* [1952] 2 All ER 462).

Where one lawyer acts for two or more parties in respect of the same subject matter, joint interest legal professional privilege arises and communications between lawyer and client X should be disclosed to client Y and vice versa, but not to outsiders (*Buttes Gas & Oil Co v Hammer (No 3)* [1981] 1 QB 223; *Re Konigsberg* [1989] 3 All ER 289). Joint interest legal professional privilege also arises where parties do not retain the same lawyer but have a joint interest in the subject matter in the communication at the time the communication occurs (see eg *R (Ford) v The Financial Services Authority* [2012] 1 All ER 1238).

19.2.2.2 Third-party or litigation privilege

The second class of legal privilege covers communications concerning pending or contemplated litigation between either a lawyer or his client and a third party. In particular it encompasses communications with a prospective witness, including that witness's identity (*China National Petroleum Corporation v Fenwick Elliot* [2002] EWHC 60 (Ch)). Such a right may only be intruded upon by subordinate legislation if the statute providing the subordinate instrument's vires makes it plain by express words or necessary implication that such an authority was intended to be conveyed (*R (Kelly) v Warley Magistrates' Court (Law Society intervening)* [2008] 1 WLR 2001).

Where the communication takes place before any dispute has arisen it is highly unlikely that it will be privileged (*Wheeler v Le Marchant* (1881) 17 Ch D 675, CA). In *Re Highgrade Traders Ltd* [1984] BCLC 151, Oliver LJ (at [172]) used the expression '*if litiga-*

tion is reasonably in prospect' to define whether litigation was pending or contemplated and in *Mitsubishi Electric Australia Pty Ltd v Victorian WorkCover Authority* [2002] VSCA 59, an Australian court defined the test as '*a real prospect of litigation as distinct from a mere possibility*'. This approach was approved in *United States of America v Philip Morris Inc*, The Times, 16 April 2004, where it was noted that 'a mere possibility' of litigation being commenced would be inadequate.

The reasonable contemplation of a criminal investigation does not necessarily equate to the reasonable contemplation of a litigation in the form of a prosecution (*Serious Fraud Office v Eurasian Natural Resources Corporation Ltd* [2017] EWHC 1017, QB). Criminal proceedings cannot be reasonably contemplated unless the prospective defendant knows enough about what the investigation is likely to unearth, or has unearthed, to appreciate that it is realistic to expect a prosecutor to be satisfied that it has enough material to stand a good chance of securing a conviction. In *R v Jukes* [2018] EWCA Crim 176, a document was sent to a solicitor admitting responsibility for health and safety during the investigation stage of a health and safety case. At the time there was no evidence that any party would have known what the investigation was likely to unearth, and therefore the document was not privileged.

In *Waugh v British Railways Board* [1980] AC 521, it was held that the dominant purpose of the communication had to be litigation. In that case the document in question was a report by an accident investigator that had been prepared so that the defendants could assess their liability in a crash and so that they could take steps to prevent any such accident from happening again. The House of Lords held that the two purposes had been of equal weight so the document was not privileged. Quite what the dominant purpose of a document or communication is will depend on the facts of each case.

In *Re L (A Minor) (Police Investigation: Privilege)* [1997] AC 16, the House of Lords held that this type of privilege only applies in adversarial proceedings and therefore would not apply to advice concerning investigations and inquiries (but see *Three Rivers District Council v Bank of England (No 4)* [2004] 3 WLR 1274, where it was accepted that communications in respect of a judicial inquiry formed by the government would be privileged). Furthermore, in *United States of America v Philip Morris Inc* (noted earlier), it was stated that the prospect of a party being required to produce documents at the trial between two other parties did not amount to litigation for these purposes and therefore no privilege would attach to communication about such matters.

19.2.2.3 The effect of legal professional privilege

Communication falling under either class will not be admissible at trial unless the party who has the privilege waives it (see **19.2.2.4**). The privilege renders the communications inadmissible and immune from discovery. However, it does not prevent documents or items in the possession of the lawyer or third party from being admissible nor does it prevent the lawyer or third party from being called as a witness of fact on some matters (see **19.2.2.5**). Furthermore, there are two exceptions to the rule that communications are privileged (see **19.2.2.6**).

The privilege is that of the client, not of the lawyer or third party (*Schneider v Leigh* [1955] 2 QB 195).

The communication will remain privileged after the proceedings to which they relate have ended and will also pass to successors in title (*Minet v Morgan* (1873) 8 Ch App 361).

19.2.2.4 Waiver of privilege

As the privilege is that of the client, only the client can waive it. Where the alleged waiver was made in excess of the powers of the person doing so, privilege will not have been waived (*GE Capital v Sutton* [2004] 2 BCLC 662). Equally, waiver that is effected by compulsion will not cancel the privilege (*British American Tobacco (Investments) Ltd v United States of America* [2004] EWCA Civ 1064). The court will look carefully at the circumstances of the waiver to determine whether and exactly how much of the privilege has been waived (*Great Atlantic Insurance Co v Home Insurance Co* [1981] 1 WLR 529). Simply mentioning a document in a witness statement does not amount to an automatic waiver of any privilege that attaches to it (*Expandable Ltd v Rubin*, The Times, 10 March 2008).

Documents may be disclosed for a limited purpose without waiving privilege generally (*British Coal Corporation v Dennis Rye Ltd (No 2)* [1988] 3 All ER 816). However, if a document or communication is disclosed voluntarily (and privilege therefore waived), privilege will normally be lost generally and with it the right to withhold production of other documents or communications relating to the same subject matter (*Derby and Co Ltd v Weldon (No 10)* [1991] 1 WLR 660). The principle governing the loss of privilege in the transaction generally is one of fairness: it is contrary to the interests of justice to allow a person to disclose a limited range of material relating to a particular matter, perhaps chosen to serve that person's own interests, while depriving the other party to the litigation of the full picture, which the remainder of the material relating to that matter would disclose. In *Re D (A Child)* [2011] EWCA Civ 648, CA, it was held that legal professional privilege had been waived through M stating in a witness statement that, after a number of legal conferences, she had changed her position as to how her child was injured. It was held that fairness required further disclosure of the attendance notes of those conferences to avoid the court and the father (whom M blamed for the child's injuries) being left with only a partial explanation as to how M had come to change her mind about how the child's injuries were sustained. Nonetheless, the importance of legal professional privilege to the proper administration of justice is such that it should be jealously guarded and it follows that courts should not be reluctant to hold that a litigant has lost the right to claim privilege unless justice and the right to a fair trial make that necessary (*R v Ahmed* [2007] EWCA Crim 2870).

Particular difficulties arise when a party is forced to give evidence as to the nature of discussions with his or her lawyer. This is most likely to be the case where in a criminal case the accused remains silent as a result of legal advice when questioned by the police and the prosecution seeks to rely on s 34 of the Criminal Justice and Public Order Act 1994 (see **15.4.1.2** and **15.4.1.6.1**). To explain that such silence was not motivated by a consciousness of guilt, the lawyer may have to give evidence. In *R v Bowden* [1999] 2 Cr App R 176, the Court of Appeal held that calling the lawyer in this way meant that the lawyer could be cross-examined as to the detail and reasons for the advice given and that it would be inappropriate for legal professional privilege to restrict this.

19.2.2.5 Limits on the scope of privilege

The privilege applies to the communications between lawyer and client, not to facts that were perceived during the solicitor–client relationship such as the client's identity (*Studdy v Sanders* (1823) 2 Dow & Ry KB 347) or the fact of the client having attended the solicitor's office to receive advice (*R v Manchester Crown Court, ex p R*, The Times, 15 February 1999). In *R (Hoare) v South Durham Magistrates' Court* [2005] RTR 4, the Divisional Court held that a solicitor could be called to prove the identity of his client and the fact of a previous conviction (at which the solicitor was present) without offending lawyer–client privilege.

Furthermore, documents or items do not become privileged simply because they are in the possession of a party's lawyer (*Dubai Bank v Galadari* [1989] 3 All ER 769). In *R v Peterborough Justices, ex p Hicks* [1977] 1 WLR 1371, the defendants were charged with forgery offences. The Court of Appeal refused to quash a warrant to search the party's solicitor's offices for allegedly forged documents stating that the solicitor had no better right to resist the warrant than the person upon whose behalf he held them. Therefore, whether the documents can be withheld depends on whether the client has some right other than legal professional privilege to keep them. This can be seen by contrasting the following two cases in which experts had received items of evidence for the purposes of advising a party and in which litigation privilege was alleged:

(a) In *R v King* [1983] 1 WLR 411, CA, it was held that a subpoena was properly issued to the prosecution requiring a handwriting expert, who had been retained by the defence, to produce documents containing the defendant's handwriting but which may have incriminated the accused.
(b) In *R v R* [1994] 4 All ER 260, CA, it was held that DNA samples that had been sent to an expert for his advice should not have been admitted. The DNA samples could not have been taken from the accused without his consent (**16.9.6.2**).

Note, in the two cases the items of evidence were admissible to prove facts in their own right. Equally, an expert whose opinion is privileged could be called by the other party to prove facts as opposed to opinions he or she has perceived (*Harmony Shipping Co SA v Saudi Europe Line Ltd* [1979] 1 WLR 1380, CA).

Facts related to a lawyer as part of his or her instructions will be privileged. However, if the lawyer perceives facts while acting for a client where those facts were not communicated to him or her by the client, those facts will not be privileged. In *Brown v Foster* (1857) 1 Hur & N 736, the plaintiff brought an action for malicious prosecution having been acquitted of embezzlement. In the course of the embezzlement trial, it was alleged that he had not made an entry in a ledger and the charge had been dismissed when it was revealed that an entry in a ledger had in fact been made. The defendant in the malicious prosecution proceedings was allowed to call the plaintiff's barrister in the embezzlement proceedings to say that the day before the ledger was admitted as evidence, there was no such entry. This was a fact perceived by the barrister rather than information received from the plaintiff under privileged instructions.

19.2.2.6 Exceptions to legal professional privilege

The privilege applies absolutely. There is no general power to override the privilege because of public interest considerations (*R v Derby Magistrates' Court, ex p B* [1996] AC 487). In *Re McE, Re M, Re C* [2009] UK HL 15, the House of Lords dealt with the impact on legal professional privilege of intrusive surveillance or 'bugging' of private conversations between solicitors and their clients. It was held that intrusive surveillance of lawyer–client communications authorised in strict accordance with the terms of the Regulation of Investigatory Powers Act 2000 was lawful. However, it also held that it would be unfair to admit evidence of communications which were covered by privilege.

However, although the privilege is absolute, it is also subject to two qualifications, which reflect public interest concerns:

(a) Legal professional privilege does not apply to communications made in pursuance of a crime or fraud (*R v Cox and Railton* (1884) 14 QBD 153). In *Crescent Farm (Sidcup) Sport Ltd v Sterling Offices Ltd* [1972] Ch 553, it was stated that fraud went beyond the tort of deceit and included '*all forms of dishonesty such as fraudulent breaches of contract, fraudulent conspiracies, trickery and sham contrivances*' (*per* Goff J).

Clearly, a lawyer will regularly be exposed to the criminal past of a client and will even have to advise the client that future conduct might be unlawful in some way. However, in *Barclays Bank plc v Eustice* [1995] 4 All ER 411, CA, a distinction was drawn between legal advice as to the legal effect of what had happened and advice as to how to carry out a fraudulent unlawful purpose in the future. The timing of the criminal conduct does not fully determine the matter. Advice as to the potential illegality of future conduct will still be privileged (*Butler v Board of Trade* [1971] Ch 680). The test is whether the communication was made in pursuance of the fraud or crime (*R v Snaresbrook Crown Court, ex p DPP* [1988] QB 532). See also the example of *R v Minchin* [2013] EWCA Crim 2412, concerning a conspiracy to pervert the course of justice by arranging a false alibi.

The issue for the court to determine is whether it was the purpose of the lawyer or the client to pursue a fraud or crime. *R v Central Criminal Court, ex p Francis & Francis* [1989] AC 346, HL, concerned the powers of search and seizure under s 10 of PACE 1984. The House stated that s 10 reflected the common law on legal professional privilege. The police, during a drugs investigation, had obtained orders requiring solicitors to produce documentation concerning the buying and selling of properties by a suspect and his family. The solicitors argued that the transactions and communications concerning them were privileged. However, the House concluded privilege would not apply if the intention of furthering a criminal purpose was that of the holder of the document or of any other party.

Merely instructing a lawyer to advance a case that may be proven to be untrue is not the furthering of a fraud or crime (*Snaresbrook Crown Court, ex p DPP*). However, where there is an agreement to pervert the course of justice that can be proven by evidence that is independent of the proof of the case in question, privilege will not attach to communications made in pursuance of that agreement (*R (Hallinan Blackburn Gittings and Nott) v Middlesex Guildhall Crown Court* [2005] 1 WLR 766). In *Kuwait Airways Corporation v Iraqi Airways Co (Disclosure: Fraud Exception)* [2005] 1 WLR 2734, the Court of Appeal held that if the alleged fraud was one of the issues in the case in question, there would have to be strong prima facie evidence of such fraud before privilege would be overruled. In *Re McE, Re M, Re C* [2009] UK HL 15, it was held that legal professional privilege would not apply to evidence of 'bugged' conversations in the custody suite of a police station between a solicitor and his detained client, where those communications involved the solicitor and his client planning how to pervert the course of justice.

(b) *Litigation privilege does not apply in non-adversarial proceedings* In any proceedings concerning the upbringing of children, the welfare of the child is the court's paramount consideration (s 1(1) of the Children Act 1989). In *Oxfordshire County Council v M* [1994] 2 All ER 269, the Court of Appeal held that the welfare of the child required that communications with third parties should not be subject to privilege. In children cases such communications will generally address various aspects of the welfare of the child such as his physical, educational, or emotional needs or harm the child may or may not have suffered. The court was also influenced by the fact that such third parties were appointed by the court in any event. The position was confirmed by the House of Lords in *Re L (A Minor) (Police Investigation: Privilege)* [1997] AC 16. There the House noted the investigative nature of children proceedings and the requirement of leave for third parties to be instructed. It was therefore held to be inappropriate for third-party privilege to apply in cases resolved using inquisitorial procedures. In *Three Rivers District*

Council v Bank of England (No 6) [2005] 1 AC 610, the House of Lords reiterated the restriction of litigation privilege to adversarial proceedings but noted that the inquisitorial nature of the CPR invited a reappraisal of litigation privilege.

19.2.2.7 Proving evidence by other means

The privilege attaches only to the communications or documents set out earlier. The facts contained in the communications or documents are not covered by the privilege. Therefore, if the fact can be proved by other means, other parties may attempt to do so. The extent to which the court must let them do so depends upon whether it is a criminal or civil case.

(a) *Criminal cases* Once the information has been made available to the prosecution, the accused's privilege is lost. For example:

(i) a note from the accused to his barrister that was found on the floor had been properly used in cross-examination (*R v Tompkins* (1977) 67 Cr App R 181, CA); or

(ii) the written account from the accused to his solicitor was accidentally sent to the prosecution. It had properly been used by the prosecution at trial (*R v Cottrill* [1997] Crim LR 56, CA).

However, the court will consider whether the evidence has been obtained unfairly and should therefore be excluded under s 78 of PACE 1984 (*R v Cottrill; R v Willis* [2004] All ER (D) 287).

(b) *Civil cases* The position is governed by CPR, r 31.20, which provides:

> *Where a party inadvertently allows a privileged document to be inspected, the party who has inspected the document may use it or its contents only with the permission of the court.*

In *Al-Fayed v The Commissioner of Police for the Metropolis* [2002] EWCA Civ 780, the relevant principles applicable to the operation of r 31.20 were articulated as follows:

i) A party giving inspection of documents must decide before doing so what privileged documents he wishes to allow the other party to see and what he does not.

ii) Although the privilege is that of the client and not the solicitor, a party clothes his solicitor with ostensible authority (if not implied or express authority) to waive privilege in respect of relevant documents.

iii) A solicitor considering documents made available by the other party to litigation owes no duty of care to that party and is in general entitled to assume that any privilege which might otherwise have been claimed for such documents has been waived.

iv) In these circumstances, where a party has given inspection of documents, including privileged documents which he has allowed the other party to inspect by mistake, it will in general be too late for him to claim privilege in order to attempt to correct the mistake by obtaining injunctive relief.

v) However, the court has jurisdiction to intervene to prevent the use of documents made available for inspection by mistake where justice requires, as for example in the case of inspection procured by fraud.

vi) In the absence of fraud, all will depend upon the circumstances, but the court may grant an injunction if the documents have been made available for inspection as a result of an obvious mistake.

vii) A mistake is likely to be held to be obvious and an injunction granted where the documents are received by a solicitor and:

a) the solicitor appreciated that a mistake has been made before making some use of the documents; or

b) it would be obvious to a reasonable solicitor in his position that a mistake has been made;

and, in either case, there are no other circumstances which would make it unjust or inequitable to grant relief.

viii) Where a solicitor gives detailed consideration to the question whether the documents have been made available for inspection by mistake and honestly concludes that they have not, that fact will be a relevant (and in many cases an important) pointer to the conclusion that it would not be obvious to the reasonable solicitor that a mistake had been made, but is not conclusive; the decision remains a matter for the court.

ix) In both the cases identified in vii) a) and b) above there are many circumstances in which it may nevertheless be held to be inequitable or unjust to grant relief, but all will depend upon the particular circumstances.

x) Since the court is exercising an equitable jurisdiction, there are no rigid rules.

Further guidance as to the duties of lawyers to act co-operatively in resolving issues relating to inadvertent disclosure was laid down in the case of *Atlantisrealm Limited v Intelligent Land Investments (Renewable Energy) Limited* [2017] EWCA Civ 1029:

i) In the electronic age, even with the help of sophisticated software, disclosure of documents can be a massive and expensive operation. Mistakes will occur from time to time.

ii) When privileged documents are inadvertently disclosed (as is bound to happen occasionally), if the mistake is obvious, the lawyers on both sides should co-operate to put matters right as soon as possible.

iii) The disclosure or discovery procedure in any common law jurisdiction depends upon the parties and their lawyers acting honestly, even when that is against a party's interest. The duty of honesty rests upon the party inspecting documents as well as the party disclosing documents.

Note also that r C26.6 of the Bar Standards Board Code of Conduct permits a barrister to withdraw from a case if he becomes aware of confidential or privileged information or documents of another person which relate to the matter on which he is instructed. If a barrister does receive such documents, they should immediately cease to read the documents, and inform their instructing solicitor, who must inform the other side and return the documents. Before informing the other side, the solicitor should consider whether to obtain instructions from the client and, if deciding to do so, should advise the client that a court will probably grant an injunction to prevent the overt use of any information gleaned and that both client and the solicitor might find costs awarded against them in respect of such an injunction (*English and American Insurance Co Ltd v Herbert Smith* [1988] FSR 232).

19.2.3 'Without prejudice' communications

It was noted earlier (at **19.2.2.1**) that where the communication was intended to be passed onto other parties, such communications will not be privileged (*Conlon v Conlon's Ltd* [1952] 2 All ER 462 (see also *Paragon Finance plc v Freshfields* [1999] 1 WLR 1183)). It follows that, generally, communications between parties are not privileged. However, written or oral communications made as part of negotiations genuinely aimed at, but not resulting in, settlement of a dispute are not generally admissible in evidence in litigation between parties over that dispute. In such situations, parties need not fear that their admissions or concessions during negotiation will be seen by the tribunal of fact should they fail to settle. A 'dispute' may engage the rule, notwithstanding that litigation has not yet begun (*Bradford & Bingley plc v Rashid* [2006] 4 All ER 705). The crucial consideration in determining whether or not the rule applies is whether, in the course of negotiations, the parties contemplated, or might reasonably have contemplated, litigation if they could not agree (*Barnetson v Framlington Group Ltd* [2007] 3 All ER 1054).

Such communication is generally referred to as 'without prejudice' correspondence. As a matter of good practice those words should be clearly marked on any letters that are not intended to go before the judge. However:

(a) the court is not bound to hold correspondence to be 'without prejudice' whenever the words are used (*Buckinghamshire County Council v Moran* [1990] Ch 623), although weight should be attached to the fact the words are used (*Williams v Hull* [2009] NPC 132);

(b) the court is not bound to hold that correspondence without those words can never be 'without prejudice' (*Chocoladefabriken Lindt & Sprungli AG v Nestle Co Ltd* [1978] RPC 287); and

(c) the real test is whether the correspondence is part of negotiations genuinely aimed at settlement (*South Shropshire District Council v Amos* [1986] 1 WLR 1271).

The rule prevents the correspondence from being admissible at trial (either on the matter of liability or on the issue of remedies). However, there are limited circumstances in which such correspondence will be admissible, as follows:

(a) If the negotiations reach settlement, the correspondence can be used as evidence of what was agreed (*Walker v Wilshire* (1889) 23 QBD 335; *Tomlin v Standard Telephones & Cables Ltd* [1969] 1 WLR 1378). It is not evidence on any other matter, nor is the agreement between the claimant and the first defendant admissible in respect of the dispute between the claimant and another defendant on exactly the same matter (*Rush & Tompkins Ltd v Greater London Council* [1989] AC 1280, HL). Nor should 'without prejudice' correspondence be admitted to help the court *interpret* the terms of an agreement (*Oceanbulk Shipping and Trading SA v TMT Asia Ltd* [2010] EWCA Civ 79). The reaching of an agreement is not necessarily recognition of the truth of the allegations to which it relates and should not therefore be allowed to prove anything other than the *fact* of agreement. However, where one of the parties who reached a settlement brings proceedings against a third party for a contribution to the damages in the main claim and the without prejudice correspondence refers to the degrees of contribution, the correspondence can be referred to on that issue (*Gnitrow Ltd v Cape plc* [2000] 1 WLR 2327).

(b) Where subsequent proceedings relate to wholly different subject matter and the correspondence reveals evidence on that different subject matter then the correspondence will be admissible whether or not a settlement was reached (*Muller v Linsley & Mortimer* [1996] PNLR 74).

(c) Where correspondence is marked 'without prejudice save as to costs' the court may, in limited circumstances, refer to the correspondence when determining costs issues. This detailed procedure is governed by CPR, Part 36 (see ***Blackstone's Civil Practice***) and the case law deriving from *Calderbank v Calderbank* [1976] Fam 93. This will necessarily only apply where there was no settlement as the point of the analysis is to determine whether the party in question received a better order from the court than was offered by the other party and should therefore have the costs of the litigation paid by the other party.

(d) In family law proceedings correspondence aimed at settlement will generally be inadmissible. However, public policy requires that any admissions made by a parent concerning any harm that a child has suffered, whether made in an attempt to settle proceedings before trial or for other reasons will be admissible as evidence (*Re D (Minor)* [1993] 2 All ER 693, see also Family Procedure Rules 2010, PD 9A, para 6.2).

19.3 Public policy exclusion

The rules that we have examined in this chapter so far have concerned the inadmissibility of evidence because one or both parties has asserted a privilege in respect of it. These privileges exist because of a concern to maintain the integrity of the litigation process and the interests of justice above and beyond the needs of the particular case. However, there is also a rule of more general application which restricts the extent to which otherwise admissible evidence can be disclosed to parties and admitted as evidence. The rationale for this rule is that there are other public policy reasons for keeping evidence out of court than its impact upon the interests of justice. This area of law is also commonly known as 'public interest immunity' (PII).

19.3.1 The general rule

The test of public policy exclusion is simply a matter of balancing the interest of justice in disclosing the evidence in question, on the one hand, against the public policy for excluding it, on the other hand (*Conway v Rimmer* [1968] AC 910). A claim of public policy exclusion should be decided by the courts.

The mere fact that a government agency or the prosecution claims that it is not in the public interest for evidence in its possession to be revealed does not determine whether or not it should be (*R v Ward* [1993] 1 WLR 619 and the Criminal Procedure and Investigations Act 1996, Part I). If no party requests that the evidence be excluded on public policy grounds, the court may (and should) consider whether to do so if necessary (*Duncan v Cammell Laird & Co Ltd* [1942] AC 624).

The 'public interest' is not determined simply by reference to the class of document or source of information in question. Although such an approach had previously been adopted in relation to documents such as high-level government papers, the House of Lords stated in *Burmah Oil Co v Bank of England* [1980] AC 1090 that 'class' claims should be evaluated and decided on their merits just like any other type of document. Therefore, public interest immunity from disclosure or use will not automatically be granted in respect of a document merely because it is diplomatic correspondence or a confidential economic report, for example. In 1996 the Lord Chancellor issued a statement (1997 147 NLJ 62) that government departments would no longer seek exclusion simply on the grounds that the document fell into a particular class. Instead, ministers will:

> focus directly on the damage that disclosure of sensitive documents would cause ... Ministers will only claim immunity when they believe that disclosure ... will cause real damage or harm to the public interest. Damage will normally have to be in the form of a direct and immediate threat to the safety of an individual or to the nation's economic interest or relations with a foreign state, though in some cases the anticipated damage might be indirect or longer term, such as damage to a regulatory process.

Therefore, a balancing exercise must be conducted in all cases. The fact that material of a particular class is more or less regularly excluded simply reflects the importance that is often attached to such sources when that balancing exercise is conducted rather than any absolute rule as to whether or not they should be excluded.

While in civil cases the interest of justice may vary from case to case, in criminal cases it has been said that where evidence may prove the accused's innocence or prevent a miscarriage of justice, the balance comes down heavily in favour of disclosure (*R v Keane* [1994] 1 WLR 746, CA). This does not prevent the court from having to consider the potential value of the evidence: the decision not to disclose material to the defence on the grounds of public interest immunity may undermine the right of the defendant to a fair trial in accordance with Article 6 of the ECHR. The European Court has recognised that the withholding of some information about prosecution investigative procedures is permissible without breaching the right of the accused to a fair trial (*Klass v Federal Republic of Germany* (1978) 2 EHRR 214, 232). However, in *Rowe and Davis v United Kingdom* (2000) 30 EHRR 1, the European Court of Human Rights stated that only such withholding of evidence as was strictly necessary would be consistent with a fair trial. In *R v H; R v C* [2004] 2 AC 134, the House of Lords set out the test for public interest immunity in two stages:

1 Is there a real risk of serious prejudice to an important public interest (and, if so, what) if full disclosure of the material is ordered? If No, full disclosure should be ordered.
2 If the answer to ... is Yes, can the defendant's interest be protected without disclosure or disclosure be ordered to an extent or in a way which will give adequate protection to the public interest in question and also afford adequate protection to the interests of the defence?

19.3.2 The effect of public policy exclusion

Where evidence is excluded for reasons of public policy, no party can waive that right. The failure of any interested party to claim that evidence ought to be excluded on the grounds of public policy is simply a factor that the courts will consider in balancing the public policy against the interests of justice. In this sense public policy exclusion is different to the privileges set out at **19.2**, as in privilege cases, the exclusion of the source of evidence depends upon a claim by someone that the evidence is privileged.

Further, it is the fact or information that is excluded on public policy grounds rather than the means of proving it as is the case where privilege is asserted (ie the source or document itself) (*Rogers v Home Secretary* [1973] AC 388). Therefore, in contrast to evidence excluded on the grounds of a privilege, information excluded on the grounds of public policy cannot be proved by some other means (for the contrast, see **19.2.2.7**).

19.3.3 Examples

The following cases are all examples of the exercise of the principle of public policy exclusion. The list is not comprehensive. For further cases, see ***Blackstone's Criminal Practice***. While the 'class' to which a document belongs no longer determines whether or not evidence will be admitted, the type of document or type of information contained in the document tends to raise similar concerns and issues.

19.3.3.1 National security, affairs of state, and foreign policy interests

It was this type of claim of public policy exclusion that previously led to automatic exclusion by class of document. However, in Sir Richard Scott VC's *Report of the Inquiry into the Export of Defence Equipment and Dual-Use Goods to Iraq and Related Prosecutions* (House of Commons Paper 115, 95/96, at G18.86) the use-of-class claims even in relation to national security interests was criticised, leading to the Lord Chancellor's statement (at **19.3.1**). Nevertheless, the trend has been for such evidence to be excluded. For example:

(a) in *Duncan v Cammell Laird & Co Ltd* [1942] AC 624, the court refused to order the disclosure of plans for a submarine which sank during trials;

(b) in *Burmah Oil Co v Bank of England* [1980] AC 1090, the bank's refusal to produce confidential records of dealings with banks and other businesses was upheld. The refusal was at the request of the government on the grounds of national economic interests; and

(c) in *Buttes Gas and Oil Co v Hammer (No 3)* [1981] 1 QB 223, information relating to a company's dealings with a foreign state would not be revealed where that country was in a border dispute with its neighbour. The public interest served by refusing to disclose the evidence was international comity.

19.3.3.2 Police information

Information which has been used during police investigations will often be of potential benefit to the accused in criminal proceedings or to parties taking action against the police in respect of their policing. Examples include the following:

(a) In *Evans v Chief Constable of Surrey* [1988] QB 588, a report sent to the DPP by the police was held not to be disclosable in a civil action as it was held to be important to preserve the freedom of communication between the police and the DPP. Equally, where the police have obtained evidence during a criminal investigation, the court must balance the confidentiality of such information obtained under the exercise of compulsory powers against the basic public interest in assuring a fair trial on full evidence in any subsequent civil proceedings (*Marcel v Commissioner of Police for the Metropolis* [1992] Ch 225, CA; *Taylor v Director of the Serious Fraud Office* [1999] 2 AC 177). In *Frankson v Home Office* [2003] 1 WLR 1952, the Court of Appeal rejected the argument that statements made to police officers under caution would necessarily be excluded in the public interest. There is therefore no general public interest in maintaining the confidentiality of statements made to prosecuting authorities which will outweigh the interest of a fair trial, although the court did leave open the possibility that an overriding public interest in non-disclosure could arise in specific cases.

(b) In *R v Horseferry Road Magistrates' Court, ex p Bennett (No 2)* [1994] 1 All ER 289, it was recognised that communications between prosecuting authorities in different countries could potentially be excluded, although the evidence was admitted on that occasion as it showed that the accused had been unlawfully returned to the jurisdiction.

(c) In *R v Chief Constable of the West Midlands, ex p Wiley* [1995] 1 AC 274, it was held that whether or not statements made in the course of police complaints investigations should be excluded depended on the facts of each case.

(d) Where a criminal case appears to have been based upon informant evidence, the courts have generally held that the identity of informants should not be disclosed although it may be ordered if it is necessary to establish the innocence of the accused (*Marks v Beyfus* (1890) 25 QBD 494). In *R v Agar* [1990] 2 All ER 442, the accused's case was that the informant and the police had cooperated in 'setting up' the accused by inviting him to the informant's house and then planting evidence there. The Court of Appeal held that the defence should have been entitled to cross-examine the police officers as to whether the informant had told them that the accused was due to visit his house.

(e) A similar approach has been adopted in relation to persons who have allowed their houses to be used as police surveillance posts (*R v Rankine* [1986] QB 861). In *R v Johnson (Kenneth)* (1989) 88 Cr App R 131, the Court of Appeal stated that before the court can admit evidence from a surveillance, two matters should be proved (as a minimum):

   (i) a police officer in charge of the observations (no lower in rank than sergeant) testifies that *before the observation took place* he spoke to the occupiers of the premises to be used about their attitude to the observation, including the risk of disclosure of the use of the premises; and

   (ii) a police officer of the rank of at least chief inspector testifies that *immediately before trial* he visited the place of the observation and spoke to the occupiers at that time about their attitude to the disclosure of its use as an observation post at trial.

Where the court rules that the identity of informants or the details of information held by the police must be revealed, the prosecution may decide not to proceed on the charges in question. In this way they can preserve their sources.

19.3.3.3 Other confidential information

This is probably the most difficult category of cases to deal with in that it is difficult to identify a dominant head of public policy. Moreover, in some cases, the decision will depend on the importance of the information to the party seeking disclosure. For various illustrations of the courts' approach, see:

(a) *D v National Society for the Prevention of Cruelty to Children* [1978] AC 171, in which exclusion was granted in respect of anonymous reports made to the NSPCC concerning child abuse to children;

(b) *Science Research Council v Nassé* [1980] AC 1028, in which public policy exclusion was unsuccessfully sought in respect of documents used to determine promotion applications for employees;

(c) *Lonhro Ltd v Shell Petroleum Company Ltd* [1980] 1 WLR 627, in which information given in confidence to a government inquiry concerning a matter of foreign policy was held to have been properly excluded;

(d) *Re M (A Minor) (Disclosure of Material)* [1990] 2 FLR 36, in which social services reports and case notes concerning a child in care were not disclosable. (However, such immunity does not operate against a guardian appointed for the child by the court in Children Act 1989 proceedings. Such a guardian can be ordered by the court to have access to all social service records under s 42 and no immunity would prevent such disclosure);

(e) *R v Hampshire County Council, ex p K* [1990] 2 All ER 129, in which social services department records were held not to be disclosed unless the judge ordered so; and

(f) *Lonrho plc v Fayed (No 4)* [1994] QB 775, in which a taxpayer's tax returns held by the Inland Revenue were held potentially to be subject to public interest immunity as they had been obtained from the taxpayer by compulsion.

19.3.3.4 Journalistic sources

The Contempt of Court Act 1981, s 10, makes general provision as to the circumstances in which a journalist may be required by court order to reveal sources of information. Section 10 provides:

No court may require a person to disclose, nor is any person guilty of contempt of court for refusing to disclose, the source of information contained in a publication for which he is responsible, unless it be established to the satisfaction of the court that disclosure is necessary in the interests of justice or national security or for the prevention of disorder or crime.

Therefore, journalists are not generally under an obligation to disclose their sources unless the evidence is necessary for one of four purposes: the interests of justice, national security, prevention of crime, or prevention of disorder. The effect is that journalistic sources are covered by public policy exclusion and must be weighed against the other reasons for revealing the source, of which one is the interests of justice, a phrase that has been interpreted narrowly (*Secretary of State for Defence v Guardian Newspapers* [1985] 1 AC 339). In *X Ltd v Morgan-Grampian (Publishers) Ltd* [1991] 1 AC 1, the interests of justice were defined as the protection of important legal rights or the protection against serious legal wrongs. Disclosure must be necessary for those purposes; therefore, important factors will include the significance of the evidence and the difficulty of obtaining the information from other sources.

The 'prevention of disorder or crime' ground has been interpreted to relate to crime in general not specific crimes (*Re an Inquiry under the Companies Securities (Insider Dealing) Act 1985* [1988] AC 660). Therefore, the section cannot be used in this way to force journalists to disclose sources so that they can be called as witnesses in the case unless this is in the 'interests of justice'.

19.3.4 Determining whether to exclude evidence

In outline, the procedures are as follows:

19.3.4.1 Criminal cases

Public policy exclusion will generally arise as part of the disclosure proceedings relating to unused material (ie material the prosecution will not rely upon). Under ss 3 and 7 of the Criminal Procedure and Investigations Act 1996, the prosecution is under an obligation to disclose material that might reasonably be considered to undermine the prosecution case or assist the defence case. The 1996 Act provides that material may only be withheld from the accused on the grounds of public interest immunity if the court has made a decision to that effect. The extent to which the defence should be involved in any such application depends on the degree of sensitivity of the material in question. There are three possibilities, as follows:

(a) For the least sensitive class of material, the prosecution must inform the defence of the application (and the defence will be allowed to participate at the hearing) and of the class of material to which it relates.

(b) For more sensitive material (where the prosecution alleges that harm would be caused to the public interest by merely identifying the material in question), the prosecution must inform the defence of the application and the defence can make representations about the procedure to be adopted for determining the public interest immunity issue. However, the prosecution does not have to reveal the nature of the material and the defendant and his representatives are not permitted to attend the hearing of the application.

(c) For the most sensitive cases (those in which the public interest would be threatened merely by revealing the fact of an application), the prosecution may apply to the court without notifying the defence of the application at all. However, a 'closed material' procedure may be adopted, where a special counsel is appointed to represent the defendant's interests.

As the decision not to disclose evidence to the defence threatens the right to a fair trial, the process for determining what evidence should be revealed should itself safeguard the right to a fair trial protected by Article 6(1) of the ECHR. In *Rowe and Davis v United Kingdom* (2000) 30 EHRR 1, the European Court of Human Rights stated, at [61], that '*any difficulties caused to the defence by a limitation on its rights must be sufficiently counterbalanced by the procedures followed by the judicial authorities*'.

In *R v H* [2003] 1 WLR 411, the House of Lords considered the procedures under the Criminal Procedure and Investigations Act 1996 in the light of developing practice in the UK courts and European jurisprudence. The result of this consideration was a seven-stage process to be adopted when the prosecution withholds unused material on the grounds of public interest, as follows:

1. The court must identify and consider the material that the prosecution seeks to withhold.
2. It must determine whether the material is such as may weaken the prosecution case or strengthen that of the defence. (Disclosure does not have to be ordered for evidence that does not do one or the other.)
3. It must determine whether there is a real risk of serious prejudice to an important public interest if full disclosure of the material is ordered. (If no serious prejudice, disclosure should be ordered.)
4. It must determine whether the defendant's interest can be protected without disclosure or limited disclosure can be ordered that will both give adequate protection to the public interest and also to the interests of the defence. The court may have to consider what measures can be taken to offer adequate protection for the defence short of full disclosure.
5. The court must consider whether measures proposed in answer to step 4 represent the minimum derogation necessary to protect the public interest in question. (The court is under a duty to get as close as possible to full disclosure while offering adequate protection for the interest in question.)
6. It must consider whether any order for limited disclosure under steps 4 or 5 above may render the trial process unfair to the defendant. (If the trial process is rendered unfair, fuller disclosure should be ordered even if this leads the prosecution to discontinue the proceedings so as to avoid having to make disclosure.)
7. It must keep the fairness of the trial process under constant review during the trial in light of the order for limited disclosure. (The House noted that it was important that the answer to step 6 should not be treated as final.)

The House therefore recognised that not only is there an issue of whether or not evidence ought to be disclosed, but also that the court ought to consider ways in which evidence could be partially disclosed. The balance between disclosure and public interest immunity can therefore be achieved not simply by ordering or refusing disclosure of unused material, but also by altering the way in which such material is disclosed. The House noted, in particular, possibilities such as formal admissions of some or all of the facts the defence seeks to prove with the material, disclosure short of full disclosure by the preparation of summaries or extracts, or the provision of edited or anonymised documents.

The House also noted that occasionally a fair trial would require that the defendant was represented at disclosure hearings relating to the more sensitive material. In such cases, as noted earlier, the defendant and his representatives may not even be informed of the application. The House therefore approved the practice of appointing 'special counsel' to argue the defendant's case for disclosure at such hearings. However, special counsel would only be appointed in exceptional circumstances. Special counsel would not be acting for the defendant and therefore would not be under any obligation to report to him matters revealed during the disclosure hearing. However, special counsel would be in a position to challenge the prosecution case from the defence perspective so as to ensure that the adversarial nature of the trial process was safeguarded.

Where the person holding the information is not a party to the proceedings he may make an application to the court to rule that the information should be withheld. Alternatively, such matters fall to be resolved when the third party is the subject of a witness summons requiring him to attend court to produce the document or information.

19.3.4.2 Civil cases

CPR, r 31.19(1) makes detailed provision for determining whether evidence should be revealed. Such applications may be made without notice and will not generally be served on the other party unless the court orders otherwise. Where the information is sought from a non-party to the proceedings the application is made under CPR, r 31.17. Where the material is very sensitive the civil courts may adopt the 'closed material' procedure used in criminal cases, appointing a special counsel to advocate on the other party's behalf; see for example *Al Rawi v Security Service* [2009] EWHC 2959 (QB), which concerned the disclosure of material in a civil claim for damages for false imprisonment and torture by former detainees who had been held at various locations by foreign states, including at Guantánamo Bay by the USA.

Part 2 of the Justice and Security Act 2013—the Government's response to the decision in *Al Rawi*—now enables civil courts to order closed material procedures in cases where disclosure of material would damage the interests of national security. The rationale for these procedures is that they permit the security services to argue their case by referring to highly sensitive evidence which would ordinarily be withheld and would give rise to possibly speculative claims and expensive settlements. Under the Justice and Security Act 2013, s 6(1), the civil court in relevant proceedings may make a declaration that the proceedings are proceedings in which a closed material application may be made to the court. Under s 6(2), such a declaration may be made on the application of the Secretary of State or any party to the proceedings or of its own motion. A 'closed material application' is an application to the court by parties who would otherwise be required to disclose 'sensitive material' (ie material that would damage national security if it were disclosed), for permission not to disclose it otherwise than to the court, any person appointed as a special advocate and the Secretary of State (see s 6(8) and (11)). Under s 6(3)–(6), there are two conditions which must be met before a declaration will be made:

(a) A party to the proceedings would be required to disclose the sensitive material in the course of proceedings or would be required to make the disclosure were it not for (i) the possibility of a claim for public interest immunity in relation to the material, or (ii) the fact that there would be no requirement to disclose if the party chose not to rely on the material, or (iii) the material would be intercepted material excluded under the Regulation of Investigatory Powers Act 2000, s 17(1), or (iv) any other enactment that would prevent the party from disclosing the material but would not do so if the proceedings were proceedings in relation to which there was a declaration under this section (s 6(4)).

(b) It is in the interests of the fair and effective administration of justice in the proceedings to make a declaration (see s 6(5)).

Where the application is sought to be made by the Secretary of State, there is a condition which must be met under s 6(7): the court must not consider an application by the Secretary of State unless it is satisfied that the Secretary of State has, before making the application, considered whether to make, or advise another person to make, a claim for public interest immunity in relation to the material on which the application is based.

Where a court makes a declaration under s 6, it must keep it under review and may revoke it if it considers that 'the declaration is no longer in the interests of the fair and effective administration of justice in the proceedings' (see s 7).

INDEX